Table of Contents

Latin American Research Network
Inter-American Development Bank

The Inter-American Development Bank created the Latin American Research Network in 1991 in order to strengthen policy formulation and contribute to the development policy agenda in Latin America. Through a competitive bidding process, the Network provides grant funding to leading Latin American research centers to conduct studies on economic and social issues selected by the Bank in consultation with the region's development community. Most of the studies are comparative, which allows the Bank to build its knowledge base and draw on lessons from experiences in macroeconomic and financial policy, modernization of the state, regulation, poverty and income distribution, social services, and employment. The individual country studies are available as working papers and are also available in PDF format on the internet at http://www.iadb.org/oce/41.htm.

Acknowledgments

The studies in this book were financed by the Latin American Research Network of the Inter-American Development Bank and would not have been possible without the collaboration of many friends and colleagues. For their comments at the June 1996 Conference on "Determinants of Domestic Savings in Latin America" in Santafé de Bogotá and their critique of the case studies, thanks are due to Ricardo Hausmann, Ernesto Talvi, Sebastian Edwards, Martin Feldstein, Michael Gavin, Santiago Herrera, Leonardo Letelier, Maurice Obstfeld, Roberto Steiner, Alejandro López, Jorge Streb, Eduardo Engel, Ricardo Ffrench-Davis, Patricio Meller, Shane Hunt, Francisco Verdera, Javier Kápsoli, Fátima Ponce, and Roberto Rivera. We also owe thanks to the following for their collaboration on the individual country studies: Natalia Salazar, Raquel Bernal, Fabio Sánchez, Julio Cáceres, Fernando Borraz, Luis Sténari, Enrique Gilles, Carlos Espina, and Claudio González. Norelis Betancourt and Raquel Gómez kept the research train on track while Rita Funaro and Graciela Thomen engineered the publication process.

Preface

Which comes first, saving or growth? Latin America's lackluster growth rates have often been blamed on similarly uninspiring rates of saving. Evidence collected in this book confirms the link between saving and growth, but not necessarily the chain of causation. In fact, the Latin American experiences studied herein suggest that growth sparks saving, not the other way around.

By taking a close look at the determinants of saving, the case studies in this volume raise this, and other, provocative questions. An examination of what drives saving in seven Latin American countries spans a variety of topics ranging from the impact of financial liberalization and terms of trade shocks on saving to demographic factors associated with the life-cycle hypothesis and income inequality. The Latin American experience is complemented by an analysis of the effects of liberalization and structural reform on saving in three European countries. The comparison uncovers often surprising parallels and offers insights as to what Latin America can expect as it continues to open up its financial systems and effect structural adjustments.

Of particular interest in light of recent financial turmoil is the reaction of private saving to financial sector reforms. Several chapters in this volume explore this issue by examining the credit booms that often accompany financial liberalization. The case studies look at liquidity constraints, credit channels, asset prices, and consumption booms to explain saving and raise important policy questions. If financial liberalization activates a cycle of booming credit and consumption—presumably leading to current account imbalances and possible financial crises—is it desirable? And if it is desirable for efficiency's sake, are there necessary prerequisites or timing considerations?

Another subject of debate is the relationship between public and private saving. Do changes in public saving influence aggregate domestic saving? If not, does this weaken the case for fiscal austerity? And what about the relationship between foreign and domestic saving? If capital inflows are volatile and tend to crowd out domestic saving, are there grounds for controlling capital inflows?

Clearly, the policy implications of the kinds of questions raised in this book are far-reaching. These collected works, from authors with in-depth knowledge of these economies, foster a better understanding of diverse and complex issues that help account for the past. They also provide us with a clearer image of some of the major policy challenges that remain for the future.

Ricardo Hausmann
Chief Economist
Inter-American Development Bank

I. OVERVIEW

I. OVERVIEW

CHAPTER 1

Saving in Latin America and Lessons from Europe

William A. Plies and Carmen M. Reinhart[1]

Numerous studies have pointed to low saving rates as a serious constraint on growth in Latin America.[2] During the last 20 years, per capita GDP growth averaged about 1 percent in Latin America and almost 5 percent in East Asia.[3] Over the same period, saving rates stagnated in Latin America—where they remained at around 17 percent of GDP—and nearly doubled in East Asia, where they rose to over 35 percent. The link between low saving rates and poor growth performance is not limited to these two regions—Sub-Saharan Africa's "growth tragedy" is often partially blamed on that continent's low level of saving. Not surprisingly, throughout much of Latin America and elsewhere in the world, a wide-ranging spectrum of policies has been either implemented or is being considered with the aim of stimulating saving. Some policies have sought to reduce distortions in the financial sector that may depress saving, while others have explicitly targeted saving through a variety of tax incentives. Other policies have encompassed ambitious reforms of entitlement programs and pension schemes.

Early theories posited a causal chain from saving to growth. In the 1960s and 1970s, proponents of financial liberalization, such as McKinnon (1973) and Shaw (1973), sought to promote saving by allowing for positive, market-determined real rates of return. The higher level of saving, in turn, was thought to support a higher level of investment and growth. This line

---

[1] William A. Plies is a master's candidate at the University of Maryland, College Park. Carmen M. Reinhart is a professor at the University of Maryland.
[2] See Edwards (1995) and Schmidt-Hebbel and Servén (1997).
[3] See Schmidt-Hebbel, Servén, and Solimano (1996).

of analysis gave impetus to policy prescriptions that called for a liberalization of the financial system that did away with directed credit policies and interest rate controls. Many countries, under the auspices of multilateral institutions, implemented ambitious reforms of their financial systems. Yet, much of the recent empirical evidence has called into question the implications of those theories, suggesting that the chain of causation runs from growth to saving and not the other way around.[4] Indeed, the evidence from Latin America fits that pattern rather well.[5] Furthermore, recent experiences with financial liberalization, including that of the United States during the 1980s and several of the episodes that are discussed in this volume, suggest that financial liberalization may ease preexisting credit constraints and actually reduce saving.

Some authors have suggested that the evidence hints at the existence of virtuous circles of saving and growth and poverty traps of undersaving and stagnation. Reports published by the Inter-American Development Bank (IDB, 1996 and 1997) indicate that many of the reform programs implemented in Latin America over the past decade have been designed to activate virtuous circles. Recent financial crises notwithstanding, the successful development experience in East Asia lends credence to the notion of virtuous circles but begs the question as to whether Latin America can duplicate the East Asian experience.

Seven of the case studies collected in this volume provide insights into that and other related policy questions by examining what drives saving in Latin America. The chapters cover Argentina, Chile, Colombia, Mexico, Peru, Uruguay, and Venezuela and span a variety of topics ranging from the impact of financial liberalization on saving to the role of terms of trade shocks. Many of the studies also employ new data sources that provide a better understanding of the saving patterns of various agents in the economy: the public sector, firms, and households. All too often, past studies have relied on highly aggregated data masking important differences across these sectors. Three of the studies (Italy, Spain, and the United Kingdom) analyze the European experience with liberalization and structural reforms and its

---

[4] See Deaton (1990) and Carroll and Weil (1993).
[5] A recent report (IDB, 1996) examined the link between the average saving rates of Caribbean, Central American, and South American countries during 1991–95 and average real GDP growth in the preceding 10 years; the stylized evidence suggests a strong and positive correlation from growth to saving.

effects on saving. The aim of these chapters is to provide insights as to what Latin American countries can expect in the wake of structural reform.

Beyond describing past and present trends in saving across a spectrum of primarily Latin American countries, this volume also analyzes many topical issues that remain the subject of much debate in academic and policy circles. What is the relationship between private and public saving? Can changes in public saving be expected to influence aggregate domestic saving? If not, the case for fiscal austerity, so prevalent in adjustment programs, may well be undermined. Most of the studies in this volume address these questions by examining the evidence on Ricardian equivalence, or whether the private sector fully internalizes and offsets the actions of the public sector.

Many countries in Latin America and elsewhere have either undergone or are contemplating full or partial financial liberalization. Recent studies have shown that financial liberalization is usually accompanied by greater access to credit and, more often than not, by credit booms.[6] Macroeconomists and policy makers have long sought to understand what happens to private saving when there are financial sector reforms. To shed light on this issue, several of the chapters that follow examine the prevalence of liquidity constraints, the presence of a credit channel, and the role of asset price and consumption booms in explaining saving. One of the studies offers an innovative look at what drives durable goods consumption. This line of work is rich in policy implications. If financial liberalization activates a cycle of booming credit and consumption—presumably leading to widening current account imbalances and increasing the possibility of a financial crisis—is it desirable? If it is desirable on the basis of efficiency considerations, what are the necessary prerequisites? Is there an optimal sequencing?

As noted, earlier literature on the links between saving and growth emphasized the need for high saving rates to finance higher investment and serve as the engine of economic growth. Yet, the newer studies suggest that it is growth that drives saving. The outcome of this debate is filled with policy implications, and many of the country studies in this volume bring new evidence to bear on this key issue. If high saving is the "passive" outcome of growth, then policy makers should be less concerned with policies aimed at stimulating saving per se and should instead focus on those policies that foster growth through more direct channels. The vast literature on

---

[6] See Gavin and Hausmann (1996) and Kaminsky and Reinhart (1996).

endogenous growth offers some leading candidates in this regard, ranging from keeping inflation under control to improving education and reducing taxation.

As in the previous empirical literature on saving, the studies in this volume also provide evidence of the relationship between saving and its traditional determinants: demographic factors associated with the life-cycle hypothesis (LCH), terms of trade shocks, foreign saving, and income inequality. On the issue of foreign saving, several of the studies assess to what extent capital inflows "crowd out" domestic saving. If capital inflows are fickle and volatile and there is extensive crowding out, is there a case for capital controls on inflows? Should policy makers aim to influence how these capital flows are intermediated? Three of the studies also have much to say about the impact of pension reform on saving, and one study (Noya, Lorenzo, and Grau-Pérez, in this volume) examines the determinants of public saving. While the bulk of the evidence presented in this book comes from macroeconomic data, four chapters also draw inferences from neglected micro data based on surveys of households and firms.

Saving and Its Components: The Stylized Facts

Data Issues

Saving data are generally calculated in questionable ways, mostly as residuals of other macroeconomic variables.[7] Measurement error is often compounded by failing to correct for capital gains/losses and unrecorded capital flight. There is considerable variation in estimated saving rates among alternative sources of data. In what follows, unless otherwise noted, all the descriptive analysis is based on the original data provided by the authors. Hence, it is based on data that have been, to the extent possible, corrected for some of the problems that typically plague data on saving. Because the sample period is not uniform across countries and not all countries have equally disaggregated data, Box 1.1 gives details as to the pertinent sample period used. The case studies provide a richer discussion of the individual databases.

---

[7] For a detailed description of recurrent measurement problems see Edwards (1995) and Schmidt-Hebbel and Servén (1997); see Held and Uthoff (1995) for a Latin American sample.

Descriptive Statistics

Table 1.1 presents basic descriptive statistics for the various definitions of saving. The mean, standard deviation, maximum value, and minimum value are reported for each variable. There are several features worth noting.

Domestic saving rates have oscillated in these eight countries from a minimum of −2.3 percent for Mexico to a high of 39.3 for Venezuela, highlighting the considerable variation both across countries and across time. Unlike East Asia, none of the countries in the sample show mean domestic saving rates above 25 percent. Indeed, the mean for the entire sample is about 17 percent. This is consistent with the predictions of a subsistence model of consumption (see Ogaki, Ostry, and Reinhart, 1995), which suggests a marked nonlinear relationship between saving rates and income. A country where income is close to the cost of a subsistence consumption basket will save little; as the gap between subsistence needs and income widens, saving rates increase sharply at first and then flatten out with further increments to income.

If domestic saving has oscillated in a wide range, part of the explanation is in the behavior of fiscal policy. Public saving has recorded lows of −7 percent in Peru and highs of 20 percent in Venezuela. The volatility of public saving is highlighted in chapter 2 on Argentina. Public saving across all the countries has averaged around 3 percent (and the mean is negative for two countries), or about 18 percent of national saving, well below the 25 to 40 percent range recorded for Asia. Hence, the inability of Latin American governments to generate substantial saving in part explains the flat profile of saving in several countries in the region. Taken together, the volatile behavior of fiscal saving, its relatively low level, and evidence on the procyclicality of fiscal policy in Latin America (see, for instance, Gavin and Perotti, 1998) all suggest that lax and erratic fiscal policy may go a long way toward explaining the region's relatively low saving levels. Indeed, some studies have shown that the volatility of fiscal policy in Latin America is associated with monetary and financial instability—factors that can only stimulate capital flight and reduce domestic saving rates.[8]

As to who contributes to private saving, the household or the firm, the data (for the subsample of countries for which they are available) pro-

---

[8] See IDB (1995 and 1997) and studies cited therein.

Table 1.1 Saving Rates: Descriptive Statistics

Country	National Saving	Domestic Saving	Public Saving	Private Saving	Household Saving	Firms' Saving	Foreign Saving
Argentina							
Mean	20.57	20.17	5.79	15.25	N.A.	N.A.	0.40
Standard Deviation	3.12	4.39	4.01	2.54	N.A.	N.A.	2.23
Minimum	15.44	11.26	−0.89	7.97	N.A.	N.A.	−4.99
Maximum	29.79	31.72	14.35	20.50	N.A.	N.A.	5.58
Chile							
Mean	15.75	N.A.	4.62	10.33	12.96	−2.46	N.A.
Standard Deviation	9.94	N.A.	3.91	7.95	7.12	2.76	N.A.
Minimum	2.20	N.A.	−2.40	0.80	2.60	−8.10	N.A.
Maximum	40.50	N.A.	12	22.10	23.20	3.5	N.A.
Colombia							
Mean	18.58	17.63	5.25	13.33	4.02	8.01	0.95
Standard Deviation	2.42	5.13	2.36	1.74	1.26	1.33	2.9
Minimum	13.53	7.29	1.34	8.52	1.24	5.14	−6.76
Maximum	22.88	28.57	10.26	15.43	6.52	10.37	6.24
Mexico							
Mean	15.58	12.86	1.96	13.61	6.11	3.32	2.72
Standard Deviation	5.69	6.39	2.82	3.05	1.35	1.61	2.82
Minimum	3.31	−2.28	−3.35	6.58	4.6	1.3	−4.69
Maximum	30.05	26.72	10.01	20.05	7.6	6.3	7.83
Peru							
Mean	21.47	18.91	−0.25	19.22	7.45	13.67	2.5
Standard Deviation	3.71	3.69	2.31	3.46	3.01	5.51	3.05
Minimum	15.17	10.36	−6.99	12.71	2.27	3.23	−4.58
Maximum	31.12	25.89	4.87	25.89	12.87	21.08	9.16
Uruguay							
Mean	N.A.	14.59	1.25	13.33	N.A.	N.A.	N.A.
Standard Deviation	N.A.	2.09	3.4	3.87	N.A.	N.A.	N.A.
Minimum	N.A.	11.3	−5.5	7.1	N.A.	N.A.	N.A.
Maximum	N.A.	17.2	6.6	19.5	N.A.	N.A.	N.A.
Venezuela							
Mean	20.93	23.25	9.52	11.41	N.A.	N.A.	−2.32
Standard Deviation	4.74	4.54	4.93	3.98	N.A.	N.A.	1.43
Minimum	14.23	16.96	1.91	2.91	N.A.	N.A.	−4.72
Maximum	36.76	39.33	20.1	17.84	N.A.	N.A.	0.02

N.A. Not available.
Note: In most cases, the breakdown of private consumption into its household and firm components is available for a subset of the total sample for the more recent period.

vide no conclusive evidence. In Colombia and Peru, households account for the bulk of private saving while in Chile and Mexico the largest contributors are firms. Pension reform notwithstanding, households on average have negative saving rates in Chile. In two of the four cases where disaggregated data are available, household saving is more volatile than that of firms. In one case they are equally volatile, and in the remaining case the opposite is true. Hence, it is not possible to draw firm conclusions on the volatility issue. However, to the extent that consumption-smoothing considerations are dominant in household decisions, it should not be surprising to find that the volatility of household saving is greater than that of firms.

Foreign saving also appears to be volatile across countries and across time. While data for Chile and Uruguay were not reported, the oscillations in foreign saving for the remaining sample range from about 7 percent capital outflows to over 9 percent capital inflows. The amplitude of the cycle is large, but the contribution of foreign saving to national saving is modest, never reaching 3 percent of GDP; on average for the five countries for which data were available, it is slightly over 1 percent of GDP. Hence, if foreign saving does not increase national saving by much, on average, it certainly contributes to its volatility. Combined, these two observations call into question the desirability of capital inflows.

Not surprisingly in light of the preceding discussion, private saving is the largest component of domestic and national saving and the most stable. Its coefficient of variation is consistently well below those recorded for both public and foreign saving. Because investment projects typically require long-term financing, this observation may, in part, help explain why saving-investment correlations have typically been high.

Trends in Saving and Its Components

Previous studies have suggested that the disparity in saving rates between Latin America and East Asia can be traced to secular developments affecting demographics, fiscal policy, growth, and marked regional differences in the extent of financial deepening.[9] In order to answer the questions as to why

---

[9] See, for instance, Edwards (1995) and Faruqee and Hussain (1995).

saving rates have stagnated in Latin America and whether there is room to increase saving over the immediate horizon, it is important to assess the past trends in various sectors. Tables 1.2 and 1.3 and Boxes 1.1 and 1.2 address this issue. With the exception of Chile (where saving shows a marked secular increase of over 21 percentage points between 1974 and 1994) and Mexico (where saving shows a secular decline, falling over 13 percentage points in the same period), domestic saving rates in the region have remained essentially flat. However, before interpreting this as a common regional characteristic, it is worth noting that aggregate saving remained flat—but for different reasons.

Table 1.2 and 1.4 highlight some of the findings on this issue. For instance, public saving has been trending downward in a pronounced way in Argentina and Mexico—contributing to the downward trend in the aggregate saving rate (Table 1.2). Yet, in Venezuela and Uruguay, where the aggregate saving rate has also declined, public saving has been flat or has actually increased. In an attempt to further synthesize the information, in Table 1.3 a matrix divides public and private saving into three categories: downward trend, trendless, and upward trend. If a "common regional" picture of Latin American saving rates were to characterize the cross-country experience, then the bulk of the cases would be expected to fall into two cells: flat public saving and downward trend in private saving. Instead, Table 1.3 suggests there is no representative pattern to the trends in public and private saving. Furthermore, what accounts for the evolution of private saving—households or firms—also diverges across countries. These observations suggest that regional explanations of the trends in Latin American saving rates may be of limited utility.

This possibility was further explored by conducting principal component analysis on several measures of the aggregate saving rates across countries and across time. The starting point was six time series on saving (for the countries for which data were available) for the period 1980–93 for domestic saving and the period 1975–93 for national saving. A broader set of countries and a longer sample (1970–95), based on an alternative data set from the World Bank, will also be examined. Principal components can describe the comovement in time series. From the original series, a smaller set of series and the principal components can be constructed to explain as much of the variation in the original series as possible. The higher the degree of comovement among the original series, the fewer the number of

Table 1.2 Trends and Cycles in Saving and Its Components: Latin America

Country/ Study	Sample Period	Trend in Saving and Its Components	Recent Developments
Argentina: López Murphy, Navajas, Urbiztondo, and Moskovitz	1968–94	Private saving has been trendless, while public saving has been in a downward trend.	Following the Convertibility Plan in early 1991 and renewed access to international capital markets, private saving rates fell sharply, recovering in 1994. A boom in durable goods expenditures by households is associated with the decline in saving rates.
Chile: Agosin, Crespi, and Letelier	1975–94	Sharp upward trend in private saving, while public saving is flat. Saving by firms appears to account for the steady rise in private saving.	Both public saving and private saving have remained close to their trends in the 1990s.
Colombia: Cárdenas and Escobar	1958–94	Private saving has been flat (as saving by households and firms has been trendless), while public saving showed an upward trend during this period.	Following trade and financial liberalization in 1991, private saving (particularly that of firms) fell sharply. Tax increases appear to contribute to this decline.
Mexico: Calderón-Madrid	1965–95	Both public saving and private saving have been trending lower throughout this period.	Following the December 1987 inflation stabilization plan, private saving, particularly that of households, fell sharply below its trend, recovering only in 1994.
Peru: Gonzales, Lévano, and Llontop	1958–94	Private saving has shown a modest upward trend, while public saving has shown a tendency to decline over time. The rise in private saving is associated with a positive trend in saving by firms, as household saving has declined steadily.	Following the "Fujishock" and its reforms, including financial liberalization, private saving fell sharply as household saving fell well below its trend. Firms' saving continued to increase during this period.
Uruguay: Noya, Lorenzo, and Grau-Pérez	1980–94	Modest downward trend in private saving and upward trend in public saving.	Following the 1991 inflation stabilization plan, private saving dipped further, well below its trend. A relaxation of liquidity constraints helps explain this.
Venezuela: Zambrano, Riutort, Muñoz, and Guevara	1968–94	Marked downward trend in private saving; public saving essentially flat.	Prior to the 1994 banking crisis, private saving had fallen below its secular trend.

Table 1.3 Trends in Public and Private Saving

Sector	Negative Trend	Flat (No Trend)	Positive Trend
Public Saving	3	2	3
Private Saving	4	2	2

Box 1.1 Macroeconomic Time Series Used

Country	National Saving	Domestic Saving	Public Saving	Private Saving	Household Saving	Firms' Saving	Foreign Saving
Argentina	1958–95	1958–95	1970–95	1970–95	N.A.	N.A.	1958–95
Chile	1975–94	N.A.	1975–94	1975–94	1975–94	1975–94	N.A.
Colombia[a]	1958–94	1958–94	1958–94	1958–94	1970–94	1970–94	1958–94
Mexico	1965–95	1965–95	1965–95	1965–95	1987–94	1987–94	1965–95
Peru	1958–94	1958–94	1958–94	1958–94	1979–94	1979–94	1958–94
Uruguay	N.A.	1980–94	1980–94	1980–94	N.A.	N.A.	N.A.
Venezuela	1968–94	1968–94	1968–94	1968–94	N.A.	N.A.	1968–94

N.A. Not available.

Note: Several of the papers also have extensive cross-sectional data on households and firms.

a.The Cárdenas and Escobar study (chapter 4) actually uses longer time series spanning 1925 to 1994.

principal components needed to explain a large share of the variation in the original series.[10]

Tables 1.5 to 1.7 present the results from this exercise for the two measures of domestic saving (the data provided by the chapters in this volume

[10] For instance, if all the original series were identical, then the first principal component would explain 100 percent of the variation of the original series. At the other extreme, if the original series show no comovement whatsoever, then nothing would be gained by looking at common factors. The procedure begins by standardizing the variables, so that each series has zero mean and a unit standard deviation. This standardization ensures that all series receive uniform treatment and that the construction of the principal component indices will not be disproportionately influenced by the series exhibiting the largest variation.

Box 1.2 Methodological Notes

Testing for Ricardian Equivalence

The variables in the system are private consumption (c), income (y), government consumption (g), taxes (t), the change in public sector debt (ΔD), and any other determinant of consumption or saving that needs to be controlled for (z). The vector autoregression (VAR) could be estimated in levels, if the variables are stationary, or in an error-correction (ECVAR) form that is associated with Johansen (1988), if they are nonstationary. A representative equation in the ECVAR system, say that of private consumption, with a single lag to model dynamics would take the form,

$$\Delta c_t = \beta_1 c_{t-1} + \beta_2 g_{t-1} + \beta_3 t_{t-1} + \beta_4 \Delta D_{t-1} + \beta_5 z_{t-1} \qquad [\text{A.1}]$$
$$+ \delta_1 \Delta c_{t-1} + \delta_2 \Delta g_t + \delta_3 \Delta g_{t-1} + \delta_4 \Delta t_t + \delta_5 \Delta t_{t-1}$$
$$+ \delta_6 \Delta (\Delta D)_t + \delta_7 \Delta g_t + \delta_3 (\Delta D)_{t-1} + \delta_8 \Delta z_t + \delta_9 \Delta z_{t-1} + \varepsilon_t.$$

The unrestricted model, as shown in equation [A.1], would be estimated and compared with a second model that restricts the coefficients on taxes and the change in public debt in both the long-run relationship (the βs) and the dynamics (the δs) to be zero under the assumption of Ricardian equivalence, which is the null or maintained hypothesis. The restricted and unrestricted models are compared via a x^2 test on the exclusion restrictions.

Saving-Growth Causality Tests

Following Carroll and Weil (1993), the most common approach for assessing what comes first, when it comes to saving-growth causality, is to rely on straightforward Granger-causality tests. In the context of a VAR framework of the following form:

$$\Delta s_t = \beta_{11} \Delta s_{t-1} + \beta_{12} \Delta y_{t-1} + \varepsilon_{1t} \qquad [\text{A.2}]$$
$$\Delta y_t = \beta_{21} \Delta s_{t-1} + \beta_{22} \Delta y_{t-1} + \varepsilon_{2t}$$

Typically, five-year to ten-year averages for saving and growth are used, and hence a single lag is sufficient to address the temporal precedence, or causality, issue.

and World Bank data) and national saving. As the correlation matrix highlights, saving rates across countries in the region are not all moving in the same direction. The incidence of negative correlations is also fairly high. Furthermore, the correlations are sensitive to the choice of sample—the longer the sample, the weaker the degree of comovement. For instance, for the 1980–93 period, which weighs heavily the debt crisis years, the first principal component explains 53 percent of the total variation in the original domestic saving series. For national saving over a slightly longer sample

Table 1.4 Trends and Cycles in Saving and Its Components: European Case Studies

Country	Sample Period	Trend in Saving and Its Components	Recent Developments
Italy: Jappelli and Pagano	1950–90	Private saving has been trendless, although saving rates declined steadily in the 1980s. Households appear to account for this decline. Public saving has been in a downward trend.	Slowing growth, financial liberalization, and changes to social security appear to be important factors explaining the decline in private saving.
Spain: Boldrin and Martin	1964–95	Upward trend in private saving, while public saving has a sharp negative trend.	Following important trade and financial liberalization measures, private saving fell in the early 1980s and then recovered. Structural changes in expectations about the income-generating process appear to explain this shift in private saving. The reforms did not appear to have a substantive effect.
United Kingdom: Begg and Griffith-Jones	1963–95	Private saving has been flat (as saving by households and firms has been trendless), while public saving has shown a downward trend during this period.	Following financial liberalization in the early 1980s, private saving (by both households and firms) fell. Saving by firms recovered in the 1990s. A relaxation of liquidity constraints and a "euphoria" factor about expected path of income appear to explain this pattern.

that adds the years 1975–79 to the previous sample, the R^2 is 46 percent and the first principal component explains less than half of the total variation of the original series. Finally, for the 1970–95 period and the full sample of countries, the first principal component explains only 38 percent of the variation in saving. Hence, even in the aggregate data, a strong regional pattern does not emerge. By contrast, the same exercise for a group of (formerly) rapidly growing Asian economies yields very different results, with the first principal component explaining anywhere from 65 to 75 percent of the variation in the original series, depending on the sample period used.[11]

The degree of regional comovement in domestic and national saving rates is considerably lower than that found among external variables, such as foreign exchange reserves and real exchange rates. Perhaps the results are not surprising in light of the idiosyncratic nature of many of the shocks

---

[11] The economies are Indonesia, South Korea, Malaysia, Singapore, Thailand.

Table 1.5 Correlation of Domestic Saving across the Region and Factor Analysis: 1980–93

	Argentina	Chile	Colombia	Mexico	Peru
Argentina	1.00				
Chile	−0.12	1.00			
Colombia	−0.60	0.54	1.00		
Mexico	0.52	−0.47	−0.47	1.00	
Peru	0.23	0.49	0.49	−0.40	1.00

Principal Component	Eigenvalue	R^2	Cumulative R^2
1	3.19	0.53	0.53
2	1.47	0.24	0.78
3	0.66	0.11	0.89

Table 1.6 Correlation of Domestic Saving across the Region and Factor Analysis: 1970–95

	Argentina	Chile	Colombia	Mexico	Peru	Uruguay	Venezuela
World Bank Data							
Argentina	1.00						
Chile	−0.55	1.00					
Colombia	0.04	0.42	1.00				
Mexico	0.02	−0.26	0.07	1.00			
Peru	0.06	−0.33	−0.09	0.73	1.00		
Uruguay	0.15	−0.38	0.11	−0.03	0.04	1.00	
Venezuela	0.62	−0.43	−0.08	−0.36	−0.05	0.16	1.00

Principal Component	Eigenvalue	R^2	Cumulative R^2
1	3.03	0.38	0.38
2	1.99	0.25	0.63
3	1.14	0.18	0.77

Table 1.7 Correlation of Domestic Saving across the Region and Factor Analysis: 1975–93

	Argentina	Chile	Colombia	Mexico	Peru
Argentina	1.00				
Chile	−0.36	1.00			
Colombia	0.06	0.70	1.00		
Mexico	0.53	−0.74	−0.48	1.00	
Peru	−0.14	−0.36	−0.42	0.49	1.00

Principal Component	Eigenvalue	R^2	Cumulative R^2
1	2.77	0.46	0.46
2	1.73	0.29	0.75
3	0.53	0.09	0.84

that have influenced saving rates over the course of the years in these countries. For example, the oil shocks had a very different impact on oil-rich Venezuela than on the other countries.[12] Not surprisingly, private saving rates recorded their highest readings following the oil price hikes in the 1970s and fell markedly in the 1980s as oil prices collapsed.

Common Cycles?

While the trends are heterogeneous, a common regional characteristic appears to emerge in the cyclical deviations around those divergent trends. Reinhart and Talvi (1998) show that the common cycle in domestic and foreign saving is not confined to the region and, indeed, cuts across developing countries in other regions. For instance as shown in Table 1.8, the correlation between the cyclical components of domestic saving in Asia and Latin America is in the 0.40 to 0.51 range, depending on the detrending method used, and is statistically significant; a very similar result is shown for the cycles in capital flows (i.e., foreign saving).

One example emerges from the debt crisis. In the initial and most severe stages of the debt crisis in the early 1980s, domestic saving rates fell

---

[12] See Zambrano et al., in this volume.

Table 1.8 Saving and Capital Flows, 1970–95: East Asia and Latin America

	Hodrick-Prescott Filter	Kalman Filter	Beveridge-Nelson Filter
Domestic Saving			
Correlation	0.44	0.51	0.40
t-statistic	2.17	2.03	1.92
Foreign Saving			
Correlation	0.36	0.42	0.46
t-statistic	3.43	2.77	2.32

Source: Reinhart and Talvi (1998).

either back to trend or below trend. This would, of course, be consistent with the permanent income hypothesis, if the sharp decline in incomes at that time was seen as partially transitory. A second example of a regional cyclical pattern comes from the early 1990s, when the region emerged from its debt crisis and regained access to international capital markets. As noted in several of the studies and summarized in Table 1.2 under the heading "Recent Developments," private saving rates in Argentina, Chile, Colombia, Mexico, Peru, and Uruguay fell to either trend level (Chile) or below trend (the rest). The relaxation of liquidity constraints or upward revisions to the expected path of future income may be consistent with the observed phenomenon. Whatever the explanation, the conclusion is that, despite the broad variations in the trend and level of saving rates, Latin American countries share regional forces.

As to what may account for a common cycle, there are alternative explanations. First, as argued in Calvo, Leiderman, and Reinhart (1993), capital flows (foreign saving) may be responding to a shared international factor, such as international interest rates. A relaxation in international borrowing constraints may, in turn, fuel a consumption boom. Second, and not inconsistent with the previous explanation, the timing of structural reforms, including trade and financial sector liberalization, may, to a large degree, coincide across countries in the region (see IDB, 1996 and 1997) and produce concerted cycles of saving and dissaving.[13]

---

[13] This issue is taken up in the next section of this chapter and is discussed in detail in several of the studies.

The lessons from the European experience as to what happens to saving in the wake of liberalization and structural reform are mixed. According to the findings of the authors, financial liberalization (and, in the case of Spain, trade liberalization as well) is thought to be an explanation behind the decline in private saving for Italy and the United Kingdom. Yet, in the case of Spain, once one controls for revisions to the path of expected income following the reforms, the behavior of private saving is well accounted for. Thus, financial liberalization per se did little to reduce or eliminate any prior credit constraints that may have existed.

Issues and Lessons: Evidence from the Case Studies

Several themes cut across all the case studies. Key questions addressed in these studies include the role of fiscal policy, the impact of financial liberalization, the extent of crowding out between domestic saving and capital inflows, and the effect of income distribution on saving. Also examined is the evidence on the causal patterns between growth and saving. Basic concepts and measures of saving are also spelled out.

Basic Concepts

National saving. National Saving (S_n) is the portion of disposable income not devoted to consumption or government purchases. From the basic national income identities, it can be shown that national saving is the sum of investment (I) and the current account balance (CA). Given that policy makers usually become concerned in the presence of large current account deficits, which are so often associated with currency crises, it is not surprising that that they are also concerned with declining saving rates,

$$S_n = I + CA. \tag{1}$$

This basic identity implies that in an open economy, with capital perfectly mobile across borders, saving and investment need not be correlated. The early results of Feldstein and Horioka (1980) revealed a puzzlingly high degree of correlation, which was interpreted as consistent with a low degree of international capital market integration. While subsequent studies have tended to find that those correlations diminish over time, they still remain in a range that would suggest more impediments to the free flow of capital than is evident judging from the evolution of financial markets. This pattern of a declining correlation between saving and investment is discussed in some of the chapters in this volume. For instance, in chapter 2, López-Murphy, Navajas, Urbiztondo, and Moskovitz show that in the case of Argentina, the correlation for the full 1958–95 period is 0.75 but becomes nil during the 1990s. A more recent explanation for high saving-investment correlations is that liquidity constraints may cause the bulk of investment to be financed through the retained earning of firms, an issue that is also investigated in several of the studies in this volume.

Public and private saving. National saving can also be decomposed into its private (S_p) and public (S_g) components. This breakdown is particularly useful in explaining to what extent the observed stagnation of saving rates in so many countries in Latin America is due to lax fiscal policies or to the behavior of the private sector. For the countries of East Asia, public sector saving comprises nearly 25 percent to 40 percent of aggregate saving, implying that some portion of the rapid growth in that region is attributable to thrifty government spending habits.[14]

Hence,

$$S_n = S_p + S_g.$$
[2]

Thus, at least in the East Asian context, where public and private saving were both trending upward over an extended period, there is little evidence of a complete private sector offset to changes in public saving, as would be the case under Ricardian equivalence. As a result, there is scope for governments to boost national saving via increases in public saving. In chapter 7 on Uruguay, Noya, Lorenzo, and Grau-Pérez carefully examine the determinants of public saving; their results provide fresh evidence of an electoral/political cycle, consistent with the findings for many OECD countries.[15]

---

[14] See Edwards (1995).
[15] See Mishra (1997) for recent evidence on this issue.

Capital inflows and domestic saving. For very low-income countries, foreign aid can be a substantial portion of national saving, while for many of the middle-income countries in Latin America, highly cyclical private capital flows can be an uncertain source of financing for consumption, investment, and growth.[16] Much of the empirical evidence suggests that there is a partial offset between domestic and foreign saving.[17] The combination of evidence on crowding out between capital inflows and domestic saving, and the volatile and uncertain nature of capital inflows—not to mention their propensity to sudden reversals—has made policy makers wary about the attractiveness of capital inflows, particularly those with a short maturity. Not surprisingly, two of the countries studied in the following chapters, Chile and Colombia, have introduced measures to discourage capital inflows and reduce foreign saving.

Furthermore, the composition of foreign saving may also influence whether it is consumed, invested or saved. For instance, Boone (1994), assessing the impact of official foreign aid in a large sample of developing countries, concludes that nearly all official aid is consumed and, hence, does little to promote growth.[18] The composition also matters as regards the stability of foreign saving, with foreign direct investment generally thought to be a more stable source of external saving than short-term and portfolio capital.[19] Hence, it is also useful to decompose national saving into its domestic (S_d) and external components (S_e),

$$S_n = S_d + S_e.$$ [3]

Firms and households. Finally, private saving can be decomposed into the saving of firms (S_f) and that of households (S_h):

$$S_p = S_f + S_h.$$ [4]

---

[16] An extreme example is Mozambique, where foreign aid amounted to 76 percent of GDP in 1989.

[17] For a comparison of the cyclical relationship between domestic and foreign saving rates in Asia and Latin America, see Reinhart and Talvi (1998).

[18] See also Obstfeld (1995).

[19] See Kaminsky and Reinhart (1998) for a study of this issue as it relates to financial crises in Asia and Latin America.

In the past, several studies have concluded that firm and household saving are substitutes, though the degree of substitution is not one-to-one and varies considerably across countries.[20] Discerning among the saving patterns of firms and households can be a valuable ingredient in designing policies, such as tax and pension reform, that directly or indirectly aim to influence saving. For instance, following their analysis of disaggregated private saving data, in chapter 3 on Chile, Agosin, Crespi, and Letelier reach the provocative conclusion that pension reform does little to explain Chile's dramatic rise in private saving. They show that the steep increase in saving rates is due to firms and that, indeed, a decline in voluntary household saving was posted after the pension reform.

Public and Private Saving: Evidence of Ricardian Equivalence

Fiscal policy plays a central role in macroeconomic management, particularly in developing countries, where access to international capital markets is costly and frequently erratic. As the recent crises in Asia highlight, countries often increase public sector saving on short notice, so as to restore confidence and calm financial markets. In the context of inflation stabilization plans, whether the plans use the exchange rate or a monetary aggregate as the nominal anchor, fiscal adjustment is required to allow the central bank to pursue its goal of price stability. However, under certain assumptions about the completeness of financial markets and consumers' horizons, theoretical models admit the possibility that any effort by governments to increase public saving—presumably with the goal of increasing domestic saving—will only induce offsetting changes in private saving.

The conditions for Ricardian equivalence, however, are quite stringent. It requires households to have perfect access to capital markets, leaving no role for liquidity constraints, and it assumes households have an infinite planning horizon and common discount rates for the public and private sectors. Furthermore, it requires that future income, tax, and public expenditure flows are known with certainty and that taxes are not distorting. Notwithstanding the low likelihood that all these conditions are simultaneously met, the empirical literature on the determinants of saving has

---

[20] See, for instance, Denison (1958) and David and Scadding (1974).

tried hard to assess the degree of offset, or substitutability, between private and public saving.

Typically, tests for Ricardian equivalence have taken three forms. First, studies that have estimated reduced-form saving equations have included the public saving rate, s_g, as a regressor in explaining the private saving rate, s_p, testing whether the coefficient on public sector saving is significantly different from -1:

$$sp_t = \beta z_t + \gamma sg_t + \varepsilon_t \qquad [5]$$

$$\text{Ho: } \gamma = -1.0 \qquad [6]$$

where z is a vector that controls all the other determinants of private saving. Second, it is possible to use a vector autoregressive (VAR) framework to test for Ricardian equivalence. This test, which is described in Box 1.2, is in the spirit of Seater and Mariano (1985), who, following Barro (1974), proposed that under Ricardian equivalence all that matters for the household planning problem is government consumption, as households are indifferent whether its financing is through taxes or debt accumulation.[21] Finally, it is possible to say something about whether Ricardian equivalence holds or not via an indirect route, by testing for the presence of liquidity constraints, infinite horizons, or both.[22]

Nine of the studies in this volume investigated empirically the issue of Ricardian equivalence, with the overwhelming conclusion that it does not hold (Table 1.9). Either public sector saving is not statistically significant in explaining private saving, it has the wrong sign (Jappelli and Pagano, in this volume), or for the most part (where the coefficient has the anticipated negative sign), estimates of the degree of offset between public and private saving rates range from around -0.70 to about -0.40 and are significantly different from -1.0. Indeed, most of the results presented are broadly in line with those obtained in recent exhaustive cross-country studies, which have found a relatively low degree of offset between public and private saving relative to the predictions of Ricardian equivalence. For in-

---

[21] Of course, this assumes taxes are lump sum. If taxes are distortionary, this test would be biased against rejecting the null hypothesis of Ricardian equivalence.

[22] See, for instance, Haque and Montiel (1989).

Table 1.9 Public and Private Saving: Evidence on Ricardian Equivalence

Study	Country	Sample Period, Frequency, and Dependent Variable	Methodology	Results
Agosin, Crespi, and Letelier	Chile	1975–94, annual, private saving rate	Johansen's ECVAR	Rejects Ricardian equivalence. Only partial substitutability is found. Coefficient on public saving is –0.608. Significantly different from –1.0.
Cárdenas and Escobar	Colombia	1929–94, 1970–94, annual, private and household saving rates	Reduced-form saving equation, OLS	Rejects Ricardian equivalence. Coefficient on public saving is –0.716 (full sample) and –0.507 (subsample) for private saving and –0.391 (subsample) for household saving. In all cases significant.
Jappelli and Pagano	G-10, excluding Italy	Panel, 1960–94, national saving rates	Reduced-form saving equation, OLS and robust estimation	Rejects Ricardian equivalence. Coefficient on public saving ranges from 0.68 to 0.73, depending on method of estimation and the use of time trends. In all cases *positive* and significant.
Gonzales, Lévano, and Llontop	Peru	1950–94, annual	Reduced-form saving equation, OLS	Rejects Ricardian equivalence. Coefficient on public saving is –0.43 and significant.
Boldrin and Martin	Spain	1964–95, quarterly, percent change in real private saving	Reduced-form saving equation, OLS	Ricardian equivalence is not explicitly tested. Fiscal measure is growth rate of public income. Coefficient is –0.40 and significant.
Begg and Griffith-Jones	United Kingdom	1963–95, annual	Reduced-form saving equation, instrumental variables	Coefficient on public saving is –0.46 in the household saving equation. Yet, when public saving is the dependent variable, the coefficient on household saving is not different from unity.
Noya, Lorenzo, and Grau-Pérez	Uruguay	1975:1–94:4, quarterly, private consumption	Consumption function, Johansen's ECVAR	Rejects Ricardian equivalence. Coefficients are not reported, but the χ^2 statistic on the restrictions on the coefficients of public consumption, revenue, and debt in the VAR is.
Zambrano, Riutort, Muñoz, and Guevara	Venezuela	1968–94, annual, private consumption	Consumption, function, Johansen's ECVAR	Rejects Ricardian equivalence. Coefficients are not reported, but the χ^2 statistic on the restrictions on the coefficients of public consumption, revenue, and debt in the VAR is.

stance, the results imply a somewhat higher degree of offset than was suggested by Loayza, Schmidt-Hebbel, and Servén (1998), who find that the coefficient on public saving lies in the –0.30 to –0.20 range. However, they are in the –0.673 to –0.416 range estimated by Edwards (1995), who also rejected Ricardian equivalence for his sample.

However, this evidence must be interpreted with care, as point estimates of the offset coefficient for Latin America may be subject to bias. Specifically, Gavin and Perotti (1998) note that, unlike industrial countries, for most of Latin America access to capital markets is sporadic. During bad times private borrowing constraints limit the private sector's ability to offset changes in public saving, while the relaxation of these constraints during good times gives the private sector a greater ability to internalize the actions of the government. The authors' empirical estimates suggest that asymmetries are significant, with the estimated offset coefficient in the 0.70–0.75 range in good times and roughly half that magnitude in bad times. Nonetheless, their evidence, like that of the studies in this volume, rejects Ricardian equivalence.

Liquidity Constraints, Credit Channels, Financial Liberalization, and Consumption Booms

While there may be more than one reason for the rejection of Ricardian equivalence, one explanation for its empirical failure is that not all households have access to credit markets, and hence, some households have no ability to smooth consumption over time. Thus, for the liquidity-constrained households, consumption decisions are entirely determined by current income. On theoretical grounds, it has been shown that a relaxation of liquidity constraints will be associated with a consumption boom and a decline in aggregate saving. Furthermore, the more binding the initial constraints, the greater the consumption boom that can be expected.[23]

Many countries in Latin America, and elsewhere, have undergone or are anticipating substantive financial sector reforms that end a regime of financial repression, where credit was directed and interest rates on loans

---

[23] See Obstfeld (1995) for theoretical discussion and simulations of such exercises. See Copelman (1994) for an empirical investigation of the Campbell and Mankiw (1989) model to explain consumption booms during several inflation stabilization plans in Latin America.

and deposits were set by decree. Many of the past liberalization episodes unleashed a period of rapid growth in bank lending, asset price booms, and increases in consumption that often coincided with a decline in private saving rates. Many of those episodes also ended in a full-fledged financial crisis.[24] Hence, no analysis of saving is complete without an assessment of the pervasiveness of liquidity constraints. Gauging the prevalence of constraints is important both to understand the extent to which these may account for a higher level of saving than would otherwise prevail and to assess what could happen to saving if the constraints were relaxed, say via renewed access to international capital markets, financial liberalization, or both mechanisms.

The tests for the presence of liquidity constraints have often been linked to a credit channel in explaining the behavior of consumption/saving. Studies that have focused on reduced-form saving equations have tested for liquidity constraints by introducing credit (either its growth rate or as a ratio to GDP) as a regressor. The premise is that greater access to credit reduces saving. Hence, the anticipated coefficient on the credit variable is negative. A more explicit test for the importance of liquidity constraints was proposed by Campbell and Mankiw (1989). They postulated that there are two types of households in the economy: A share of households, λc, is liquidity constrained and their consumption is entirely determined by the evolution of current income, while the remaining households, $(1-\lambda)$, have free access to capital markets and can smooth their consumption intertemporally. As a result:

$$c_t = \lambda c_t^c + (1 - \lambda)\, c_t^u \qquad [7]$$

where aggregate consumption, c_t, is the weighted sum of the unconstrained and constrained households, denoted by superscripts u and c, respectively. Most often, equation [7] has been estimated substituting into c_t^u the simplest form of utility function with one good and no monetary considerations.[25] Further simplifying assumptions have allowed for linearization of the Euler condition that determines the dynamics of consumption of the uncon-

---

[24] See Kaminsky and Reinhart (1996) for a chronology and stylized facts surrounding these episodes.
[25] See Reinhart and Talvi (1998) for a survey of this literature for developing countries.

strained households. If the real interest rate is assumed constant, then the growth of aggregate consumption is given by,

$$\Delta c_t = \theta + \lambda \Delta y_t + \varepsilon_t \qquad [8]$$

where embedded in θ is an estimate of the intertemporal elasticity of substitution (IES).

Most of the studies in this volume (see Table 1.10) addressed this issue through direct estimation or indirectly, by discussing the stylized evidence and reviewing the existing literature. With the exception of Peru (see Gonzales, Lévano, and Llontop, in this volume), who find no evidence of an important credit channel in the macro data, the bulk of the studies (using macro and/or micro data) suggest that liquidity constraints are prevalent.[26] Two of the studies, Uruguay and Venezuela, present estimates of λ in the 0.36 to 0.53 range. These estimates are in line with those obtained in other countries with a similar level of development.[27] Interestingly, introducing an interaction term between income and credit growth in equation [8] (see chapter 7) reduces λ.

The chapters on Colombia, Italy, Mexico, the United Kingdom, and Uruguay also provide some support for the view that relaxation of liquidity constraints following financial liberalization played a substantive role in explaining the observed decline in private saving rates in those countries. In a similar vein, the study on Argentina suggests that regaining access to international capital markets following the implementation of the Convertibility Plan played a key role in decoupling aggregate saving and investment. Indeed, a recent study that exploits new panel cross-country data for developing and OECD countries finds that in most specifications, the credit variable had the anticipated negative sign in the saving equation.[28]

The evidence from most of the studies that use micro data on saving by firms (Chile, Colombia) and households (Mexico) seem to corroborate the results from the macro data in terms of the existence of binding liquidity constraints. They also allocate a key role to the relaxation of these con-

---

[26] These results contrast those reported for Peru in Haque and Montiel (1989), who estimate a statistically significant $\lambda = 0.25$.

[27] See Vaidyanathan (1993) for the link between liquidity constraints and development.

[28] See Loayza, Schmidt-Hebbel, and Servén (1998) and Edwards (1995).

Table 1.10 How Prevalent Are Liquidity Constraints?

Study	Country	Sample Period, Frequency, and Dependent Variable	Methodology	Results
López-Murphy, Navajas, Urbiztondo, and Moskovitz	Argentina	1960–94, annual national saving rate	ECM, variant of Feldstein-Horioka	There is a significant and positive relationship between saving and investment through 1989, becoming insignificant in the 1990s. Argentina's renewed entry into international capital markets is thought to account for this structural shift.
Cárdenas and Escobar	Colombia	1985–93, annual, 397 firms, saving by firms	OLS	Finds firms' propensity to save out of profits fell following financial reform. Cash flow and saving decisions are independent after reforms.
Agosin, Crespi, and Letelier,	Chile, micro data from 196 firms	Panel, 1986–94, annual, saving by firm	OLS and robust estimation	Finds evidence that firms are liquidity constrained in that they have to rely on retained earnings to finance their investment projects.
Jappelli and Pagano	Italy	N.A.	Discussion and stylized evidence	Based on their earlier studies, they present evidence as to the role of liquidity in keeping saving rates high in Italy relative to other OECD countries and the role of financial liberalization in explaining their recent decline.
Calderón-Madrid	Mexico, micro data household survey	1989, 1992, 1994, household saving rates	OLS	Access to credit reduces household saving. The coefficient on a dummy variable that takes on the value of 1 if the household had access to credit ranges from –0.245 for 1989 to –0.16 for 1992.
Gonzales, Lévano, and Llontop	Peru	1950–94, annual	ECM	Growth in credit to the private sector is not significant in explaining the growth in real private saving.
Begg and Griffith-Jones	United Kingdom	N.A.	Discussion of previous studies	From the review of six studies, the balance of the results (four of the six) attach an important role to financial deregulation in explaining the decline in U.K. saving rates.
Noya, Lorenzo, and Grau-Pérez	Uruguay	1975:1–94:4, quarterly, private consumption growth	Instrumental variables, Campbell and Mankiw (1989) approach	The proportion of liquidity-constrained households is in the 0.39 to 0.49 range. Furthermore, introducing credit significantly reduces the coefficient on current income. Yet, using dummy variables, the authors find no evidence that the dependence of consumption on income is lower in the post–financial liberalization period.
Zambrano, Riutort, Muñoz, and Guevara	Venezuela	1968–94, annual, growth consumption	GMM, Campbell and Mankiw (1989) approach	The proportion of liquidity-constrained households is in the 0.355 to 0.534 range, depending on whether or not durable goods were included in the consumption measure.

N.A. Not available.

Note: ECM, error-correction model; GMM, general method of moments; OLS, ordinary least squares.

straints in explaining the decline in the 1990s in private saving rates in Colombia and Mexico following financial liberalization. Furthermore, in chapter
5, Calderón-Madrid finds evidence that the boom in real estate prices that
accompanied financial liberalization in Mexico further contributed to the
decline in saving by households. His results suggest that households that
owned property, and could use such property as collateral to secure loans,
saved less. For Peru, the results from the micro data are somewhat more
conflicting. Gonzales, Lévano, and Llontop find no evidence of high saving-
investment correlations for firms, suggesting liquidity constraints were not
quantitatively important, yet their household data reveal that access to credit
after 1991 played an important role in explaining the decline in household
saving. The evidence from Agosin, Crespi, and Letelier's analysis of firms'
saving behavior in Chile (see chapter 3) provides support for the argument
put forth in Morandé (1996), that the steep rise in firms' saving during most
of the 1980s had much to do with the rising liquidity constraints they faced,
as bank credit dried up in the wake of the severe crisis that shook Chile's
financial sector.

Analyses of the recent consumption booms in Argentina and Uruguay following their exchange-rate based (ERBS) inflation stabilization plans
in the early 1990s also provide interesting insights as to why private saving
rates declined (Table 1.11). While there is much theoretical literature on the
potential sources of these booms, and more limited empirical information,
chapter 2 by López-Murphy, Navajas, Urbiztondo, and Moskovitz on Argentina represents one of the first efforts to explain what drives durable
goods consumption during these boom periods.[29] Indeed, the surge in durable goods consumption (these are usually imports) is at the center stage
of the consumption booms that have characterized so many of the recent
and past inflation stabilization plans. Unfortunately, lack of data on durable goods consumption has, to date, limited researchers' ability to analyze
this issue formally.

The study on Argentina suggests that revisions to expectations about
the path of future income played a key role in explaining the boom. Yet, the
results suggest that the evolution of interest rates also played an important
role; this result is subject to more than one interpretation. There is the
intertemporal story, as pioneered by Calvo (1986), suggesting that if the

---

[29] See Reinhart and Végh (1995).

Table 1.11 Consumption Booms and Durable Goods

Study	Country	Sample Period, Frequency, and Dependent Variable	Methodology	Results
López Murphy, Navajas, Urbiztondo, and Moskovitz	Argentina	1960–94, annual growth in consumption of durable goods	ECM	The authors weigh and test competing models to explain the boom in durable goods consumption following the Convertibility Plan. They find that the decline in nominal interest rates, the rise in salaries (in U.S. dollars) and the decline in the price of durable goods all help explain the boom, suggesting intertemporal, intratemporal, and wealth effects.
Calderón-Madrid	Mexico, micro data from household survey	1989, 1992, 1994	OLS	The results suggest that a consumption boom following the inflation stabilization and financial liberalization had much to do with greater access to credit and an asset (particularly housing) price boom, which allowed households to borrow using their real estate as collateral.
Boldrin and Martin	Spain	1964–95, quarterly, percent change in real private saving	Descriptive and OLS	A consumption boom followed the trade and financial sector liberalization in 1986. Based on their model, authors conclude that revisions to expected permanent income can account for much of the boom.
Begg and Griffith-Jones	United Kingdom	N.A.	Literature review	Two competing hypotheses are compared to explain the consumption boom in the U.K. The two are easier access to credit and revised expectations of future income. Empirical studies are inconclusive, although the financial liberalization/credit channel received more weight.
Noya, Lorenzo, and Grau-Pérez	Uruguay	1975:1–94:4, quarterly, private consumption	Instrumental variables	In explaining the 1990 poststabilization boom, the study finds that more rapid income growth, increased credit availability, and lower interest rates all contributed to explain the boom.

N.A. Not available.

Note: ECM, error-correction model; GMM, general method of moments; OLS, ordinary least squares.

interest rate decline is perceived to be temporary, people will consume to-day when the effective price of consumption is low, relative to its expected future level. However, the results are also consistent with other interpretations. Recalling that interest rates affect the relative price of the flow of durable goods and services (see Ogaki and Reinhart, 1998), lower interest rates will also induce an intratemporal substitution toward relatively cheaper durable goods. Furthermore, the lower interest rates could be a function of a declining country risk premium, more favorable access to international capital markets, and, hence, a relaxation of liquidity constraints. Indeed, the authors present such evidence when analyzing the saving-investment link.

Durable goods are also relatively credit intensive vis-à-vis services and nondurables. Hence, the results for Uruguay (see chapter 7), which use total consumption and include durable goods, suggest that easier availability of credit may have fueled the boom in consumption and the decline in the saving rate.

In sum, the heterogeneous evidence presented in this book suggests that agents in most countries are affected in varying degrees by liquidity constraints and that a relaxation of these constraints may partially account for a decline in the saving rate. Whether the decline in saving is secular or transitory remains to be seen and merits further study.

Do Capital Inflows Crowd Out Domestic Saving?

There are many parallels between analyzing the links between saving and liquidity constraints and assessing the relationship between domestic and foreign saving. In industrial countries, access to international capital markets is continuous and, by and large, taken for granted. Yet, for most developing countries—including those such as Korea that have achieved near-industrialized status—access to international capital is limited in scope, given that it is costly, and subject to periodic collapses. In other words, examining the link between domestic and foreign saving involves looking at liquidity constraints (and the relaxation of these) at the country level rather than at the level of the household or the firm.

Hence, like a relaxation in domestic liquidity constraints, greater access to foreign saving (i.e., capital inflows) may lead to a decline in domestic saving. This proposition is well justified on theoretical grounds (see Reinhart and Talvi, 1998) and has been documented in the empirical literature with mixed results. Capital inflows may finance consumption booms. This can occur through a variety of channels, but one channel, which is particularly relevant to the Asian and Latin American experience of the 1990s, has to do with the role played by banks. When international interest rates are markedly below domestic interest rates, it is very profitable for banks to borrow offshore (a capital inflow) and lend domestically at the higher interest rates. The greater availability of credit for both households and firms provides an opportunity to consume (and/or invest) beyond the confines of current income—hence, the decline in private saving.

As with testing for Ricardian equivalence in the context of a reduced-form saving equation framework, most of the studies that have examined the link between domestic and foreign saving have done so by including foreign saving (or else the current account) as an explanatory variable for private saving or domestic saving (Table 1.12). However, unlike Ricardian equivalence, the null hypothesis tested is whether the coefficient on foreign saving is significantly different from zero. The relationship between domes-

Table 1.12 Do Capital Inflows Crowd Out Domestic Saving?

Study	Country	Sample Period, Frequency, and Dependent Variable	Methodology	Results
López Murphy, Navajas, Urbiztondo, and Moskovitz	Argentina	1960–94, annual national saving rate	Pairwise correlation	The authors report a correlation with foreign saving of –0.33.
Agosin, Crespi, and Letelier	Chile	1975–94, annual, private saving rate	Johansen's ECVAR	Coefficient on foreign saving rate is –1.116. Cannot reject that there is full offset (i.e., not significantly different from –1.0).
Cárdenas and Escobar	Colombia	1929–94, 1970–94, annual, private and household saving rates	Reduced-form saving equation, OLS	Coefficient on foreign saving rate is –0.36 (full sample) and –0.395 (subsample) for private saving and –0.316 (subsample) for household saving. In all cases significant.
Gonzales, Lévano, and Llontop	Peru	1950–94, annual, private saving rate	OLS	Coefficient on foreign saving is –0.37 and significant.

tic and foreign saving that is suggested by theoretical explanations is likely to be cyclical, while secular factors are more closely linked to income trends and demographics. For this reason, another approach has focused on correlations among the cyclical components of domestic and foreign saving.

In the studies in this volume that examined this issue closely, the conclusion is that foreign saving crowds out, albeit not perfectly (the exception is Chile), domestic saving.[30] The bulk of the coefficients on foreign saving are clustered in the −0.40 to −0.30 range. Focusing on the cyclical components of domestic and foreign saving, Reinhart and Talvi (1998) also conclude that the bulk of the evidence for both Asia and Latin America is that domestic saving and external saving are negatively rather than positively related. Other things being equal, a relaxation of international "liquidity constraints," via a rise in capital inflows, can be expected to reduce domestic saving, although usually the decline is not proportional.

Growth and Saving: What Comes First?

Earlier literature on the links between saving and growth stressed the need for countries to boost their saving rates. Paradoxically, in light of the preceding discussion, it was thought that financial deregulation could accomplish this task. By allowing real interest rates to rise and, in many cases, become positive for the first time, financial deregulation would bolster saving. In turn, higher saving rates would finance higher levels of investment and fuel economic growth.[31] While financial deregulation does, more often than not, result in higher real interest rates, it has failed to produce the anticipated positive effects on saving.[32] Over and beyond the credit channel discussed in the preceding subsections, there may be important reasons why the link between saving and real rates of return may be weak, particularly for low-income countries.[33] Furthermore, even if saving increases in response to the

---

[30] Agosin, Crespi, and Letelier (in this volume) find that for Chile they cannot reject the null hypothesis that the offset is complete, that is, the coefficient on foreign saving is not significantly different from −1.0.

[31] See, for instance, McKinnon (1973).

[32] See Galbis (1993) on the evolution of interest rates during financial liberalization.

[33] For instance, Ogaki, Ostry, and Reinhart (1995) argue that the sensitivity of saving to real interest rates depends on a country's wealth. The poorer the country and the closer it is to

higher real interest rates, recent studies have even questioned that the chain of causation runs from saving to growth. The evidence presented in Carroll and Weil (1993) suggests that growth drives saving rates—and not the other way around.

From a policy standpoint, taking these results at face value implies that policy makers need not be concerned with tax incentives and other policies geared toward stimulating domestic saving. Instead, their focus should be on structural reforms that increase efficiency and macroeconomic stabilization. This is, of course, a simplistic argument. Even in the absence of a saving-growth causal chain, policy makers may wish to pursue higher levels of saving. For instance, a marked decline in private saving, such as those observed in Argentina, Colombia, and Mexico in the 1990s, may precipitate an undesired deterioration in the current account that could undermine credibility and precipitate a currency crisis. Furthermore, while the existing empirical literature has had relatively little to say about this, domestic saving is likely to be a less volatile source of funds than fickle foreign saving.

Following Carroll and Weil (1993), the most common approach to assessing what comes first, when it comes to saving-growth causality, is to rely on straightforward Granger-causality tests (see Box 1.2). Typically, five-year to ten-year averages for saving and growth are used, and, hence, a single lag is sufficient to address the temporal precedence, or causality, issue.

The case studies that examined this issue—unlike the more clear-cut findings of the absence of Ricardian equivalence, the importance of liquidity constraints, and the substitutability between domestic and foreign saving—presented no clear consensus. Table 1.13 highlights the diversity of the findings. For Chile and Venezuela, the results appear to point in the causal direction from growth to saving (and investment). For Colombia, the results are sensitive to how the "long-run" values of output and saving are measured. For one measure, there is no apparent link between saving and growth, while for another there is mutual causation. The evidence presented in Jappelli and Pagano (see chapter 9) shows a strong positive influ-

---

only being able to support a subsistence level of consumption, the less saving will respond to changes in interest rates.

Table 1.13 Evidence on the Links between Growth and Saving

Study	Country	Sample Period, Frequency, and Dependent Variable	Methodology	Results
Agosin, Crespi, and Letelier	Chile	1960–94, annual, private saving rate and private investment/GDP ratio, also growth rates and levels per capita	Bivariate VAR	No direct tests on growth are performed, but in all the specifications there is a unidirectional causal relationship from investment to saving.
Cárdenas and Escobar	Colombia	1929–94, annual, 10-year averages in private saving rates and GDP growth (as well as their permanent components)	Bivariate VAR	No causal relationships are detected when 10-year averages are used. When permanent components are used, there is a significant two-way causality.
Jappelli and Pagano	G-10, excluding Italy	Panel, 1960–94, national saving rates	Reduced-form saving equation, OLS, and robust estimation	While no two-way causality tests are performed, growth is a significant determinant of saving in all specifications and estimated strategies.
Boldrin and Martin	Spain	1964–95, quarterly, national or private saving rate and GDP growth	Bivariate VAR	Pairwise correlations are high for national saving (0.69), but there is no evidence of a causal relationship running in either direction. This result is robust to using levels of the variables.
Zambrano, Riutort, Muñoz, and Guevara	Venezuela	1968–94, annual, private saving rate and GDP growth including and excluding oil	Bivariate VAR	There is a significant (at the 10% level) causal relationship running from growth to saving irrespective of the measure of GDP used. There is no causal relationship from saving to GDP.

ence from growth to saving; but the opposite chain of causation is not empirically investigated. For Spain, the evidence presented in Boldrin and Martin (see chapter 10) suggests that contemporaneous growth-saving correlations are high, but no causal link is evident.

In sum, the collective evidence does not provide conclusive support for (or disprove, for that matter) the results presented in Carroll and Weil (1993), in which growth causes saving. Given the richness of the policy implications as to how this issue is settled, perhaps the only clear conclusion is that the links between long-term growth and saving merit further scrutiny in Latin America.

The Life-Cycle Hypothesis (LCH): Macro and Micro Evidence

The LCH is derived from the aggregation of finite-lived overlapping generations and introduces age-related consumer heterogeneity. Consumption in any period is a function of both wealth and disposable income, where the marginal propensities to consume from either are dependent on factors such as age, life expectancy, and working years. The LCH posits that individuals will have negative saving when they are young, have positive saving during their working years, and run down their savings in retirement. Hence, saving follows a hump-shaped pattern for each consumer.

Variables associated with the LCH have, most often, found strong empirical support in the cross-country macroeconomic data. Most often, studies that estimate reduced-form saving equations using panel or cross-sectional data find that the age dependency ratio is significantly and negatively linked to saving. While the values of the estimated coefficients are sensitive to the set of regressors used in the sample countries and to how the dependency ratio was measured, the results are robust across a broad array of specifications and data sets.[34] As the LCH would predict, the higher the share of the very young and the very old (who dissave) in the population, the lower the saving rate. As shown in Table 1.14, Colombia and Peru do, indeed, present similar evidence.

Unlike the issue of liquidity constraints, where the results from the study of the micro and macro data converged, the evidence on the LCH is

---

[34] Other demographic variables frequently included in the regression analysis are population growth rates and average retirement ages.

Table 1.14 Life-Cycle Hypothesis and Saving

Study	Country	Sample Period, Frequency, and Dependent Variable	Methodology	Results
Cárdenas and Escobar	Colombia	1929–94, 1970–94, annual, private saving rate	Reduced-form saving equation, OLS	The age dependency ratio is significant in all specifications. Its coefficient is –0.27 (full sample) and is increasingly important in the more recent period; the range is –2.44 to –1.905 (subsample).
Jappelli and Pagano	Italy, micro data on household saving	1984, 1986, 1987, 1989, 1991, and 1993 household saving rates	Descriptive analysis	The authors conclude that the evidence in the micro data does not provide support for the LCH in explaining the decline in aggregate saving. The decline in the propensity to save is evident across all age groups.
Calderón-Madrid	Mexico, micro data on household survey	1989, 1992, 1994	OLS	In contrast to the predictions of the LCH, the number of children per household aged 12 or less and of heads of household aged 65 or older (eldest group) were either not significant or were significant with a positive sign.
Gonzales, Lévano, and Llontop	Peru	1950–94, annual, real private saving	Johansen's ECVAR	The inverse of the dependency ratio is part of the cointegrating vector. Consistent with the LCH, the coefficient ranges from 0.297 to 0.427, depending on sample period.

less conclusive. As noted, there is some support for the LCH at the macro level. In the case of Peru, the pattern of household saving across age groups in cross-sectional micro data appeared to be broadly consistent with the hump-shaped pattern predicted by the LCH. Yet, two of the studies that analyzed micro household data find little support for LCH predictions. In the case of Mexico, the number of children aged 12 or less per household has a positive and significant coefficient in the saving equations, while households headed by someone aged 65 or more (the oldest group) saved more, although the statistical significance depended on the year examined. In a similar vein, Jappelli and Pagano (in this volume) have little success explaining Italy's declining saving rate on the basis of the life-cycle model's predictions. During a period of slowing economic growth, the LCH would predict that saving would fall, as the incomes of the highest-saving age group—the middle-aged and actively employed—would be proportionately hit the hardest. Hence, a priori, one should expect to find in the micro data that the decline in saving rates is largely confined to this working-age cohort. The data presented in Jappelli and Pagano instead reveal declines in the saving rates of all age groups. Perhaps the lack of conclusive evidence on the causality from growth to saving in these studies reflects an ambiguity in its underpinnings in the LCH.

Other Determinants of Saving

Two additional variables in both theory and existing evidence emerge as potential determinants of private saving. The first variable, income distribution, has usually been coupled with household saving, while the terms of trade may affect both the household and the firm.

Income Distribution

The bulk of the theoretical literature on household saving has suggested that a more skewed income distribution would produce a higher level of aggregate saving. The argument rests on differential propensities to consume out of current income, with the rich consuming a proportionally lower share of their income. However, a recent strand of the political economy literature has suggested that there is a positive link between political instability and income inequality.[35] The argument runs as follows: Political instability increases uncertainty; uncertainty adversely affects investment; and lower investment means lower growth. Taking this causal chain a step further, if, indeed, growth causes saving as Carroll and Weil (1993) suggest, then countries with more income inequality and lower growth would also be expected to have lower saving rates. Hence, on theoretical grounds, the sign of the coefficient on income inequality is ambiguous. Previous empirical studies (see Plies and Reinhart, 1998, for a recent survey) have found scattered evidence in favor of both positive and negative links. A recent study by Schmidt-Hebbel and Servén (1996), using a comprehensive cross-country data set on income distribution, found no significant link. This lack of

---

[35] See, for instance, Alessina and Rodrik (1994) and Persson and Tabellini (1994).

significance was robust to the specification of saving used, as well as to the choice of sample countries. Table 1.15 summarizes the results of the studies in this volume that examined this issue. For Spain and Venezuela, macro data were used to examine this issue; in neither case was the proxy for income distribution significant.

On the basis of the household data, the Mexican case offers some provocative results. While the issue of income distribution is not explicitly addressed, Calderón-Madrid links household saving to educational attainment, specifically, years of education. Presumably, education and income levels are positively related; indeed the household survey data from Peru illustrate this positive correlation. Yet, Calderón-Madrid finds that more educated households save less. This is explained by the fact that these households have access to credit, while less educated households do not.

The Terms of Trade

As with income distribution, the predicted theoretical sign of the relationship between the terms of trade and saving is ambiguous. When a country experiences an adverse temporary terms of trade shock (a decline in the relative price of its exports), this temporary decline in current income should lead to dissaving, based on consumption-smoothing considerations. This is the basis of the Harberger-Laursen-Metzler (HLM) effect, and it follows from the permanent income hypothesis (PIH). The PIH suggests there is a difference between the short-run and long-run marginal propensities to consume, where the difference depends on the perceived permanence of the change in income. If the decline in income is seen as permanent, abstracting from habit persistence, consumption would be reduced accordingly; if the shock is temporary, consumption does not adjust and saving declines.

However, this is only part of the story. Following the shock, imports become expensive relative to other goods in the basket. This relative price shift can be expected to lead individuals to substitute away from the imported good and consume less of it—this is known as the consumption-tilting effect. Hence, consumption-smoothing considerations suggest a positive relationship between the terms of trade and saving and consumption tilting a negative one.

Presumably, the issue can be settled empirically. All of the four case studies in the following chapters that examine this issue find a positive in-

Table 1.15 Other Determinants of Saving

Study	Country	Sample Period, Frequency, and Dependent Variable	Methodology	Results
Income distribution				
Calderón-Madrid	Mexico, micro data from household survey	1989, 1992, 1994	OLS	While the explanatory variable does not directly measure household income, it is years of education. Presumably education and income levels are positively related. The author finds that more educated households save *less*. The interpretation given is that these household heads have access to credit, while less educated household heads do not.
Boldrin and Martin	Spain	1964–95, quarterly, percent change in real private saving	OLS	The proxy for income distribution, the share of gross profit margin over total value added, has a positive coefficient, but it is not statistically significant.
Zambrano, Riutort, Muñoz, and Guevara	Venezuela	1968–94, annual, private consumption	Johansen's ECVAR	The authors find no statistical evidence that their proxy for income distribution affects saving.
Terms of trade				
López Murphy, Navajas, Urbiztondo, and Moskovitz	Argentina	1960–94, annual national saving rate	Pairwise correlation	The correlation between the terms of trade and saving is not statistically significant (0.03).
Gonzales, Lévano, and Llontop	Peru	1950–94, annual, real private saving	Johansen's ECVAR	The terms of trade affect long-run saving positively, are significant, and are a component of the cointegrating vector. Changes in these do not influence significantly the short-run dynamics of saving.
Zambrano, Riutort, Muñoz, and Guevara	Venezuela	1968–94, annual, private consumption	Johansen's ECVAR	The terms of trade are significant and are a component of the cointegrating vector. Furthermore, terms of trade changes significantly affect the short-run dynamics of saving.

fluence of the terms of trade on saving, consistent with the HLM hypothesis. In Peru, the terms of trade are part of the cointegrating vector, suggesting that they influence the long-run level of saving, if not necessarily its short-run dynamics. In the case of Venezuela, estimates of an Euler equation derived from a model that allows for consumption of traded and nontraded goods, as in Ostry and Reinhart (1992), are used to simulate the effects of a terms of trade shock on saving. These exercises suggest that saving in Venezuela is highly sensitive to the terms of trade. Finally, while in Argentina the correlation between saving and the terms of trade is positive, it is close to zero and is not likely to be statistically significant.

Not surprisingly, when examining the saving/terms of trade link, the three countries that demonstrate a strong systematic and positive relationship are the three with the least diversified export structure and export revenues that are heavily dependent on one or a handful of primary commodities. In the case of Peru, it is minerals and ores and in Venezuela, oil.

Some Final Thoughts

There are important common threads in saving rates across Latin America, particularly as to the cyclical behavior of saving. Domestic saving rates have, more often than not, remained relatively flat over the past 25 years. No doubt, the sharp slowdown in economic growth during the 1980s that hit most of the region has much to do with the prevalence of stagnant saving rates. Over and beyond that, it would appear that regional explanations may not be adequate. There is considerable cross-country variation in the evolution over time of public, firm, and household saving that is masked in the broader aggregates.

Many of the previous studies that have analyzed saving behavior in Latin America and elsewhere have relied on highly aggregated data and have pooled countries for the purpose of conducting cross-country and panel analysis. This broad-brush approach has proved extremely useful for pinning down some of the stylized evidence on the determinants of saving. Yet, from the vantage point of designing policies that seek to directly or indirectly influence the level of saving, and recalling the heterogeneity of country experiences, *it seems inappropriate to suggest a "regional" policy prescription*. This highly varied experience makes it all the more necessary to gain a deeper understanding of individual country characteristics and circumstances.

The case studies contained in this volume represent a step in this direction. From a broad pool of time series on the saving patterns of households, firms, government, and the external sector, as well as from micro data for individual households and firms, these studies allow for a richer understanding of what has driven saving rates in these countries. In addition, these case studies have much to contribute to a wide range of topics that are directly linked to economic policy. The most conclusive evidence from their collected results is summarized as follows.

Despite the heterogeneity of approaches and case studies, the overwhelming empirical evidence suggests that, while there is some degree of offset between public and private saving, households do not fully internalize the consumption decisions of the public sector. Indeed, in most instances the estimated degree of offset is quite low. This implies that governments can have an active role in influencing the level of domestic saving.

Possibly explaining the absence of Ricardian equivalence, liquidity constraints appear to be quantitatively important. The bulk of the evidence from both macro and micro data on firms and households suggests that (1) some portion of the population has no access to credit markets, and consumption decisions are ruled by current income; (2) credit aggregates (in the macro data) or access to credit (in the micro data) provide much information about the prevalence of constraints and can explain much of the behavior in saving rates during periods in which those constraints changed markedly. Increases in firms' saving rates in Chile have been linked to the tightening of liquidity constraints during the banking crisis years, and declines in saving rates in Argentina, Colombia, Italy, Mexico, Peru (for households), the United Kingdom, and Uruguay have been associated with their relaxation. In this regard, a fruitful line of inquiry would explore the role of monetary and financial sector policies in influencing aggregate saving.

The study on Argentina had much to say about what drives consumption booms and, particularly, booms that are driven by a surge in household expenditure in durable goods. Broader cross-country studies in this area would enrich our understanding of consumption/saving cycles. Indeed, household decisions on whether to act now or postpone durable goods purchases have much to say about the cycles in consumption/saving.

The bulk of the evidence in these studies suggests that foreign saving is more likely to displace domestic saving than to complement it—although in most cases the extent of offset is partial. Since foreign saving is potentially more volatile than its domestic counterpart, these results call into question the desirability of having "too much" foreign saving, or capital inflows. It calls for a reassessment of the desirability (if not the feasibility and usefulness) of capital controls. It again raises the issue of liquidity constraints, whether these come from the domestic financial sector or are imposed from abroad by fickle capital markets.

Although many of the results suggest a growth-saving causal link, the ambiguity as to what comes first—saving or growth—highlights the need for further study in this area. Are vast regional differences between Asia (notwithstanding its recent woes) and Latin America, with regard to saving rates, partly explained by growth in the former in the 1980s and stagnation in the latter? These issues have not been conclusively settled and call for greater scrutiny.

The evidence provides, at best, mixed support for the LCH and no support to suggest that income distribution has anything to add to our understanding of what drives saving rates. Certainly, if a skewed income distribution provided the boost to private saving that consumer theory tells us it should, then Latin America should have much higher saving rates than Asia! In a group of Latin American countries, the ratio of income in the top quintile to that in the bottom quintile is 16, or about twice that of Asia.[36]

Whether terms of trade shocks have a significant or minimal impact on how much is saved may depend importantly on the concentration and primary commodity content of exports. Apparently, countries with the least diversified export structure and greatest primary commodity exposure are the most affected in terms of the impact on saving of terms of trade developments.[37]

---

[36] See Plies and Reinhart (1998).

[37] See also Elbadawi and Mwega (1998) for a comparison of African countries, which are highly weighted toward primary commodity exports, to other developing countries.

References

Alessina, A. and Rodrik, D. 1994. "Distributive Politics and Economic Growth." *Quarterly Journal of Economics.* 109: 465–90.

Barro, R. 1974. "Are Government Bonds Net Wealth?" *Journal of Political Economy.* 81 (6): 1095–1117.

Boone, P. 1994. "The Impact of Foreign Aid on Savings and Growth." London School of Economics. Mimeograph.

Calvo, G.A. 1986. "Temporary Stabilization: Predetermined Exchange Rates." *Journal of Political Economy.* 94: 1319–29.

Calvo, G.A., Leiderman, L. and Reinhart, C.M. 1993. "Capital Inflows and Real Exchange Rate Appreciation in Latin America: The Role of External Factors." *IMF Staff Papers.* 40: 108–50.

Campbell, J. and Mankiw, N.G. 1989. "Consumption, Income, and Interest Rates: Reinterpreting the Time Series Evidence." In O.J. Blanchard and S. Fischer, editors. *NBER Macroeconomics Annual.* Cambridge, Mass.: MIT Press.

Carroll, C.D. and Weil, D.N. 1993. "Saving and Growth: A Reinterpretation." *Carnegie-Rochester Conference Series on Public Policy.* 40: 133–92.

Copelman, M. 1994. "The Role of Credit in Post-Stabilization Consumption Booms." Department of Economics, Massachusetts Institute of Technology, Cambridge, Mass. Mimeograph.

David, P. and Scadding, J.L. 1974. "Private Savings: Ultrarationality, Aggregation, and Denison's Law." *Journal of Political Economy.* March-April: 225–49.

Deaton, A. 1990. "Saving in Developing Countries: Theory and Review." *Proceedings of the World Bank Annual Conference on Development Economics 1989.* 61–96. Washington, DC.

Denison, E.F. 1958. "A Note on Private Saving." *Review of Economics and Statistics.* 261–67.

Edwards, S. 1995. "Why Are Saving Rates So Different Across Countries? An International Comparative Analysis." NBER Working Paper 5097. National Bureau of Economic Research, Cambridge, Mass.

Elbadawi, I. and Mwega, F.M., 1998. "Can Africa's Saving Collapse Be Reverted?" Development Economics Vice Presidency, Research Group, World Bank, Washington, DC.

Faruqee, H. and Hussain, A. 1995. "Saving Trends in Southeast Asia: A Cross-Country Analysis." Working Paper WP/95/39. International Monetary Fund, Washington, DC.

Feldstein, M. and Horioka, C. 1980. "Domestic Savings and International Capital Flows." *Economic Journal.* 90: 314–29.

Galbis, V. 1993. "High Real Interest Rates under Financial Liberalization: Is There a Problem?" Working Paper WP/93/7. International Monetary Fund, Washington, DC.

Gavin, M. and Hausmann, R. 1996. "The Root of Banking Crises: The Macroeconomic Context." In R. Hausmann and L. Rojas-Suárez, editors. *Banking Crises in Latin America.* Washington, DC: Inter-American Development Bank.

Gavin, M. and Perotti, R. 1998. "Fiscal Policy and Private Saving in Latin America in Good Times and Bad." In R. Hausmann and R. Reisen, editors. *Promoting Savings in Latin America.* Washington DC: Inter-American Development Bank.

Haque, N.U. and Montiel, P. 1989. "Consumption in Developing Countries: Tests for Liquidity Constraints and Finite Horizons." *Review of Economics and Statistics.* 71: 408–15.

Held, G. and Uthoff, A. 1995. "Indicators and Determinants of Saving for Latin America and the Caribbean." Working Paper 25. ECLAC, Santiago.

IDB (Inter-American Development Bank). 1995. *Economic and Social Progress in Latin America.* Washington DC.

―――. 1996. *Economic and Social Progress in Latin America.* Washington DC.

―――. 1997. *Latin America after a Decade of Reforms, Economic and Social Progress in Latin America.* Washington DC.

Jappelli, T. and Pagano, M. 1994. "Saving, Growth, and Liquidity Constraints." *Quarterly Journal of Economics.* 109: 83–109.

Johansen, S. 1988. "Statistical Analysis of Cointegration Vectors." *Journal of Economic Dynamics and Control.* 12: 231–54.

Kaminsky, G.L. and Reinhart, C.M. 1996. "The Twin Crises: The Causes of Banking and Balance of Payments Problems." Board of Governors of the Federal Reserve System. *International Finance Discussion Papers.* 544: 1–28.

―――. 1998. "Financial Crisis in Asia and Latin America: Then and Now." *American Economic Review. Papers and Proceedings.* 88 (May): 444–48.

Loayza, N., Schmidt-Hebbel, K. and Servén, L. 1998. " What Drives Saving across the World?" Development Economics Vice Presidency, Research Group, World Bank, Washington, DC.

McKinnon, R. 1973. *Money and Capital in Economic Development.* Washington, DC: Brookings Institution.

Morandé, F. 1996. "Savings in Chile: What Went Right?" Office of the Chief Economist, Inter-American Development Bank, Washington, DC. Mimeographed.

Obstfeld, M. 1995. "Effects of Foreign Resource Flows on Saving: A Methodological Overview." University of California, Berkeley. Mimeograph.

Ogaki, M. and Reinhart, C.M. 1998. "Measuring Intertemporal Substitution: The Role of Durable Goods." *Journal of Political Economy*. 106: 1078–98.

Ogaki, M., Ostry, J. and Reinhart, C.M. 1995. "Saving Behavior in Low- and Middle-Income Developing Countries: A Comparison." Working Paper WP/95/3. International Monetary Fund, Washington, DC.

Ostry, J. and Reinhart, C.M. 1992. "Private Saving and Terms of Trade Shocks: Evidence from Developing Countries." *IMF Staff Papers*. 39(3): 495–517.

Persson, T. and Tabellini, G. 1994. "Is Inequality Harmful for Growth? Theory and Evidence." *American Economic Review*. 84: 600–21.

Plies, W.A. and Reinhart, C.M. 1998. "Does Income Inequality Raise Aggregate Saving?" University of Maryland. Mimeograph.

Reinhart, C.M. and Talvi, E. 1998. "Capital Flows and Saving in Asia and Latin America: A Reinterpretation." *Journal of Development Economics*. 57: 45–66.

Reinhart, C.M. and C. Végh. 1995. "Nominal Interest Rates, Consumption Booms, and Lack of Credibility: A Quantitative Examination." *Journal of Development Economics*. 46 (April): 357–78.

Schmidt-Hebbel, K. and Servén, L. 1996. "Income Inequality and Aggregate Saving: The Cross-Country Evidence." World Bank Policy Research Working Paper 1561. Policy Research Department. Washington, DC.

———. 1997. *Saving across the World: Puzzles and Policies*. World Bank Discussion Paper 354. Washington, DC.

Schmidt-Hebbel, K., Servén, L. and Solimano, A. 1996. "Saving and Investment: Paradigms, Puzzles, and Policies." *The World Bank Research Observer.* 11 (1): 87–117.

Seater, J. J. and Mariano, R. 1985. "New Tests of the Life Cycle and Tax Discounting Hypotheses." *Journal of Monetary Economics.* 15 (2): 195–215.

Shaw, E.S. 1973. *Financial Deepening in Economic Development.* Oxford, U.K.: Oxford University Press.

Vaidyanathan, G. 1993. "Consumption, Liquidity Constraints, and Economic Development." *Journal of Macroeconomics.* 15: 591–610.

II. EVIDENCE FROM LATIN AMERICA

Consumption, Pension Reform, and Saving in Argentina

Ricardo López Murphy, Fernando Navajas, Santiago Urbiztondo, and Cynthia Moskovitz[1]

Argentina's economic growth and macroeconomic stabilization of the early 1990s were accompanied by domestic saving that was inadequate to finance strong growth in investment. The counterpart to this shortage of saving was a sizable current account deficit. In 1995 the Argentine economy had to adjust to adverse conditions arising from the Mexican devaluation: first, a sharp tightening of deposits and loans and then, an abrupt drop in economic activity. The question of how to achieve adequate, growth-sustaining domestic saving has been a constant in analyses of macroeconomic performance as well as in the public policy debate in Argentina.

Explanations of the recent cycle of domestic saving in Argentina have emphasized such factors as relative prices and aggregate expenditure, the behavior of the public sector, and capital flows. Such arguments, however, have mostly been conducted on a weak empirical base, in part because of measurement problems. This study attempts to measure domestic saving over a relatively long period, to arrive at some stylized facts regarding its behavior over the past three or four decades and thus place the recent cycle in context.

Four concerns motivate this study. First, while there are problems associated with measuring saving, rather than explain what is poorly measured, an attempt is made to measure it better. The results of this study show that conclusions regarding recent saving behavior in Argentina may

---

[1] The authors are all economists with Fundación Investigaciones Económicas Latinoamericanas (FIEL) in Buenos Aires, Argentina.

change when appropriate adjustments are made to measures of public saving and durable goods expenditure.

Second, taking the empirical literature on the saving-investment correlation presented in Feldstein and Horioka (1980) as a starting point, the short- and long-term adjustment of both aggregates is illustrated. This sheds light on whether or not imbalances between saving and investment such as those seen recently are only temporary or will persist over the long term. In other words, how long will it take to eliminate a discrepancy between saving and investment of the nature and magnitude seen in the Argentine economy in the 1990s?

Third, the cyclical behavior of private durable goods expenditure seems to be directly responsible for the pattern of saving behavior. Beyond simply acknowledging this empirical fact, however, how does it explain the determinants of durable goods expenditure? To answer, an attempt is made to develop an original data base. Then an econometric comparison is made between two alternative hypotheses arising from models based, on the one hand, on optimal intertemporal decisions following exchange rate–based stabilization and on the other hand, on problems surrounding the perception of wealth or permanent income that accentuate the cycle of spending.

Fourth, in explaining saving behavior, one cannot ignore certain structural aspects that may be modifying such behavior in the medium and the long term. Among the public policies directed toward producing permanent or long-term effects on saving in Argentina, one that stands out is the recent reform of the pension system from one based on a pattern of allotments to one based on capitalization. The effect this reform will have on saving depends crucially not only on how the transition from one system to another is financed, but also on the specific requirements of the new system, as well as on the context in which it is carried out. In this regard, the possible reaction of saving to Argentine pension reform is simulated.

Saving in Argentina, 1958–95: Measurement and Basic Evidence

Devising an acceptable way to measure saving is an important step toward clarifying the issues and developing consistent explanations for the facts observed. Available official information is used to attempt to approximate saving behavior, while at the same time following aggregate measurement practices. First, using the available series of national accounts, balance of payments data, and government financial statistics, and making the pertinent connections, annual series of product, national income, investment, external saving, and domestic saving data for the 1958–95 period have been prepared. Second, information from the fiscal accounts has been used to separate the public and private components of saving and investment for the 1970–95 period. Third, these estimates of public and private saving have been adjusted to take into account the inflation tax. Fourth, private saving and investment for 1980–95 have been reestimated so that they account for the effects of durable goods consumption; the latter is estimated from the data series constructed for the analysis of durable goods expenditure in the next section.[2]

The aim of these analyses is to provide a measurement of saving that highlights the stylized facts of its short- and long-term behavior and quantitatively establishes the effects of proper treatment of the fiscal imbalance and durable goods expenditure. The main conclusion is that, when certain aspects of public saving and durable goods consumption are taken into account, the amplitude of the recent cycle of private saving in Argentina, which has led many observers to diagnose serious problems, tends to diminish.

In addition, the correlation between saving and investment in the Argentine case is studied in the context of an econometric error-correction model. This model highlights, on the one hand, the long-term aspects that arise from the type of proportionality suggested by Feldstein and Horioka (1980) and, on the other hand, the short-term adjustment to imbalances in this relationship. It is argued that this latter aspect allows an investigation of the likely duration of the imbalance between saving and investment observed in the first half of the 1990s. The main conclusion is that the speed with which the saving-investment imbalance is corrected in the Argentine case, as determined by the results of the error-correction model, is quite high. Any gap between the two aggregates closes in around three years. However, the behavior observed in 1994 and 1995 shows a somewhat slower adjustment than what can be simulated with the model parameters.

---

[2] For more on the methodological questions regarding measurement and the resulting data base see López Murphy et al. (1998).

Saving and Investment Behavior, 1958–95: Stylized Facts

Basic data on the measurement of saving and investment conducted in this study are presented graphically in Figure 2.1 and can be found in López Murphy et al. (1998). This measurement starts from the methodology of national accounts at constant prices for the 1958–95 period, estimates public and private saving and investment for 1970–95 using data from the public accounts, introduces corrections for the inflation tax, and finally, estimates the impact of durable goods consumption for the 1980–95 period. Several observations regarding the behavior of saving and investment may be made on the basis of this measurement.

Argentina's saving and investment rates have been, on average, very low, especially compared with those observed in certain high-growth countries.[3] This is stated without dismissing the interpretation this observation wishes to offer, and whether different levels of saving and investment mean different things given, for example, overall economic productivity.

The evidence for 1958–95 covers a long cycle in the behavior of saving and investment, which, in general terms, are positively correlated. From the beginning of the period to the end of the 1970s, saving and investment followed a growth trend. National saving increased by nearly 10 percentage points of GDP between 1958 and 1960 and between 1976 and 1978, when it approached a historical maximum; growth in investment paralleled this growth in saving (Figure 2.1). This behavior reversed itself sharply during the 1980s, with simultaneous drops in both aggregates. The presence of this long cycle corresponds to economic growth performance. However, the relationship between growth and saving suggested in Figure 2.1 is not seen in the simple correlation between saving and growth in national income (Figure 2.2), in part because of the strong variability of the latter.

An analysis of saving and investment that distinguishes between public and private components for the 1970–95 period indicates that the public component of saving and investment is in large part responsible for the observed cyclical behavior (Figure 2.3). In other words, the behavior of private saving is much more stable than that of national saving, and the

---

[3] In this sample, an annual growth rate of GDP per capita of 5 percent corresponds, on average, to an annual saving rate of nearly 26 percent.

Figure 2.1
Saving, Investment, and Growth: 1958–95

National Saving, External Saving, and Investment (constant prices)

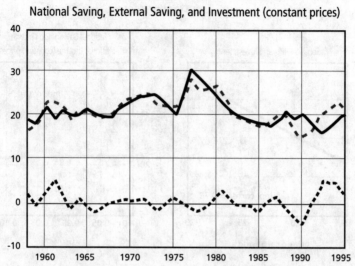

Gross Domestic Product (1986 dollars)

SBN = Gross National Saving   SE = External Saving
IBIF = Gross Domestic Investment

Figure 2.2
Correlations with National Saving: 1958–95
(constant prices)

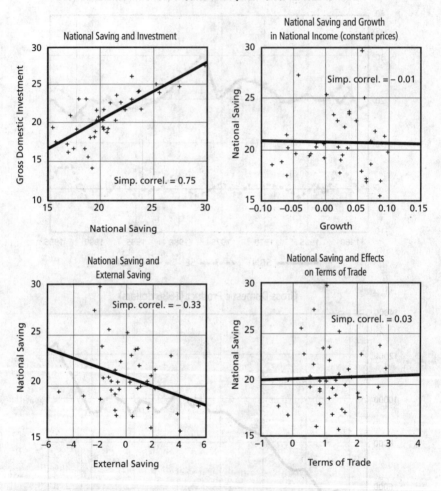

behavior of public saving is critical in distinguishing changes in aggregate saving.

The evidence indicates the presence of short- or medium-term cycles of national saving and investment, corresponding to fluctuations in external saving. The estimations show periods (1960–62, 1980–81, and 1992–94) in which external saving assumes extreme values and, accordingly, national saving falls below national investment (Figure 2.1). In these three

Figure 2.3
Public and Private Saving and Investment: 1970–95
(percentage of GDP)

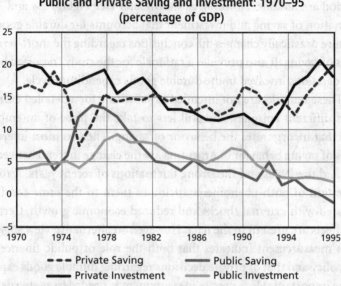

cases, the rise in external saving corresponds to favorable effects in the terms of trade, which, however, were not sustained. There were also periods of negative external saving (1965–67, 1976–78, and 1988–90). In particular, external saving experienced strong fluctuations in the second part of the period under study. The relationship between national saving and external saving for the entire sampling period is negative and basically driven by the fluctuations of recent years (Figure 2.2).

Variations in the terms of trade have not had any perceptible effect on national saving at the level of simple correlation (Figure 2.2). Nor is there a close correlation between private saving and the terms of trade for the 1970–95 sample. This finding would indicate the absence of any Harberger-Laursen-Metzler effect, according to which positive (and temporary) shocks to the terms of trade increase income and (given a positive propensity to save) saving.[4]

---

[4] See Harberger (1950), Laursen and Metzler (1950), and more recently, the critical reexamination in Ostry and Reinhart (1992).

Finally, the fluctuations in national saving and investment for the 1991–94 period are notable. However, as shown later (see Figures 2.4 and 2.5), a reestimation of saving and investment that accounts for durable goods expenditure drastically changes the conclusions regarding the short-term dynamics of saving. It also provides a rationale for the study (reported below) of the decisions involved in the durable goods expenditure cycle.

These remarks are not intended to substitute for a detailed examination of different episodes, and still less to take the place of an empirical model that incorporates the behavior of saving. The two most interesting aspects of saving behavior in Argentina are the change in trend between the 1970s and the 1980s and the strong fluctuations of recent years. A routine explanation of both phenomena attributes them to the same conditions associated with external shocks and reduced economic growth. Certainly, both effects are present in the data. However, an alternative view suggested by this measurement indicates that both the role of public finances and fiscal policy and that of private decisions regarding durable goods expenditure are important. More precise measurement is needed to aggregate these phenomena, and this is provided later.

The Saving-Investment Correlations

Since the Feldstein and Horioka study (1980), economists have been analyzing the strong positive correlation between saving and investment for different samples of countries, with varying results.[5] Jansen and Schulze (1996) have recently argued that the natural approach to studying this phenomenon is through an econometric error-correction model. This model accounts for the long-term relationship that, according to theory, must exist between saving and investment, making possible a better description of the adjustment dynamics of this relationship.

The relationship between saving and investment is significantly positive for the period studied (1958–95). In Figure 2.1 one may note the tem-

---

[5] The analysis of the saving-investment correlation in this section is performed on the 1958–95 data bases that result from using the constant price methodology (see López Murphy et al., 1998). Respecting the homogeneity of this series, the analysis does not include an adjustment for durable goods consumption, which will only be approximated for the 1980–95 period.

porary trajectory of both rates in relation to GDP. In principle, it seems reasonable to distinguish among three different stages of saving and investment behavior in Argentina. In the first stage, from 1958 to 1977, both rates were characteristic of an economy with extensive foreign exchange controls and financial regulation. In the second stage, from 1977 to 1989, this trend was reversed, as financial regulations were loosened or removed, although foreign exchange controls continued to be exercised during certain periods. Finally, from 1990 to 1995, saving and investment became divorced from one another in the short term, in a context of greater financial and capital account flexibility. Reference to the degree of regulation and financial and foreign exchange control is prompted by the fact that part of the Feldstein-Horioka hypothesis is supported by the absence of perfect capital mobility. In a context of controls or an absence of financial integration with the rest of the world, investment in the short term must depend on the availability of external saving.

The error-correction equation proposed to measure the correlation between saving and investment is:

$$D(SNB)_t = \text{Constant} + \alpha D(IBIF)_t + \beta\left[SBN_{t-1} - IBIF_{t-1}\right] + u_t \qquad [1]$$

where SBN is the rate of gross national saving, IBIF is the rate of investment, and D(.) is the difference operator $D(X)_t = X_t - X_{t-1}$.

This equation or a variant of it has been selected following the general-to-specific approach (see Ahumada, 1995) to ensure that an appropriate specification is selected. In this equation, α represents the immediate or short-term effect of saving on investment, whereas the β term captures the relationship of long-term proportionality or equality. The insignificance of the constant constitutes supporting evidence of this proportionality.

Equation [1] was tested to establish the stability of the α coefficient throughout the three specified periods. As Jansen and Schulze show for the Norwegian case, there may be differences in both magnitude and sign in the short-term correlation between saving and investment, in addition to a certain asymmetry in their interpretation. Although positive values of α would not necessarily indicate the absence of capital mobility, zero or negative values for the same parameter can only be explained by such mobility.

Box 2.1 LS // Dependent Variable, D(SBN)
Sample (Adjusted): 1960–95

Variable	Coefficient	Std. Error	t-Statistic	Prob.
Constant	–0.114406	0.269833	–0.423989	0.6745
D6077*D(IBIF)	0.661892	0.159663	4.145560	0.0002
D7889*D(IBIF)	0.440258	0.208267	2.113915	0.0427
D9095*D(IBIF)	–0.133823	0.262802	–0.509218	0.6142
SBN(–1)-IBIF(–1)	–0.399881	0.113285	–3.529861	0.0013
R^2	0.495134	Mean dependent var		0.061111
Adjusted R^2	0.429990	S.D. dependent var		1.959924
S.E. of regression	1.479723	Akaike info criterion		0.911956
Sum squared residual	67.87698	Schwarz criterion		1.131889
Log likelihood	–62.49699	F-statistic		7.600610
Durbin-Watson statistic	1.737780	Prob. (F-statistic)		0.000218

The results for the Argentine case indicate that the model is satisfactory, but they also show an important structural change during the 1990–95 period, in which the short-term correlation between saving and investment is nil. Whereas this correlation is definitely positive in the first part of the sample (1960–77), it decreases during the 1980s and changes sign, although it is not significant during the 1990s.

In the 1990s, Argentina experienced a productivity shock resulting from reforms that encouraged investment. In order to reestablish the long-term proportionality or equality between saving and investment, national saving has to grow at some point. However, in the short term the discrepancy between saving and investment may be accentuated by the reevaluation of long-term income by economic agents, which causes an increase in consumption and a drop in saving at the start of an exchange rate program or after a favorable shock. The short-term correlation between saving and investment is negative under conditions of capital mobility, despite being positive in the long term. There is no inconsistency between the two types of adjustment from the viewpoint of decisions made by economic agents over time. Equation [1], unlike any other specification, is flexible enough to allow the short-term dynamic to attain different values while maintaining long-term proportionality.

Adjustment in the Saving-Investment Relationship

The error correction term $\beta\left[SBN_{t-1} - IBIF_{t-1}\right]$ in equation [1] explains, besides the existence of long-term cointegration or proportionality, how the short-term saving adjustment affects the discrepancy between saving and investment. In this way it indicates the speed of the adjustment to long-term equilibrium and the length of the so-called interim period. Very low β values indicate that the short-term imbalance will last a long time before it is corrected, whereas high values indicate that the imbalance will be short-lived. In their study, Jansen and Schulze do not observe that the β parameter provides precise information about these characteristics. In the analysis of saving and investment behavior in small economies open to capital flows, the duration of the imbalance between saving and investment after a positive shock is of particular interest.

In the regression results for equation [1], note that $\beta = 0.400$, which, interestingly enough, is similar to that found by Jansen and Schulze for Norway over the period 1954–89. This value indicates that 40 percent of the imbalance between saving and investment is corrected over the course of one year, and that the average duration of the imbalance varies between two and three years. In other words, in the face of a shock that causes a divergence in the saving-investment relationship, that relationship reestablishes itself in a relatively short period.

Although the preceding equation proves the stability of the α coefficient, the same should be proved for the β coefficient. Jansen and Schulze ignore this point, implicitly reasoning that the equality always prevails in the long term, and that, in equation [1], SBN will always be equal to IBIF in the stationary stage, regardless of the value of β. That is true, but it disregards the fact that the speed of adjustment of the saving-investment relationship may be changing structurally.

One test of the constancy of β throughout the three periods shows a drop in these parameters from those in effect at the beginning of the period (0.523) to lower values in the 1990s (0.314). This not only indicates the nature of the short-term relationship but also shows that the speed of the adjustment to long-term equilibrium has been changing in recent years.

The Effect of Durable Goods Consumption: 1980–95

Starting with an estimation of durable goods expenditure,[6] durable goods consumption was estimated in order to adjust the calculation of saving and investment from the national accounts for the 1980–95 period.

The results are shown in Figures 2.4 and 2.5. The main conclusion is that the amplitude of the recent cycle of national and private saving is diminished when durable goods expenditure is included as saving. This estimation shows that private saving calculated in this way reaches its historical maximum (24 percent) in 1994. In the same way, investment grows substantially in recent years.

The estimates show that the recent dynamics of national saving, especially private saving, cannot be explained without considering durable goods expenditure as a central element. Explaining durable goods expenditure and its relationship to economic stabilization is another important task, prompted by the facts observed and measured in this section.

The Private Consumption Cycle, 1980–95:
Evidence on Durable Goods Expenditure

The rise in consumption witnessed over the first four years after the beginning of Argentina's convertibility program is a response to different stimuli and may reflect an appropriate response by economic agents to changes in the economic fundamentals. However, there are reasons, indicated by the consumption expenditure dynamic, to believe that the cycle is exaggerated beyond the existence or nonexistence of the tequila effect and would have nonetheless led to a significant tightening later on.

Whether domestic saving remained adequate to fund investment at the beginning of the stabilization program is a question that relates directly to the literature on exchange rate–based stabilization, in which a boom in private expenditure is stimulated by intertemporal relative price distortions. In the Argentine case, lack of information in the national accounts precludes examining the private expenditure cycle in its full magnitude and in the face of alternative hypotheses. Instead, the evidence on durable goods expenditure is studied since that is the most dynamic component of aggregate

---

[6] A detailed explanation is available in López Murphy et al. (1998).

Figure 2.4
National and Private Saving Adjusted for Durable Goods: 1980–95
(percentage of GDP)

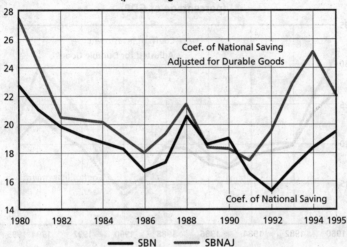

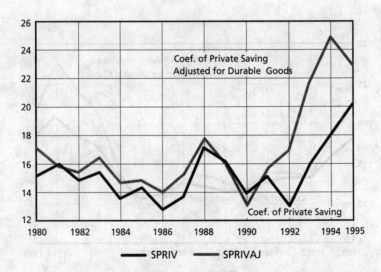

SBN = Gross National Saving
SBNAJ = Adjusted Gross National Saving

SPRIV = Private Saving
SPRIVAJ = Adjusted Private Saving

Figure 2.5
Gross Domestic and Private Investment Adjusted for
Durable Goods: 1980–95
(percentage of GDP)

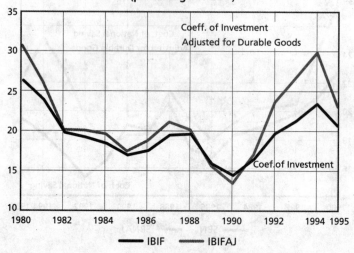

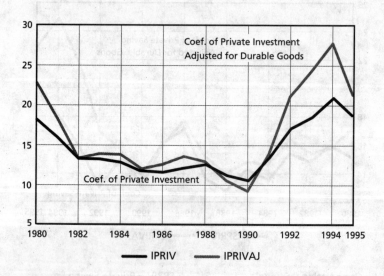

IBIF = Gross Domestic Investment   IBIFAJ = Adjusted Gross Domestic Investment
IPRIV = Private Investment   IPRIVAJ = Adjusted Private Investment

expenditure, and one in which the presence or absence of overspending can be detected. Therefore, an estimate was made of durable goods expenditure, which, besides describing the magnitude of the cycle, may be used for the purpose of econometric analysis in some reduced or unrestricted form.

Cycle of Durable Goods Expenditure: Intertemporal Distortions and Overvaluation of Permanent Income

Consumption booms have been a common element in the cycles of many Latin American economies, and Argentina has proved to be no exception. Understanding what causes these distinct consumption cycles is essential for answering questions regarding the drop in private saving and the particular inability of economies to deal with unfavorable external shocks that persist even after the period of bonanza.

Five possible explanations for the boom in aggregate consumption have been emphasized (Montiel, 1997). The first is based on the old explanation of income redistribution across a population with different propensities to consume. This mechanism has been used for many years in the Argentine case to describe, for example, the tightening effect of a devaluation (the so-called Díaz-Alejandro effect). The second explanation is associated with an exchange rate–based stabilization program that anchors the nominal interest rate and, with adaptive expectations that still feed a certain expected inflation, generates a sharp drop in the real interest rate ex ante. This has been the argument used by Rodríguez (1982) to explain the dynamics of spending in the stabilization that characterized the late 1970s and early 1980s, based on the so-called *tablita* of preannounced devaluations used in Argentina in the late 1970s. The third explanation is based on a broadening in the availability of credit following financial deregulation, which lifts liquidity constraints on consumers. The fourth explanation is based on recent developments in the literature regarding stabilizations that lack credibility. This explanation was first offered by Calvo (1987): exchange rate–based stabilization causes a drop in the nominal interest rate, which economic agents perceive as transitory, thus leading to an intertemporal distortion that favors private consumption. This process is facilitated by the presence of a cash-in-advance-type restriction that loosens when the opportunity cost of holding cash falls. The fifth explanation is based on a euphoria that may well be a superrational (that is, perfectly informed) response to structural changes perceived as substantially improving permanent income, or a product of unsustainable overvaluation by economic agents on the basis of errors in the perception of what constitutes permanent income.

In the Argentine case, there is reason to believe that the last two explanations are the most relevant. On the one hand, exchange rate–based stabilization caused a definite drop in the nominal interest rate, accompanied by an adjustment of inflationary expectations and marked credit expansion. In a bimonetary economy like Argentina, the nominal interest rate may be less relevant than it is elsewhere in determining liquidity restrictions. However, it is also the ideal price variable for capturing a reduction in the use of cash for transactions and an expansion of credit following an exchange rate–based stabilization program. On the other hand, stabilization ushered in a strong revaluation by economic agents of their permanent income, which may have led to euphoria in either of the senses mentioned above.

Recent literature regarding real exchange rate–based stabilization has led to an analysis of the theoretical implications of this type of stabilization. This analysis has enriched the description of the dynamics of such programs to account for certain observed regularities, among which is the fact that a noncredible program may display fiscal equilibrium on the way to a balance of payments crisis, as described by Krugman (1979).[7] What produces this apparent equilibrium is precisely a consumption boom caused by a drop in the nominal interest rate. According to one representation, offered by Calvo and Vegh (1990), the consumption equation that describes the optimal plan of a well-informed, representative agent unfolds as the product of two terms:

- Permanent income, obtained from intertemporal budget restrictions such as the present value of income plus net asset ownership at the start of the consumption program, and
- The marginal propensity to consume, expressed as the ratio between the average price of consumption (along the entire path) and the marginal (current) price of consumption, both of which depend on the nominal interest rate path and differ depending on the values assumed by the elasticity of substitution of consumption over time, as a function of utility.

---

[7] See Calvo (1995), who illustrates the described effect on the basis of Talvi (1996).

The consumption boom occurs when economic agents choose their optimal plan in response to an equilibrium nominal interest rate sequence (i.e., one that is consistent with the government budgetary restriction). The initially low level of nominal interest rates causes a drop in the marginal price of consumption below the average price, temporarily elevating it above the unit marginal propensity to consume. The drop in consumption occurs later, when the program is no longer sustainable and the nominal rate again rises as a function of the rate of inflation required to finance the government.

Key elements of this model are the nominal interest rate, which is temporarily predetermined, and the capacity of economic agents for substituting consumption over time. Reinhart and Vegh (1995) have adjusted the deterministic equation described above to data from several Latin American countries to obtain intertemporal elasticity of substitution values consistent with the data, and to explain the cycle of consumption observed, in order to analyze the credibility hypothesis. For the Argentine case, and using quarterly data from the first quarter of 1978 to the second quarter of 1989, they obtain a relatively low intertemporal elasticity of substitution (0.21). They are also able to explain a small part of the consumption cycle that characterized the tablita episode (1978–81), but a more significant part of the cycle associated with the Austral Plan (1985–88). The authors suggest possible reasons for thinking that better statistical compilation of durable goods consumption would improve the results, raising the intertemporal elasticity of substitution of consumption (Fauvel and Samson, 1991) and introducing a greater change in relative prices.

Significant fluctuations in durable goods expenditure have received much attention from researchers, who have tested departures of consumer behavior with respect to those goods against the permanent income hypothesis. Mankiw (1982) analyzed the implications of a random path hypothesis advanced by Hall (1978) and found that data for the United States were not consistent with a simple theory that established a linear relationship between durable goods and services consumption and the stock of those goods, and according to which that hypothesis should have given rise to errors in the consumption equation. Other authors (e.g., Caballero, 1990) have argued that there is only one lag in the behavior of durable goods expenditure in applying the permanent income hypothesis in a world in which it is costly for agents to adjust their stocks.

Among other recent models of this nature, Bar-Ilan and Blinder (1992) analyze one in which it costs economic agents to adjust their decisions (in the style of the menu cost models). This gives rise to a consumption function that can be broken down into two parts: permanent income and a fraction that represents the "active" agents in the market. The authors mention that the break in the proportionality of the permanent income hypothesis is due to variations in that fraction, which account for the dynamic of durable goods expenditure. There are two interesting features of this representation. The first is that the marginal propensity to spend on durable goods varies as a function of the number of active agents in the market. The second is that the variables which determine that decision to participate, much like the nominal interest rate in exchange rate–based stabilization, appear to exaggerate the dynamics of durable goods expenditure. The same argument may be utilized, in the context of that model, to show that errors in the perception of permanent income may cause drastic changes in durable goods expenditure, possibly leading to a change in the fraction of active agents. Although a 1 percent overestimation of permanent income should not result in a greater than 1 percent increase in consumption, the same does not hold true when it changes the number of active agents in the market.

In more general terms, the hypothesis of excess spending based on errors in the perception of permanent income may follow because wealth "perceived" by economic agents depends upon relative prices, which change according to the exchange rate–based stabilization plan (see Heymann, 1984). The increase in the price of nontradable goods leads to a revaluation of wealth held by these agents, which, in the face of imperfect or incomplete information, leads to excess optimism and overspending. This confusion may be conditioned by what each agent observes in the behavior of the other agents, leading that agent to believe that the positive shock generated by stabilization is permanent.

Given the importance this type of explanation seems to have in the Argentine case, it is important to examine the hypothesis of excess optimism. The basic problem with any empirical analysis—from which none of the models considered here is exempt—is the inability to observe the key variables under the maintained hypotheses. The nominal interest rate may proxy for effects other than those mentioned in the literature on the credibility of exchange rate–based stabilization, arising from the inflation rate.

The concept of perceived wealth also suffers from the problem of quantitative approximation. In this preliminary attempt to explain the cycle of durable goods expenditure, a measurement of wages in dollars, given its variability, adequately captures the cyclicality of wealth.

Durable Goods Expenditure: 1980–95

Preliminary results from this analysis may help in understanding the recent cycle of durable goods expenditure in Argentina. Econometric tests can therefore be conducted on abbreviated forms that capture the relevant variables for the decision surrounding durable goods expenditure, according to the results obtained in the literature. The reasons that led to the focus of attention on the nominal interest rate and the wage in dollars as representing alternative explanations of the cycle in recent years have already been explored. However, the most costly activity in terms of information has been preparing, for purposes of this study, a series that approximates quarterly durable goods expenditure in Argentina. The absence of national accounts statistics regarding consumption of these goods demanded an indirect route to compiling a series. The series begins with production and sales data for a reduced but representative set of goods and goes on to aggregate imports taken from Argentine foreign trade data. Despite the measurement errors—namely, the over- and underrepresentation of certain goods whose expenditures are captured—this measure should sufficiently approximate the cycle of expenditure.

The basic series are described in López Murphy et al. (1998) and depicted in Figure 2.6. Spending per capita on durable goods (QDN) appears in the first panel. There is a long cycle that extends from a maximum at the beginning of the sample, during the tablita episode, to the maximum during the convertibility program, achieved in the third quarter of 1994. Between those maxima is a more depressed level of spending, with less marked cycles much like what occurred in the mid-1980s under the Austral Plan.[8]

---

[8] As indicated above, Reinhart and Vegh (1995) are better able to explain the short cycle of the Austral Plan than the large fluctuation due to the tablita. The series mentioned shows the relative importance of the two episodes with regard to the cycle of durable goods expenditure.

Figure 2.6
Durable Goods Expenditures, Wages, Interest Rate
and Price of Durable Goods: 1980–95

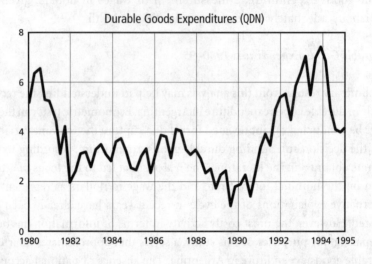

Durable Goods Expenditures (QDN)

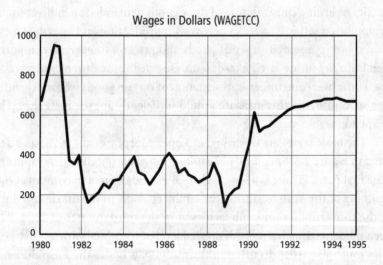

Wages in Dollars (WAGETCC)

Between the minimum of the hyperinflation episode and the maximum under convertibility, durable goods expenditure increased nearly sevenfold. This jump follows the fixing of the exchange rate under the 1991 convertibility program and continues up to the 1994 maximum.

Figure 2.6 (continued)

Interest Rate (IN)

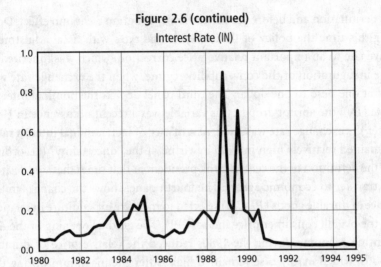

Price of Durable Goods (PDCPI)

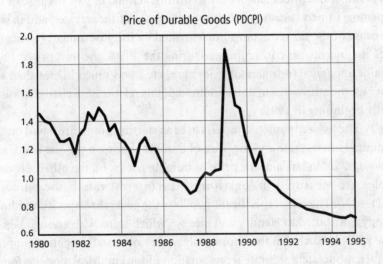

The remaining panels show the selected explanatory variables. Wages in constant 1995 dollars (*WAGETCC*) are shown in the second panel,[9] which depicts an impressive cycle in comparison to that for durable goods expenditure. The wage in dollars jumped in the second half of 1990, after the

---

[9]In the regressions shown later, this variable is called WAGESTC.

hyperinflation and before the convertibility program went into effect. During this time the policy of flexible exchange rates with fiscal adjustment gave rise to an important relative price correction, which was inherited at the inauguration of the convertibility regime, when the exchange rate was set at one peso to one dollar. The third panel depicts the nominal interest rate (*IN*); the abrupt drop in this variable was a recent occurrence in 1991 after the exchange rate was fixed. As a matter of fact, nominal interest rates remained relatively high in 1990 by virtue of the "uncertainty" (according to the definition of the central bank president at that time) that was desired to transfer to economic agents. The fourth panel shows the changes in the price of durable goods (*PDCPI*) selected to measure expenditure in relation to the overall consumer price index (CPI). The gradual opening of the Argentine economy during the 1980s reduced the relative price of durable goods, which in any case remained high. After the maximum during the hyperinflation, prices fell sharply to historical lows, in part because of the opening, in part because of the rise in the price of the services, and in part because of the tax reductions implemented by the government to encourage the increase in consumption. During the 1980s, the unit price of any major appliance (refrigerator, television, etc.) was much higher than the average monthly wage in dollars, although this relationship changed drastically beginning in 1991.

The two econometric models used as starting points are based on the nominal interest rate and the price of durable goods, on the one hand, and on wages in dollars and the price of durable goods, on the other. All variables are measured in logarithms; the interest rate is measured as $\ln(1 + IN)$. The initial specification follows the general-to-specific methodology (attributed to Hendry and others), which starts with enough lags in the variables such that the error is only white noise, and goes on to simplify until a moderately accurate representation of the empirical model is found (see Ahumada, 1995). In addition, it includes dummy variables that, in each case, correct pronounced discrepancies as a result of easily recognized events in recent economic history.[10]

---

[10] Each model was estimated using both Eviews version 2.0 (see Lilien et al., 1995) and PC-GIVE version 7.0 (Doornik and Hendry, 1992). The results are reported in Eviews, except that referred to in the inclusion test, which was conducted in PC-GIVE.

The Nominal Interest Rate Model

Starting with a model that recognizes the nominal interest rate as a central variable, one arrives through simplification at an error-correction model in which durable goods expenditure and the interest rate appear to be co-integrated, with a long-term interest elasticity for durable goods expenditure of 3.76.[11] For its part, the durable goods price does not enter into the equation when all of the dynamic effects of the nominal interest rate are included. The statistics show a standard error of the regression (SER) of 0.088 and satisfactory values for the rest. All of the variables are significant (see López Murphy et al., 1998). The Durbin-Watson (DW) statistic indicates autocorrelation; however, autocorrelation tests (the Breusch-Godfrey Lagrange multiplier test on the same order, one, as the DW, and to two or more rejections) did not detect autocorrelation. There is also no evidence of heteroskedasticity in the errors (as determined by the White test). The equation suffers from a serious forecast problem for the year 1995, however, even when a dummy variable is included for the second quarter, when the drop in durable goods expenditure was most severe.

The summarized equation of this model is as follows:

$$D(LQDN) = 0.553 + 0.248 D[LQDN(-3)] - 1.249 D(LI)$$
$$- 0.266 LQDN(-1) - 1.006 LI(-1)$$
$$R^2 = 0.92 \quad SER = 0.088 \quad DW = 1.65 \quad F = 32.72$$

where $D(LX)$ is the logarithmic difference of variable X, and $X(-1)$ is the rejected variable defined as follows:

QDN = per capita expenditure on durable goods.
$I = (1 + IN)$: one plus the nominal interest rate.

The Wage-in-Dollars and Durable Goods Price Model

The search for an equation that explains the behavior of durable goods expenditure per capita as a function of total wages in dollars and the price

---

[11] Calculated on the basis of the equation specified below, as the ratio (−1.006/0.266).

of durable goods also gave rise to an error-correction model. The long-term elasticity of wage–durable goods expenditure, implicit in the equation obtained, is 0.48. This value, noticeably less than unity, may be due to measurement error for the income variable, as measured wages are more volatile than unobserved permanent income. Changes in wages in dollars have a null short-term impact on durable goods expenditure, and a noticeably smaller long-term effect than that of the nominal interest rate.[12] For its part, the durable goods price has only a short-term impact on the dynamic of durable goods expenditure but does not appear in the long-term determination of that expenditure. The statistics show that the adjustment to the equation is slightly lower than that obtained with the interest rate model, the standard error of the regression is 0.097, and there is no evidence of either autocorrelation or heteroskedasticity. The summarized equation is :

$$D\left(LQDN\right) = -0.360 + 0.237\,D\left[LQDN\left(-3\right)\right] - 0.756\,D\left(LPDCPI\right)$$
$$-0.291\,LQDN\left(-1\right) + 0.140\,LWAGESTC\left(-1\right)$$
$$R^2 = 0.90 \quad SER = 0.097 \quad DW = 2.11 \quad F = 28.25$$

where, again, $D(LX)$ is the logarithmic difference of variable X, and $X(-1)$ is the rejected variable, with the following definitions in addition to those previously specified:

WAGESTC: wages in 1995 dollars.
PDCPI: price of durable goods in terms of CPI, general level.

Inclusion Tests and the Joint Model Based on the Interest Rate and Wage in Dollars

One way to evaluate the explanatory capacity of the alternative models is to perform encompassing tests, designed to determine whether one model can

---

[12] In the error-correction model, the short-term impact is shown by the ratio of the term $D(LI)$ or $D(LWAGESTC)$, according to the type of model, whereas the long-term effect is obtained from the error-correction term between the levels of variables, $LQDN(-1)$ or

Table 2.1 Inclusion Test Statistics, 1981:1 to 1995:4

Model 1 v Model 2	Form	Test	Form	Model 2 v Model 1
–3.67326	N(0,1)	Cox	N(0,1)	–6.53083
2.68846	N(0,1)	Ericsson IV	N(0,1)	4.26974
9.06302	Chi(4)	Sargan	Chi(5)	15.9772
2.59411	F(4,40)	Joint Model	F(5,40)	4.40403
[0.0508]			[0.0027]	

account for the results of the other, and vice versa. If either model encompasses the other, that model is to be preferred; if it is not possible to encompass them, that is evidence in favor of a joint model that includes both types of explanatory variables. The simplest test of all those available is the F test of omitted variables, which analyzes the inclusion, or lack thereof, of the variables from one model in the other. The nominal interest rate model cannot reject the inclusion of the wage in dollars, and the wage-in-dollars model cannot reject the variables of the interest rate model. In this composition, the victim ends up being the durable goods price, which cannot be included in the interest rate model, and which loses significance when the interest rate is incorporated into the wage-in-dollars model.

However, a more complete battery of encompassing tests may be conducted with the PC-GIVE program. Together with the F test, these may help determine the precise degree of encompassing of one model or the other by its rival. The results are summarized in Table 2.1. In the table, model 1 is the nominal interest rate model, and model 2 is the wage-in-dollars model. Four statistics are provided for each option, which consists of evaluating one model versus its rival. In the first column, it is asked whether model 1 can account for the other variables, presenting the statistical value, its form, and the author of the test. Significant values indicate that the variables proposed by the rival model must be included. A similar analysis is conducted on the

---

LWAGESTC(–1). In the case of the interest rate model, the short-term impact is approximately one third that of the long-term effect, whereas the wage-in-dollars model has no impact on wages.

basis of model 2. The exact source of the tests may be consulted in Doornik and Hendry (1992).[13] The last line shows the degree of significance of the F test of one model against the joint model that includes variables from both.

The results show that neither model encompasses the other and that a joint model must be used. Notice, however, that the statistical values are always larger in the case where the test begins with model 2, which indicates that this model would be more inclined to accept the interest rate variable than model 1 would be to include wages in dollars. This is clearly the result of the F test, which, in the case beginning with the interest rate model, is close to the rejection limit for the rival model through a combined, nonrestrictive model.

On this basis, the joint model was simplified. Since the joint model is still unable to explain the sharp drop for the year 1995, the unemployment rate is included as an omitted variable. This variable is included both directly as $(1 - TDES)$ and as its square root, where TDES is the unemployment rate known by economic agents up to the indicated quarter (in other words, using the employment rate as an explanatory variable). This variable has been cited by some as leading economic agents to cut back on their purchases and recalculate their permanent income. The results of the omitted variable test forced the introduction of the unemployment rate as an explanatory variable, in a quadratic relationship with durable goods expenditure.

The summarized equation is:

$$D(LQDN) = -0.749 + 0.208 D\left[LQDN(-3)\right] - 1.204 D(LI)$$
$$- 0.278 LQDN(-1) - 0.804 LI(-1)$$
$$+ 0.111 LWAGESTC(-1) + 0737(1 - TDES)^2$$

$$R^2 = 0.93 \quad SER = 0.079 \quad DW = 1.70 \quad F = 38.56$$

---

[13] The first test is based on a statistic proposed by Cox and analyzes the ability of one model to explain the residual variance of the other (called inclusion of variances). Ericsson IV is a test utilizing key variables, given that the previous one was conducted by the ordinary least squares method. The Sargan test assesses the restrictive form of the original model against a nonrestrictive form based on a projection of the dependent variable starting from the variables in the rival model. Finally, the F test assesses each model's ability to include the combination of both models.

The results indicate an error-correction model in which durable goods expenditure per capita has been cointegrated with the interest rate and wages in dollars, with implicit long-term elasticities equal to 2.9 for the interest rate and 0.4 for wages in dollars. The statistics show a satisfactory adjustment, although the model is still unable to capture the drop in consumption that occurred in the second quarter of 1995.

Overall, the results of this section indicate the importance of the nominal interest rate in explaining the observed cycles. This supports the hypothesis that the cycle of durable goods is compatible with the explanation that economic agents respond to incentives that modify their intertemporal decisions. However, the relevance of wages in dollars and the unemployment rate confirm that elements of optimism and pessimism may have exacerbated individual decisions. The results do not necessarily indicate whether the level of expenditure reflected in the boom of the 1990s was sustainable, nor do they indicate whether the variables treated as exogenous were equilibrium phenomena. For exchange rate stabilization models, sustainability depends upon the fundamentals, which determine the path of the nominal interest rate.

Domestic Saving and Structural Reforms: The Impact of Pension Reform

From an explanation of past behavior, the analysis now changes to a projection of future behavior. Here, one structural element that has changed radically in Argentina is the reorganization of the pension system and the mechanism for financing pension benefits. Given the potential effect of this type of reform on saving, it is useful to first review the literature on the effect that pension reform has on saving and then project the final impact of such reform on domestic saving in Argentina.[14]

Historically, old-age retirement systems have been organized informally and voluntarily, with working generations supporting the retired members of the family. However, because this arrangement imposed a high level of risk, the state eventually came to be considered the principal provider for old age. Pension fund contributions have become mandatory dur-

---

[14] See López Murphy et al. (1998) for the principal characteristics of Argentine pension reform.

ing this century in most countries. Their organization, however, generally ranges between two extremes. At one extreme is the allotment, or pay-as-you-go, system, in which the economically active generations contribute toward financing the retirement of the passive generation at that time. In this way the rate of return to the contributing generation—but not necessarily to each individual—is equal to the increase in the wage bill.[15] At the other extreme is the privately capitalized, or fully funded, system, in which an individual's contributions are designed to finance his or her own future retirement, and thus the return to each individual is the market interest rate on that individual's personal contributions.

One issue discussed at length in the literature has been the effect that introducing a state-run pension fund system is expected to have on the economy's saving rate, starting from the situation where there is no pension system. Given that the main concern focused on estimating the impact of the allotment system, only the effect on private saving was considered—no effects on public saving were envisioned. The central discussion may be summarized as follows: From a theoretical viewpoint, there are two key effects, a wealth effect and a retirement effect. The former indicates that the existence of the pension system reduces the need to save for retirement, and thus reduces the rate of private saving. The latter indicates that, since people will retire earlier when there is a pension system in place (because additional contributions do not allow them to increase their benefits), a higher saving rate will be required to provide for a longer retirement and a shorter active life. From an empirical standpoint, estimates seem to suggest (but do not confirm, and with significant controversy surrounding the issue) that the wealth effect exceeds the income effect (see Smith, 1990). This result becomes more apparent in the long run, because the second effect is temporary: the higher saving rate of contributing generations is eventually canceled out by the lower ratio of contributors to beneficiaries (the cancellation is only partial if the economy is growing). An explanation of the weak (nearly null) effect of this type of pension reform on private saving, seen in some estimates, is that before the existence of pension systems, families organized themselves according to a system of voluntary allotment. The

---

[15] Implying that, in the stationary stage, aggregate yield is equal to the sum of the rates of population growth and output.

introduction of a mandatory system thus merely inserted the government as an intermediary.

The literature has also considered the effect of pension reform on the saving rate when an allotment system is replaced with a privately capitalized system. Although such reform necessarily contributes toward increasing domestic saving, because the incentives for capital accumulation increase as the link between contributions and benefits is restored, this is not the only factor at play. Given that a reform of this nature visibly affects the deficit position of the public sector, attention must also be directed toward public saving, because how reform is financed affects public saving and, indirectly, private saving.

In the first place, if the deficit that results from continuing to pay benefits for the passive generation, with no further contributions from the active generations, is financed by issuing public debt, the old, implicit debt under the public pension system is replaced by a new, explicit debt. Public saving (as measured) thus diminishes.[16] Thus, depending on whether public debt constitutes net wealth, the additional effects on saving will be different. The Ricardian equivalence theorem, according to which government bonds signify the commitment of future taxes in exactly the same amount (at present value), postulates that the reduction of public saving will be compensated by an identical increase in private saving to pay future taxes. Hence reforms financed with debt have the same effect on domestic saving as reforms financed with taxes. On the other hand, the Keynesian viewpoint holds that government debt securities constitute net wealth. This means that the reduction in public saving (equal to the issuance of new debt) leads to an increase in the private sector's desire to consume and to save. However, since the desired increase in saving is minimal, a transition financed with debt will have less of an effect (ceteris paribus) on domestic saving.

On the other hand, if the deficit is financed with taxes (through an increase in revenue as well as a reduction in public spending), it would become public saving if one considers it as a retirement of old, implicit debt (in the event that this implicit debt has not been perceived, public saving as perceived by the private sector will not be affected). In fact, however, this saving will not appear as such in the national accounts precisely because the

---

[16] This is what has occurred in Argentina in the opinion of several economists (see Teijeiro, 1996).

debt it cancels was implicit. In this case, even if it generates a partial reduction in private saving due to the reduction in disposable income, the net effect of the reform on domestic saving will be positive.

However the transition period is financed, the greater correlation between contributions and benefits introduced by this type of reform may have a negative wealth effect. The level of saving required to finance retirement is less, and therefore other forms of saving diminish (although these other forms tend to be more liquid and therefore should not be expected to be totally replaced). It has also been argued that there is a recognition effect, by which the private capitalization system leads to an increase in other forms of saving, by making people value financial independence and security at retirement age more highly than before. Finally, attention should be paid to the saving instruments available to the private sector at the time of reform. If other forms of saving are prohibited (meaning that only saving above a certain threshold may be directed toward attractive and secure ends), the desired saving rate before pension reform could be higher than the effective saving rate. In that case the substitution effect—i.e., the transfer of other forms of saving to pension funds—would be very small.[17]

Evidence in this instance is less controversial. According to some authors, the effect of contributing one dollar to the private pension system in the United States increases domestic saving by between 30 and 80 cents (indicating that other forms of saving are reduced by between 20 and 70 cents).[18] In the case of Chile, where the transition has been financed to a significant extent through taxes, an important increase has also been observed in the level of national saving, overcompensating for the reduction in external saving and resulting in a higher rate of gross investment. It has been estimated that the accumulated funds received by the pension fund

---

[17] It has also been noted that private saving may increase if some people (those with lower incomes) are forced to save more than their desired level of saving.

[18] Smith (1990) reports studies (for the United States) by Munnell (1976), Hubbard (1986), and Gultekin and Logue (1979), who found that new saving in the pension systems reduces other forms of saving by 66 percent, 16 percent, and 10–19 percent, respectively. Smith also notes that the estimations of Ando and Kennickell (1987) and Barros (1979) allow for greater optimism. Kennickell, using observations from the United States and Japan, found no significant substitution effect, whereas Barros presents evidence of a recognition effect in the United Kingdom, where private capitalization systems have led to an increase in other forms of saving.

administrators have had a positive and permanent effect on reducing the private consumption rate.[19]

In all of these cases, however, we must consider the influence exercised by other forms of incentives (especially taxes) that are built into the reforms, in addition to the availability of other forms of saving and the development of insurance markets at the time of the reform. When the tax incentives of reform are stronger, and access to other forms of saving or insurance is limited (either because they are simply unavailable or because they carry very low rates of return), the net expected effect on private saving will be greater.[20]

A Projection of the Impact of Pension Reform

What effect could pension reform have on the financial position of the public sector and on domestic saving under different forms of financing? Table 2.2 presents an estimate of the impact of pension reform, in effect since mid-1994, on the financial position of the Argentine public pension system. It is constructed on the basis of information available up to the end of 1995. Except where otherwise specified, the values are expressed as current values.[21] The projected values, on the other hand, are expressed as constant values.

Assume that the population currently committed to making contributions (around 10 million people) will grow at an annual rate of 1.5 percent, and that the percentage of those actually making contributions will

---

[19] See Corsetti and Schmidt-Hebbel (1994). Rondanelli (1996) estimates that Chile's pension reform was responsible for two thirds of the increase in that country's national saving over the past fifteen years. Net retirement saving in Chile increased by 2.4 percent of GDP, but the accumulated fund effect—a recognition effect—was responsible for an increase in private saving equal to 4.2 percent of GDP.

[20] These aspects are examined in Uthoff (1996), who suggests, based on the Chilean experience, that more important than pension reform itself (as to the definition of benefits according to an allotment or a capitalization system) is the creation of an appropriate context for saving and investment (including credible macroeconomic prices, GDP growth, macroeconomic stability, tax incentives, privatization of public companies, etc.). Such factors can explain the dramatic increase in nonpension private saving in Chile. Of course, pension reform contributed to the creation of that context by providing to the financial system the resources that contributed to its development.

[21] Values for 1993 are those noted, except for other sources of income, in which case, for the purpose of analyzing the differential impact of reform, values were calculated in such a way as to leave the public system in equilibrium (a status approximating reality at that time).

Table 2.2 The Impact of Reform on the Financial Position of the Pension Fund System: 1993–2010

Year	Contributors (thousands) AFJPs (1)	Pub. Syst. (2)	Wages Estimated ($/year) (3)	Contributions ($ millions) AFJPs (4)	Pub. Syst. (5)	Other Sources ($ millions) (6)	Total Benefits (thou.) (7)	Average Benefit ($/year) (8)	Total Costs ($ millions) (9)	Public System Surplus^a =(5)+(6)–(9)	GDP ($ millions) (10)	Contr. AFJPs/GDP (percent) (11)	Pub. Syst. Surplus/GDP (percent) (12)
1993	0	5,540	6,600	0	9.508	5.237	3,200	4,608	14.745	0	270.582	0.00	0.00
1994	2,371	2,280	6,746	0.807	10.045	5.31	3,219	5,180	16.689	(1.329)	283.000	0.29	–0.47
1995	2,810	1,926	8,182	2.358	9.75	5.395	3,241	4,680	15.16	(0.23)	280.000	0.84	–0.01
1996	3,222	1,790	8,182	2.900	6.546	5.476	3,192	4,680	14.941	(2.919)	284.200	1.02	–1.03
1997	3,634	1,669	8,182	3.270	6.708	5.558	3,144	4,680	14.71	(2.450)	288.463	1.13	–0.85
1998	4,045	1,540	8,182	3.641	6.871	5.641	3,097	4,680	14.496	(1.983)	292.790	1.24	–0.68
1999	4,457	1,410	8,182	4.01	7.034	5.726	3,051	4,680	14.278	(1.519)	297.182	1.35	–0.51
2000	4,869	1,284	8,182	4.382	7.196	5.812	3,005	4,680	14.064	(1.056)	301.640	1.45	–0.35
2001	5,280	1,150	8,182	4.752	7.359	5.899	2,960	4,680	13.853	(0.595)	306.164	1.55	–0.19
2002	5,692	1,027	8,182	5.123	7.52	5.988	2,916	4,680	13.645	(0.137)	310.757	1.65	–0.04
2003	6,104	899	8,182	5.493	7.684	6.077	2,872	4,680	13.441	0.320	315.418	1.74	–0.10
2004	6,510	770	8,182	5.864	7.846	6.168	2,829	4,680	13.239	0.776	320.149	1.83	–0.24
2005	6,927	642	8,182	6.234	8.009	6.261	2,871	4,680	13.438	0.832	324.951	1.92	–0.26
2006	7,338	514	8,182	6.605	8.17	6.355	2,914	4,680	13.639	0.887	329.826	2.00	–0.27
2007	7,750	385	8,182	6.975	8.334	6.450	2,958	4,680	13.844	0.940	334.773	2.08	–0.28
2008	8,162	257	8,182	7.346	8.497	6.547	3,002	4,680	14.052	0.992	339.795	2.16	–0.29
2009	8,573	128	8,182	7.71	8.659	6.645	3,047	4,680	14.262	1.042	344.892	2.24	–0.30
2010	8,985	0	8,182	8.087	8.822	6.745	3,093	4,680	14.476	1.090	350.065	2.31	–0.31

Note: AFJP, administradores de fondos de jubilaciones y pensiones.
a Number in parentheses indicate a deficit.

grow from 47 percent currently to 70 percent by the end of the period under study. This assumption implies that the number of contributors (actual subscription-paying and not simply registered members) by 2010 will be 8.985 million.[22] In addition, assume that the number of people choosing the capitalization system over the public system increases uniformly through the end of the period. This implies that the transfer from one system to the other occurs at a decreasing rate (with regard to total contributing members) and that all contributors will have chosen the capitalization system by 2010.[23] See columns (1) and (2) of Table 2.2.

With regard to declared wages, the values corresponding to 1993, 1994, and 1995 are those estimated in terms of contributions made to the system.[24] Beginning with the 1995 value, wages are assumed to remain constant.[25] The legal rate of retirement contributions as a share of wages was modified in early 1994: there was a 10 percent increase in the personal con-

---

[22] This assumption cannot be considered optimistic. Note that the increment in the number of years of contributions, from the current level (27 years) to what is expected to represent the average once enough years have elapsed as a result of larger requirements to reach the retirement benefit (35 years), accounts for 30 percent of the increase. If we consider that 38 percent of current members do not make contributions, and thus are not accounted for among the initial contributors, the increase in the number of contributors for these two reasons, up to 2010, would be nearly 70 percent. Thus, an assumption of a 50 percent increase in the share of the economically active population making retirement contributions (from 47 percent to 70 percent) seems reasonable. Distributing this growth uniformly over the next 15 years (instead of over the first 10 years, when the principal effect of the increase on the requirements will be observed) should be also interpreted as a conservative assumption.

[23] Implicitly, then, the assumption is that employees younger than 50 (45 in the case of women) who have chosen to remain in the public system will gradually switch to the capitalization system as they gain confidence in it, but that all older contributors (approximately 40 percent of the contributing population) have chosen the public system and will remain there until retirement. This is undoubtedly a simplistic assumption, since in fact, up to the end of 1995, 8 percent of the male members of the state pension fund were 50 or older, whereas the percentage of female members 45 or older was near 15 percent.

[24] Based on the calculation of the average mandatory retirement contribution (AMRC) made by the National Social Security Administration.

[25] Given that the AMRC has been increasing since 1993 without a similar increase in the average wage, either or both of two conclusions may be drawn. The first is that there has been a significant increase in the reporting coverage of wages subject to retirement contributions. The second is that the increase in delinquency observed primarily during 1995 was concentrated mainly among contributors with fewer resources. Therefore, assuming a constant wage, a reduction in pension evasion is also assured. This means the coverage of retirement contributions is expected to continue to increase.

tribution rate, and employer contributions were reduced by an average of 25 percent (from 16 percent to 12 percent). This was factored in when calculating total system contributions. On the other hand, resources from other sources in 1993 are assumed to be constant on a per capita basis, although again we assume a 1.5 percent annual average population growth rate, throughout the period. For 1994 and 1995 the values observed were not recorded, except for those assumed to correspond to the situation where reform did not go forward; only in terms of this shift do the 1994 and 1995 figures not correspond to those actually observed.

In addition, the average level of payment (that is, the average benefit) was constructed by dividing total outlays by the number of beneficiaries for that year (taking no notice of outlays other than retirement benefits). Since the reform also called for increasing the minimum age of eligibility for benefits by one year every two years until the minimum age has been increased by a total of five years, the number of beneficiaries decreases at an annual rate of 1.5 percent between 1996 and 2004.[26] Given the expected changes in the number of beneficiaries, and accounting for the assumption made regarding the increase in declared wages (which constitutes the basis for adjusting the benefits granted under the old system), the estimated growth of total public pension system outlays during the next 15 years was calculated. See columns (6), (7), (8), and (9) of Table 2.2.

Finally, using estimated GDP values (in current prices) for 1993 through 1995, and assuming that GDP per capita remains constant during the projected horizon, we calculated payroll contributions to the privately managed retirement and pension administrators (*administradoras de fondos de jubilaciones y pensiones*, or AFJPs) and the fiscal position of the public system as percentages of GDP.[27] See columns (11) and (12).

---

[26] That is, even with annual growth of nearly 1.5 percent in the number of beneficiaries as a result of population growth, if we consider that the fraction of beneficiaries between ages 60 and 64 (55 and 59 for women) approaches 32 percent of the total passive population, the five-year increment in the minimum age for receiving retirement benefits will signify an annual reduction in the total number of retirees of approximately 1.5 percent (3 percent annual reduction for the increment in requirements minus 1.5 percent for population growth). After 2004, however, the natural growth rate will return to 1.5 percent.

[27] Note that the numbers would not change in the absolute under the assumption that real wages increase at the same rate as GDP, since that would have implied a proportionally similar increase in retirement benefits granted and in the amount of financing from other sources allotted to the system. Therefore, the assumption that growth per capita is equal to zero has no

Table 2.2 shows that, under these assumptions, pension reform leads to a deficit position from 1994 to 2002, after which the deficit becomes a surplus.[28] These deficits are significant. They reach a maximum of 1.03 percent of GDP in 1996, in which year they constitute 20 percent of total outlays. They then continue to accumulate to a maximum of 4.1 percent of GDP (assuming an interest rate equal to the per capita GDP growth rate, i.e., zero) in 2000. In addition, the ratio of contributors to beneficiaries rises from 1.46 in 1995 to 2.9 in 2010.[29]

---

effect on the estimations obtained as percentages of GDP.

[28] The 1995 deficit was small because of extraordinary contributions made during the period (a pension moratorium was in effect), and because of the partial suspension of reductions in employer contributions. Had it been otherwise, expected total contributions to the public system in 1995 would have been less than $9.8 million (column 5, including less than the $6.5 million estimated for 1996, due to the lower percentage of transfers to the capitalization system), making 1995 a year of larger deficit. In fact, the National Social Security Administration received an advance (a credit) from results of the moratorium on the order of $1.4 million, which explains 42 percent of the difference noted. If we assume that revenue from pension contributions would have been 20 percent less had employers' reductions not been suspended during eight months of the year, the figure would have approximated the estimated collection for 1996, and the public system deficit for 1995 would have exceeded 1 percent of GDP.

[29] In a recent projection Schulthess and Demarco (1996) assumed that the total number of contributors up to 2010 would be 53 percent higher than the number observed for 1995 (and would increase more quickly during the first few years), that 30 percent of contributors would remain in the allotment system to the end (against 38 percent actual), that transfers of public resources from other sources to the system would remain constant at an annual $3.6 million, that the average number of retirees under the new system would be 34 percent higher than that under the previous system (with retirees and pensioners in the new system representing 55 percent of the total in the year 2010), that the annual reduction in the number of beneficiaries would be between 1.1 percent and 1.5 percent annually, that the average employer contribution rate would be 12 percent of the wage bill, and that the population would remain constant. Given these assumptions, they estimate that the public system will be in deficit throughout the period (a situation that will reverse itself only in the year 2014), with the deficit reaching a maximum of 26 percent of total outlays for 1996 (1.34 percent of GDP). Comparing this estimation with our own, we can see that Schulthess and Demarco considered a level of funds from other sources that was lower by $1.8 million annually (comparing the figures for 1995). If this difference is incorporated into Schulthess and Demarco's estimate, the deficit would reverse itself in the year 2007 and would represent only 0.7 percent of GDP in 1996. The remaining difference (five fewer years of deficit in our estimation) is basically the result of assuming that the average benefit under the new system will not change, that the number of contributors (net of population growth) in our estimation is equal to 50 percent throughout the period (less than the 53 percent assumed by Schulthess and Demarco) and is distributed uniformly over time (reducing its impact with regard to that of the other estimation), and that the reduction in the number of beneficiaries by 3 percent annually (not discounting the

Table 2.3 estimates the immediate impact of pension reform on the private saving rate. Column (1) is constructed considering that the fraction of contributions to capitalized AFJPs decreases as a result of life insurance: given that 23 percent of contributions are sent to life insurance companies to pay disability and ordinary benefits, this percentage, added to the (new) administrative cost incurred must be excluded from the saving calculation on the basis of the contributions received by the AFJPs. However, except for the administrative costs of the insurance companies, the benefits paid out each year (supposedly equal to the amount of funds received, if the market is competitive) have to be transferred to the administrators, who only gradually transfer them to the members (or their descendants) in the form of disability or death benefits. As a result, assuming that in 2010 the inflow of cash (to the administrators) from the life insurance companies will be double the outflow in the form of pension payments to beneficiaries, and that the administrative costs of the administrators and the insurance companies are 8 percent and 5 percent of contributions, respectively, the percentages of contributions to AFJPs capitalized in 1994 and 2010 are 87 percent and 78 percent, respectively. Finally, assuming linear growth over that period, the result is column (1).[30] Column (2) simply transcribes the financial impact of reform on the public system stated in Table 2.2.

From there, Table 2.3 analyzes the additional effect of different methods of financing the public system deficit during the transition period. With regard to financing through taxes, the discussion at the beginning of this study indicates that the public sector financial position will remain constant, and that the recently calculated private saving in column (1) is genuine. However, the tax increase signifies a reduction in disposable income, which, assuming a 20 percent marginal propensity to save, generates a reduction in private saving, as shown in column (3). In addition, this increase (net of taxes) in private saving must be corrected to reflect a reduction in other forms of forced saving. Assuming that other saving instruments have the advantage of increased liquidity, which constitutes a nearly insignificant sum

---

annual population growth of 1.5 percent to make the figures comparable) during the first ten years in our sample exceeds the reduction of 1.1 to 1.5 percent during the entire assumption period in the alternative estimation.

[30] Note that if the interest rate at which the contributions to AFJPs are capitalized is equal to the growth rate of GDP per capita, in 2010 the funds accumulated in the AFJPs will represent 22 percent of GDP.

Table 2.3 Final Effect of Different Transition Financing Forms on Domestic Savings (percent)
Panel A

Year	Impact Effect		Tax Financing (T) Effects on Private Saving (3)	Debt (D) Effects on Priv. Sav. (4)	Substitution of Saving		Tax Financing		Total Effect (7)
	Private Saving/ GDP (1)	Public Deficit/ GDP (2)			With Tax Financing (5)	With Debt Financing (6)	Private Saving =(1)+(3)+(5) (a)	Public Saving (b)	
1994	0.25	0.47	-0.09	0.09	-0.02	-0.02	0.14	0.00	0.14
1995	0.73	0.01	0.00	0.00	-0.07	-0.07	0.66	0.00	0.66
1996	0.88	1.03	-0.21	0.21	-0.14	-0.18	0.54	0.00	0.54
1997	0.97	0.85	-0.17	0.17	-0.16	-0.19	0.64	0.00	0.64
1998	1.06	0.68	-0.14	0.14	-0.28	-0.32	0.65	0.00	0.65
1999	1.14	0.51	-0.10	0.10	-0.31	-0.34	0.73	0.00	0.73
2000	1.22	0.35	-0.07	0.07	-0.46	-0.49	0.69	0.00	0.69
2001	1.29	0.19	-0.04	0.04	-0.50	-0.52	0.75	0.00	0.75
2002	1.36	0.04	-0.01	0.01	-0.54	-0.55	0.81	0.00	0.81
2003	1.43	-0.10	0.02	-0.02	-0.58	-0.57	0.87	0.00	0.87
2004	1.49	-0.24	0.05	-0.05	-0.62	-0.60	0.93	0.00	0.93
2005	1.55	-0.26	0.05	-0.05	-0.64	-0.62	0.96	0.00	0.96
2006	1.61	-0.27	0.05	-0.05	-0.67	-0.64	1.00	0.00	1.00
2007	1.66	-0.28	0.06	-0.06	-0.69	-0.67	1.03	0.00	1.03
2008	1.71	-0.29	0.06	-0.06	-0.71	-0.68	1.06	0.00	1.06
2009	1.76	-0.30	0.06	-0.06	-0.73	-0.70	1.09	0.00	1.09
2010	1.80	-0.31	0.06	-0.06	-0.75	-0.72	1.12	0.00	1.12

Table 2.3 (continued)
(percent)
Panel B

	Financing with Ricardian Debt			Final Effect on Domestic Saving — Financing with Keynesian Debt			Financing with Ricardian/Keynesian Debt		
	Private Saving = (1) + (2) + (3) + (5)	Public Saving = −(2)	Total Effect (8)	Private Saving = (1) + (4) + (6)	Public Saving = −(2)	Total Effect (9)	Private Saving = [(a) + (c)]/2	Public Saving = [(b) + (d)]/2	Total Effect (10)
Year	(a)	(b) = (a) + (b)	(c)	(d)	(9) = (c) + (d)	(e)	(f)	(10) = (e) + (f)
	(a)	(b)	(8) = (a) + (b)	(c)	(d)	(9) = (c) + (d)	(e)	(f)	(10) = (e) + (f)
1994	0.61	−0.47	0.14	0.32	−0.47	−0.15	0.46	−0.47	−0.01
1995	0.67	−0.01	0.66	0.66	−0.01	0.65	0.66	−0.01	0.66
1996	1.57	−1.03	0.54	0.91	−1.03	−0.12	1.24	−1.03	0.21
1997	1.49	−0.85	0.64	0.95	−0.85	0.10	1.22	−0.85	0.37
1998	1.32	−0.68	0.65	0.88	−0.68	0.20	1.10	−0.68	0.42
1999	1.24	−0.51	0.73	0.90	−0.51	0.39	1.07	−0.51	0.56
2000	1.04	−0.35	0.69	0.80	−0.35	0.45	0.92	−0.35	0.57
2001	0.95	−0.19	0.75	0.82	−0.19	0.62	0.88	−0.19	0.69
2002	0.86	−0.04	0.81	0.83	−0.04	0.78	0.84	−0.04	0.80
2003	0.77	0.10	0.87	0.84	0.10	0.94	0.80	0.10	0.91
2004	0.68	0.24	0.93	0.85	0.24	1.09	0.77	0.24	1.01
2005	0.71	0.26	0.96	0.88	0.26	1.14	0.79	0.26	1.05
2006	0.73	0.27	1.00	0.91	0.27	1.18	0.82	0.27	1.09
2007	0.75	0.28	1.03	0.94	0.28	1.22	0.85	0.28	1.13
2008	0.77	0.29	1.06	0.97	0.29	1.26	0.87	0.29	1.16
2009	0.79	0.30	1.09	0.99	0.30	1.30	0.89	0.30	1.19
2010	0.81	0.31	1.12	1.02	0.31	1.33	0.91	0.31	1.22

for a significant fraction of the workers, and that there is a lag in recognizing that private saving is actually increasing as a result of pension reform, we may expect that the substitution effect will initially be small, but increasing. As a result, it is assumed that the rate of substitution takes the following values: 10 percent in 1994 and 1995, 20 percent in 1996 and 1997, 30 percent in 1998 and 1999, and 40 percent from then on. Given that international estimates of this effect range from 20 to 70 percent (and sometimes even less), this assumption appears reasonable. The corresponding deduction in private saving is shown in column (5).

Putting all the pieces together, then, the final impact of Argentina's pension reform on domestic saving, assuming that the transition is financed through taxes, is shown in column (7). This estimate represents the combined effect on private saving, shown in column (a), and public saving, in column (b). The effect is significant, even during the initial years of high deficit. And from there it increases, reaching 0.54 percent of GDP in 1996, 0.69 percent in 2000, and 1.12 percent in 2010.[31]

With regard to financing the transition with public debt, the estimation varies according to how the deficit is perceived by the private sector. If Ricardian equivalence holds, the increase in the deficit represents public dissaving, which will be compensated by an increase in private saving in anticipation of future taxes. In that case, disposable income is affected just as it would be if the reform were financed by taxes. How the deficit is financed is then irrelevant with regard to its overall impact on domestic saving, although its composition is very different: private saving is higher in the deficit years and lower in the surplus years. The effect of financing the deficit with debt, in compliance with Ricardian equivalence, is shown in column (8).[32]

However, if individuals do not perceive (or do not care) that they will pay higher taxes in the future if the deficit is financed with debt, the new

---

[31] Note that the surplus of the last eight years generates a tax reduction under this form of financing. This will be important when comparing this result with the effect of reform when the deficit is financed through public debt.

[32] Note that if the previously implicit retirement debt were recognized by the private sector, the increase in private saving would have occurred earlier, at the time that debt was incurred, and it would also be correct to say that pension reform does not mean a larger deficit, since the old, implicit debt is replaced by a new, explicit debt. As a result, the previous analysis with regard to aggregate saving remains valid.

government debt securities constitute new wealth for the private sector. We have referred to this as the Keynesian case. This perceived increase in private wealth leads to an increase in desired consumption and saving, but since the latter only occurs in terms of the marginal propensity to save (which is certainly less than one), this public dissaving is not fully compensated by an increase in private saving. Therefore, again assuming a 20 percent marginal propensity to save, column (4) shows the additional increase from column (1) in private saving. Column (6) calculates the reduction in other forms of saving due to the joint increase of saving in columns (1) and (4), using the same assumption as that used in calculating column (5) with tax financing. The final effect on domestic saving in this case is the result of adding columns (1), (4), and (6) (i.e., private saving) and subtracting column (2) (i.e., public dissaving). Note that in column (9) the total effect is positive only beginning in 1997. A surplus emerges in 1995 only as a result of extraordinary revenue from the moratorium and the suspension in reductions in employer contributions. Moreover the surplus will be less than in the previous case up to 2002, at which time the public system surplus is used to amortize the debt issued (that is, it represents positive public saving).[33] Results of an intermediate alternative are shown in column (10), where we assume that half of the private sector acts in the Ricardian manner, and the other half in the Keynesian manner.[34] This column shows that the final effect of pension reform on domestic saving is, except in 1994, always positive, although initially it is much lower than the corresponding financing through taxes in column (7). In general terms, reform tends to raise the domestic saving rate. The rise is equivalent to 0.21 percent of GDP in 1996 and only exceeds 1 percent of GDP in 2004.[35]

---

[33] With regard to the negative effect on domestic saving in 1994 and 1996, remember that new administrative costs are incurred for reform, and that these costs are subtracted from saving. There was also a reduction in employer contributions (i.e., negative public saving), which only later is compensated by increased saving through reductions in evasion and through increases, in general, in the ratio of contributors to beneficiaries.

[34] The estimation of the relationship between private saving and public saving discussed in chapter 1 of this volume on the basis of a sample from several countries, as well as evidence in other estimations, indicates that this case is most likely to represent the actual situation.

[35] This final effect, an increase in private saving of nearly 1 percent of GDP up to year 15 of the reformed system, contrasts with the larger direct effect (3.4 percent of GDP) estimated by Rondanelli (1996) for the first 15 years of the Chilean experience. Some important reasons behind this difference are that, in the Chilean case, the percentage of the work force with

Broadly speaking, we may expect that pension reform in Argentina would generate an increase in the domestic saving rate mainly through the increase in contributions required in order to obtain retirement benefits, and through the participants' perception that a substantial fraction of such benefits will accrue to the individual saver. This effect, however, will be observed more rapidly if the public sector makes an effort to finance the deficit of the public system during the transition with (at least) a combination of taxes and borrowing. And it will be more permanent and significant if the current private saving rate is less than the desired one—which may be the case in Argentina given the lack of attractive saving instruments for a large portion of the population. In effect, as shown in the estimations by Rondanelli (1996) and the considerations raised by Uthoff (1966) for Chile, most of the effect of moving from an allotment system to a capitalization system comes from financial system deepening. This leads us to think that it is by this route that pension reform will have the greatest impact on private saving.

Conclusions

This study has investigated the determinants of saving behavior in Argentina, beginning with the four concerns raised in the introduction. The main conclusions may be summarized in terms of our responses to these four concerns.

First, our measurement efforts show that, when certain important issues related to public saving and durable goods consumption are properly taken into account, the amplitude of the recent cycle of private saving in Argentina tends to diminish. Public saving was mostly responsible for the fluctuations in overall domestic saving in recent decades. In the early 1990s, however, fluctuations in private saving can be explained by consumer decisions regarding durable goods purchases. Incorporating the effects of the inflation tax and the consumption of durable goods in the measurement of saving works in the same way to lessen or reverse the measured drop in private saving during the 1990s. In the first case, this occurs because ac-

---

retirement contributions grew from 40 percent to 94 percent between 1981 and 1994, that the allotment component in that country only exists as a minimum benefit insurance charged to the state (the percentage of capitalized wages, including medical insurance, is thus larger), and that the wage bill as a percentage of GDP is larger in Chile than in Argentina.

counting for the inflation tax as public saving smooths the cycle of public saving seen in conventional measurements. In the second case, it occurs because accounting for durable goods expenditure causes significant changes in the measured level of saving. This result then leads to an investigation into the determinants of durable goods expenditure.

Second, analysis of the saving-investment correlation allows one to investigate the persistence of the imbalance between saving and investment observed during the first half of the 1990s. The principal conclusion is that the speed with which saving-investment imbalances are corrected in the Argentine case, as revealed by the error-correction model, is very high. Indeed, any such imbalance is closed within around three years. However, the behavior observed in 1994 and 1995 indicates a somewhat slower adjustment.

Third, the boom in durable goods consumption during the 1991–94 period occurred within a framework of broad growth in private consumption. This was accompanied by a set of structural changes that made it difficult to identify the extent to which this boom was due to credibility problems or to an excess of optimism due to the misperception of wealth. The results of this study indicate the importance of the nominal interest rate in explaining the observed cycles. This supports the hypothesis that the cycle of durable goods consumption is compatible with the explanation that economic agents respond to incentives that modify their decisions over time. However, the relevance of wages in dollars and the unemployment rate suggests that elements of optimism and pessimism seem to have exacerbated individual decisions. The results do not necessarily tell us whether the pattern of spending reflected in the boom of the 1990s is sustainable or not.

Finally, the analysis of pension reform indicates that we may expect pension reform in Argentina to generate an increase in the domestic saving rate. This will occur mainly through an increase in the contributions required to qualify for retirement benefits, and through the perception of participants that a significant fraction of these benefits will belong to them as individuals in the future. This effect will be observed more quickly, however, if the public sector attempts to finance the public system's deficit during the transition with (at least) a combination of taxes and borrowing. Moreover, the effect will be more permanent and significant if the current private saving rate is less than the desired rate, which may be the case in Argentina given the lack of attractive saving instruments for a large portion of the population.

References

Ahumada, H. 1995. "Econometría dinámica: una exposición simplificada." Serie Seminarios 16/95. Instituto y Universidad Torcuato di Tella, Buenos Aires.

Ando, A. and Kennickell, A. 1987. "How Much (or Little) Life Cycle Is There in Micro Data? The Cases of the United States and Japan." In R. Dornbusch, S. Fischer, and J. Bossons, editors. *Macroeconomics and Finance: Essays in Honor of Franco Modigliani.* Cambridge, Mass.: MIT Press.

Banco Central de la República Argentina. 1975. *System of Accounts for Product and Income in Argentina.* Vol. 2. Buenos Aires.

———. Various years. *Annual Report.* Buenos Aires.

———. Various years. *Quarterly Estimations of Global Supply and Demand, 1970–1980.* Buenos Aires.

Bar-Ilan, A. and Blinder, A. 1992. "Consumer Durables: Evidence on the Optimality of Usually Doing Nothing." *Journal of Money, Credit and Banking.* 24: 253–72.

Barros, D. 1979. "Private Saving and Provision of Social Security in Britain 1946–75." In G. Von Furstenberg, editor. *Social Security versus Private Saving.* Cambridge, U.K.: Ballinger.

Caballero, R. 1990. "Expenditures on Durable Goods: A Case for Slow Adjustment." *Quarterly Journal of Economics.* 105: 727–43.

Calvo, G. A., 1987. "Balance of Payment Crises in a Cash-in-Advance Economy." *Journal of Money, Credit and Banking.* 19: 19–32.

———. 1988. "Costly Trade Liberalization: Durable Goods and Capital Mobility." *IMF Staff Papers.* 35: 461–73.

————. 1995. "Varieties of Capital-Market Crises." Working Paper Series 306. Inter-American Development Bank, Washington, D.C.

Calvo, G. and Vegh, C. 1990. "Interest Rate Policy in a Small Open Economy." *IMF Staff Papers.* 37: 753–76.

CEPAL (Comisión Económica para América Latina y el Caribe). 1995. *Indicadores Macroeconómicas de la Argentina.* Buenos Aires.

Corsetti, G. and Schmidt-Hebbel, K. 1994. "Pension Reform and Growth." Paper presented at a conference on Pensions: Funding, Privatization and Macroeconomic Policy, Universidad de Chile, Santiago, January 26–27.

Cottani, J. and Llach, J. J. 1993. "National Saving, External Saving and Investment Financing during Economic Reform: The Argentine Plan." Secretariat of Economic Planning, MEYOSP, Buenos Aires. August.

Doornik, J. and Hendry, D. 1992. *PC-GIVE: An Interactive Econometric Modelling System, Version 7.* Oxford, U.K.: Institute of Economics and Statistics, University of Oxford.

Fauvel, Y. and Samson, L. 1991. "Intertemporal Substitution and Durable Goods: An Empirical Analysis." *Canadian Journal of Economics.* 24: 192–205.

Feldstein, M. and Horioka, C. 1980. "Domestic Savings and International Capital Flows." *Economic Journal.* 90: 314–29.

FIEL (Fundación Investigaciones Económicas Latinoamericanas). 1990a. "El gasto público en Argentina: 1960–1988." FIEL-CEA, Buenos Aires.

————1990b. "Gasto y déficit cuasifiscal." Separata Boletin Technint. 261. Buenos Aires.

Fracchia, A. 1978. "Contabilidad nacional a precios constantes en América Latina." *Cuadernos de la CEPAL.* 24. Santiago.

Gultekin, N. B. and Logue, D. E. 1979. "Social Security and Personal Saving: Survey and New Evidence." In G. Von Furstenberg, editor. *Social Security versus Private Saving.* Cambridge, U.K.: Ballinger.

Hall, R. 1978. "Stochastic Implications of the Life Cycle–Permanent Income Hypothesis: Theory and Evidence." *Journal of Political Economy.* 86 (6): 971–87.

Harberger, A. 1950. "Currency Depreciation, Income and the Balance of Trade." *Journal of Political Economy.* 58 (February): 47–60.

Held, G., Uthoff, A. and Titelman, D. 1995. "Indicators and Determinants of Saving for Latin America and the Caribbean." Working Paper 25. CEPAL, Santiago.

Heymann, D. 1984. "Precios relativos, riqueza y producción." *Ensayos Económicos.* March.

Hubbard, R. G. 1986. "Pension Wealth and Individual Saving: Some New Evidence." *Journal of Money, Credit and Banking.* 18 (May): 167–78.

Jansen, W. J. and Schulze, G. 1996. "Theory-Based Measurement of the Saving-Investment Correlation with an Application to Norway." *Economic Inquiry.* 34: 116–32.

Kiguel, M. and Liviatan, N. 1992. "The Business Cycle Associated with Exchange Rate Based Stabilization." *The World Bank Economic Review.* 2: 279–305.

Krugman, P. 1979. "A Model of Balance of Payments Crises." *Journal of Money, Credit and Banking.* 11: 311–25.

Laursen, S., and Metzler, L. 1950. "Flexible Exchange Rates and the Theory of Employment." *Review of Economics and Statistics.* 32 (November): 281–99.

Lilien, D. et al. 1995. *Econometric Views.* Irvine, Calif.: Quantitative Micro Software.

López Murphy, R., Navajas, F., Urbiztondo, S. and Moskovitz, C. 1998. "Determinantes del ahorro interno: el caso Argentina." Working Paper R-324. Office of the Chief Economist, Inter-American Development Bank, Washington, D.C.

Mankiw, N. G. 1982. "Hall's Consumption Hypothesis and Durable Goods." *Journal of Monetary Economics.* 23: 417–25.

———. 1985. "Consumer Durables and the Real Interest Rate." *Review of Economics and Statistics.* 67: 353–62.

MEYOSP (Ministerio de Economía y Obras y Servicios Públicos). 1995. *Argentina en Crecimiento, 1995–1999.* Vol. 1: *Proyecciones Macroeconómicas.* Buenos Aires.

———. 1996. "Estimaciones trimestrales del balance de pagos, 1993–1995." Buenos Aires.

Ministerio del Interior, Secretaria de Asistencia para la Reforma Económica Provincial. 1993. "Datos para el análisis del sector pública de las distilitas jurisdiciones de la Argentina." Buenos Aires. October.

———. 1993. "Situación de las provincias argentinas." Buenos Aires. January-February.

Montiel, P. 1997. "What Drives Consumption Booms?" In K. Schmidt-Hebbel and L. Servén, editors. *Saving in the World: Puzzles and Policies.* World Bank Discussion Paper 354. Section C2. Washington, D. C.

Munnell, A. 1976. "Private Pensions and Saving: New Evidence." *Journal of Political Economy.* 84 (October).

Ostry, J. and Reinhart, C. 1992. "Private Saving and Terms of Trade Shocks. Evidence from Developing Countries." *IMF Staff Papers.* 39: 495–517.

Posadas, L. 1993. "El nuevo sistema de jubilaciones y pensiones: sus efectos sobre el deficit previsional público." Pronatass/Birf Final Report, Project Argentina/89/005. June.

Reinhart, C. M. and Vegh, C. 1995. "Nominal Interest Rates, Consumption Booms, and Lack of Credibility: A Quantitative Examination." *Journal of Development Economics.* 46 (April): 357–78.

Rodríguez, C. 1982. "The Argentine Stabilization Plan of December 20th." *World Development.* 10: 801–11.

Rondanelli, E. H. 1996. "Chilean Pension Fund Reform and Its Impact on Saving." Paper presented at the 8th CEPAL Regional Seminar on Fiscal Policy, Santiago, Chile, January 22–25.

Schulthess, W. and Demarco, G. C. 1996. "El financiamiento del régimen previsional público en Argentina después de la reforma." Paper presented at the 8th CEPAL Regional Seminar on Fiscal Policy, Santiago, Chile, January 22–25.

Smith, R. 1990. "Factors Affecting Saving, Policy Tools and Tax Reform: A Review." *IMF Staff Papers.* 37 (1).

Talvi, E. 1996. "Exchange Rate–Based Stabilization with Endogenous Fiscal Response." Working Paper Series 324. Inter-American Development Bank, Washington, D. C.

Teijeiro, M. 1996. "La política fiscal durante la convertibilidad." Center for Public Studies, Buenos Aires. April.

Uthoff, A. 1996. "Promoción del ahorro y los sistemas de pensiones." Paper presented at the 8th CEPAL Regional Seminar on Fiscal Policy, Santiago, Chile, January 22–25.

CHAPTER 3

Explanations for the Increase in Saving in Chile

Manuel R. Agosin, Gustavo Crespi, and Leonardo Letelier[1]

Since the mid-1980s, when the economy was in the throes of the debt crisis, saving and investment in Chile have increased dramatically. Saving has increased at a faster rhythm than investment, reversing the heavy use of foreign resources prevailing during the first half of the last decade. These characteristics of the saving and investment process contrast with the situation in other countries of the region, where the rate of investment has stagnated and the national saving rate has dropped (IDB, 1996).

This chapter seeks to explain the behavior of saving in Chile. It begins with a description of the stylized facts: on the one hand, the evolution of gross investment and its breakdown into national saving and foreign saving, and on the other, the contribution to national saving of public, household, and business saving.[2] The conclusion is that the strong increase in gross investment since the mid-1980s has been financed increasingly with national saving and that the private business sector and the government have been the agents that have contributed the most to increasing national saving. Households do not save in net terms, even after adding forced saving via the privatized individual capitalization social security system in operation since 1981. Nonetheless, compulsory saving has been responsible for a decrease in household dissaving.

The analysis of long-term data for the Chilean economy helps provide a historical insight into the performance of saving and investment during the last decade. Although the rates of saving and investment have experienced a remarkable increase since the mid-1980s, it has only been in the last

---

[1] The authors are professors in the Department of Economics at the Universidad de Chile.
[2] The terms "national saving" and "domestic saving" are used interchangeably.

three or four years that they have managed to exceed the levels attained in the 1960s. Within this context, the recent performance of saving and investment would represent a return to long-term trends, and the low rates observed during the period 1970–89 would in fact constitute the outliers.

An econometric analysis is then offered for aggregate saving. In the first place, the link between saving and investment is studied. Second, the degree of substitutability between private and public saving, between private and foreign saving, and between business and household saving is analyzed. The objective here is to ascertain if some of the theoretical hypotheses about saving are fulfilled in the Chilean case. One of them is Ricardian equivalence, which posits that any change in government saving is necessarily offset by a change with the opposite sign of the same magnitude in private saving. Another hypothesis—that of perfectly integrated capital markets—posits that foreign saving is a perfect substitute for domestic private saving and that, consequently, any increase in foreign saving tends to be fully offset by a decrease in domestic saving. Finally, the hypothesis that households internalize completely the saving of business firms is tested.

In the analysis of the long-term relationships between private saving, public saving, and foreign saving, it is found that public saving tends to displace private saving, though in an incomplete manner, thereby allowing us to reject the hypothesis of strict Ricardian equivalence. Therefore, an increase in public saving increases national saving.

On the other hand, the hypothesis that foreign saving is a perfect substitute for private saving cannot be rejected. An economic interpretation of this relationship is that private firms face liquidity constraints. When foreign saving decreases, firms resort to a greater extent to internally generated funds in order to finance investment projects. This result holds only in the long run. In the short run, the impact of a change in foreign saving on domestic saving is nil. This implies that any change in foreign saving has an immediate effect on the level of investment. Since there are long adjustment lags to short-term disequilibrium, the period in which changes in foreign saving can affect investment is rather protracted.

A third interesting result is that the functions that explain business saving and household saving are quite different and that households internalize only 50 percent of changes in business saving. This refutes the hypothesis that households are capable of "lifting the corporate veil." Broadly speaking, the data for the Chilean economy belie the notion that households perfectly offset the saving of other agents in the economy. The offset coefficients are invariably lower than unity. A reason may be that liquidity constraints prevent households from maximizing their consumption intertemporally. Or it may be that they simply do not take into account the saving behavior of government or of firms. Whatever the case, the results cast serious doubts on the validity of empirical analyses of aggregate saving undertaken within a conceptual framework that stresses the consumption decisions of households (e.g., Morandé, 1996, and Edwards, 1995).

The analysis of the data on saving in Chile reveals the critical importance of business saving. Therefore, microeconomic data are used to estimate an econometric model of saving by Chilean publicly listed corporations. The main purpose of the model is to establish whether those companies are actually constrained in their access to financial resources that are external to the firm and must resort primarily to internally generated sources of funding, thus accounting for the strong correlation that exists between saving and investment in the Chilean economy. The results suggest that corporate saving is an important source of financing for investment and that informational asymmetries in capital markets are likely to be the chief cause. In addition, firms face significant adjustment costs in attaining their desired levels of saving. Other (less strong) results indicate that internal resources are more relevant for small corporations than for large ones and that they tend to become less important if a company belongs to an economic group.

The Stylized Facts

The estimations for saving made in this chapter use the following identities:

$$SDOM = I - SFOR \qquad [1]$$
$$SPRIV = SDOM - SPUB \qquad [2]$$
$$SBUS = SPRIV - SHOUS \qquad [3]$$

where $SDOM$ = domestic saving; I = gross investment; $SFOR$ = foreign saving (current account deficit); $SPRIV$ = private saving; $SPUB$ = public saving; $SHOUS$ = household saving; and $SBUS$ = business saving. I, $SFOR$, $SPUB$, and $SHOUS$ are independent estimations. Therefore, $SDOM$, $SPRIV$, and $SBUS$ are estimated as residuals.

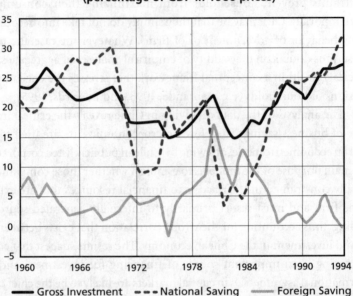

Figure 3.1
Saving and Investment in Chile: 1960–95
(percentage of GDP in 1986 prices)

The process of growth of the Chilean economy over the last decade has been accompanied by a strong increase in both gross investment and national saving (see Figure 3.1). As a percentage of real GDP in 1986 prices,[3] gross national saving has increased from levels close to zero in 1982 to more than 30 percent in 1995. In turn, gross fixed capital formation as a proportion of real GDP has practically doubled, reaching more than 27 percent in 1995.

These figures, which at first glance seem spectacular, need to be placed in their long-term historical context (see Table 3.1 and Figure 3.1). Table 3.1 shows the figures for growth, investment, and saving over a set of periods that highlight the changes in regimes that have been in place in the Chilean economy since 1960. The 1960s represent an appropriate benchmark, because subsequent periods were marked by extremes in economic

---

[3] Nominal saving was deflated by the implicit deflator of gross investment. The resulting figure is expressed as a share of GDP in 1986 prices.

Table 3.1 Saving, Investment, and Growth in Chile: 1960–95 (percent)

	Rate of Growth of GDP Per Capita	Gross Fixed Capital Formation	National Saving (% of GDP)	Foreign Saving (% of GDP)
1960–70	2.2	23.2	25.4	3.7
1971–73	−1.1	18.4	15.3	3.8
1974–81	2.0	18.4	18.5	6.4
1982–89	1.1	18.7	13.4	6.4
1990–95	4.7	24.9	26.8	1.7

Note: All computations were made with data from the national accounts in 1986 pesos. The series were spliced in 1985 to make the figures for previous years comparable with those of 1985 and later.
Source: Authors' calculations, based on data from Central Bank of Chile.

policy or were affected by acute external shocks. The period 1971–73 corresponds to the socialist experiment. During 1974–81, an important part of the pro-market reforms that have attracted international interest were implemented. The 1982–89 period corresponds to the debt crisis. During this period, pragmatic adjustments to the pro-market reforms were introduced. The last period, 1990–95, corresponds to the return to democracy and coincides with a new boom in the availability of foreign capital.

As can be perceived in Table 3.1 and Figure 3.1, which express GDP, saving, and investment in 1986 prices, the recent performance of saving and investment is clearly a return to the long-term trends of the 1960s. Thus, it is not that Chile, over the last decade, has attained rates of saving and investment that are much higher than the historical ones. Rather, the period 1970–89 should be regarded as a departure from long-term trends, with a clear recovery from the mid-1980s and an improvement in the rates that prevailed in the 1960s only as of 1992.

Historical series also reflect other meaningful changes in the saving process within the Chilean economy: the decline in foreign saving and the increase in national saving as a source of funding investment. Again, this is a relatively recent trend that becomes very marked as of 1986, despite the strong capital inflow that begins to take place in 1987 (Agosin, 1995; Ffrench-Davis, Agosin, and Uthoff, 1995). Both the increase in investment and national saving and the decrease in foreign saving are significant during this period.

Both the private sector and the public sector have contributed to the increase in national saving (Figure 3.2). Unfortunately, detailed information on the components of national saving exists only after 1975. Both public saving and private saving have displayed a markedly procyclical behavior, rising with the recovery of the Chilean economy in the second half of the 1970s and falling during the 1982–84 crisis. Since the mid-1980s, with the long upswing in the economy, both components of national saving have expanded once again. Between 1985 and 1994, public sector saving increased from –0.9 percent of GDP to 5.4 percent. These figures include the quasi-fiscal losses of the Central Bank (to be described below) and the operating surplus (profits plus depreciation funds) of state-owned enterprises (SOEs). On the other hand, private saving has also increased markedly: from 9.1 percent in 1985 to 22.1 percent in 1994.

Information on household saving[4] allows us to study the evolution of the two chief components of private saving: household and business saving. As can be seen in Figure 3.3, despite the social security reform of 1981, household saving has been strongly negative in Chile during the last two decades. Private corporations, however, have significantly increased their levels of saving (undistributed profits plus depreciation funds).

Briefly stated, during the phase of economic expansion which is still in progress, the increase in national saving between the mid-1980s and the mid-1990s has been on the order of 22 percentage points of GDP. The most important contributions have originated from business firms and the public sector. Households did not contribute to the increase in private saving, which has been the sole responsibility of business firms.

Public Saving

The behavior of public saving accounts for a nonnegligible proportion of the favorable evolution of national saving over the last decade. There are three levels of coverage that can be discerned within the public sector, each of them featuring distinctive traits with respect to saving. The first is what is designated as the general government, grouping the ministries and central-

---

[4] Information estimated by the Central Bank at the request of ECLAC (see ECLAC, 1995, table 1). This information is available for 1986–94. The series was extended back to 1975 using the methodology of the Central Bank for 1986–94.

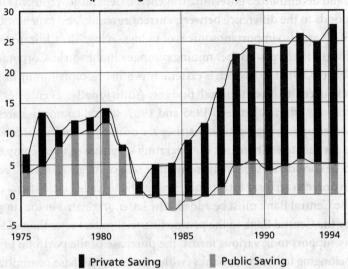

Figure 3.2
Private and Public Saving: 1975–94
(percentage of GDP in 1986 prices)

Private Saving   Public Saving

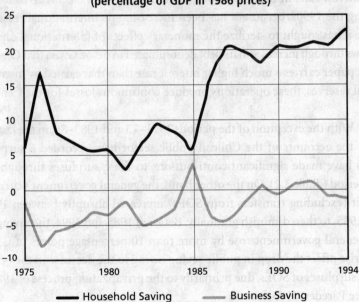

Figure 3.3
Private Saving: 1975–94
(percentage of GDP in 1986 prices)

Household Saving   Business Saving

ized agencies, social security institutions (which meet the social security needs of those who did not opt for the new pension system), municipal governments, and decentralized government agencies. General government saving corresponds to the difference between current revenues and expenditures.

SOEs are also important sources of public saving. The Chilean state is the owner of the largest copper mining company in the world, Corporación del Cobre (CODELCO), which is extremely profitable, contributing important resources to the national budget. Additionally, even after the privatizations effected between 1985 and 1989, several companies are still state-owned and, in aggregate terms, they are profitable, significant funding sources for the state. Therefore, the operating surpluses of these companies need to be considered separately from other sources of government saving.

In order to arrive at total public saving, the so-called quasi-fiscal deficit of the Central Bank must be added. The latter originated in the support given by the Central Bank to the private financial system after the 1982 crisis. This support took various forms: the purchase of the portfolio of bad loans belonging to bankrupt banks (with a future repurchase commitment from the banks); the setting up of a preferential dollar to dedollarize foreign private liabilities by converting them to national currency; and a loan to the state in exchange for a long-term bond in dollars at a 2 percent nominal interest rate. In the second place, the Central Bank has incurred losses during the 1990s, because it has been increasing its international reserves while it has sought to sterilize the monetary effects of international capital inflows through increases in its debt denominated in pesos. Given that Central Bank paper carries a much higher interest rate than that earned by international reserves, these operations produce continuous losses for the Central Bank.

With the exception of the periods 1971–73 and 1983–86, in the last 35 years the accounts of the Chilean public sector have recorded a surplus. SOEs have made significant contributions to these surpluses throughout the period (Table 3.2). On the other hand, the general government's current deficit (excluding transfers from SOEs) increased abruptly between 1982 and 1985, to then diminish gradually. Between 1985 and 1994, the saving of the general government rose by more than 10 percentage points of GDP. This rise offset the drop in public saving owing to the decrease in the operating surpluses of SOEs, due primarily to the privatization process of 1985–89 (see Paredes, 1995).

Table 3.2 Public Saving: 1975–94
(percentage of GDP in 1986 prices)

	General Government, Excluding SOE Contribution (1)	Central Bank Deficit[a] (2)	CODELCO Profits (3)	Other SOE Profits (4)	Total SOE Profits (5)	Public (1)+(2)+(5) (6)
1975	3.3	—	—	—	0.6	3.9
1976	−7.7	—	5.6	7.2	12.7	5.0
1977	0.4	2.0	3.2	4.7	7.9	8.3
1978	2.0	1.5	3.4	2.9	6.4	10.3
1979	−0.8	1.2	6.3	3.7	9.9	10.6
1980	0.7	1.2	5.3	4.9	10.2	12.0
1981	−0.1	−1.8	2.0	3.7	5.7	7.4
1982	−9.0	1.4	2.5	5.7	8.2	0.6
1983	−12.0	−0.5	4.5	7.5	12.0	−0.5
1984	−12.0	−3.0	3.2	7.6	10.8	−2.4
1985	−9.1	−4.9	5.0	8.1	13.1	−0.9
1986	−6.3	−4.7	4.2	6.5	10.7	−0.2
1987	−5.6	−3.5	4.4	6.1	10.5	1.4
1988	−4.3	−3.0	8.3	4.0	12.2	4.9
1989	−2.3	−2.7	8.2	2.6	10.8	5.8
1990	−3.2	−2.2	6.3	3.6	9.9	4.4
1991	−1.1	−0.9	3.9	3.1	7.0	4.9
1992	0.7	−1.1	3.5	3.1	6.6	6.1
1993	1.2	−1.0	2.1	3.1	5.2	5.4
1994	1.1	−1.0	1.9	3.3	5.2	5.4

Note: It is assumed that the deficits of the Central Bank were zero during 1975–77, years for which no information is available.

a. Deficits carry a negative sign.

Source: Authors' calculations, based on information from Central Bank of Chile and Ministry of Finance.

An important negative component in public saving as of 1981 is the deficit generated by the part of the social security system that is still administered by the state. The Chilean social security system operated on a pay-as-you-go basis until 1980. The reform of 1981 transformed it into an individual capitalization system run by regulated private pension funds (Administradoras de Fondos de Pensiones—AFPs). All wage earners must choose an AFP and contribute 12 percent of their income (with a maximum limit) on a monthly basis. The adoption of this system marked the beginning of a period of transition, in which active contributors have been progressively transferred from the old public system to the AFPs.

The impact of this change in the pension system on public saving has been twofold. In the first place, the government must continue to pay pensions, but it has lost its revenue base, as most wage earners have transferred to the private system. Second, in order to encourage the transfer to the AFPs, a "recognition bonus," meant to compensate workers for their past contributions to the pay-as-you-go system, became part of their social security savings under the new system. The social security deficit of the public sector, which started off at 8 percentage points of GDP in 1982–84, has been gradually falling and will continue to decline over time.

Private Saving

Table 3.3 shows the breakdown of private saving into its two basic components: household and business saving. Since 1982, household saving has included compulsory saving for social security contributions. Business saving is obtained as a residual between total private saving and net household saving.

Households consume more than they earn.[5] Compulsory saving through the AFPs has tended to gradually increase and at present is 4 percent of GDP (at 1986 prices). On the other hand, voluntary household saving has kept essentially constant, fluctuating in the period 1975–94 around an average of –3.7 percent of GDP. This means that the forced saving system has made a net contribution to household saving, because households have not voluntarily dissaved what the system forces them to save. In a pay-as-you-go system, social security contributions may well be considered simply as a tax. To the contrary, the individual capitalization system makes saving for retirement explicit. Because the liquidity constraints faced by households do not allow them to increase their liabilities in a manner that is equivalent to the increase in their assets originating from compulsory saving, the new system contributes to total household saving. It is interesting to note

---

[5] These estimates could be exaggerating household dissaving, as the existence of a sustained dissaving for 20 years is hard to believe. Nonetheless, the fact remains that Chilean households save little if at all.

Table 3.3 Private Saving: 1975–94
(percentage of GDP in 1986 prices)

	Total	Voluntary Household [a]	Forced [b]	Total Household	Business
1975	2.8	-1.8	—	-1.8	4.6
1976	8.5	-8.1	—	-8.1	16.6
1977	2.1	-5.9	—	-5.9	8.0
1978	1.8	-5.1	—	-5.1	6.9
1979	2.1	-3.4	—	-3.4	5.5
1980	2.2	-3.5	—	-3.5	5.7
1981	0.8	-1.8	0.9	-2.7	2.6
1982	1.6	-5.0	1.8	-6.8	6.6
1983	5.1	-4.3	1.8	-6.1	9.4
1984	5.4	-2.7	2.0	-4.7	8.1
1985	9.1	3.5	2.1	1.4	5.6
1986	11.8	-4.1	1.8	-5.9	15.8
1987	16.0	-4.6	1.8	-6.4	20.6
1988	17.9	-1.8	2.6	-4.4	19.7
1989	18.6	0.5	2.8	-2.3	18.1
1990	19.7	-0.7	3.0	-3.7	20.4
1991	19.5	0.8	3.0	-3.8	20.3
1992	20.0	1.0	3.2	-2.2	21.0
1993	19.4	-1.0	3.4	-4.4	20.4
1994	22.1	-1.1	3.7	-4.8	23.2

a. Total saving minus forced saving.
b. Contributions to pension funds.
Sources: Authors' calculations, based on data from the Central Bank, the Ministry of Finance, ECLAC (1995), and Marfán and Bosworth (1994).

that, since the change in the system in 1981, households have reduced their total dissaving by 2.4 percent of GDP. While nonnegligible, this contribution is modest, especially in view of the pubic dissaving that has accompanied the shift from the old pay-as-you-go public system to the new individual capitalization private system.

It has been argued that the new pension fund system may have contributed to saving through the deepening of financial markets (see Morandé, 1996). Actually, people now have a much greater variety of financial instruments through which they may save. Besides, a deeper financial market, due to a great extent to the AFP system, may have improved the efficiency of the process of financial intermediation between saving and investment. These arguments, based on theoretical concepts, must be examined in the light of the fact that households seem not to save at all.

Finally, private corporations have contributed the most to national saving. A preliminary explanation (endorsed by Morandé, 1996) is that, owing to severe credit restrictions in the domestic financial market (due to the deep crisis of the national banking system) and in international capital markets (due to the debt crisis), large corporations had to resort to retaining profits to finance the increase in investment that took place from 1985 on. This is especially true in the tradable sectors of the economy, which were favored by strong real exchange rate depreciations beginning in 1982.

The 1984 tax reform also involved strong incentives for the retention of profits. The essential aspect of such reforms was the elimination of the tax on profits and its replacement by a unified tax on income, which is paid by individuals. Corporate profits were subject to a 10 percent withholding tax, which was treated as a credit against stockholders' taxes when profits are distributed. The reform was gradually implemented during the period 1984–87. In 1990, the withholding tax rate on profits was raised to 15 percent.

Part of the increase in business saving is due to the transfer of companies from the public to the private sector, a process that took place between 1985 and 1989. SOE operating surpluses (excluding CODELCO) dropped during this period by 5.5 points of GDP, due mostly to the privatization process. However, business saving rose by 12.5 percent over the same period.

Domestic Saving, Investment, and Growth

Causality between Saving and Investment

Is saving important for growth? Finding the causal relationships between saving, investment, and growth in the Chilean economy has important implications both for understanding the dynamics of the process of growth and for formulating public policies. If it is concluded that an increase in saving is indispensable in order to increase the rate of growth, the most appropriate economic policies would be those geared to stimulate a greater rate of saving by households, business firms, and the government. Alternately, the conclusion could be that saving has no relevance at all in the growth process, because the main determinant of the rate of growth is either investment or technical progress. If this insight were correct, it would not make sense to orient economic policy to increase saving and it would be more productive to work on variables affecting investment and technical progress.

If any importance can be attached to saving as an explanatory variable of the long-term rate of growth, it becomes essential to elucidate whether the changes in both business and government saving are internalized by households. If business saving is a perfect substitute for household saving, the location of private saving is immaterial, and any increase in the saving of households would be offset by an equivalent decline in the saving of business firms (or vice versa). Therefore, stimulating households to save through, say, tax incentives would not increase the saving rate of the economy as a whole. On the other hand, if there is Ricardian equivalence, the government's actions to increase or reduce its saving would in no way affect the rate of saving in the economy, as private agents would totally offset the changes in government saving.[6]

Both theoretical and empirical analyses suggest that there is a strong causal relationship running from investment to growth (see, for example, Barro and Sala-i-Martin, 1995 ; Barro, 1991; DeLong and Summers, 1991). Where there is less consensus is on the importance of saving. In the neoclassical tradition (encompassing endogenous growth models, at least as regards the role of saving), consumers' preferences between present and future consumption (plus the availability of foreign saving, in an open-economy context) ultimately determine the rate of investment. For the models that follow the Keynesian tradition, on the other hand, investment decisions by firms determine the rate of growth, and saving is an endogenous variable that adjusts to the levels required by investment. An explanation for that causal relationship is that an important part of private investment is financed with retained earnings. In these models, firms are the only (or the main) savers, and wage earners consume all (or practically all) of their in-

---

[6] If Ricardian equivalence held, it would imply that efforts to increase private saving through changes in the institutional setup of the social security system would have no effect on aggregate private saving, as households would save less voluntarily in order to offset forced saving.

come (see, for example, Pasinetti, 1974, pp. 99–101). In this formulation, the line of causality goes from investment to growth, and from growth to higher levels of saving via an increase in retained profits.[7]

Does the direction of causality, then, go from saving to investment or from investment to saving? Granger causality tests provide evidence in favor of the plausibility of the hypothesis that investment is the fundamental variable. Private saving and private investment figures were used in the tests, which were performed with absolute levels, per capita levels, first differences, and ratios to GDP. The Hannan-Quinn (1979) criterion yields an optimum lag of one year in all cases.

The results are shown in Table 3.4. In all cases, it was possible to determine that the history of private investment is a significant determinant of private saving but that the history of private saving does not affect private investment. F tests disprove the hypothesis that private saving is not caused (in the Granger sense) by investment. Additionally, the hypothesis that private investment is not caused by private saving cannot be rejected. These findings support the conclusion that investment pulls saving, while changes in saving do not cause changes in investment, supporting Keynesian notions regarding the saving-investment nexus.

Error-Correction Model and Analysis from the General to the Particular

A model is developed for private saving through the estimation of autoregression vectors (VAR) that explore the long- and short-term relationships existing between private saving, on the one hand, and the variables that could affect it. The approach adopted in this section involves the following stages and is influenced by Hendry and Doornik's (1994) modeling approach from the general to the particular. In the first place, Johansen's

---

[7] It should be noted that the predictions of these models are identical to those made by life-cycle consumption models, where saving increases with growth because the generations that save have higher incomes than those that are dissaving. More sophisticated versions of the life-cycle model, however, with a large number of overlapping generations, result in more ambiguous predictions (see Deaton, 1995). Of course, the transmission mechanisms going from growth to saving are very different in these two groups of models. Actually, one of the most serious problems with the attempts to verify empirically the predictions of life-cycle models lies in the use of econometric studies of aggregate variables in the economy (GDP and domestic saving) as proxies for microeconomic variables for households (for examples, see Carroll and Weil, 1994, and Edwards, 1995).

Table 3.4 Granger Causality Tests between Private Saving and Investment: 1960–94

	spriv		ipriv	
In rates, as a percentage of GDP				
$spriv_{-1}$	0.87	0.67		0.07
	(8.43)	(5.55)		(0.92)
$ipriv_{-1}$		0.51	0.95	0.88
		(2.77)	(10.41)	(7.57)
R^2	0.689	0.751	0.772	0.778
Granger F test		7.69**		0.85
In per capita levels				
$spriv_{-1}$	1.02	0.75		0.11
	(13.02)	(6.04)		(1.15)
$ipriv_{-1}$		0.39	1.06	0.96
		(2.73)	(16.00)	(8.38)
R^2	0.841	0.872	0.889	0.893
Granger F test		7.50*		1.33
In first differences for per capita levels				
$spriv_{-1}$	−0.32	−0.39		0.17
	(−1.86)	(−2.29)		(0.95)
$ipriv_{-1}$		0.45	0.21	0.17
		(2.04)	(1.18)	(1.23)
R^2	0.101	0.210	0.043	0.089
Granger F test		4.16*		1.51
In levels				
$spriv_{-1}$	1.08	0.80		0.16
	(17.87)	(6.63)		(1.52)
$ipriv_{-1}$		0.33	1.09	0.95
		(2.62)	(21.54)	(8.78)
R^2	0.909	0.925	0.935	0.940
Granger F test		6.85*		2.26
In first differences				
$spriv_{-1}$	−0.21	−0.31		0.22
	(−1.14)	(−1.72)		(1.47)
$ipriv_{-1}$		0.44	0.25	0.18
		(2.13)	(1.42)	(1.02)
R^2	0.041	0.167	0.061	0.124
Granger F test		4.54*		2.16

*Significant at 5%.   ** Significant at 1%.
Notes: Regression constants are omitted. Numbers in parentheses are t–statistics. Definition of variables: spriv: private saving in 1986 pesos; ipriv: gross private investment, in 1986 pesos.

technique is used to obtain long-term cointegration relationships between the variables of the system. That is, the estimation of the VAR can help establish which linear combination or combinations of the variables of interest originate stationary errors. In the second place, by imposing and testing hypotheses derived from the theoretical frameworks discussed above, one can discriminate from among the several competing theories which one fits the data of the Chilean economy. Third, an estimate of the parsimonious representation of the vector error-correction model (PVECM) makes it possible to model the short-term dynamics of the long-term economic structure identified during the first two stages of the analysis. Fourth, the system can be conditioned to the weak exogenous variables identified in the first two stages in order to obtain the conditional PVECM model.

This exercise will be performed on the basis of the following vector of the variables:

$$Z = [spriv, gdp, spub, sfor, d1, d2, T] \qquad [4]$$

where the series included in the VAR correspond to *spriv* (private saving), *gdp* (gross domestic product), *spub* (public saving), *sfor* (foreign saving), *d1* (dummy variable for the period covered by the new social security system, 1981–94), *d2* (dummy variable for 1984 onwards, in order to capture the effects of the 1984 tax reform), and *T* (time trend). All the series are defined in per capita levels and at 1986 prices (using the deflator of gross fixed capital formation). Two additional dummy variables—*d3*, to capture the change in the methodology of the national accounts as of 1985, and *d4*, for the 1990 tax reform—are added to the error-correction model.

$$= 0.4544 * gdp - 0.6077 * spub - 1.116 * sfor + 6,436 * d1$$

$$+ 3,208 * d2 - 1,038 * T.$$

It was determined that the optimum lag was two years and that there exists only one cointegration vector. The standardized version of this vector is the following:

$$spriv = 0.4544 * gdp - 0.6077 spub - 1.116 * sfor + 6,436 * d1$$

$$+ 3,208 * d2 - 1,038 * T. \qquad [5]$$

Both the signs and the magnitudes of the parameters found are satisfactory. In particular, the negative relationships between private domestic
saving, on the one hand, and public and foreign saving, on the other, tend
to confirm the presence of some degree of substitutability between domestic private saving and each one of these variables. Also, of the variables included in the VAR, GDP and public saving are weakly exogenous, and both
domestic private saving and foreign saving are endogenous.

The imposition of structural theoretical constraints on the long-term
relationship is vitally important in order to identify the economic nature of
the process generating private saving and to be able to conduct comparative
statics exercises. The first hypothesis (H1, in Table 3.5) refers to the long-
term dependence of private saving on GDP. In general, the permanent income hypothesis suggests the existence of a marginal long-term propensity
to consume of one, which, of course, implies a marginal propensity to save
of zero. Stated in other words, only temporary changes in GDP would affect
saving and not the permanent changes captured by the long-term relationship. However, liquidity constraints make it impossible for consumers to be
continuously on their optimum consumption path over time. Therefore, it
would not be surprising to find a long-term positive association between
per capita income and saving: since consumers cannot dissave optimally
during shortfalls of income from its permanent level, in order to meet un-
foreseen declines in income, they would normally tend to save a proportion
of their permanent income. If, moreover, increases in income, no matter
how permanent, are concentrated in the high-saving segment of the popu-

Table 3.5 Tests for Theoretical Hypotheses on Cointegration Vector for *Spriv*

Hypotheses	*spriv*	*gdp*	*spub*	*sfor*	*d*1	*d*2	Trend	P value	
H1	(a	0	b	c	d	e	f)	$\varepsilon\rho(\$)$	0.0002**
H2	(a	b	0	c	d	e	f)	$\varepsilon\rho(\$)$	0.0000**
H3	(a	b	−1	e	d	e	f)	$\varepsilon\rho(\$)$	0.0357**
H4	(a	b	c	0	d	e	f)	$\varepsilon\rho(\$)$	0.0007**
H5	(a	b	c	−1	d	e	f)	$\varepsilon\rho(\$)$	0.6516
H6	(a	b	c	d	e	f	0)	$\varepsilon\rho(\$)$	0.0036**

** Significant at 1%.

Note: $\rho(\beta)$: cointegration space.

lation, it would not be surprising if a positive and significant relationship were to be found between income and private saving.

The second hypothesis (H2) tests for the nonexistence of a significant relationship between public and private saving, which would imply that any alteration in public saving is fully reflected in national saving. The third hypothesis (H3) posits that there exists perfect substitutability between private and public saving. H4 tests the hypothesis that the coefficient attached to foreign saving in the equation explaining private saving is not significantly different from zero. The fifth hypothesis (H5) is that there exists a perfect substitutability between foreign saving and private saving (offset coefficient equal to –1). Finally, H6 tests the existence of a significant trend in private saving.

From the results, summarized in Table 3.5, there does not exist evidence in favor of the permanent income hypothesis. The long-term relationship between saving and GDP is different from zero and has a coefficient that is far too high (0.45) to be consistent with such an approach. On the other hand, the existence of a negative relationship between private saving and public saving rules out the hypothesis that any increase in public saving involves an increase of equal value in national saving. Nor does the evidence favor Ricardian equivalence, since substitutability is far from perfect, with the increase in public saving of one peso being offset by a decrease in private saving of only 60 cents. The test that this coefficient is not significantly different from –1 is rejected at the 1 percent level.

Finally, in the long term, private saving and foreign saving appear to be perfect substitutes (the hypothesis that the coefficient of foreign saving is equal to –1 cannot be rejected). This is surprising, given that the degree of openness of the capital account is not perfect (due to the presence of taxes on short-term capital inflows and to some restrictions on capital outflows) and that the substitutability of domestic and foreign assets is far from perfect (as witnessed by the recent "tequila" effect, which also affected the country's financial assets). Therefore, a coefficient that is not significantly different from unity would be justified only in light of the existence of liquidity constraints on the investment decisions of firms. This would be the case if firms financed investment projects either with internally generated saving or with funds external to them, including foreign resources. Therefore, when foreign financing constraints are relaxed, firms could react by increasing the shares of their profits that they distribute as dividends and by reducing their saving. It should be noted that this interpretation is consistent with the absence of strict Ricardian equivalence and with the strong and positive association found between private saving and GDP.

On the basis of the above results and considering the endogenous nature of private saving (*spriv*) and foreign saving (*sfor*), one can estimate an error-correction system for these variables. The error term in both estimations—the difference between the current level of private saving and its long-term equilibrium—is represented by *res*, which is built by assuming as valid the constraint connected with H5 in Table 3.5. The results of the estimation by maximum likelihood are shown in Table 3.6. The version shown is the outcome of the reduction from the general to the particular of two error-correction equations which include the first differences of all the variables, both in time *t* and lagged one period, plus a set of two additional dummy variables so as to capture the effects of the change in methodology used to estimate the national accounts (which affects the data from 1985 onward),

Table 3.6 Vector Error–Correction Model (PVECM) Estimated by Maximum Likelihood (Nonrestricted Reduced Forms)

Variable	Coefficient	t
Equation 1 for *dspriv*		
$dspriv_{-1}$	−0.514	−3.50
res_{-1}	−0.622	−2.10
dspub	−0.436	−2.54
dgdp	0.242	2.67
Constant	−36,570	−2.16
d3	15,293	3.82
Equation 2 for *dsfor*		
$dspriv_{-1}$	0.449	3.43
res_{-1}	−0.660	−2.44
dspub	−0.374	2.37
$dspub_{-1}$	0.412	4.88
dgdp	0.284	3.49
Constant	−40,394	−2.41
d3	−4,190	−1.16

Note: d means yearly increase; the lags are indicated by a subindex, and *res* is residuals of equation [5] in the text, assuming H5 in Table 3.5.

labeled $d3$, and the 1990 tax reform ($d4$). Thus, a parsimonious representation of the short-term behavior of the two endogenous variables of the system (PVECM) was obtained. Additionally, the properties of the error term and the stability of the parameters were tested. In both cases, well-behaved errors and stable parameters were obtained. That is to say, the model was able to capture adequately the short-term dynamics of Chilean saving during the period under analysis.

Several conclusions can be derived from the results. The first is that, despite the apparent perfect substitutability between foreign saving and private saving found for the long-term relationship, the impact effect of the variations in foreign saving ($dsfor$) on short-term private saving ($dspriv$) is not significantly different from zero and was thus eliminated from the PVECM. In economic terms, this means that, in the short term, a decline in foreign saving reduces investment peso for peso. Second, the coefficient measuring the speed of adjustment to disequilibria in private saving has a value of -0.62, which indicates that the model is convergent and that more than half of long-term disequilibria is corrected over the term of one year. A third interesting finding is that the marginal propensity to save in the short term (0.25) is considerably lower than the value obtained for the long-term relationship (0.45). Fourth, as expected, the short-term response of private saving to changes in public saving is smaller than the long-term effect. Fifth, the high absolute value of lagged private saving in the private saving equation (-0.5) implies the presence of a high degree of inertia in the adjustment process. This implies that, even though more than half of the disequilibria is closed in a year, this inertia originates new disequilibria, so that complete adjustment may take several years.[8]

Finally, and with a view to evaluating the effects of exercises of "comparative statics," the dynamic system implied by the PVECM for its long-term static equilibrium was solved. The reduced forms obtained and the long-term static multipliers are shown below:

$$spriv = -7.138 + 0.5312 * gdp - 0.6619 * spub + 30.940 * d1$$

$$+14.080 * d2 + 20.170 * d3 - 2.694 * T. \qquad [6]$$

---

[8] Thus, for instance, simulation exercises show that, after five years, there still exists a gap of about 5 percent between actual and equilibrium levels of private saving.

$$sfor = 8.467 - 0.563 * gdp + 0.617 * spub - 22.150 * d1$$
$$-5.701 * d2 - 14.310 * d3 + 1.364 * T. \tag{7}$$

These results imply that private saving is an endogenous variable that is determined jointly with foreign saving. On the other hand, the long-term fundamentals of private saving are public saving and GDP. The low substitutability of private and public saving, together with the strong response of private saving to GDP, are inconsistent with the permanent income and Ricardian equivalence hypotheses. There is a strong inertia in the short-term behavior of private saving, and short-term coefficients are all considerably lower in absolute value than long-term ones. These results are consistent with the existence of liquidity constraints on private agents and differences in planning horizons between different types of economic agents.

As regards policy instruments, increases in public saving are offset by declines of private saving of only two thirds; therefore, efforts to increase public saving are an effective way to increase national saving. Besides, increases in public saving also lead to (marginal) increases in foreign saving (maybe because the greater creditworthiness displayed by the state reduces sovereign risk). Finally, institutional innovations such as pension reform and the strong reduction of tax rates on undistributed profits have increased private saving. However, these results are to be interpreted with great care because they have been obtained by means of dummy variables used as proxies and therefore may be capturing other phenomena that are temporally correlated with private saving.

Keeping these limitations in mind, eq. [6] estimates the orders of magnitude of the contribution that different institutional reforms have made to private saving. A high-end estimate of the contribution of social security reform to the increase in private saving between 1981 and 1994 is 7 percent of GDP, whereas the tax reform could have added an extra 3 percent. Both together account for, at the most, half of the increase in private saving between 1981 and 1994 (21 percentage points of GDP). As already pointed out, the direct contribution of the social security reform to private saving was 3.7 percent of GDP (see Table 3.3), and consequently the difference (3.3 percent) could be ascribed to indirect effects (for instance, a deeper capital market). However, it should not be forgotten that, in order to measure their net contribution to national saving, it is necessary to give due consideration to the lower public saving these innovations have entailed.

Therefore, the chief explanatory variables for the increase in private saving have been the acceleration of growth and the increases in business profits and investment plans.

A Model for Components of Private Saving

To what extent do households internalize enterprise saving? Is household or corporate saving more sensitive to foreign saving? These questions have yet to be answered. The hypothesis that the high offset coefficient would be the product of the presence of liquidity constraints on investment suggests that the main effect of increases in foreign saving should fall upon business saving. These issues can be addressed with a very simple model for the two components of private saving that are estimated with data for 1975–94 for household and business saving.

Begin with a Keynesian function for household saving, in which saving depends on income. Add public saving and business saving to this structure. To the extent that households internalize some proportion of the change in business saving and public saving, their saving will be influenced by these latter variables. Also, include foreign saving as an explanatory variable. Increases in foreign saving relax the liquidity constraints faced by all national agents, including households, and therefore lessen their need to save.

In the case of business saving, a different structure reflects the basic stylized fact that corporations save in order to invest. Business saving is a function not only of firms' investment plans but also of the taxation system and of the domestic and foreign liquidity constraints they must face. As not all the information needed to specify a complete model is available, public saving and foreign saving are added as explanatory variables. Therefore, the equation used for business saving may be interpreted as a sort of reduced form of a richer model that includes the variables described above. For instance, if there is crowding out of business saving by public saving, this could be the outcome of changes in business income tax rates. On the other hand, foreign saving is a variable closely related to international liquidity constraints: the greater the availability of foreign financing, the less the need to finance investment projects with internally generated funds.

The model consists of the following two equations:

$$shous = \alpha_0 + \alpha_1 * gdp + \alpha_2 * spub + \alpha_3 * sfor + \alpha_4 * scorp \qquad [8]$$

$$sbus = \beta_0 + \beta_1 * ipriv + \beta_2 * spub + \beta_3 * sfor \qquad [9]$$

where *shous* = household saving, *sbus* = business saving, *gdp* = gross domestic product, *spub* = public saving, *sfor* = foreign saving (deficit in current account), and *ipriv* = private investment. All variables are expressed in per capita terms and in 1986 pesos.

To the extent that households internalize a portion of both public saving and business saving, $0 > \alpha_2$, $\alpha_4 \geq -1$. On the other hand, if the effect of foreign saving on private saving falls more on business saving than on household saving, α_3, $\beta_3 \leq 0$ and $\beta_3 < \alpha_3$.

The estimations are summarized in Table 3.7.[9] As can be seen, the model accounts for a high percentage of the total variation of household and business saving. All variables used are $I(1)$ and, judging from the augmented Dickey-Fuller criteria, the equations cointegrate. The Breusch-Godfrey test rules out the presence of autocorrelation.

The results indicate that household saving does not respond to the same variables as business saving. The long-term marginal propensity to save of households is, in effect, greater than zero, which is consistent with the results obtained for private saving in the preceding section. Besides, households internalize the changes in business saving very incompletely. For every peso of increase in business saving, households reduce theirs by only 50 cents. This outcome is in keeping with our expectations. In the Chilean economy there are many small firms, whose savings cannot be told apart from the savings of their owners. However, in the case of large corporations and foreign companies, which are the main business savers, it is more difficult to hold the conventional assumption that the offset coefficient is –1.

Ricardian equivalence fails to hold at this level as well. Households internalize approximately one third of the changes in public saving. Considering its impact on business saving, an increase in public saving by one

---

[9] In estimating [8] and [9], a dummy variable ($d1$) is added and takes a value of 1 in 1985 and of 0 in other years, since naked observation of the series for household saving suggests an important degree of overestimation for that year.

Table 3.7 Functions for Private Saving: 1975–94

Explanatory Variable	Endogenous Variable	
	shog	semp
	(1)	(2)
Constant	−58,326	12,790
	(−4.88)**	(2.90)**
gdp	0.293	
	(3.71)**	
ipriv		1.069
		(15.59)**
spub	−0.372	−0.649
	(−2.41)*	(−4.14)**
sfor	−0.566	−0.928
	(−2.80)**	(−6.11)**
sbus	−0.520	
	(−2.95)**	
d1	11,110	−16,502
	(2.23)*	(−2.17)*
R^2	0.768	0.956
DW	1.39	1.30
ADF test[a]	−2.74**	−3.89**

* Significant at 5%. ** Significant at 1%.
Note: t-statistics (in parentheses) are only indicative, as the series are integrated of order 1.
a. For (1), test with no lags; for (2), test with two lags.

peso leads to a decrease in household saving of approximately 70 cents. This estimate is consistent with the results of the VAR described above. Finally, the estimated equations suggest that changes in foreign saving affect private saving mostly through their impact on business saving. Note that the coefficient associated with foreign saving is considerably greater in absolute terms in equation (2) than in equation (1). In addition, in equation (2), it is not significantly different from −1.

The Saving Behavior of Chilean Corporations

What about the saving behavior of Chilean publicly listed corporations? If a significant portion of them face liquidity constraints on their desired levels of investment, that would explain a part of the long-term relationship between national saving and investment. Questions to answer include the following: How do Chilean corporations finance their investment plans, and how has the pattern of financing changed over time? Is corporate saving related to investment decisions? Are liquidity constraints more severe for small firms than for larger ones, or for companies that do not belong to a conglomerate than for those that do belong to one?

Before reporting on the conclusions of the econometric analysis, it is useful to examine the information contained in the table on sources and uses of funds for the Chilean corporate sector (Table 3.8). These data show information for all of the close to 250 companies listed on the stock exchange. Internal financing increases dramatically towards the mid-1980s, as compared to 1981, and there is a reduction in indebtedness, which was the most significant source of funds for Chilean corporations in 1981. Clearly, Chilean corporations faced severe liquidity constraints beginning with the 1982 crisis. While the use of internal resources, as a proportion of total financing, goes down beginning in 1986, what increases is not indebtedness

Table 3.8 Sources and Uses of Funds in Chilean Corporations: 1981–94 (percentage of total)

	1981	1986	1990	1994
Sources of funds				
Own resources	51.1	78.1	65.3	63.7
Operating	(7.3)	(37.0)	(35.8)	(32.6)
Debts	47.5	18.2	21.8	15.2
Bonds	—	1.8	7.2	5.2
Shares	1.3	1.9	5.7	16.0
Total	**100.0**	**100.0**	**100.0**	**100.0**
Uses of funds				
Fixed investments	18.0	25.0	36.0	22.1
Financial investments	68.6	40.8	24.1	37.5
Decrease in debts	18.7	21.5	16.3	16.8
Dividends	6.8	9.3	26.1	20.5
Investment in working capital	−12.1	3.4	−2.5	3.2
Total	**100.0**	**100.0**	**100.0**	**100.0**

Source: Authors' calculations, based on Securities and Insurance Commission, FECU form.

but rather the placement of shares and bonds, which become important sources of financing in the 1990s.

As regards the use of funds, the percentage devoted to investments in fixed assets (which comes close to the concept of gross fixed capital formation in the national accounts) has fluctuated considerably, with a maximum in 1990 (36 percent) and a figure slightly higher than a fifth in 1994. Financial investments (which include purchases of other companies), extraordinarily important at the beginning of the 1980s, go down considerably by the mid-1980s, to then increase again in the 1990s, though in 1994 they were much lower than in 1981. At the beginning of the 1980s, Chilean corporations devoted very small proportions of their funds to the distribution of dividends. At present, the participation of dividends in the use of funds has increased considerably.

These figures offer a bird's-eye view of the significant changes the Chilean financial system has undergone since the beginning of the 1980s. While at the outset of the past decade the use of bank loans for the purchase of other companies was predominant, in the 1990s there is a greater use of own resources and of the stock exchange and long-term credit markets, with a greater predominance of physical investments rather than financial investments (particularly, the purchase of other companies). Long-term financing via shares or bonds, a new phenomenon, is closely related to the modification of the social security system, which has allowed a rapid development of equity and bond markets. On the other hand, the decline in the importance of indebtedness with the banking sector may be due in part to the availability of other more suitable sources of funds, but it is also related to the greater prudential regulation of the financial system, which was instituted as an outcome of the 1982 crisis.

Corporate Saving with Liquidity Constraints

An empirical model of the saving behavior of Chilean corporations is presented here. The theory behind the model is based on Fazzari, Hubbard, and Petersen (1988), who offer reasons why firms often finance investments with undistributed earnings rather than with borrowed funds or with equity issues. This, of course, implies that the Modigliani-Miller (1958) theorem that external funds are a perfect substitute for internally generated capital does not hold in practice.

It is possible to identify several reasons why internal funds have a decisive cost advantage over external funds. Among the most prominent ones are the transaction costs associated with the placement of shares or bonds; the existence of differences in the tax treatment of undistributed profits, dividends, and interest; agency problems; and asymmetric information. This study emphasizes the relevance of the last two factors.

Asymmetric information may originate significant cost disadvantages for funds raised externally. This idea is present in the so-called theories of financing hierarchies (Myers and Majluf, 1984; Stiglitz and Weiss, 1981; and Greenwald, Stiglitz and Weiss, 1984). In line with this approach, it is assumed that managers possess complete information regarding the value of their assets and returns to new investment projects. This contrasts with the position of external investors, who, not being able to discern between the qualities of the investment projects that are submitted to them by different firms, value all of them at the average for the population. The outcome is that new external investors (shareholders, banks, or bond holders)[10] end up demanding a premium for lending to or buying issues from relatively good firms so as to offset the losses they will have in financing bad firms. This tends to increase the cost of external funds for high-quality firms over and above the opportunity cost of internal funds.

External financing also generates agency problems, because as the ratio of debt to capital increases, managers have enhanced incentives to diverge from the interest of creditors. They may postpone profitable investment projects, give preference to others with a lower or even negative profitability, or otherwise issue new debt that reduces the value of already existing debt. Creditors, aware of this potential conflict of interest, place conditions on borrowers that limit their discretionary power. Thus, restrictions are imposed on debt-capital ratios and on liquidity indicators. While these restrictions are a solution to potential opportunistic behavior, they limit the firm's financial flexibility and reduce the availability of external and internal funds to finance profitable investment projects (Smith and Warner, 1979).

---

[10] In the specific case of debt markets, asymmetric information leads, additionally, to the phenomenon of adverse selection. When lenders increase the interest rate, the safer investment projects withdraw from the market and only the riskier ones remain. This leads to a deterioration in the composition of the portfolio of the lender. If lenders are risk averse, they will end up setting an "equilibrium" interest rate that leads to excess demand for funds, with some debtors receiving loans and other potentially equivalent ones being rationed in terms of quantity.

The literature on corporate dividend policy also sheds light on the saving behavior of corporations. Lintner's (1956) model is taken as the point of departure for this paper. The original model assumes that companies set their dividend policies based on a routine rule, which is normally a fixed percentage of profits:

$$D_t = r_t * U_t \qquad [10]$$

where D_t = current dividend and U_t = current profit.[11]

The above expression may be rewritten in terms of the company's saving (retained earnings, S_i) as follows:

$$S_i = \alpha_t * U_i \qquad [11]$$

where $\alpha = 1 - r$. This expression may be reformulated in terms of rates dividing both sides by sales.

Unlike the original model, which assumes a fixed dividend policy, here it is assumed that α adjusts to reflect the firm's preferences for internally generated funds. Therefore:

$$\alpha_t = C * I_t^{\gamma_0} * T_t^{\gamma_1} * D_t^{\gamma_2} * M_t^{\gamma_3} * G_t^{\gamma_4} * P_t^{\gamma_5} \qquad [12]$$

where C is a constant, I is the investment-to-sales ratio, T is size (total assets to sales), D is ratio of indebtedness to sales, M is a proxy for the ownership structure (percentage participation of majority stockholders), G is affiliation with an economic group (dummy variable with value 1 for companies belonging to a group), and P is the rate of profits to sales. The finding of $\gamma_0 > 0$ will be evidence in favor of the existence of a financing hierarchy, since it would indicate the existence of a positive correlation between the decision to invest and the decision to generate funds internally.

On the other hand, a negative coefficient γ_1 is consistent with the foregoing theoretical framework, insofar as larger firms are easier to audit by their creditors than smaller ones. Besides, the larger the size of the firm, the

---

[11] This represents a departure from Lintner's original model, as an instantaneous adjustment between profits and the desired dividend is assumed (see Giner and Salas, 1995).

faster is the dissemination of information regarding its behavior, and the larger the collateral it is able to offer creditors.[12] The level of indebtedness (D) is viewed by financial markets as a negative indicator of creditworthiness and is associated with a greater potential agency problem; hence, higher indebtedness is expected to be associated with a greater use of internally generated financial resources ($\gamma_2 > 0$).

The variable M represents the concentration of ownership in majority stockholders. As a more concentrated ownership is associated with a less acute agency problem and greater efficiency, a negative parameter γ_3 is expected. The dummy variable G captures affiliation with an economic group. If the existence of the group is due to the incentive to internalize imperfect capital markets, firms that belong to a group will face fewer financial restrictions on investment than those that do not and will require less internal financing. If this is the case, one would expect that $\gamma_4 < 0$ (Bisang, Burachik, and Katz, 1995). Finally, within a context of financing hierarchies, with given investment projects, a higher ratio of profits to sales will encourage an increase in dividend payout and a reduction in corporate saving; hence, it is expected that $\gamma_5 < 0$.

Since investment is an endogenous variable determined jointly with the firm's saving, it will be modeled as a function of the sales accelerator:[13]

$$I_i = \Omega_0 * \Delta Q_i \qquad\qquad [13]$$

where Q is the level of sales and Ω_0 is a positive parameter.

Replacing [13] in [12] and this in turn in [11] yields:

$$S_i = C * \left(\Omega_0 \Delta Q_i\right)^{\gamma_0} * T_i^{\gamma_1} * D_i^{\gamma_2} * M_i^{\gamma_3} * G_i^{\gamma_4} * P_i^{1+\gamma_5} . \qquad [14]$$

Taking natural logarithms of equation [14], the following reduced linear form is to be estimated:

---

[12] Likewise, the "social weight" (in terms of employment) of large firms often makes them eligible for state subsidies during financial crises, which reduces the likelihood of bankruptcy and improves their access to external financial resources.

[13] It should be noted that richer modeling (including, for instance, a price variable) has not been used because of the lack of information for a significant number of companies.

$$\ln S_i = C' + \gamma_0 \ln(\Delta Q)_i + \gamma_1 \ln T_i + \gamma_2 \ln D_i + \gamma_3 \ln M_i$$

$$+ \gamma_4 \ln G_i + (1 + \gamma_5)\ln P_i \qquad [15]$$

where $C' = C + \gamma_0 ln\Omega_0$.

The main drawback of the linear estimation of [15] lies in the fact that some of the variables assume negative values, which inhibits the possibility of working with natural logarithms. In order to take this problem into account, the estimations were done with the variables in levels, using powers in order to capture nonlinearities, which is consistent with a Taylor expansion of the original nonlinear model.

The steps followed to obtain the results shown below may be summarized as follows:

(1) estimation by ordinary least squares (OLS) of the linear version of the saving equation, with corporate saving (undistributed profits plus depreciation funds) as a percentage of sales taken as the dependent variable;

(2) applying a White test for heteroskedasticity;

(3) correction of heteroskedasticity by respecifying the model through the inclusion, in the final regression, of the variables that are significant in the description of the residuals found in the preceding stage and using OLS with White's consistent covariance matrix;[14]

(4) correction for autocorrelation, through the specification of a short-term partial adjustment model; and

(5) and (6) final estimation of the model by OLS and by restricted least squares (RLS). The equations numbered [1], [2], [3], [4], [5], and [6] in Table 3.9 show the results of these estimations, in that order.

The data base, provided by the Securities and Insurance Commission (Superintendencia de Valores y Seguros), records quarterly balance sheets and operational results for all publicly traded corporations. Since the number of companies included in the sample varies from one year to another, an "unbalanced" panel of companies is used corresponding to the period

---

[14] Which replaces $V(\beta_{mco}) = \sigma^2 (X'X)^{-1}$ by $\sigma^2 (X'X)^{-1} X' \sum X(X'X)^{-1}$.

1985–94, with the restriction that each company should appear at least for a period of five consecutive years, so as to minimize potential autocorrelation problems. The number of companies included in the analysis is 196 (48 in financial services, 53 in industry, 21 in energy and gas, 40 in other services, 13 in agriculture and livestock, 12 in telecommunications and transportation, and 9 in mining). The total number of observations is 1,419.

The OLS estimation (regression 1 in Table 3.9) yields parameters with signs that conform to the financing hierarchies model. However, with the exception of the constant, the rate of profit, and the dummy that captures the existence of subsidiaries, the variables were not significantly different from zero. Moreover, it is possible to detect the presence of heteroskedasticity and autocorrelation (a significant chi-square White test and a Durbin-Watson test of 0.96). According to the White test, the cause for heteroskedasticity is the omission of the squares of the variables for size and profits. Therefore, the model was reestimated by incorporating these nonlinearities (regression 2). In order to eliminate residual heteroskedasticity, for purposes of inference, the consistent White variance-covariance matrix (regression 3) was also computed. At this point, the results improve substantially; all the variables have the correct signs and are statistically significant, with the exception of the indebtedness variables, which were not significantly different from zero.

The main problem found at this stage was the persistence of autocorrelation, which reduces the reliability of the previous tests. The alternative hypothesis that the error term follows an AR(1) process could not be rejected, which indicates that the model is incorrectly specified as a static regression, when actually it is a dynamic model. In order to capture the short-term dynamics involved, a partial adjustment model (regression 4) is estimated. In order to account for the problem of heteroskedasticity, the inference tests were made by estimating White's consistent variance-covariance matrix. The results obtained (regression 5) suggest that the only statistically significant variables at the 5 percent level of error are sales and the rate of profit. Furthermore, it was not possible to reject the hypothesis of the existence of an accelerator mechanism (Wald's F test). The coefficient for lagged saving is significant and assumes a value close to 0.65, which is consistent with a partial adjustment mechanism. This specification also allowed for the removal of autocorrelation (according to the Breusch-Godfrey chi-square test).

Table 3.9 Equations for Corporate Saving
(gross corporate saving as percentage of sales, SCOR)

	1	2	3	4	5	6
C	-0.3153 *	-0.17887 *	-0.17887	-0.03632	-0.03733	-0.0097
REV_t	1.33e-08	2.20e-0.8 *	2.20e-0.8 *	2.89e-08 *		
REV_{t-1}	-9.30e-09	-9.44e-09	-9.44e-09 *	-2.76e-08 *		
DREV					2.93e-08 *	2.74e-08 *
T	-6.5e-10	-7.07e-09 *	-7.07e-09 *	-1.71e-09	-1.31e-09	
T^2		1.42e-17 *	1.42e-17 *	4.01e-18	3.51e-18	
DST	-0.0160	-0.02978	-0.02978	-0.04913	-0.04764	
DLT	0.0099	0.01661	0.01661	0.00761	0.00705	
$SCOR_{t-1}$				0.64304 *	0.64367 *	0.6449 *
P	-0.3119 *	-0.19181 *	-0.19181 *	-0.08586 *	-0.08617 *	-0.0864 *
P^2		-0.00091 *	-0.00091 *	-0.01117 *	-0.00111 *	-0.0011 *
MS	0.0049 *	0.00413 *	0.00413 *	-0.00105	0.00106	
SUB	-0.1130 *	-0.15530 *	-0.15530 *	-0.04299	0.01115	
REL	0.0788	-0.15101 *	-0.15101 *	0.00936	-0.04074	
R^2	0.70	0.78	0.78	0.86	0.86	0.86
Adj-R^2	0.70	0.78	0.78	0.86	0.86	0.86
F	1.73	1.49	1.49	1.23	1.23	1.23
DW	0.96	0.89	0.89	1.68	1.68	1.68
F	373.2 *	452.2 *	452.2 *	645.9 *	705.2 *	1,946.9 *
White	41.10 *					
Wald					0.19	
Breusch-Godfrey				0.03		

* Significant at 5%.

Note: All data used are expressed in constant 1994 pesos. Their exact definitions are as follows:

SCOR	=	Profits plus depreciation minus dividends distributed, as percentage of sales
REV	=	Sales
DREV	=	Yearly change in sale
T	=	Size of firm, measured as total short-term assets to sales
T^2	=	Square of size
DST	=	Short-term indebtedness, measured as total short-term liabilities to sales
DLT	=	Long-term indebtedness, measured as long-term liabilities to sales
P	=	Profit to sales
P^2	=	Square of profit to sales
MS	=	Participation in corporate ownership of 12 majority shareholders
SUB	=	Dummy variable with value 1 for those corporations that have subsidiaries
REL	=	Dummy variable with value 1 for those corporations that have related companies.

Finally, a model restricted to the significant variables (a reduction that could not be rejected) was estimated, which concluded that there exists a strong relationship between corporate saving and the sales accelerator (see regression 6). In light of the theoretical model, this suggests a need to finance investment projects with internally generated resources.

Likewise, the relationship between the rate of profit and the rate of saving is still negative and significant. The low adjustment coefficient suggests that firms face high adjustment costs in reaching their desired rate of saving when sales or profits change: long-term parameters are more than two times greater than their short-term equivalents. The remaining variables were not statistically significant. However, this can also be due to the fact that the short time series available does not allow for the specification of richer short-term dynamics.

Economic Policy Implications

The business sector is likely to face important liquidity constraints. This suggests the need to correct the capital market's failures that prevent many firms from financing privately and socially profitable investment projects. This is an important source of dynamic inefficiency. Although the results were not conclusive (because of the use of a sample that included only publicly listed corporations), liquidity constraints are likely to be more significant for small and medium-sized companies. There is some evidence that this is also so for firms that do not belong to a conglomerate.

Based on empirical analyses, a key factor underlying the increase in saving in Chile since the mid-1980s has been rapid economic growth, which has been the driving force behind business saving and investment decisions. In the face of liquidity constraints on both domestic and foreign capital markets, corporations have resorted to internally generated funds to finance their investment projects. Even though those constraints have been relaxed significantly in the 1990s, business saving has continued to increase, driven by strong increases in private investment and business income.

In the Chilean economy, private saving appears to be an endogenous variable depending on investment and growth. This would suggest that policy makers ought to focus attention on the factors that determine investment and productivity growth. Nonetheless, the reason to be concerned about saving is external vulnerability. Adverse external shocks, including those of a financial nature, may affect the sustainability and the rate of growth. The high degree of substitutability between foreign and corporate saving found in the empirical analysis works only in the long run. In the short run, the degree of substitutability is zero. Therefore, a sudden decline in foreign saving (say, because foreign portfolio investors become pessimistic about the Chilean economy) should lead to a sharp contraction in investment, at least for a fairly long period, considering the long adjustment periods exhibited by Chilean macroeconomic variables. Given the exogeneity and volatility of an important component of foreign capital,[15] the maintenance of high rates of growth, within a context of high rates of investment, involves ensuring that domestic saving rises pari passu with investment.

Another source of instability is the existence of imperfections in capital markets, which make business investments highly dependent on cash flow. Thus, when sales drop, business saving and investment also fall. This makes the economy more unstable than it would otherwise be with a different institutional setup that would allow firms better access to external financial resources. Of course, there are moral hazard problems involved that need to be solved in any new institutional arrangements for financing investment.

The future growth of the Chilean economy is not threatened by a shortage of domestic saving. However, there are two sources of vulnerability with respect to saving. On the one hand, public saving is too dependent on the evolution of copper prices. It should not be forgotten that the profits of CODELCO are the single main source of public revenue. Public saving could easily become dissaving in settings that are less favorable to the price of copper than in the recent past.

In the second place, household dissaving is a matter that deserves greater consideration. If households discount future consumption at a private rate exceeding the social discount rate, interventions to discourage consumption and promote saving are warranted. Though such interventions generate losses in present welfare, they do contribute to prevent strong fluctuations in income and employment and could therefore increase future

---

[15] Foreign saving was found to be an endogenous variable in the VAR. However, it should be remembered that foreign saving is the current account deficit, while capital inflows can be smaller or larger than the current account deficit. Capital inflows (plus available reserves) generally place an upper limit on the current account deficit that can be financed.

welfare. What really matters is that the present value of the net gains be positive. The finding that offset coefficients of household saving with respect to business or government saving are lower (in absolute terms) than one suggests that forced saving through the individual capitalization pension fund system does in fact increase total household saving. Moreover, an increase in the rates of contributions to pension funds, or an improvement in coverage, could contribute to raising the economy's saving rate.

References

Agosin, Manuel R. 1995. "El retorno de los capitales extranjeros a Chile." *El Trimestre Económico.* 62(248): 467–94.

Barro, R.J. 1991. "Economic Growth in a Cross Section of Countries." *Quarterly Journal of Economics.* 106(2): 407–43.

Barro, R.J. and Sala-i-Martin, X. 1995. *Economic Growth.* New York: McGraw-Hill.

Bisang, N., Burachik, G. and Katz J. 1995. "Los grandes grupos corporativos en el escenario manufacturero argentino." In *Hacia un nuevo modelo de organización industrial. El sector manufacturero argentino en los años 90.* Buenos Aires: Alianza Editorial.

Carroll, C.D. and Weil, D.N. 1994. "Saving and Growth: A Reinterpretation." *Carnegie-Rochester Conference Series on Public Policy.* 40: 133–92.

Deaton, A. 1995. "Growth and Saving: What Do We Know, What Do We Need to Know, and What Might We Learn?" Research Program in Development Studies, Princeton University, Princeton, N.J. Mimeograph.

DeLong, J.B. and Summers, L.H. 1991. "Equipment Investment and Economic Growth." *Quarterly Journal of Economics.* 106(2): 445–502.

Domar, E.D. 1947. "Expansion and Employment." *American Economic Review.* 37 (March): 34–55.

ECLAC (Economic Commission for Latin America and the Caribbean). 1995. "La medición de los ingresos en la perspectiva de los estudios de pobreza." Santiago.

Edwards, S. 1995. "Why Are Saving Rates So Different across Countries? An International Comparative Analysis." NBER Working Paper 5097. National Bureau of Economic Research, Cambridge, Mass.

Fazzari, S. M., Hubbard, R.G. and Petersen, B.C. 1988. "Financing Constraints and Corporate Investment." *Brookings Papers on Economic Activity*. 1: 141–95.

Ffrench-Davis, R., Agosin, M.R. and Uthoff, A. 1995. "Movimiento de capitales, estrategia exportadora y estabilidad macroeconómica en Chile." In R. Ffrench-Davis and S. Griffith-Jones, editors. *Las nuevas corrientes financieras hacia la América latina—fuentes, efectos y políticas*, Santiago-México: Fondo de Cultura Económica.

Giner, E. and Salas, V. 1995. "Explicaciones alternativas para la política de dividendos: análisis empírico con datos empresariales españoles." *Investigaciones Económicas*. 19 (September): 339–49.

Greenwald, B., Stiglitz, J.E., and Weiss, A. 1984. "Information Imperfections in the Capital Market and Macroeconomic Fluctuations." *American Economic Review*. 74 (May): 194–99.

Hannan, E.J. and Quinn, B.G. 1979. "The Determination of the Order of an Autoregression." *Journal of the Royal Statistical Society*. B 42: 190–95.

Harris, R. 1995. *Using Cointegration Analysis in Econometric Modeling*. Englewood Cliffs, N.J.: Prentice-Hall

Hendry, D.F. and Doornik, J.A. 1994. "Modelling Linear Econometric Systems." *Scottish Journal of Political Economy*. 41: 1–33.

IDB (Inter-American Development Bank). 1996. "National Saving in Latin America and the Caribbean: Recent Developments and Policy Issues." Office of the Chief Economist, Washington, D.C.

Larrañaga, O. 1990. "El déficit del sector público y la política fiscal en Chile, 1978–87." Serie Política Fiscal 4. ECLAC, Santiago.

Lintner, J. 1956. "Distribution of Income of Corporations among Dividends, Retained Earnings and Taxes." *American Economic Review*. 46: 97–113.

Marfán, M. and Bosworth, B. 1994. "Saving, Investment and Economic Growth." In B.P. Bosworth, R. Dornbusch, and R. Labán, editors. *The Chilean Economy: Policy Lessons and Challenges.* Washington, D.C.: The Brookings Institution.

McKinnon, R.I. 1991. "Macroeconomic Instability and Moral Hazard in Banking." In R.I. McKinnon. *The Order of Economic Liberalization: Financial Control in the Transition to a Market Economy.* Baltimore and London: Johns Hopkins University Press.

Modigliani, F. and Miller, M.H. 1958. "The Cost of Capital, Corporation Finance, and the Theory of Investment." *American Economic Review.* 48 (June): 261–97.

Morandé, F. 1996. "Savings in Chile. What Went Right?" Office of the Chief Economist, Inter-American Development Bank, Washington, D.C. Unpublished.

Myers, S.C. and Majluf, N.S. 1984. "Corporate Financing and Investment Decisions When Firms Have Informations That Investors Do Not Have." *Journal of Financial Economics.* 13 (June): 187–221.

Paredes, R. 1995. "Privatization and Regulation in a Less Developed Economy. The Chilean Case." Unpublished doctoral thesis. University of California at Los Angeles.

Pasinetti, L.I. 1974. *Growth and Income Distribution: Essays in Economic Theory.* London: Cambridge University Press.

Rama, M. 1993. "Empirical Investment Equations for Developing Countries." In L. Servén and A. Solimano, editors, *Striving for Growth after Adjustment: The Role of Capital Formation.* Washington, D.C.: World Bank.

Smith, C. and Warner, J. 1979. "On Financial Contracting: An Analysis of Bond Covenants." *Journal of Financial Economics.* 7 (June): 117–61.

Stiglitz, J. and Weiss, A. 1981. "Credit Rationing in Markets with Imperfect Information." *American Economic Review.* 71 (June): 394–410.

CHAPTER 4

Saving Determinants in Colombia: 1925–94

Mauricio Cárdenas and Andrés Escobar[1]

Colombia is a good case study of the determinants of national saving, for several reasons. First, the interaction between private and public saving has played a key role in the determination of national saving.[2] Second, foreign saving has been a key force behind the investment process. Third, household saving rates have experienced a secular decline since the early 1970s while firms' saving (as a share of GNP) has fallen by as much as 5 percentage points after a structural reform package was introduced in 1990. Overall, the private saving rate is 6 percentage points below its prereform level. Public saving has increased by 3 percentage points as a result of a series of tax reforms. Consequently, national saving has fallen by 3 percentage points since 1990.

In this sense, the rich experience of Colombia is useful in order to understand long-run trends in the level and composition of savings, as well as the initial effects of trade, pension, and financial reforms. Moreover, the recent fall in national (especially private) saving has coincided with a period of high investment growth.[3] As a consequence, the growing gap between national saving and investment has been matched by increasing foreign saving, which was in 1994 at a record high. Concerns over the sustainability

---

[1] The authors are economists at Fedesarrollo in Bogotá, Colombia.
[2] At present, national saving rates in Colombia are similar to their postwar average (18.3 percent of GNP) as well as the developing countries' average. They are, however, below the world average. See Schmidt-Hebbel and Servén (1996).
[3] According to Cárdenas and Olivera (1995) the increase in investment rates is the result of a reduction in the user cost of capital due to the real appreciation of the peso, as well as the reduction in real interest rates and tariffs on capital goods.

of the current account deficits have been at the center stage of the policy debate in Colombia. Many argue in favor of increasing saving rates to raise investment and speed up economic growth. However, little consensus exists on how to achieve that goal.

Several factors have been mentioned as possible explanations for the collapse in private saving rates. Many have argued that trade liberalization, combined with the recent real appreciation of the peso, reduced the relative prices of durable goods. In addition, capital inflows as well as financial reform relaxed the liquidity constraints and provided the necessary resources for an increase in consumption. Others place the emphasis on the growing levels of taxation, which may have reduced private saving. From a different angle, labor reform increased disposable income by introducing a new type of labor contract ("integral salaries") that includes all fringe benefits as salaries. This change in the wage regime may have increased consumption in credit-constrained households. Also, funds for severance payments are now held in the workers' own accounts at private institutions. This, of course, represents a shift of saving from firms to households. Finally, Colombia is at the onset of a significant oil boom that has affected the perception of permanent income.

The recent decline in private saving is strongly related to the increase in taxation. Other factors, such as reduced protection and liquidity constraints, are also significant. However, in this case the effects are temporary, so no major offsetting policy interventions are required. In order to increase national saving, the recommendation is for an increase in public saving, especially through a reduction in the current levels of government expenditures. In fact, a 3 percentage point reduction in total government outlays would increase the national saving rate by 1.5 percentage points. The key aspect to emphasize is that counterreforms reintroducing protection and financial repression would be unwise. Private saving will increase as pension reform matures and firms' margins recover based on productivity gains. Moreover, there is a close inverse relationship between private and foreign saving, so the lower current account deficit that is expected in future years would probably be matched by an increase in private saving.

National saving, investment, and growth are correlated in several ways. The tests indicate that foreign saving and investment are positively correlated, while the correlation between national saving and investment has been much weaker in the last 25 years. In spite of that, the hypothesis that national saving causes growth in the Granger sense cannot be rejected. The main conclusion is that national saving depends negatively on foreign saving and positively on public saving, thus rejecting the Ricardian equivalence hypothesis. Also, tariffs seem to have a positive effect on saving, meaning that trade liberalization may result in a reduction in saving rates. However, the results of a vector autoregressive (VAR) model indicate that this effect tends to vanish relatively fast. Other variables, such as the interest rate, are not significant in the regressions. Finally, much of the recent reduction in saving in Colombia is explained by the collapse in firms' saving rates. Results from a panel of 397 firms for the 1985–93 period indicate that the relaxation of liquidity constraints was associated with an increase in indebtedness and a reduction in the retention of profits.

Conceptual Framework

The starting point for savings accounting is the national income identity (in current prices):

$$I_t^p + I_t^g = \left(Y_t - T_t - C_t\right) + \left(T_t - G_t\right) - \left(X_t - M_t\right) = S_t^p + S_t^g + S_t^x \quad [1]$$

where I_t^p and I_t^g denote gross private and public investment, respectively. Private saving (S_t^p) is defined as GDP (Y_t) minus taxes net of transfers and subsidies from the public to the private sector (T_t) minus private consumption (C_t). Public saving (S_t^g) is equal to net taxes minus current government expenditures (G_t). Foreign saving (S_t^x) is defined as the negative of net exports of goods and nonfactor services ($X_t - M_t$). In this case, the sum of S_t^p and S_t^g is called internal or domestic saving.

Often, it is useful to write eq. [1] in terms of GNP, which is the sum of GDP and net international factor payments and unrequited transfers, which we call FB_t. In this case the proper expression becomes:

$$\left(Y_t + FB_t - T_t - C_t\right) + \left(T_t - G_t\right) - \left(X_t + FB_t - M_t\right) = S_t^p + S_t^g + S_t^x \quad [2]$$

where we have assumed that net factor payments accrue to the private sector. Under this definition the sum of S_t^p and S_t^g corresponds to national saving, which we denote as S_t, and S_t^x (foreign savings) is the negative of the current account balance.

However, measurements of saving based on the national accounts can be imprecise for several reasons. First, only the flow of services from the stock of consumer durables should be considered as consumption.[4] Second, inflationary taxation is a form of forced saving by the private sector, which is transferred to the public sector and should be considered accordingly.[5] To correct this problem we follow Schmidt-Hebbel and Servén (1996) and define the inflation tax (*IT*) as:

$$IT_t = \frac{\pi}{1+\pi} B_{t-1}$$

where π is the inflation rate and B is the monetary base. Correcting for the inflation tax, the private saving rate is defined as:

$$\frac{S^p - IT_t}{GNP_t - T_t} \qquad [3]$$

and the public saving rate,

$$\frac{S^g - IT_t}{GNP_t - T_t}. \qquad [4]$$

The Model

The determinants of national saving can be captured with a model borrowed from the intertemporal approach to the current account literature. In particular, the model comes from Obstfeld and Rogoff (1995 and 1996) and considers a one-good, small, open economy. Hence, the emphasis is placed on intertemporal rather than intratemporal substitutability.[6] Consider a representative individual who maximizes the following time-separable utility function:

$$U_t = \sum_{s=t}^{\infty} \beta^{s-t} u(C_s) \qquad [5]$$

---

[4] This source of possible mismeasurement will be dealt with in a later section.
[5] There are other problems with Colombian data. See López (1996).
[6] Echeverry (1996) applies to the Colombian data a model that captures the intratemporal substitution between importable and nontraded goods.

where $\beta \in (0, 1)$, $u'(C) > 0$, $u''(C) < 0$, subject to the following dynamic budget constraint:[7]

$$\sum_{s=t}^{\infty} \left(\frac{1}{1+r}\right)^{s-t} \left(C_s + I_s\right) = \left(1+r_t\right)B_t + \sum_{s=t}^{\infty} \left(\frac{1}{1+r}\right)^{s-t} \left(Y_s - G_s\right) \qquad [6]$$

where B_t is the value of the economy's net foreign assets at the end of period $t-1$. A constant interest rate is assumed to keep the analysis as simple as possible and is justified on the grounds that no significant empirical relation is evident between saving and the interest rate. As usual, maximization of eq. [5] gives the consumption Euler equation,

$$u'\left(C_s\right) = \beta\left(1+r\right)u'\left(C_{s+1}\right) \qquad [7]$$

which, under an isoelastic utility function (σ is the elasticity of intertemporal substitution),

$$u(C) = \frac{C^{1-1/\sigma} - 1}{1 - 1/\sigma} \qquad [8]$$

takes the form:

$$C_{s+1} = \beta^\sigma \left(1+r\right)^\sigma C_s. \qquad [9]$$

Using [9] to eliminate C_{t+1}, C_{t+2}, ... from eq. [6] results in the consumption function:

$$C_t = \frac{r + \vartheta}{1+r}\left[\left(1+r_t\right)B_t + \sum_{s=t}^{\infty} \left(\frac{1}{1+r}\right)^{s-t} \left(Y_s - G_s - I_s\right)\right] \qquad [10]$$

where $\vartheta \equiv 1 - \beta^\sigma\left(1+r\right)^\sigma$. Before deriving an expression for saving, it is helpful to define the permanent level of a variable X as the hypothetical annuity

---

[7] This constraint embodies the transversality condition, which does not allow the domestic economy to borrow abroad indefinitely. The present value of net external assets has to be equal to zero as $T \to \infty$. That is,

$$\lim_{T \to \infty} \left(\frac{1}{1+r}\right)^T B_T = 0.$$

with the same present value as the variable itself. Denoting the permanent level as $\tilde{X}_t$, the definition implies that:

$$\sum_{s=t}^{\infty}\left(\frac{1}{1+r}\right)^{s-t}\tilde{X}_t = \sum_{s=t}^{\infty}\left(\frac{1}{1+r}\right)^{s-t}X_s \qquad [11]$$

so that,

$$\tilde{X}_t \equiv \frac{r}{1+r}\sum_{s=t}^{\infty}\left(\frac{1}{1+r}\right)^{s-t}X_s. \qquad [12]$$

At this point it is convenient to rewrite national saving as (recalling the national income identity):

$$S_t = I_t - S_t^x = Y_t + rB_t - C_t - G_t. \qquad [13]$$

Substituting the consumption function [10] into [13] and making use of [12], we get a fundamental equation for national saving:

$$S_t = \left(Y_t - \tilde{Y}_t\right) - \left(G_t - \tilde{G}_t\right) + \tilde{I}_t - \frac{\vartheta}{1+r}W_t \qquad [14]$$

and a corresponding expression for foreign saving,

$$S_t^x = \left(G_t - \tilde{G}_t\right) + \left(I_t - \tilde{I}_t\right) - \left(Y_t - \tilde{Y}_t\right) + \frac{\vartheta}{1+r}W_t \qquad [15]$$

where W_t is a measure of wealth at beginning of period t:

$$W_t \equiv \left[\left(1+r_t\right)B_t + \sum_{s=t}^{\infty}\left(\frac{1}{1+r}\right)^{s-t}\left(Y_s - G_s - I_s\right)\right]. \qquad [16]$$

Equations [14] and [15] provide some interesting insights on the dynamics of saving:

- When output is above its permanent level, agents save more to smooth consumption. Agents save by accumulating interest-yielding foreign assets, so that foreign savings fall. This prediction is in line with the permanent income hypothesis.

- If public expenditures are higher than the long-term sustainable level, the effects are the same as in the case of abnormally low output. High government expenditures reduce national saving and increase foreign saving. Agents adjust by running a larger current account deficit, which in turn allows agents to spread the negative impact on their disposable income over the entire future.
- Increases in the "permanent" (or long-term) level of investment require higher domestic saving, just as in the Feldstein-Horioka (1980) results.
- Unusually high levels of investment are financed with foreign saving. Rather than adjusting consumption in the face of extraordinarily profitable opportunities, countries prefer to borrow abroad.
- When $\vartheta > 0$, the subjective discount factor β is smaller than the market discount factor $1/(1+r)$, so the country is relatively impatient. In this case, consumption is tilted towards the present and national saving is lower. Correspondingly, the current account balance is reduced (foreign saving increases).

A simple transformation of eq. [14] yields some additional insights. Subtracting public saving $(T_t - G_t)$ from both sides yields an expression for private saving:

$$S_t^p = (Y_t - \tilde{Y}_t) - (T_t - \tilde{G}_t) + \tilde{I}_t - \frac{\vartheta}{1+r} W_t.$$ [17]

In this model, when taxes are above their permanent level, private agents adjust by lowering their saving.[8] Unusually high public saving is matched with lower private saving, so that Ricardian equivalence holds. In other words, government budget imbalances are irrelevant for resource allocation (they do not affect national saving). This, of course, does not necessarily hold when world capital markets are imperfect, agents do not live infinitely, and taxes generate distortions.[9]

---

[8] In this model the present value of government expenditures is equal to the present value of taxes (i.e., the government pays back its debt) so that the permanent level of expenditures is equal to the permanent level of taxes.

[9] The empirical evidence often refutes Ricardian equivalence in the context of developing countries. The most frequent result is that an increase in public saving reduces private saving but less than proportionally. Edwards (1995) estimates a –0.55 coefficient. Corbo and Schmidt-Hebbel (1991) distinguish between an increase in taxes (with coefficients between –0.48 and

The model presented in this section leaves out some other aspects of potential relevance in explaining saving in Colombia. Some of these factors are:[10]

- *Life cycle*: The model does not capture heterogeneous agents whose saving depends on their age, according to the life-cycle hypothesis. Typically, the young and the retired dissave, so that the higher the dependency ratio, the lower the saving rate.

- *Precautionary motive:* The model assumes perfect foresight. When uncertainty is introduced and $u'''(C) > 0$, it is possible that individuals engage in precautionary saving.[11] Agents save more when output is more variable. For example, if the variability in rural production is higher than in urban output, it is possible that saving falls as the urbanization rate increases. It is also possible that greater macroeconomic instability, as captured by the variability of inflation, results in higher precautionary saving.

- *Openness:* The model assumes free trade and perfect capital mobility. When restrictions apply, distortions alter the allocation of resources. For instance, when durable goods are imported, tariff and nontariff protection increases their relative price and reduces overall consumption. It is also possible that firms' margins (as well as their saving) are higher under protection.

- *Liquidity constraints*: Capital market imperfections, such as borrowing constraints, have played a major role in the saving literature. In this case, the consumption Euler equation fails to hold, as agents cannot borrow against future income if some form of collateral is not available.[12]

-0.65) and reductions in government expenditures that lower private saving by less (between -0.16 and -0.50). The implication is that larger public saving is effective in generating increases in national saving. However, in the Colombian case, Carrasquilla and Rincón (1990) have failed to reject Ricardian equivalence.

[10] Schmidt-Hebbel and Servén (1996) and Deaton (1995) provide excellent surveys of this literature.

[11] See Deaton (1995).

[12] Income distribution has also been mentioned as a possible determinant of saving. However, in this case the results are not conclusive. Menchnik and David (1983), Bunting (1991), Sahota (1993), Cook (1995), and Hong (1995), among others, find that saving depends positively on inequality. But Della Valle and Oguchi (1976), Musgrove (1980), Edwards (1995), and Schmidt-Hebbel and Servén (1996) do not find a significant relation. In the Colombian case, Steiner

These four factors have some empirical support. In the case of the dependency ratio, Edwards (1995) and Jappelli and Pagano (1994) have found a negative relationship with saving, but the evidence is not conclusive yet (see Gersovitz, 1988). Based on the Colombian income and expenditure survey (1984–85), Ramírez (1992) found that the young and the retired save little. Indirect measures of the precautionary motive (such as the degree of urbanization) have shown a negative relationship with saving (Edwards, 1995).

The evidence is more conclusive regarding liquidity constraints. For example, Jappelli and Pagano (1994) use the loan-to-value ratio and consumption credit as proxies of borrowing constraints and find that these variables affect saving negatively (in a panel of 19 countries). These results are consistent with those found by Hayashi, Ito, and Slemrod (1988), Muellbauer and Murphy (1990), Bayoumi (1991), Miles (1992), and Guiso, Jappelli, and Terlizzese (1994). In the Colombian context, López (1994) presents evidence in the same direction.

Saving in Colombia: Stylized Facts

Figure 4.1 shows national saving, foreign saving, and investment in Colombia during the 1925–94 period.[13] Although there are problems with the quality of data before 1950, on average, it can be said that investment and national saving rates have been lower in the postwar period. In this sense, these rates seem to have shifted from a higher plateau (pre-1950) to a lower one in the past 45 years. Figure 4.1 also suggests that national saving and investment rates move in opposite directions (especially since the 1950s). Consequently, periods of high investment correspond to periods of high foreign saving.

Figure 4.2A breaks down national saving into private and public saving,[14] while Figure 4.2B plots the permanent or trend components of the

---

and Escobar (1994) found a negative relation between the labor/nonlabor income ratio and saving in the national accounts.

[13] Expressed as percentages of GDP for the 1925–49 period and as percentages of GNP for the 1950–94 period. These unadjusted series come from ECLAC for the period 1925–49, Banco de la República's national accounts (1950–69), and DANE's national accounts (1970 onwards). Due to quality problems, data prior to 1950 should be used with caution.

[14] Adjusted for inflation tax since 1950.

Figure 4.1
Saving and Investment Rates: 1925–94

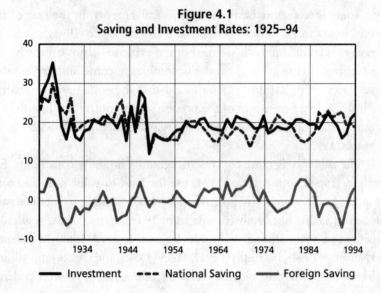

same variables.[15] Clearly, there is a negative long-run trend in private saving rates, which fell from over 20 percent in the pre-1950 period to less than
10 percent in recent years. However, this trend may be a consequence of
poor data quality before 1950. More reliable information (1950 onward)
suggests greater stability in private saving, especially since 1970. In fact, between 1972 and 1990 private saving rates fluctuated between 13 percent
and 15 percent, a narrow margin given the variability of other macro variables in Colombia.[16]

Nonetheless, private saving rates have abruptly fallen since 1991, reaching a record low of 8.5 percent in 1994, due to both households' and private
firms' saving decisions. Figure 4.3 shows that household saving rates have

---

[15] In order to define the "permanent" level of the variables, the filter suggested by Hodrick-
Prescott is used. Besides the low application cost, this filter allows for better adjustment of the
cyclical component to high and low frequencies of the series. This is done by minimizing the
sum of squared transitory fluctuations, subject to a Lagrange multiplier (λ) that penalizes the
variability of the trend component. In order to apply this filter, it is necessary to establish a
priori a value of λ. Although Hodrick and Prescott have recommended a value between 100
and 400 for U.S. data, in a recent paper Suescún (1996) finds that 500 is the level that better
reproduces Colombian business cycles. This result is used to generate the permanent levels of
GDP, government consumption, and investment.
[16] Such stable performance could explain the lack of studies on private saving in Colombia.

Figure 4.2. Components of Saving: 1925–94
(percent)

A. Public, Private, National, and Foreign Saving

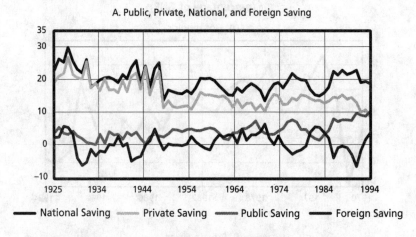

── National Saving ━━━ Private Saving ━━━ Public Saving ━━━ Foreign Saving

B. Permanent Components

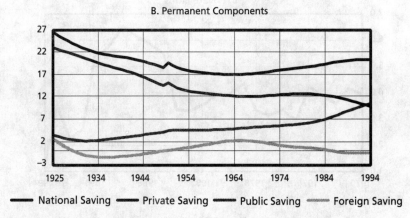

── National Saving ━━━ Private Saving ━━━ Public Saving ━━━ Foreign Saving

had a negative trend since the early 1970s. On the other hand, private firms' saving (see Figure 4.3 also) was relatively stable between 1970 and 1984 and then, after a rapid increase during the late 1980s, collapsed in 1992.

Finally, public saving rates have steadily increased from 2.5 percent before 1950, to 5 percent in the 1950s, to 10 percent in the 1990s (see Figures 4.2A and 4.2B).[17] In 1994, public saving surpassed private saving.

---

[17] Cárdenas and Olivera (1995) show that public investment rates also have an upward long-run trend in the case of Colombia.

Figure 4.3
Components of Private Saving: 1970–94
(percentage of GNP)

A. Households

B. Private Firms

C. Financial Institutions

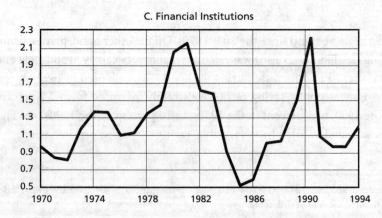

The Interaction between Public and Foreign Saving

A cursory look at Figure 4.2A suggests the existence of a negative correlation between public and foreign saving, except for the 1991–94 period. Figure 4.4 decomposes foreign savings into public sector foreign borrowing, private sector foreign borrowing, foreign direct investment, and change in foreign reserves (all the items below the current account in the balance of payments). Interestingly enough, external savings took mainly the form of public sector foreign borrowing, at least until the 1990s. It is worth mentioning that during the present decade the nature of external saving has been related to foreign direct investment.

Much of the correlation between foreign and public saving is explained by the existence of the National Coffee Fund, a public account created in 1940 that operates as a producers' price stabilization device. When world coffee prices are above trend, an increase in the current account surplus is generated and, thus, Colombia experiences a reduction in its foreign saving.

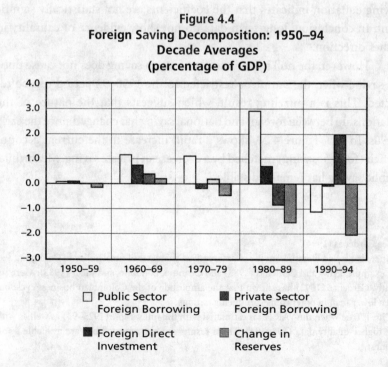

Figure 4.4
Foreign Saving Decomposition: 1950–94
Decade Averages
(percentage of GDP)

On the other hand, due to its specific institutional design, the fund saves more, generating an increase in public saving. In other countries where stabilization funds exist, such as Côte d'Ivoire, surpluses are generally redistributed to other sectors with low saving propensities, undermining their macroeconomic effectiveness.[18]

In addition, Colombia's central government has traditionally run a countercyclical fiscal policy: high world coffee prices are matched by lower government expenditures and, consequently, by a reduction in foreign borrowing. In sum, the effects of exogenous shocks to the current account (e.g., coffee booms) have been partially offset by increases in public saving.[19] However, Gómez and Thoumi (1986) argue in favor of the opposite causality: higher public saving substitutes for external saving.

The nature of the negative correlation between public and foreign saving is explored by implementing some Granger-causality tests on the data of Figure 4.2A. More specifically, a second-order VAR is estimated for foreign and public saving. The coefficients on the two lags of public saving (in the foreign saving equation) are not significantly different from zero. Similarly, the joint F test on the two lags of foreign saving in the public saving equation indicates that the coefficients are not statistically significant. In conclusion, long-term data do not show evidence of causality in either direction.[20]

However, the null hypothesis that foreign saving does not cause public saving when the sample is restricted to the 1950–92 period can be rejected. This is a puzzling result, which suggests that the nature of the relationship between foreign and national saving has changed since the early 1990s. In fact, Figure 4.2A shows a rapid increase in the current account deficit (foreign saving) matched by a decrease in private saving. Meanwhile, public saving has remained stable.

---

[18] See Cárdenas (1994).

[19] There is a broad literature on the countercyclical character of fiscal policy in Colombia. See, for example, Perry and Cárdenas (1986) and Ocampo, Londoño, and Villar (1985). More recently, Cárdenas (1992) has shown that the amplitude of the Colombian business cycle has been lower than in other coffee-producing nations.

[20] This is true when the VAR (2) is estimated with the full sample (1925–94) as well as with the higher-quality data (1950–94). These results are not reported but are available upon request.

Saving, Investment, and Growth: Correlations and Causality Tests

The starting point of the literature on savings-investment correlations in Colombia is Feldstein and Horioka (1980), who used cross-section data to estimate:

$$(I/Y)_t = \alpha + \beta(S/Y)_t + u_t. \tag{18}$$

Under full capital mobility, the slope coefficient (β) should be less than one: national saving looks for the best investment opportunity available in the international economy. However, Feldstein and Horioka found that the coefficient is not significantly different from one.[21] There are many possible explanations for this result, so the existence of a high correlation between national saving and investment is by no means sufficient proof of capital immobility.[22]

Nonetheless, the framework of eq. [18] is of limited use for time-series analysis. Jensen and Schulze (1996) provide a more adequate test of the saving-investment correlation in the context of a single country over a time period. They use an error-correction model (ECM) that captures the long-run theoretical relationship between the two variables (the current account should revert to some equilibrium value in the long run) and allows for a short-run dynamic adjustment between them. In particular, the following ECM specification is used:

$$\Delta(I/Y)_t = \alpha + \beta\Delta(S/Y)_t + \gamma(I/Y - S/Y)_{t-1} + u_t \tag{19}$$

where β corresponds to the first-differences version of the Feldstein-Horioka coefficient and measures the impact of changes in national saving on contemporaneous investment (short-run relationship). The error-correction

---

[21] Feldstein and Bachetta (1991) reinforce the early findings with more recent data.

[22] The literature offers a wide array of models able to produce comovements in saving and investment in response to exogenous shocks. Market imperfections, in the context of labor mobility and international trade, are one possibility. But even under almost perfect markets it is possible to reach similar results when technological shocks occur simultaneously in different countries. See Tesar (1991), Frankel (1993), and Obstfeld (1988 and 1995).

term, $\gamma(I/Y - S/Y)_{t-1}$, captures the long-run identity or cointegrating relationship between both aggregates. Specifically, γ indicates the speed of adjustment to short-run discrepancies between saving and investment (until the identity is reestablished). Low values of γ imply that short-run gaps take a long time to be corrected.

Table 4.1 shows the results of the estimation. The first column displays a regression estimated for the entire 1925–94 period that shows a value of 0.87 for the one-period pass-through coefficient (β). This coefficient, not statistically different from one, indicates that it is not possible to reject the hypothesis that changes in national saving and changes in investment

Table 4.1 Saving-Investment Correlations (dependent variable: ΔI_t)

	1925–94 (1)	1925–69 (2)	1970–94 (3)
Constant	0.1248	0.1283	0.1283
	(0.45)	(0.51)	(0.09)
ΔS_t	0.8713		
	(9.18)***		
Dummy 1925–69 * ΔS_t		1.0138	
		(10.88)***	
Dummy 1970–94 * ΔS_t			0.0860
			(0.24)
$(I-S)_{t-1}$	−0.3404	−0.2887	−0.2381
	(−3.60)***	(−3.41)***	(−1.66)
R^2	0.5779	0.6559	0.0402
DW	1.7566	1.9283	2.4087
No. of Observations	69	69	69
Estimation Method	OLS	OLS	OLS

*Significant at 10%.
**Significant at 5%.
***Significant at 1%.
Note: I, investment; S, national saving; Sx, foreign saving. All variables are in terms of GDP for the 1925–49 period and of GNP after 1950. Numbers in parentheses are t-statistics.

are perfectly correlated. In relation to the error-correction term, the estimated value of γ indicates that 34 percent of the discrepancy between saving and investment is corrected in the course of one year. Thus, when the two aggregates are different, the identity is reestablished in a relatively short period of time. In other words, historical data do not support the view that current account imbalances are sustainable in the long run for a country like Colombia.

The regression in column 2 focuses on the existence of a short-term relationship between investment and national saving only for the 1925–69 period, while the third column repeats the same exercise, but for the 1970–94 period.[23] Interestingly enough, while the estimated β is 1.01 in the former sample, it falls to 0.09 and becomes insignificant in the latter. This suggests that foreign saving has played an increasingly important role in the short-run financing of investment since 1970, probably due to the diversification of foreign credit sources for the country.[24]

The high value of the pass-through coefficient for national saving can be indicative of a strong relationship between growth and saving. This issue can be analyzed by estimating a first-order vector autorregression of the growth rate and the saving rate for the 1925–94 period.[25] Two different procedures are applied to concentrate on the low-frequency relationships. First, a VAR with 10-year moving averages is estimated. Second, the growth rate is defined as the percentage change in the permanent component of GDP, and the ratio between permanent national saving and permanent income is used as a measure of the saving rate.[26] The results, reported in Table 4.2, show no evidence of causality in either direction when the 10-year moving averages are used. However, the opposite is true when the VAR (1) is estimated with the permanent components. In fact, as indicated by the F-statistic, the coefficient on the lagged saving rate (in the growth equation) is significantly different from zero, suggesting that past saving performance is helpful in predicting growth. Similarly, the coefficient on the lagged growth (in the saving equation) is statistically significant. Thus, the evidence can-

---

[23] The change in saving is interacted with the corresponding dummy variable in both cases.
[24] See Ocampo and Lora (1988).
[25] The results do not change when the sample is restricted to 1950–94.
[26] As before, the permanent components are obtained using the Hodrick-Prescott filter.

Table 4.2 Granger Causality between Saving and Growth

Causality	Sample	Number of Lags	F-Statistic	P-Value
A. 10-year Moving Averages				
From Growth to National Saving	1925–94	1	0.1795	0.6739
From National Saving to Growth	1925–94	1	0.7440	0.3933
From Growth to National Saving	1950–94	1	0.7440	0.3933
From National Saving to Growth	1950–94	1	0.1795	0.6739
B. Permanent Components				
From Growth to Private Saving	1925–94	1	6.2087	0.0034**
From Private Saving to Growth	1925–94	1	2.5398	0.0870*
From Growth to Private Saving	1950–94	1	4.7396	0.0142*
From Private Saving to Growth	1950–94	1	6.6022	0.0033**

*Significant at 10%.
**Significant at 5%.
Note: Growth is the percentage rate of change in permanent income.

not reject a strong relation between growth and saving, with causality running in both directions.

Empirical Results: The Intertemporal Model

An analysis of the determinants of national, foreign, and private saving is based on equations [14], [15], and [17], respectively.[27] Variables with a tilde ($\sim$) denote permanent components. Figure 4.5 presents $Y_t - \tilde{Y}_t$, $G_t - \tilde{G}_t$, and $I_t - \tilde{I}$ (all as percentages of $\tilde{Y}_t$). The graphs replicate the conventional wisdom about business cycles in Colombia and confirm the perception that the 1990s are characterized by increases in government expenditures and investment over their permanent levels. Figure 4.6 shows two additional variables of interest: $T_t - \tilde{T}_t$ and $T_t - \tilde{G}_t$. They clearly indicate that taxes are not only over their permanent level, but also well above the permanent level of government expenditures.

---

[27] Unfortunately, it was not possible to construct a series for wealth (W).

Figure 4.5
Deviations from Permanent Levels: 1950–94

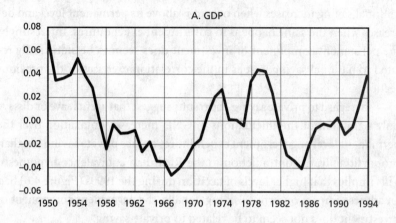

A. GDP

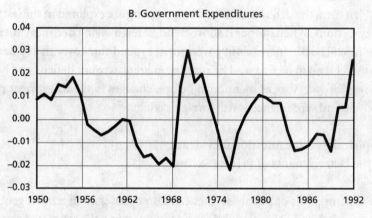

B. Government Expenditures

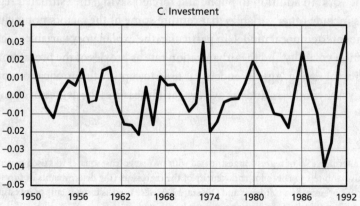

C. Investment

Table 4.3 presents the results of the estimation. All the equations were estimated with ordinary least squares.[28] The results are in line with the theory: national saving increases when output is above its permanent level and decreases when the same happens to government expenditures. Interestingly, the permanent component of investment does seem to be statistically related to national saving, just as in the correlation exercises of the previous section.

In regard to private saving, the results suggest that agents save or dissave only a fraction of the fluctuations in GNP. Increases in taxation over the permanent level of government expenditures reduce private saving less than proportionally, in contradiction to the Ricardian equivalence hypothesis. This implies that higher levels of taxation during the 1990s (Figure 4.6) had an adverse impact on private saving. Finally, the permanent component of investment does not seem to be related to private saving.

In turn, the determinants of foreign saving are explored in the last set of regressions. When output is above trend, foreign saving declines (foreign debt is paid back). Increases in government expenditures over their permanent level tend to be financed by running current account deficits and borrowing abroad. Also, as mentioned before, changes in the investment rate (above trend) are financed with foreign saving.

Empirical Results: Additional Evidence on the Determinants of Private Saving

The determinants of private savings can also be assessed in a more general framework. In addition to public and foreign saving, the estimated regressions include other variables that capture some of the factors not included in the intertemporal model. In particular, the explanatory variables include inflation volatility and the urbanization rate as proxies of the precautionary motive for saving. Age dependency is used to capture the implications of the life-cycle hypothesis, and the average tariff measures the degree of openness

---

[28] An alternative set of regressions estimated with two-stage least squares was used to perform a Hausmann test to check for endogeneity of the regressors (the determinants of private investment presented in Cárdenas and Olivera, 1995, were used as instruments of investment). The null hypothesis of exogeneity could not be rejected.

Table 4.3 Saving Determinants: 1952–94

Dependent Variable	National Saving	Private Saving[a]	Foreign Saving
Constant	−5.2992	1.2918	0.8494
	(−0.42)	(0.12)	(1.43)
$Y - \bar{Y}$	0.5474	0.3602	−0.5331
	(4.71)***	(2.99)***	(−4.38)***
$G - \bar{G}$	−1.2175		1.2189
	(−5.46)***		(5.45)***
I	1.2319	0.7716	
	(1.87)*	(1.29)	
$I - \bar{I}$			0.9850
			(7.29)***
$T - \bar{G}$		−0.6507	
		(−4.21)***	
R^2	0.6096	0.4426	0.6886
DW	2.0236	1.9245	2.0288
No. of Observations	43	43	43
Estimation Method	AR1	AR1	AR1
Exogeneity Test			
Hausmann Test	0.4122	2.1505	0.4167
P-Value	0.9815	0.7081	0.9811
Accept Ho (Exogeneity)?	Yes	Yes	Yes

*Significant at 10%.

***Significant at 1%.

Note: All variables as percentages of potential GNP. Numbers in parentheses are *t*-statistics.

a. Adjusted for inflation tax.

Figure 4.6
Taxes: 1950–94
(percentage of GDP permanent level)

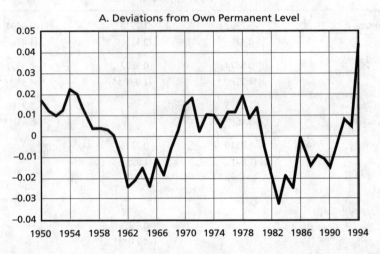

A. Deviations from Own Permanent Level

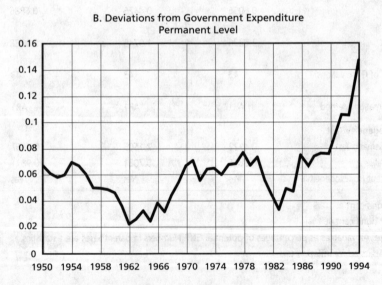

B. Deviations from Government Expenditure
Permanent Level

of the economy. The real interest rate, as well as those variables that measure liquidity constraints, were included but were not significant.

Table 4.4 reports the results of the estimation. The regression reported in column 1 uses the entire 1925–94 sample and indicates that foreign saving and public saving have a negative impact on private saving. In addition, both the degree of urbanization and the age dependency of the population have a negative impact on private saving. The volatility of inflation does not seem to affect private saving in the long run (although the regressions with post-1970 data report the expected positive sign).

The remaining regressions in Table 4.4 use data for the last 25 years, which are more reliable and can be further disaggregated. The negative effect of foreign saving on private saving is quite stable, always between –0.3 and -0.4. Interestingly, this effect operates through household saving (column 7). Private firms' saving, on the other hand, does not seem to depend on foreign saving. The negative impact of public saving on private saving confirms the results of the previous section. On average, one extra peso of public saving reduces private saving by 50 cents. However, as column 5 shows, the negative effect on private saving is larger when the increase in public saving comes from an increase in taxes rather than a decrease in government expenditures. In fact, the estimated coefficients indicate that the recent increase in taxation explains much of the decline in private saving. Concretely, taxation/GDP increased by nearly 7 percentage points between 1990 and 1994. This alone is associated with a 4 percentage point reduction in the private saving rate, equivalent to two thirds of the total reduction in private saving.

Average tariffs, a measure of protection, were also included in the regressions. Although the expected sign is theoretically uncertain, they seem to have a positive effect on saving, entirely due to the behavior of firms (column 8). Therefore, it is possible that protection increases firms' margins and undistributed profits. However, caution should be exercised in the interpretation of this result, as tariffs could be proxies for other variables, such as liquidity constraints. Finally, real interest rates were not significant (columns 4 and 6), an important though common result found in both theoretical and empirical literature on saving.

To capture the dynamics of these relationships, a VAR (1) model was estimated on private, public, and foreign saving, as well as average tariffs and inflation volatility. Urbanization and dependency rates were excluded

Table 4.4 Private Saving Determinants

Dependent Variable	Private Saving Rate						Household Saving Rate	Firms' Saving Rate
	1929–94 (1)	1970–94 (2)	1970–94 (3)	1970–94 (4)	1970–94 (5)	1970–94 (6)	1970–94 (7)	1970–94 (8)
Constant	35.5182 (5.26)***	10.9364 (6.26)***	187.3710 (2.04)**	236.4620 (2.42)**	11.6754 (4.25)***	11.6645 (4.12)***	8.5906 (10.12)***	-0.0773 (-0.14)
Foreign Saving Rate	-0.3599 (-2.83)***	-0.3949 (-4.72)***	-0.4248 (-5.54)***	-0.4171 (-5.53)***	-0.3916 (-4.25)***	-0.3927 (-4.14)***	-0.3159 (-5.55)***	
Public Saving Rate	-0.7158 (-3.69)***	-0.5066 (-4.27)***	-0.5387 (-4.03)***	-0.5748 (-4.28)***			-0.3906 (-5.18)***	
Taxes / GNP					-0.5840 (-4.48)***	-0.5852 (-4.33)***		
Government Expenditures / GNP					0.4993 (2.22)**	0.4997 (2.03)**		
Public Firms' Saving Rate					-0.2052 (-0.46)	-0.2036 (-0.44)		
Urbanization Rate	-0.1092 (-2.72)***		-1.4968 (-1.87)*	-1.8965 (-2.25)**				

(continued)

Table 4.4 (continued)

Dependent Variable	Private Saving Rate						Household Saving Rate,	Firms' Saving Rate,
	1929–94 (1)	1970–94 (2)	1970–94 (3)	1970–94 (4)	1970–94 (5)	1970–94 (6)	1970–94 (7)	1970–94 (8)
Age Dependency	−0.2699 (−2.13)**		−1.9055 (−1.96)**	−2.4395 (−2.35)**				
Inflation Volatility	−0.0320 (−0.49)	0.4237 (2.40)**	0.7307 (3.22)***	0.7627 (3.40)***	0.3711 (2.11)**	0.3719 (1.98)**	0.3648 (3.30)***	
Average Tariff		0.2101 (3.44)***	0.2002 (3.91)***	0.1862 (3.61)***	0.1933 (3.01)***	0.1936 (2.94)***		0.2585 (7.04)***
Real Interest Rate				−0.0629 (−1.30)		0.0029 (0.06)		
R^2	0.6142	0.7614	0.8226	0.8384	0.7981	0.7986	0.7811	0.6837
DW	2.0037	1.9522	1.9035	1.9427	1.9546	1.9508	2.0866	1.6738
No. of Observations	66	25	25	25	25	25	25	25
Estimation Method	AR1	AR1	AR1	AR1	AR1	AR1	AR1	AR1

*Significant at 10%.
**Significant at 5%.
***Significant at 1%.

Note: Rates were obtained in terms of GDP for the 1925–49 period and GNP after 1950. Numbers in parentheses are t-statistics.

given the low variance of the series.[29] The impulse response functions from this estimation are plotted in Figure 4.7. In particular, the effects on private saving of a one standard deviation change in all the other variables were analyzed. The VAR was estimated with data from 1950 to 1994.

The results indicate that increases in foreign saving tend to affect negatively private saving only for three years after the shock, while the (negative) impact of public saving tends to be of a more permanent nature. In addition, higher tariffs increase private saving, but the effect vanishes rapidly. This result captures the negative effect of trade liberalization on saving but suggests the temporary nature of that factor.

Liquidity Constraints and the Behavior of Saving

One possible explanation for the recent fall in private saving rates is that consumption of durable goods has increased as a consequence of the relaxation of liquidity constraints, in turn induced by the structural reform package implemented in the early 1990s. The validity of this hypothesis is tested using the analytical framework proposed by Bandiera et al. (1999), where total consumption is the sum of consumption by restricted (R) and unrestricted (NR) agents:

$$c_t = c_t^{NR} + c_t^{R}. \tag{20}$$

If the utility function is quadratic, the Euler equation for the unrestricted consumer is a random walk without drift:

$$c_t^{NR} = c_{t-1}^{NR} + \varepsilon_t \tag{21}$$

while the restricted agents consume a fraction of their income :

---

[29] In all cases, the augmented Dickey-Fuller tests did not reject the presence of unit roots in the series. The number of lags (L) in the test correspond to:

$$L = \min\left(j + 2.10\right)$$

where j is the number of lags that minimizes the Akaike criteria (AIC). Under some specifications it is possible to reject that foreign savings are $I(1)$. For that reason, the VAR was also estimated excluding this variable, without much change in the results.

Figure 4.7

Private Saving: Impulse-Response Functions, 1994
(one standard deviation shock)

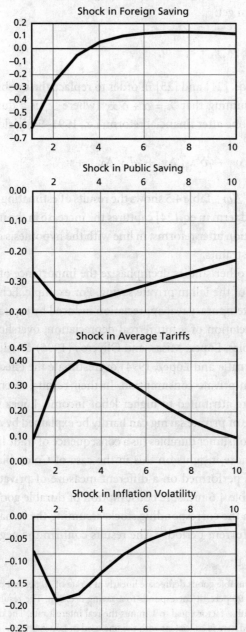

$$c_t^R = \gamma y_t^R + \omega_t.$$ [22]

Assuming that restricted consumers get a fraction λ of total income y (in logs) one can get:

$$c_t = c_{t-1}^{NR} + \gamma \lambda_t y_t + \varepsilon_t + \omega_t.$$ [23]

Lagging eqs. [21] and [23] in order to replace the unobservable value of c_{t-1}^{NR}, and assuming that $\lambda = \alpha + \delta' x_t$ (where x_t is a dummy variable with a value of one after financial reform, i.e., 1991–94) yields:

$$\Delta c_t = \gamma \alpha \Delta y_t + \gamma \delta' x_{t-1} \Delta y_t + \gamma d' y_t \Delta x_{t-1} + v_t$$ [24]

where $v_t = \varepsilon_t + \Delta \omega_t$. Table 4.5 shows the results of estimating this last equation. The second term in eq. [24] captures the increase in the income elasticity of consumption after reforms, in line with the hypothesis of a relaxation in liquidity constraints.

However, other studies deemphasize the importance of this factor as an explanation of the fall in private saving. For example, Echeverry (1996) argues that the temporary real appreciation induced by capital inflows generated the expectation of a future real depreciation, overshooting the demand for durables. López, Misas, and Oliveros (1996) conclude that other studies (e.g., Urrutia and López, 1994) overestimate the effects of financial liberalization on private consumption. In their results, recent increases in consumption are attributed to higher labor income. López (1996) argues that the collapse of private saving can hardly be explained by an adjustment in the stock of consumer durables (as a consequence of trade liberalization).

To gain more insights on this in the case of Colombia, a last set of regressions was performed on a different measure of private saving. The equations of Table 4.6 measure consumption of durable goods as the flow of services from the corresponding stock, assuming the remaining portion is saved in the current period.[30] The results confirm the negative effect of

---

[30] We assume that durable goods depreciate linearly at a rate of 10 percent per year, meaning that the remaining 90 percent corresponds to a saving decision. The results do not change when we correct with a factor equal to 1 minus the real interest rate. The definition of consumer durables used here is consistent with the one used in López (1996).

**Table 4.5 Liquidity Constraints on Consumption Test
(dependent variable: consumption growth)**

	1926–94 (1)	1950–94 (2)	1970–94 (3)
Constant	−1.8415 (−1.36)	1.0300 (1.00)	0.8003 (0.62)
Growth in GDP	0.4488 (1.72)*	−0.2421 (−1.16)	−0.2242 (−0.86)
Growth in GDP* Dummy9194	0.6422 (1.07)	0.7716 (2.69)***	0.7985 (2.78)**
GDP* Dummy91	0.0000 (0.29)	0.0000 (0.04)	0.0000 (0.12)
R^2	0.0617	0.1665	0.2786
DW	2.6132	1.9832	1.8329
No. of Observations	69	45	25
Estimation Method	MCO	MCO	MCO

*Significant at 10%.
**Significant at 5%.
***Significant at 1%.
Note: Numbers in parentheses are t-statistics.

foreign and public saving on private saving (with coefficients similar to those found in Table 4.4), but financial variables such as M2/GNP and total credit/GNP were not significant[31] This result may seem to contradict the theory that structural reforms have relaxed existing liquidity constraints in Colombia. However, it should be noticed that the correction of saving data by adding the saved portion of durable goods consumption left the behavior of the series practically unchanged (see Figure 4.8).

Determinants of Private Firms' Saving

The recent fall in private saving in Colombia is, to a large extent, the result of lower saving on the part of private firms. The determinants of saving at

[31] Once more, the real interest rate was not significant.

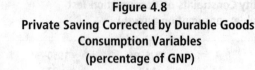

Figure 4.8
Private Saving Corrected by Durable Goods
Consumption Variables
(percentage of GNP)

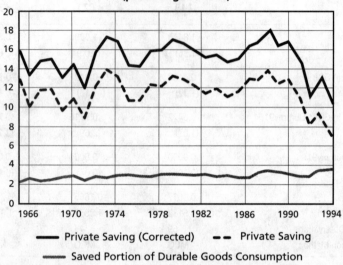

the level of the firm are analyzed by using yearly balance-sheet data from 397 manufacturing enterprises during the period 1985–93. The main purpose is to discuss the role of liquidity constraints in a representative sample of Colombian firms. The null hypothesis is that saving is the only source of funds for financing investment for credit-constrained firms. Consequently, relaxing credit constraints reduces saving.[32]

Echavarría and Tenjo (1993), Ospina (1994), Sánchez, Murcia, and Oliva (1996), and Tenjo (1995) have analyzed the determinants of firms' saving and investment in Colombia. Ospina (1994) finds that the elasticity of investment with respect to variables that measure liquidity is larger in firms that are credit constrained. Tenjo (1995) argues that due to the financial reform of 1991, firms have reduced their retention of profits. In the

---

[32] The literature has emphasized the determinants of firm-level investment (rather than saving) under liquidity constraints. For example, Fazzari, Hubbard, and Petersen (1988) and Hoshi, Kashyap, and Scharfstein (1991) conclude that, in liquidity-constrained firms, investment is dependent on the cash flow of the firm. Recently, Kaplan and Zingales (1995) have questioned some of the standard results.

Table 4.6 Determinants of Private Saving Corrected by Durable Goods Consumption
(dependent variable: private saving corrected by durable goods consumption)

	1965–94 (1)	1970–94 (2)	1970–94 (3)	1970–94 (4)	1965–94 (5)
Constant	17.8502	14.9667	14.8431	14.3752	15.1549
	(11.51)***	(4.63)***	(4.49)***	(4.80)***	(4.97)***
Foreign Saving Rate	−0.4354	−0.3223	−0.3276	−0.3448	−0.3223
	(−4.84)***	(−3.01)***	(−2.98)***	(−3.42)***	(−3.15)***
Public Saving Rate	−0.5461				
	(−4.09)***				
Taxes / GNP		−0.4623	−0.4710	−0.5609	−0.5368
		(−2.90)***	(−2.90)***	(−3.98)***	(−3.75)***
Government Expenditures /GNP		0.2944	0.3108	0.2927	0.1926
		(1.07)	(1.07)	(1.10)	(0.67)
Public Firms' Saving Rate		0.0196	0.0194	−0.1748	−0.0477
		(0.04)	(0.04)	(−0.35)	(−0.10)
Inflation Volatility	−0.0620	0.4849	0.4832	0.4472	0.4267
	(−0.55)	(2.36)**	(2.22)**	(2.34)**	(2.22)**
Average Tariff	0.1288	0.2014	0.2020	0.2092	0.2060
	(2.04)**	(2.59)***	(2.55)**	(3.03)***	(2.94)***
Real Interest Rate			0.0068		
			(0.13)		
Outstanding Loans by the Financial Sector / GNP				0.1299	
				(1.59)	
M2 / GNP					0.1093
					(1.62)
R^2	0.6619	0.7755	0.7707	0.7781	0.7833
DW	1.8654	1.9735	1.9607	1.9292	1.9245
No. of Observations	30	25	25	25	25
Estimation Method	AR1	AR1	AR1	AR1	AR1

*Significant at 10%.
**Significant at 5%.
***Significant at 1%.
Note: Numbers in parentheses are t-statistics.

most comprehensive study on the topic, Sánchez, Murcia, and Oliva (1996) estimate a model that simultaneously determines investment, saving, and borrowing by firms. They use the framework suggested in Dhrymes and Kurz (1967), as well as Myers and Majluf (1984), and split the sample into two periods (1983–91 and 1992–94) in order to test the effects of the financial reform of 1991. In their results, firms' saving decreased after financial reform, partially due to capital inflows (large firms substituted saving for external credit, while medium-sized firms substituted saving with domestic credit).

This issue was explored by estimating the following equation with panel data, where saving is defined as retained profits (plus depreciation):

$$\overset{+}{S_{firms}} = f(\overset{+}{Profits}, \overset{-}{Taxes}, \overset{-}{Liquidity}, \overset{-}{Borrowing}, \overset{+}{Liabilities/Assets}) \quad [25]$$

where it is expected that firms save more when they get more profits. In turn, taxation (which corresponds to the difference between total and pre-tax profits) affects negatively retained profits, while greater liquidity (i.e., cash flow) and access to credit (measured by the actual increase in the firm's liabilities) are associated with lower saving. However, the higher the indebtedness of the firm (in relation to its own assets), the greater the difficulty in obtaining new loans, so the higher the need for saving. A dummy variable for the period after reforms (1991–93) was included in all the equations. In addition, the dummy variable was interacted with the other explanatory variables in order to capture changes in the coefficients after the reform was implemented. According to the results of the Hausmann test, all regressions were estimated with random effects.

Column 1 in Table 4.7 indicates that all the variables are statistically significant and have the expected signs. In particular, the propensity to save by firms (out of their net profits) fell from 0.6 to 0.34, after reforms. Higher taxation reduces firms' saving, but less than proportionally (although there does not seem to exist an effect after 1991). The cash flow variable has the expected negative sign until 1992. However, cash flow and saving decisions seem to be independent after reforms. In addition, firms that have higher indebtedness (liabilities over assets) save more. Note that the dummy variable alone is not significant, so that the effects of reform operate through the variables included in the regression.

Table 4.7 Determinants of Firms' Saving : 1985–93
(dependent variable: firms' saving)

	All Firms (1)	All Firms (2)	Small Firms (3)	Medium-Size Firms (4)	Large Firms (5)	Low Indebtedness (6)	High Indebtedness (7)
Constant	-0.5053 (-0.47)	-0.1417 (-1.67)*	-0.0297 (-1.84)*	0.9656 (-0.69)	0.3150 (0.22)	-0.0161 (-1.27)	0.6301 (0.36)
Net Profits	0.6031 (13.66)***	0.5915 (16.96)***	0.7464 (10.69)***	0.4714 (8.29)***	0.6369 (11.48)***	0.5120 (9.14)***	0.757 (11.23)***
Taxes	-0.2568 (-2.59)**	-0.2681 (-3.29)***	-0.4200 (-2.74)***	0.0668 (0.44)	-0.5454 (-4.34)***	-0.1461 (-1.17)	-0.6937 (-3.93)***
Cash Flow	-1.0217 (-458.081)***	0.0206 (0.63)	0.1167 (2.01)**	0.0208 (0.36)	-0.0637 (-1.18)	0.0685 (1.19)	-0.0606 (-1.25)
Borrowing		-0.069 (-32.11)***	0.1435 (0.08)	-0.069 (-18.48)***	0.0148 (0.82)	0.1682 (0.77)	-0.0636 (-19.94)***
Indebtedness	0.0463 (3.21)***	0.0675 (5.79)***	0.66 (2.86)**	0.0561 (2.98)***	0.0338 (1.66)*	0.0817 (3.51)***	0.0317 (1.45)
Dummy 1991–93	0.0156 (1.13)	0.0189 (1.88)*	0.0414 (2.17)**	0.1556 (0.88)	0.1341 (0.08)	-0.3381 (-0.22)	0.0447 (1.60)

(continued)

Table 4.7 (continued)

	All Firms (1)	All Firms (2)	Small Firms (3)	Medium-Size Firms (4)	Large Firms (5)	Low Indebtedness (6)	High Indebtedness (7)
Dummy 1991–93 * (Net Profits)	−0.2602	−0.2153	−0.4320	−0.9403	−0.4051	0.0614	−0.5461
	(−4.40)***	(−4.90)***	(−5.03)***	(−0.13)	(−5.25)***	(0.89)	(−6.78)***
Dummy 1991–93 * (Taxes)	0.3450	0.3123	0.6566	−0.1449	0.7967	−0.3132	0.9541
	(2.26)**	(2.76)***	(3.08)***	(−0.70)	(4.19)***	(−1.77)*	(3.94)***
Dummy 1991–93 * (Cash Flow)	1.096	0.0485	−0.0796	0.0821	0.0653	0.0144	−0.0166
	(14.01)***	(0.75)	(−0.83)	(0.72)	(0.38)	(0.12)	(−0.18)
Dummy 1991–93 * (Indebtedness)		0.0364	−0.0490	0.0608	−0.0800	−0.6932	0.0396
		(2.23)**	(−1.64)*	(2.00)**	(−2.16)**	(−0.14)	(1.89)*
Dummy 1991–93 * (Liabilities)	−0.0132	−0.0193	−0.0406	−0.0167	0.0351	0.0506	−0.0583
	(−0.62)	(−1.21)	(−1.36)	(−0.60)	(1.29)	(1.27)	(−1.52)
R^2	0.98	0.99	0.33	0.99	0.29	0.32	0.99
No. of Observations	3,573	3,176	1,040	1,064	1,072	1,056	1,064
Estimation Method	Random eff.	Random eff.	Random eff.	Random eff.	Random eff.	Random eff.	Random eff.

*Significant at 10%.
**Significant at 5%.
***Significant at 1%.

Note: Numbers in parentheses are *t*-statistics.

In column 2 the flow of borrowing is added to the list of regressors. As expected, the coefficient comes out negative and statistically significant but of small size, suggesting low substitutability between saving and this source of funds. During the 1991–93 period, the negative relation between these two variables is even reduced.

The remaining regressions in Table 4.7 repeat the same exercise for different groups of firms, according to their size (small, medium, and large) and levels of indebtedness (low and high). Columns 3 through 5 indicate that saving by small firms depends crucially on their profits, tax payments, and cash flow (this last variable with a positive sign). Borrowing (which was severely limited for these firms) has a negative relation with saving in the recent period. In contrast, indebtedness (stock) and borrowing (flow) are the only determinants of saving for medium-sized firms (col. 4). In the case of presumably less credit-constrained large corporations, neither the cash flow nor borrowing affects saving (col. 5). Only in the 1991–93 period does a negative relation between borrowing and saving indicate some substitutability between these two sources of funds.

Other interesting results emerge when the sample is divided according to borrowing levels. In the case of firms with low levels of indebtedness, saving depends on their own profits (col. 6). For highly indebted firms (col. 7) the impact of profits on saving was substantially reduced after reforms. Also, the greater the cash flow, the lower their saving, reflecting greater substitutability between these two sources of financing. For these firms, increases in the stock of debt are not associated with greater saving.

Conclusions

Using the framework of an intertemporal model to analyze the determinants of saving in Colombia yields a number of conclusions. National saving partially responds to temporary changes in output, according to the permanent income hypothesis. Higher government expenditures (in relation to their permanent level) are associated with lower national saving, thus disproving the Ricardian equivalence hypothesis. In other words, national saving can be increased by raising the public sector saving rate, preferably through cuts in expenditures rather than higher taxation.

Apart from the predictions obtained from the intertemporal approach, the paper tests other common hypotheses regarding saving behavior. In particular, changes in national saving and changes in investment are perfectly correlated, and saving causes growth (in the Granger sense). Moreover, 34 percent of the national saving-investment deviations are corrected in the course of one year. Thus, the historical data do not support the view that current account imbalances are sustainable in the long run for a country like Colombia. Additional econometric evidence suggests that increases in urbanization and age dependency have had a significantly negative impact on private saving in Colombia.

Much of the recent reduction in private saving can be attributed to the increase in current government expenditures, as well as to the effects of higher taxation. Indeed, the increase in taxation explains two thirds of the 6 percentage point decrease in the private saving rate. On the other hand, lower margins induced by trade liberalization explain the reduction in firms' saving.

The recent decline in private saving is temporary, so no major offsetting policy interventions are required. However, a change in fiscal policy is recommended to obtain an overall increase in national saving. In particular, higher public saving is required, especially through a reduction in the current levels of government expenditures. The key aspect to emphasize is that counterreforms reintroducing protection and financial repression would be unwise. Increases in private saving will come only as pension reform matures and firms' margins recover based on productivity gains. Moreover, a close inverse relationship exists between private and foreign saving, so the lower current account deficit expected in future years would probably be matched by an increase in private saving.

References

Bandiera, O., Caprio, G., Honohan, P. and Schiantarelli, F. 1999. "Does Financial Reform Increase or Reduce Savings?" Policy Research Working Paper 2062. World Bank, Policy Research Department, Washington, DC.

Bayoumi, T. 1991. "Financial Deregulation and Household Behavior." Bank of England. Mimeograph.

Bunting, D. 1991. "Savings and the Distribution of Income." *Journal of Post-Keynesian Economics.* 14: 3–22.

Cárdenas, M. 1992. "Ciclos económicos y bonanzas exportadoras: teoría y evidencia en cuatro países productores de café." *Ensayos sobre Política Económica.* June. Banco de la República.

———. 1994. "Stabilization and Redistribution of Coffee Revenues: A Political Economy Model of Commodity Marketing Boards." *Journal of Development Economics.* 44: 351–80.

Cárdenas, M. and Escobar, A. 1996. "Macroeconomía y mercado de capitales." Misión de Estudios del Mercado de Capitales. Mimeograph.

Cárdenas, M. and Olivera, M. 1995. "La crítica de lucas y la inversión en Colombia: nueva evidencia." *Ensayos sobre Política Económica.* 27 (June): 95–138. Banco de la República.

Carrasquilla, A. and Rincón, H. 1990. "Relaciones entre el déficit público y ahorro privado: aproximaciones al caso colombiano." *Ensayos sobre Política Económica.* 18. Banco de la República.

Carroll, C.D. and Weil, D.N. 1994. "Saving and Growth: A Reinterpretation." *Carnegie-Rochester Conference Series on Public Policy.* 40:133–92.

Cook, C. 1995. "Saving Rates and Income Distribution: Further Evidence from LDCs." *Applied Economics.* 27: 71–82.

Corbo, V. and Schmidt-Hebbel, K. 1991. "Public Policies and Saving in Developing Countries." *Journal of Development Economics.* 36: 89–115.

Deaton, A. 1995. "Growth and Saving: What Do We Know, What Do We Need to Know, and What Might We Learn?" Research Program in Development Studies, Princeton University, Princeton, N.J. Mimeograph.

Della Valle, P. and Oguchi, N. 1976. "Distribution, the Aggregate Consumption Function and the Level of Economic Development: Some Cross-Country Results." *Journal of Political Economy.* 84: 1325–34.

Dhrymes, P. and Kurz, M. 1967. "Investment, Dividends, and External Finance Behavior of Firms." In R. Ferber, editor. *Determinants of Investment Behavior.* New York: Columbia University Press for NBER.

Echavarría, J.J. and Tenjo, F. 1993. "Inversión, liquidez y fuentes de financiación en la industria colombiana." *Coyuntura Económica.* June: 103–37.

Echeverry, J.C. 1996. "The Fall in Colombian Savings during the 1990s: Theory and Evidence." Banco de la República, Bogotá. Mimeograph.

Edwards, S. 1995. "Why Are Saving Rates So Different across Countries? An International Comparative Analysis." NBER Working Paper 5097. National Bureau of Economic Research, Cambridge, Mass.

Fazzari, S.M., Hubbard, R.G. and Petersen, B.C. 1988. "Financing Constraints and Corporate Investment." *Brookings Papers on Economic Activity.* 1: 141–95.

Feldstein, M. 1983. "Domestic Savings and International Capital Movements in the Long Run and the Short Run." *European Economic Review.* 21: 129–51.

Feldstein, M. and Bachetta, P. 1991. "National Saving and International Investment." In B.D. Bernheim and J.B. Shoven, editors. *National Saving and Economic Performance.* Chicago, Ill.: University of Chicago Press.

Feldstein, M. and Horioka, C. 1980. "Domestic Savings and International Capital Flows." *Economic Journal.* 90: 314–29.

Frankel, J. A. 1989. "Quantifying International Capital Mobility in the 1980s." NBER Working Paper 2856. National Bureau of Economic Research, Cambridge, Mass.

_____. 1993. "Quantifying Capital Mobility in the 1980s." In J. A. Frankel, *On Exchange Rates.* Cambridge, Mass.: MIT Press.

Gersovitz, M. 1988. "Savings and Development." In H. Chenery and T. Srinivasan, editors. *Handbook of Development Economics.* Vol. 1. Amsterdam: North-Holland.

Giovannini, A. 1985. "Saving and the Interest Rate in LDCs." *Journal of Development Economics.* 18: 197–217.

Gómez, H.J. and Thoumi, F. 1986. "Una nota sobre la relación entre el financiamiento externo y la inversión pública en Colombia." *Coyuntura Económica.* 3 (October): 196–203.

Guiso, L., Jappelli, T., and Terlizzese, D. 1994. "Why Is Italy's Saving Rate So High?" In A. Ando, L. Guiso and I. Visco, editors. *Saving and the Accumulation of Wealth, Essays on Italian Household and Government Saving Behavior.* Cambridge, U.K.: Cambridge University Press.

Hayashi, F., Ito, T. and Slemrod, J. 1988. "Housing Finance Imperfections, Taxation and Private Saving: A Comparative Simulation Analysis of the United States and Japan." *Journal of Japanese and International Economies.* 2: 215–38.

Hong, K. 1995. "Income Distribution and Aggregate Saving." Harvard University, Cambridge, Mass. Mimeograph.

Hoshi, T., Kashyap, A. and Scharfstein, D. 1991. "Corporate Structure, Liquidity and Investment: Evidence from Japanese Industrial Groups." *Quarterly Journal of Economics.* February: 33–60.

Jappelli, T. and Pagano, M. 1994. "Saving, Growth and Liquidity Constraints." *Quarterly Journal of Economics.* 109: 83–109.

Jensen, W. J. and Schulze, G. 1996. "Theory-Based Measurement of the Saving-Investment Correlation with an Application to Norway." *Economic Inquiry.* 34: 116–32.

Kaplan, S.N. and Zingales, L. 1995. "Do Financing Constraints Explain Why Investment Is Correlated with Cash Flows?" NBER Working Paper 5267. National Bureau of Economic Research, Cambridge, Mass.

López, A. 1994. "La teoría del ingreso permanente y las restricciones de liquidez en Colombia." In R. Steiner, editor. *Estabilización y crecimiento.* Bogotá: Tercer Mundo-Fedesarrollo.

———. 1996. "¿Por qué cayó el ahorro en Colombia a comienzos de la década del noventa?" *Coyuntura Económica.* 26 (4): 137–68.

López, A., Misas, M. and Oliveros, H. 1996. "Understanding Consumption in Colombia." World Bank. Washington, D.C. Mimeograph.

Menchnik, P. and David, M. 1983. "Income Distribution, Lifetime Savings, and Bequests." *American Economic Review.* 73: 672–90.

Miles, D. 1992. "Housing Markets, Consumption and Financial Liberalisation in the Major Economies." *European Economic Review.* 36: 1093–1127.

Miller, M.H. and Modigliani, F. 1961. "Dividend Policy, Growth and the Valuation of Shares." *Journal of Business.* 31 (October): 411–33.

Muellbauer, J. and Murphy, A. 1990. "The UK Current Account Deficit." *Economic Policy.* 5 (October): 348–95.

Musgrove, P. 1980. "Income Distribution and the Aggregate Consumption Function." *Journal of Political Economy.* 88: 504–25.

Myers, S.C. and Majluf, N.S. 1984. "Corporate Financing and Investment Decisions When Firms Have Information That Investors Do Not Have." *Journal of Financial Economics.* 13 (June): 187–221.

Obstfeld, M. 1988. "How Integrated Are World Capital Markets." In R. Findlay et al., editors. *Debt, Stabilization, and Development: Essays in Memory of Carlos Diaz-Alejandro.* Oxford, U.K.: Basil Blackwell.

_____. 1995. "International Capital Mobility in the 1990s." In P. B. Kenen, editor. *Understanding Interdependence. The Macroeconomics of the Open Economy.* Princeton, N.J.: Princeton University Press.

Obstfeld, M. and Rogoff, K. 1995. "The Intertemporal Approach to the Current Account." In G. Grossman and K. Rogoff, editors. *Handbook of International Economics.* Vol. 3. Amsterdam: North-Holland.

_____. 1996. *Foundations of International Macroeconomics.* Cambridge, Mass.: MIT Press.

Ocampo, J.A. and Lora, E. 1988. *Colombia y la deuda externa: de la moratoria de los treinta a la encrucijada de los ochenta.* Bogotá: Fedesarrollo–Tercer Mundo.

Ocampo, J.A., Londoño, J.L., and Villar, L. 1985. "Ahorro e inversión en Colombia." *Coyuntura Económica.* June

Ogaki, M., Ostry, J.D. and Reinhart, C. 1995. "Saving Behavior in Low- and Middle-Income Developing Countries: A Comparison." Working Paper WP/95/3. International Monetary Fund, Washington, DC.

Ospina, S.P. 1994. "Firm Heterogeneity, Liquidity Variables and Investment Decisions: The Colombian Case." University of Illinois, Urbana. Mimeograph.

Perry, G. and Cárdenas, M. 1986 *Diez años de reformas tributarias en Colombia: 1974–1984.* Bogotá: Universidad Nacional de Colombia (CID)–Fedesarrollo.

Ramírez, M. 1992. "El ahorro en Colombia." *Cambios estructurales y crecimiento*. Bogotá: Ediciones Uniandes.

Sahota, G.S. 1993. "Saving and Distribution." In J.H. Gapinski, editor. *The Economics of Saving*. Boston, Mass.: Kluwer Academic Publishers.

Sánchez, Fabio, Murcia, G. and Oliva, C. 1996. "La dinámica de la inversión y el ahorro empresarial en Colombia: 1983–1994." Departamento Nacional de Planeación and Inter-American Development Bank. Mimeograph.

Schmidt-Hebbel, K. and Servén, L. 1996. "Income Inequality and Aggregate Saving: The Cross Country Evidence." Policy Research Working Paper 1561. World Bank, Policy Research Department, Washington, DC.

Steiner, R. and Escobar, A. 1994. "Colombia: ahorro en declive, financiamiento en auge." Fedesarrollo, Bogotá. Mimeograph.

Suescún, R. 1996. "Commodity Booms, Dutch Disease, and Real Business Cycles in a Small Semi-open Economy: The Case of Coffee in Colombia." Banco de la República. June. Mimeograph.

Tenjo, F. 1995. "Restricciones financieras, comportamiento de las empresas manufactureras y perspectivas para el desarrollo del mercado de capitales en Colombia." Misión de Estudios del Mercado de Capitales. Mimeograph.

Tesar, L.L. 1991. "Savings, Investment, and International Capital Flows." *Journal of International Economics*. 31: 55–78.

Urrutia, M. and López, A. 1994. "La relajación de las restricciones de liquidez y el aumento del consumo privado." *Revista del Banco de la República*. August.

CHAPTER 5

Why Did Private Saving in Mexico Fall prior to the 1994 Crisis?

Angel Calderón-Madrid[1]

What explains the distinctive behavior of domestic saving in Mexico over the last 10 years, and in particular its sharp fall after 1988? Answers to this question have more than mere academic merit; they can also provide lessons of political economy and suggestions for promoting sustained economic growth without balance of payments difficulties. Three complementary analyses attempt to answer this question.

The first analysis breaks down private saving into its two components: household saving and corporate saving. The results quantify the important role of corporate retained earnings in generating private saving during the eight years prior to the 1994 crisis. They also indicate that, except in 1990, the drop in private saving that began in 1989 is attributable to the behavior of households.

Because official statistics on these separate components are unavailable for the time period examined here, data were obtained from matrices of financial assets and flows developed for this study. These matrices report the financial stocks of the banking, public, and external sectors within a single framework, along with those of companies and of households, thus facilitating analysis of the factors that determined the availability of resources for households during the study period.[2]

---

[1] The author is an economist at the Centro de Estudios Económicos of El Colegio de México.
[2] Calculations were performed according to the methodology of Arriazu (1987) and Khadr and Schmidt-Hebbel (1989).

The second analysis was based on an econometric examination of quarterly data on private saving and the variables that determined its behavior, for the period 1985–95. The most important of these variables were related to capital gains produced by the boom in real estate prices during this period, and those associated with the financial deregulation initiated in 1988.

The conceptual framework used by the Mexican Instituto Nacional de Estadística (INEGI) in 1989, 1992, and 1994 in the design of its household income and expenditure surveys provides the basis for the third analysis. Cross-sectional statistical analysis of information from these surveys can explicitly relate household saving to the educational level and age of the head of household and to other demographic variables such as the number of minors at home and the size of the household. This allows us to quantify how human capital, captured in this study by the level of formal education, influences saving decisions.

Survey responses also indicate whether the respondents were homeowners, and if so, whether they carried a mortgage. The survey also reports whether respondents had credit cards and access to other forms of nonmortgage credit. Complementing the results from our quarterly time-series analysis, these data allowed an analysis of the effect on saving of the boom in real estate prices and the increased availability of bank credit. According to the aggregate data, these two determinants of saving, which had little influence in 1989, had much more in 1992. They continued to have an impact in 1994, although less than in 1992.

This chapter analyzes the relationship between low private saving and the performance of the current account of the balance of payments, contrasting the events of 1995 with those of other recent years in Mexican history. The discussion begins with 1988 and highlights the contrasting behavior of the operating surplus in the public sector and private saving. The next part presents the matrices for financial assets by sector, to address the factors that determined the greater availability of resources to the private sector.

Saving in the private sector is then broken down into its two main components: saving by households and corporate retained earnings. Estimates of saving by companies for 1990 and 1991 show, unlike in the other years analyzed, a reduction in that saving equivalent to more than 2 percentage points of GDP compared with 1988 and 1989. The analysis then goes on to examine whether this result can be attributed to an increase in the proportion of profits distributed by companies to their shareholders rather than to a drop in those profits. Among the possible explanations is the effect of changes in the tax treatment of dividends.

Using an econometric time-series analysis to determine the behavior of private saving, this chapter addresses the factors that contributed to greater certainty about the prospects for sustained economic growth beginning in 1989. It also identifies the variables believed to approximate these changes. Other relevant variables are cited to help explain the events of this period. Finally, results obtained from regression analysis are presented.

A cross-sectional analysis for the years 1989, 1992, and 1994 aims at quantifying the ways in which human capital, captured in the regressions by the level of formal education, influences saving decisions. Additional information is provided to complement the analysis of homeownership and access to credit as factors explaining the drop in saving. Finally, age of the head of the household is analyzed as yet another variable in saving decisions.

Trends in Private Saving in the Last 30 Years

Saving and Investment and the Balance of Payments

Table 5.1 and Figure 5.1 demonstrate that, in years such as 1983, reductions in Mexico's fiscal deficit (the result of conditionality clauses in IMF adjustment programs) were not sufficient to eliminate the need for external financing. To head off a balance of payments crisis in 1982, private saving had to outstrip private investment: indeed, in 1983 private investment fell and the proportion of private saving in GDP rose.

The relationship between low private saving and the performance of the current account is highlighted by comparing 1983 with 1995. Although in 1995 the private investment–GDP ratio fell and although the fiscal accounts showed a surplus in 1995 and a deficit in 1983, the results for the current account were much weaker in 1995 than in 1983. The shift from a surplus in the current account of more than 4 percent of GDP in 1983 to a deficit in 1995 is due to the fact that private saving in 1983 was 7 percentage points higher as a share of GDP than in 1995.

It is noteworthy that in 1977—the other year in which the fiscal deficit fell in response to a balance of payments crisis, and a year in which mac-

Table 5.1A Private Saving and Its Accounting-Counterpart Aggregates (percentage of GDP)

	A Private Saving[a]	B Private Investment[b]	C Public Sector Deficit[c]	D External Saving[d]	E Inflation Tax
1965	15.0	16.6	0.7	2.3	
1966	13.8	15.4	0.6	2.2	
1967	14.0	14.8	1.7	2.5	
1968	12.4	13.9	1.4	2.9	
1969	13.0	14.1	1.3	2.4	
1970	15.4	16.1	2.6	3.3	
1971	14.8	15.9	1.3	2.4	
1972	16.0	14.9	3.3	2.2	
1973	14.1	14.4	2.5	2.8	
1974	15.7	17.1	3.1	4.5	
1975	17.6	15.8	6.8	5.0	
1976	15.2	15.2	4.1	4.1	
1977	15.9	15.2	2.6	1.9	
1978	15.2	14.4	3.4	2.6	
1979	15.7	15.5	3.8	3.6	
1980	14.9	17.1	3.6	5.8	1.0
1981	20.1	16.8	10.0	6.7	0.9
1982	15.4	12.1	5.8	2.5	2.7
1983	18.4	10.0	3.7	−4.7	1.9
1984	12.9	10.3	0.2	−2.4	1.3
1985	14.2	12.0	1.3	−0.8	0.7
1986	12.2	9.6	3.6	1.0	1.8
1987	10.2	11.0	−3.3	−2.6	2.1
1988	14.7	12.9	3.1	1.4	0.8
1989	12.2	13.1	1.9	2.8	0.5
1990	9.4	13.9	−1.6	2.9	0.7
1991	6.6	15.0	−3.3	5.1	0.5
1992	7.6	17.5	−2.5	7.4	0.3
1993	9.7	17.0	−0.9	6.4	0.2
1994	10.4	17.6	0.5	7.8	0.2
1995	11.4	12.2	−0.5	0.3	1.4

a. A = B + C − D. Adjusted private saving is the result of subtracting column E from column A.
b. Including stock building. Investment and GDP were deflated by their corresponding price indices.
c. A minus sign indicates a surplus. Column C does not include extraordinary income due to privatizations and corresponds to operational balance (private saving minus public investment).
d. Current account deficit.
Source: INEGI and Banco of México.

Table 5.1B
(percentage of GDP)

	A Private Saving (Adjusted)[a]	B Public Saving (Adjusted)[b]	C Domestic Saving[c]	D Private Gross Capital Formation[d]	E Public Gross Capital Formation[e]
1980	13.9	8.1	21.9	27.7	10.7
1981	19.1	2.9	22.0	28.7	12.0
1982	12.7	6.6	19.3	21.9	9.8
1983	16.5	4.8	21.3	16.6	6.5
1984	11.7	7.6	19.3	16.9	6.6
1985	13.5	5.7	19.2	18.4	6.4
1986	10.4	4.0	14.4	15.4	5.8
1987	8.2	10.4	18.6	16.0	5.0
1988	13.8	2.4	16.2	17.6	4.7
1989	11.7	3.3	15.0	17.8	4.7
1990	8.7	7.4	16.1	19.0	5.1
1991	6.1	8.4	14.5	19.7	4.7
1992	7.3	7.1	14.4	21.8	4.3
1993	9.5	5.2	14.8	21.1	4.1
1994	10.2	4.0	14.2	22.0	4.4
1995	10.0	5.1	15.1	15.4	3.2

a. Private saving minus inflation tax.
b. Public saving minus operational balance plus inflation tax.
c. C = A + B.
d. Including stock building.
e. E = D − (total private investment).
Source: INEGI and Banco de México.

roeconomic policy was adjusted according to IMF conditionalities—the situation was similar to that of 1983. In both years, private saving rose while the fiscal deficit fell. In all the other years in Table 5.1, the opposite occurs: when the public sector reduced its deficit or increased its surplus, private saving declined.[3] Furthermore, the unprecedentedly low private saving recorded in 1992 coincided with the highest recorded level of fiscal surplus.

---

[3] One exception is 1986, when the fiscal deficit increased (principally because of a reduction in

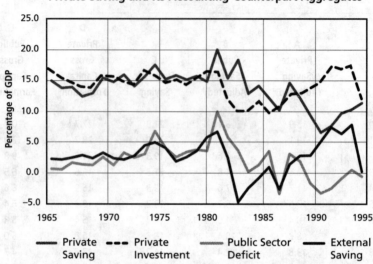

Figure 5.1
Private Saving and Its Accounting-Counterpart Aggregates

Additionally, during the final years of the so-called period of stabilizing development—the six years prior to 1971, presented in Table 5.1— Mexico funded an excess of public sector expenditure (including real interest payments on the public debt) over public sector revenue with external saving.[4] This made it possible for private investment to exceed what private domestic saving could finance, in a manner similar to what happened in the last seven years presented in the table.[5] However, unlike what happened beginning in 1988, the discrepancy between saving and investment never exceeded 1.5 percentage points of GDP between 1965 and 1971.

With the exception of 1986, when a drop in petroleum prices had a strongly negative effect on the current account, external saving was nega-

---

petroleum sales), yet private saving (with the devaluation and recession that resulted that year) also grew.

[4] This episode was characterized by high per capita growth rates, low inflation, and a fixed exchange rate.

[5] The opposite occurred not only for the two years (1981 and 1982) in which economic growth was bolstered by prospects of development associated with the country's potential to become a petroleum exporter and with greater access to international capital markets. It was also evident in the six years following the 1982 crisis, a period in which the share of private investment in GDP posted its lowest levels over the 30 years represented.

Figure 5.2
Gross Fixed Capital Formation and Domestic Saving

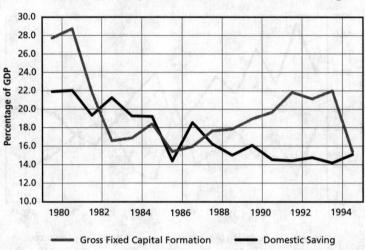

Gross Fixed Capital Formation ———   Domestic Saving ———

tive from 1983 to 1987. Mexico was again able to count on positive and increasing levels of external saving beginning in 1988, and the net external financial inflows recorded beginning in 1988 did not coincide with increasing fiscal deficits.

As Figure 5.2 makes clear, the period of sustained growth in gross fixed capital formation ended in 1994.[6] In December of that year, the country once again faced a balance of payments crisis, which resulted in a severe recession accompanied by financial instability in the domestic banking sector (see Calderón-Madrid, 1997). The six years prior to the crisis coincided, on the one hand, with a sustained increase in external saving (as noted in Table 5.1), and on the other, with increasingly lower domestic saving as a percentage of GDP, which is evident in Figure 5.2. Figure 5.3 provides a

---

[6] In 1988, after more than five years of a downward trend in the share of total gross fixed capital formation in GDP, this index once again approximated 1982 levels. Implicit in this comparison is an absence of growth in total saving in real terms during the period between these two years: real GDP was almost the same in 1988 as in 1982. Real saving, measured either in per capita terms or in terms of any other demographic indicator, did experience a notable drop. During those years the annual growth rate of the population exceeded 2 percent.

Figure 5.3
Public and Private Saving

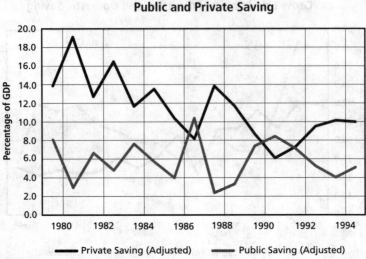

breakdown of the latter aggregate into its public and private components. When public saving increased, private saving fell, although as Figures 5.2 and 5.3 imply, the decline in one component exceeded in almost every case the increase in the other.

During the six years prior to the 1994 crisis, the public sector released funds for lending that financed an increase in private spending. This was accompanied by a series of structural changes and events that, as will be made evident below, made possible the drop in saving in the last six years.[7] Significant among these events were financial deregulation and a boom in real estate prices.

The Household Credit Boom and Commercial Bank Performance

The contribution of the domestic commercial banking sector to the boom in private spending beginning in 1989 is evident from the banking sector's figures in our matrix of financial stocks (Table 5.2). Along with the increase in spending by households after the financial deregulation initiated in 1987,

---

[7] For an analysis that covers the period since 1960, see Buira (1994).

Table 5.2 Matrix of Financial Stocks (percentage of GDP)

	1989	1990	1991	1992	1993	1994:3	1994	1995:3	1995
Households									
Commercial Banks	10.36	10.25	10.71	12.83	11.97	10.58	10.82	10.15	10.78
Consolidated Public Sector	3.93	4.49	2.41	0.37	0.54	0.28	0.31	0.44	0.49
Foreign Sector	13.96	9.52	11.01	12.15	16.16	16.82	N.A.	N.A.	N.A.
Commercial Banks									
Households	4.87	6.45	8.92	12.42	14.68	15.03	15.92	12.38	10.66
Consolidated Public Sector	6.98	6.51	6.65	2.88	1.36	0.89	1.26	1.29	1.02
Private Firms	7.61	9.48	12.08	14.37	15.97	18.52	22.90	17.96	17.53
Foreign Sector	1.05	1.16	1.24	1.17	1.35	1.51	2.02	1.98	2.22
Private Firms									
Commercial Banks	5.54	7.00	9.89	9.52	11.80	14.97	15.83	15.19	15.76
Consolidated Public Sector	5.27	4.99	2.55	1.24	1.88	-0.41	-0.48	0.54	0.93
Foreign Sector									
Commercial Banks	3.72	4.59	5.24	4.70	5.18	5.36	8.43	6.18	7.14
Consolidated Public Sector	18.94	15.30	11.05	10.88	9.33	12.32	N.A.	N.A.	N.A.
Private Firms	2.54	2.59	5.05	6.90	10.43	12.34	18.78	18.02	20.32

Notes: After the 1994 crisis, data incompatibility might exist due to adjustments made by Central Bank authorities. Columns correspond to assets and rows to liabilities. Rows corresponding to consolidated public sector with the foreign sector include international reserves of the Bank of Mexico.

Source: Author's calculations with data from SHCP, Banco de México, and INEGI. See Calderón-Madrid (1996a).

the net creditor position of households with the banking sector began to weaken steadily, and beginning in the first half of 1992 it shifted to a debtor position (ending 1992 with 12.8 percent in assets and 12.4 percent in liabilies).

To analyze what made possible the increase in funds available to households, as well as the changes in commercial bank standards for granting credit, Table 5.2 presents a fully integrated matrix of financial assets in Mexico. The format of Table 5.3—presenting the same information as in Table 5.2— was chosen to be compatible with the flow-of-funds matrices recorded by the Bank of Mexico in its annual reports. Unlike those annual reports, however, our matrix breaks the private sector down into its two components: companies and households. In addition, the banking system does not appear as a single aggregate entity but rather is divided into three subsectors: commercial banks, development banks, and the Bank of Mexico.

This matrix highlights the fact that consolidated public sector liabilities with the commercial banking sector fell by more than 6 percentage points of GDP between 1988 and 1993, while additional funds obtained by the banking system from abroad during this period increased the stock level by 2 percentage points of GDP. In contrast, credits granted by commercial banks to households grew by more than 11 percentage points of GDP between 1988 and 1993. The table also indicates that public domestic debt held by households and companies fell by more than 3 percentage points of GDP during this same period—which was another way to finance private expenditure above income.

A more disaggregated version of this table, not shown here, distinguishes assets held in national currency from those held in foreign currency.[8] Deflating these values allowed the calculation of real saving flows with two properties. First, they are compatible with the trend in assets over the long term. Second, they make it possible to identify the composition of assets and liabilities, whose variation is reflected in saving flows. In this way, it is possible to generate a table of real financial flows like that in Table 5.4, and to disaggregate the component of private saving that corresponds to companies from that which corresponds to households. Such a disaggregation is performed in the next subsection.

---

[8] The disaggregation of these matrices, as well as their presentation on a quarterly basis beginning in December 1985, is available upon request from the author.

Table 5.3 Matrix of Financial Assets by Sector: 1980–95 (percentage of GDP)

	1980	1981	1982	1983	1984	1985	1986	1987	1988	1989	1990	1991	1992	1993	1994:3	1994	1995:3	1995
Banking System																		
Resources Channeled to Private Sector	16.48	16.48	11.64	9.94	11.24	10.77	9.60	9.46	10.85	15.18	17.96	23.27	29.58	34.43	37.99	44.06	34.68	33.07
Credit to Private Firms																		
Commercial Banks	7.10	7.19	5.95	5.05	5.48	4.84	4.32	4.34	4.78	7.61	9.48	12.08	14.37	15.97	18.52	22.94	17.96	17.66
Development Banks	1.47	1.44	1.39	1.29	1.63	1.93	2.12	2.32	2.33	2.51	1.86	2.09	2.52	3.40	3.96	4.75	3.95	4.29
Credit to Households																		
Commercial Banks	6.07	6.25	3.32	2.66	3.16	3.04	2.45	2.26	3.04	4.87	6.45	8.92	12.42	14.68	15.03	15.95	12.38	10.74
Development Banks	1.84	1.60	0.98	0.95	0.97	0.94	0.70	0.54	0.69	0.19	0.17	0.19	0.28	0.38	0.48	0.41	0.39	0.38
+ Net Credit to Nonfinancial Public Sector	18.84	22.52	34.55	30.11	25.57	28.24	33.06	26.63	22.15	20.22	15.95	12.72	7.84	4.54	5.47	7.46	6.24	8.35
Commercial Banks	0.40	1.28	5.01	5.10	4.65	7.27	10.34	9.08	7.11	6.35	5.89	6.08	2.44	0.98	0.87	1.26	1.28	0.97
Development Banks	7.02	8.88	14.84	12.17	10.14	11.55	15.15	14.73	9.09	8.11	5.57	4.69	4.17	4.25	4.70	7.16	6.88	7.92
Bank of Mexico	11.42	12.36	14.70	12.84	10.78	9.42	7.57	2.83	5.95	5.75	4.49	1.95	1.23	-0.69	-0.11	-0.96	-1.92	-0.54
+ International Reserves, Bank of Mexico	1.94	1.95	1.39	3.09	4.08	3.37	4.94	8.97	2.94	2.83	3.47	5.13	4.83	5.63	3.77	2.27	4.83	5.74
− Unclassified Resources	2.46	2.77	1.49	0.86	1.01	2.03	-0.34	0.93	0.99	2.39	3.66	4.57	4.73	4.04	4.93	2.67	-3.16	-7.16
− Net Debt with Foreign Sector	8.73	10.82	22.19	19.68	16.67	19.66	26.32	24.77	16.58	15.33	12.37	12.18	11.11	11.82	12.63	19.94	20.10	23.01
Commercial Banks	2.36	2.88	5.45	5.16	4.10	4.05	4.69	2.69	2.50	2.67	3.43	4.00	3.53	3.84	3.85	6.43	4.19	4.95
Development Banks	6.37	7.94	15.98	13.77	11.40	13.96	18.85	18.79	12.00	10.52	6.79	6.28	6.11	6.85	7.85	12.16	10.47	11.88
Bank of Mexico	0.00	0.00	0.75	0.75	1.17	1.65	2.79	3.29	2.08	2.15	2.15	1.90	1.48	1.14	0.93	1.36	5.43	6.17
= Resources Obtained from Private Sector	26.06	27.36	23.91	22.61	23.22	20.69	21.62	19.36	18.37	20.50	21.35	24.37	26.40	28.74	29.66	31.18	28.81	31.32
Private Sector																		
Resources Channeled to Banking System	26.16	27.36	23.91	22.61	23.22	20.69	21.62	19.47	18.37	20.50	21.35	24.37	26.43	28.74	29.66	31.12	28.81	31.08
Private Firms																		
Deposits in Commercial Banks	4.90	5.09	4.68	4.38	4.86	4.34	3.93	3.85	3.03	5.54	7.00	9.89	9.52	11.80	14.97	15.80	15.19	15.64
Deposits in Development Banks	1.33	0.71	0.82	0.74	0.53	0.52	0.45	0.31	0.36	0.45	0.66	0.82	1.02	1.38	1.48	1.61	1.37	1.39
Households																		
Deposits in Commercial Banks	15.47	16.66	14.19	13.37	13.27	11.28	12.35	10.93	10.20	10.36	10.25	10.71	12.83	11.97	10.58	10.82	10.15	10.78
Deposits in Development Banks	1.33	1.46	1.18	1.23	1.51	1.29	1.37	1.00	1.26	0.73	0.37	0.40	0.96	1.60	1.90	1.74	1.89	2.29

(continued)

Table 5.3 (continued)

	1980	1981	1982	1983	1984	1985	1986	1987	1988	1989	1990	1991	1992	1993	1994:3	1994	1995:3	1995
Net Resources Channeled to Bank of Mexico																		
Private Firms	-0.61	-0.61	-0.63	0.03	0.18	0.63	1.17	1.25	1.03	0.69	0.32	-0.41	-0.91	-1.16	-2.01	-2.26	-1.97	-1.84
Currency	3.93	4.06	3.67	2.85	2.86	2.63	2.35	2.13	2.49	2.73	2.76	2.96	3.02	3.15	2.73	3.41	2.19	2.81
+ Holding of Public Bonds	0.75	0.76	1.71	1.49	1.78	1.69	2.40	3.64	6.54	8.50	9.17	5.38	2.52	3.58	1.88	2.10	2.95	3.26
Private Firms	0.50	0.51	1.15	1.00	1.19	1.13	1.07	2.48	3.25	4.58	4.68	2.97	2.15	3.04	1.59	1.78	2.50	2.77
Households	0.25	0.25	0.57	0.49	0.59	0.56	1.33	1.16	3.29	3.93	4.49	2.41	0.37	0.54	0.28	0.31	0.44	0.49
+ Foreign Assets																		
Households	2.88	6.79	17.37	17.25	14.49	6.75	31.71	32.25	18.74	13.96	9.52	11.01	12.15	16.16	16.82	N.A.	N.A.	N.A.
− Resources Obtained from Banking System	16.48	16.48	11.64	9.94	11.24	10.77	9.60	9.46	10.85	15.18	17.96	23.27	29.58	34.43	37.99	43.97	34.68	32.82
Commercial Banks	13.17	13.44	9.27	7.71	8.64	7.89	6.77	6.60	7.82	12.48	15.93	20.99	26.79	30.65	33.55	38.82	30.34	28.19
Development Banks	3.31	3.04	2.38	2.24	2.60	2.88	2.83	2.86	3.03	2.70	2.03	2.27	2.80	3.78	4.43	5.15	4.34	4.63
− Resources Obtained from Foreign Sector	6.64	6.80	14.20	10.83	7.91	8.35	9.44	6.96	3.24	2.54	2.59	5.05	6.90	10.43	12.34	18.78	18.02	20.32
Private Firms																		
Direct Indebtedness	6.64	6.80	14.20	10.83	7.91	8.35	9.44	6.96	3.24	2.54	2.59	2.87	3.06	3.44	3.80	5.75	6.23	7.04
Stock Market	0.00	0.00	0.00	0.00	0.00	0.00	0.00	0.00	0.00	0.00	0.00	1.77	2.75	4.95	6.02	9.08	8.38	9.37
Money Market	0.00	0.00	0.00	0.00	0.00	0.00	0.00	0.00	0.00	0.00	0.00	0.41	1.09	2.04	2.53	3.95	3.42	3.91
+ Unclassified Resources, Commercial Banks	0.77	0.36	0.00	0.00	0.00	0.00	0.00	0.00	0.00	0.00	0.00	0.00	0.00	0.00	0.00	0.00	0.00	0.00
= Net Financial Wealth	7.44	11.99	17.16	20.58	20.33	10.02	36.70	38.94	29.56	25.25	19.48	12.44	4.62	3.62	-1.97	N.A.	N.A.	N.A.
Nonfinancial Public Sector																		
Resources Obtained from Banking System	18.84	22.52	34.55	30.11	25.57	28.24	33.06	26.63	22.15	20.22	15.95	12.72	7.84	4.54	5.47	7.44	6.24	8.29
+ Private Sector Holding of Public Bonds	0.75	0.76	1.71	1.49	1.78	1.69	2.40	3.64	6.54	8.50	9.17	5.38	2.52	3.58	1.88	2.10	2.95	3.26
+ Resources Obtained from Foreign Sector	8.99	11.40	23.05	21.92	21.14	24.79	40.42	40.99	22.96	19.63	16.62	14.28	14.23	13.82	15.15	N.A.	N.A.	N.A.
Net Direct Indebtedness	8.99	11.40	23.05	21.92	21.14	24.79	40.42	40.99	22.96	19.63	16.62	12.75	10.71	8.86	9.49	N.A.	N.A.	N.A.
Holding of Public Bonds	0.00	0.00	0.00	0.00	0.00	0.00	0.00	0.00	0.00	0.00	0.00	1.53	3.52	4.96	5.66	7.19	2.05	1.18
− Unclassified Resources, Commercial and Development Banks	1.37	1.86	-1.63	-1.23	-0.51	0.00	-2.41	-2.30	-1.04	0.10	1.59	2.48	2.68	2.48	2.58	N.A.	N.A.	N.A.
= (−) Net Financial Wealth	27.20	32.83	60.94	54.75	49.01	54.72	78.30	73.57	52.69	48.25	40.14	29.91	21.90	19.46	19.92	1.05	1.91	17.27

(continued)

Table 5.3 (continued)

	1980	1981	1982	1983	1984	1985	1986	1987	1988	1989	1990	1991	1992	1993	1994-III	1994	1995-III	1995
Foreign Sector																		
Net Financial Wealth, Private Sector	7.44	11.99	17.16	20.58	20.33	10.02	36.70	38.94	29.56	25.25	19.48	12.44	4.62	3.62	-1.97	N.A.	N.A.	N.A.
+ Net Financial Wealth, Nonfinancial Public Sector	-27.20	-32.83	-60.94	-54.75	-49.01	-54.72	-78.30	-73.57	-52.69	-48.25	-40.14	-29.91	-21.90	-19.46	-19.92	N.A.	N.A.	N.A.
− Unclassified Resources, Bank of Mexico	0.32	0.55	3.12	2.09	1.52	2.03	2.07	3.23	2.03	2.29	2.07	2.09	2.05	1.56	2.36	1.23	0.95	0.17
− Statistical Discrepancy	-3.33	-3.32	-6.42	-4.90	-0.79	0.00	0.00	0.00	0.00	0.00	0.00	0.00	0.00	0.00	0.00	0.00	0.00	0.00
= Net Financial Wealth, Foreign Sector	22.76	23.61	47.09	36.99	27.94	42.68	39.52	31.39	21.10	20.71	18.59	15.37	15.23	14.28	19.54	33.93	44.27	48.64
− Net Direct Indebtedness, Nonfinancial Public Sector	8.99	11.40	23.05	21.92	21.14	24.79	40.42	40.99	22.96	19.63	16.62	12.75	10.71	8.86	9.49	N.A.	N.A.	N.A.
− Net Direct Indebtedness, Private Sector	6.64	6.80	14.20	10.83	7.91	8.35	9.44	6.96	3.24	2.54	2.59	2.87	3.06	3.44	3.80	5.75	6.23	7.04
− Net Direct Indebtedness, Banking System	8.73	10.82	22.19	19.68	16.67	19.66	26.32	24.77	16.58	15.33	12.37	12.18	11.11	11.82	12.63	19.90	20.10	22.84
− Portfolio Investment	0.00	0.00	0.00	0.00	0.00	0.00	0.00	0.00	0.00	0.00	0.00	3.72	7.36	11.95	14.20	20.22	13.84	14.48
− Household Foreign Assets	2.88	6.79	17.37	17.25	14.49	6.75	31.71	32.25	18.74	13.96	9.52	11.01	12.15	16.16	16.82	N.A.	N.A.	N.A.
− Statistical Discrepancy	-3.33	-3.32	-6.42	-4.90	-0.79	0.00	0.00	0.00	0.00	0.00	0.00	0.00	0.00	0.00	0.00	0.00	0.00	0.00
= International Reserves, Bank of Mexico	2.04	1.95	1.39	3.09	4.08	3.37	4.94	9.08	2.94	2.83	3.47	5.13	4.86	5.63	3.77	2.27	4.83	5.70

N.A. Not available.

Source: Author's calculations with data from SHCP, Banco de México, and INEGI. See Calderón-Madrid (1996a).

Table 5.4 Intersectoral Real Flows of Financial Assets: 1980–95 (percentage of GDP)

	1980	1981	1982	1983	1984	1985	1986	1987	1988	1989	1990	1991	1992	1993	1994:3	1994	1995:3	1995
Banking System																		
Resources Channeled to Private Sector	6.76	1.34	-4.94	-2.21	1.65	-0.19	-1.59	0.04	1.51	4.67	3.44	5.93	6.94	5.05	4.73	10.72	-12.56	-14.42
Credit to Private Firms																		
Commercial Banks	4.48	0.66	-1.29	-1.16	0.61	-0.50	-0.72	0.10	0.50	2.98	2.20	2.93	2.62	1.70	3.09	7.47	6.64	-7.07
Development Banks	-0.27	0.09	-0.06	-0.17	0.38	0.35	0.11	0.23	0.05	0.25	-0.53	0.29	0.49	0.90	0.67	1.46	-1.14	-0.83
Credit to Households																		
Commercial Banks	3.45	0.67	-2.98	-0.80	0.59	-0.04	-0.71	-0.14	0.80	1.93	1.79	2.70	3.74	2.35	0.85	1.74	-4.73	-6.45
Development Banks	-0.91	-0.09	-0.63	-0.08	0.06	0.00	-0.28	-0.15	0.16	-0.48	-0.02	0.02	0.10	0.10	0.11	0.04	-0.05	-0.06
+ Net Credit to Nonfinancial Public Sector	0.48	5.20	11.89	-5.96	-3.49	3.32	3.71	-5.81	-4.14	-1.23	-3.39	-2.67	-4.55	-3.24	1.08	3.05	-1.76	0.29
Commercial Banks	0.43	0.91	3.72	-0.13	-0.28	2.74	2.78	-1.07	-1.85	-0.53	-0.19	0.39	-3.48	-1.44	-0.08	0.31	-0.07	-0.39
Development Banks	-0.47	2.42	5.91	-3.33	-1.60	1.67	3.15	-0.14	-5.46	-0.69	-2.19	-0.68	-0.39	0.10	0.60	3.04	-0.80	0.19
Bank of Mexico	0.52	1.87	2.26	-2.50	-1.61	-1.09	-2.22	-4.60	3.16	-0.01	-1.02	-2.38	-0.67	-1.90	0.56	-0.30	-0.89	0.49
+ International Reserves, Bank of Mexico	0.04	0.17	-0.56	1.64	1.10	-0.61	1.44	4.12	-5.91	-0.02	0.76	1.78	-0.16	0.83	-1.67	-3.17	2.39	3.26
- Unclassified Resources	20.25	0.50	-1.29	-0.70	0.18	1.04	-2.45	1.27	0.07	1.44	1.38	1.03	0.29	-0.66	1.03	-1.24	-6.02	-9.97
- Net Debt with Foreign Sector	-0.79	2.79	11.30	-3.48	-2.32	3.42	5.88	-1.06	-7.87	-0.72	-2.31	0.25	-0.74	0.78	1.21	8.48	-1.29	1.45
Commercial Banks	0.54	0.71	2.55	-0.54	-0.88	0.06	0.48	-1.90	-0.16	0.24	0.88	0.69	-0.36	0.33	0.15	2.71	-2.70	-1.98
Development Banks	-1.25	2.08	7.99	-2.92	-1.88	2.85	4.34	0.29	-6.55	-1.09	-3.28	-0.27	-0.01	0.78	1.24	5.52	-2.57	-1.24
Bank of Mexico	-0.08	0.00	0.75	-0.03	0.44	0.51	1.07	0.55	-1.16	0.13	0.09	-0.17	-0.37	-0.33	-0.17	0.25	3.98	4.67
= Resources Obtained from Private Sector	-12.18	3.41	-3.63	-2.35	1.40	-1.94	0.13	-1.86	-0.74	2.71	1.74	3.77	2.69	2.52	1.90	3.35	-4.62	-2.35

(continued)

Table 5.4 (continued)

	1980	1981	1982	1983	1984	1985	1986	1987	1988	1989	1990	1991	1992	1993	1994:3	1994	1995:3	1995
Private Sector																		
Resources Channeled to Banking System	-12.75	3.31	-3.63	-2.35	1.40	-1.94	0.13	-1.75	-0.85	2.71	1.74	3.77	2.71	2.49	1.90	3.35	-4.62	-2.35
Private Firms																		
Deposits in Commercial Banks	-2.67	0.58	-0.44	-0.50	0.63	-0.40	-0.58	-0.01	-0.77	2.60	1.70	3.14	-0.11	2.35	3.57	4.40	-1.78	-1.33
Deposits in Development Banks	-4.20	-0.52	0.11	-0.12	-0.18	0.00	-0.09	-0.13	0.06	0.10	0.23	0.19	0.22	0.36	0.15	0.28	-0.36	-0.33
Households																		
Deposits in Commercial Banks	-5.16	2.44	-2.57	-1.44	0.37	-1.66	0.63	-1.19	-0.59	0.48	0.34	0.81	2.41	-0.78	-0.98	-0.75	-1.48	-0.84
Deposits in Development Banks	-0.76	0.42	-0.28	0.00	0.32	-0.18	0.04	-0.35	0.27	-0.48	-0.33	0.04	0.57	0.65	0.36	0.20	1.02	0.42
Net Resources Channeled to Bank of Mexico																		
Private Firms	0.03	-0.05	-0.03	0.70	0.15	0.45	0.51	0.10	-0.21	-0.30	-0.35	-0.72	-0.51	-0.25	-0.89	-1.14	0.46	0.59
Currency	0.02	0.45	-0.41	-0.98	0.10	-0.15	-0.39	-0.18	0.39	0.31	0.15	0.30	0.14	0.16	-0.31	0.37	-1.48	-0.85
+ Holding of Public Bonds	0.55	0.08	0.94	-0.29	0.34	-0.04	0.65	1.29	2.95	2.17	1.03	-3.47	-2.71	1.08	-1.58	-1.36	0.69	1.00
Private Firms	0.37	0.05	0.63	-0.20	0.23	-0.04	-0.10	1.43	0.81	1.43	0.30	-1.55	-0.73	0.90	-1.34	-1.15	0.59	0.85
Households	0.18	0.03	0.31	-0.10	0.11	-0.01	0.74	-0.14	2.14	0.74	0.73	-1.92	-1.98	0.17	-0.24	-0.20	0.10	0.15
+ Foreign Assets																		
Households	3.52	4.14	10.54	-0.89	-2.16	-7.37	24.69	1.13	-13.10	-4.18	-3.84	1.83	1.44	4.10	1.21	N.A.	N.A.	N.A.
- Resources Obtained from Banking System	6.76	1.34	-4.94	-2.21	1.65	-0.19	-1.59	0.04	1.51	4.67	3.44	5.93	6.94	5.05	4.73	10.72	-12.56	-14.42
Commercial Banks	7.94	1.34	-4.26	-1.96	1.20	-0.54	-1.43	-0.04	1.30	4.91	3.99	5.62	6.36	4.04	3.95	9.22	-11.37	-13.52
Development Banks	-1.18	0.00	-0.68	-0.25	0.44	0.35	-0.16	0.08	0.21	-0.23	-0.55	0.31	0.58	1.00	0.78	1.50	-1.19	-0.90
- Resources Obtained from Foreign Sector	0.43	0.70	7.35	-3.99	-2.54	0.63	0.76	-2.30	-3.62	-0.60	0.16	2.55	1.98	3.58	2.27	8.71	-2.16	0.14
Private Firms																		
Direct Indebtedness	0.43	0.70	7.35	-3.99	-2.54	0.63	0.76	-2.30	-3.62	-0.60	0.16	0.36	0.27	0.40	0.47	2.43	0.04	0.86
Stock Market	0.00	0.00	0.00	0.00	0.00	0.00	0.00	0.00	0.00	0.00	0.00	1.77	1.02	2.22	1.24	4.30	-1.38	-0.39
Money Market	0.00	0.00	0.00	0.00	0.00	0.00	0.00	0.00	0.00	0.00	0.00	0.41	0.69	0.96	0.55	1.97	-0.83	-0.33
- Unclassified Resources, Commercial Banks	16.64	-0.34	-0.36	2.67	0.47	-9.80	26.29	2.93	-8.89	-3.37	-4.68	-6.36	-7.49	-0.96	-5.47	N.A.	N.A.	N.A.
= Net Financial Wealth	0.78	5.15	5.09															

(continued)

Table 5.4 (continued)

	1980	1981	1982	1983	1984	1985	1986	1987	1988	1989	1990	1991	1992	1993	1994:3	1994	1995:3	1995
Nonfinancial Public Sector																		
Resources Obtained from Banking System	-0.76	5.20	11.89	-5.96	-3.49	3.32	3.71	-5.81	-4.14	-1.23	-3.39	-2.67	-4.55	-3.24	1.08	3.05	-1.76	0.29
+ Private Sector Holding of Public Bonds	0.55	0.08	0.94	-0.29	0.34	-0.04	0.65	1.29	2.95	2.17	1.03	-3.47	-2.71	1.08	-1.58	-1.36	0.69	1.00
+ Resources Obtained from Foreign Sector	-0.51	3.14	11.58	-2.14	-0.01	4.18	14.66	1.33	-17.51	-2.59	-2.16	-1.75	0.33	-0.31	1.80	N.A.	N.A.	N.A.
Net Direct Indebtedness	-0.51	3.14	11.58	-2.14	-0.01	4.18	14.66	1.33	-17.51	-2.59	-2.16	-3.28	-1.70	-1.77	0.93	N.A.	N.A.	N.A.
Holding of Public Bonds	0.00	0.00	0.00	0.00	0.00	0.00	0.00	0.00	0.00	0.00	0.00	1.53	2.03	1.46	0.87	2.40	-5.67	-6.54
− Unclassified Resources, Commercial and Development Banks	4.23	0.60	-3.86	0.47	0.67	0.50	-2.41	0.07	1.23	1.11	1.50	0.94	0.27	-0.19	0.19	N.A.	N.A.	N.A.
= (−) Net Financial Wealth	-4.95	7.82	28.27	-8.86	-3.84	6.96	21.43	-3.26	-19.93	-2.76	-6.02	-8.83	-7.20	-2.29	1.12	-17.76	0.78	16.08
Foreign Sector																		
Net Financial Wealth, Private Sector	0.78	5.15	5.09	2.67	0.47	-9.80	26.29	2.93	-8.89	-3.37	-4.68	-6.31	-7.49	-0.96	-5.47	N.A.	N.A.	N.A.
+ Net Financial Wealth, Nonfinancial Public Sector	4.95	-7.82	-27.91	8.86	3.84	-6.96	-21.43	3.26	19.93	2.76	6.02	8.83	7.20	2.29	-1.12	N.A.	N.A.	N.A.
− Unclassified Resources, Bank of Mexico	-0.62	0.25	2.57	-1.17	-0.49	0.54	-0.04	1.20	-1.16	0.33	-0.12	0.09	0.01	-0.47	0.85	-0.28	-0.36	-1.15
− Statistical Discrepancy	-3.33	-0.26	-3.08	1.80	3.94	0.77	0.00	0.00	0.00	0.00	0.00	0.00	0.00	0.00	0.00	0.00	0.00	0.00
= Net Financial Wealth, Foreign Sector	-1.78	2.68	23.33	-12.16	-7.76	15.44	-4.82	-7.39	-9.89	0.28	-1.22	-2.61	0.27	-0.85	5.74	20.14	7.81	12.18
− Net Direct Indebtedness, Nonfinancial Public Sector	-0.51	3.14	11.58	-2.14	-0.01	4.18	14.66	1.33	-17.51	-2.59	-2.16	-3.28	-1.70	-1.77	0.93	N.A.	N.A.	N.A.
− Net Direct Indebtedness, Private Sector	0.43	0.70	7.35	-3.99	-2.54	0.63	0.76	-2.30	-3.62	-0.60	0.16	0.36	0.27	0.40	0.47	2.43	0.04	0.86
− Net Direct Indebtedness, Banking System	-0.79	2.79	11.30	-3.48	-2.32	3.42	5.88	-1.06	-7.87	-0.72	-2.31	0.25	-0.74	0.78	1.21	8.48	-1.29	1.45
− Portfolio Investment	0.00	0.00	0.00	0.00	0.00	0.00	0.00	0.00	0.00	0.00	0.00	3.72	3.74	4.64	2.66	8.67	-7.88	-7.26
− Household Foreign Assets	3.52	4.14	10.54	-0.89	-2.16	-7.37	24.69	1.13	-13.10	-4.18	-3.84	1.83	1.44	4.10	1.21	N.A.	N.A.	N.A.
− Statistical Discrepancy	-3.33	-0.26	-3.08	1.80	3.94	0.77	0.00	0.00	0.00	0.00	0.00	0.00	0.00	0.00	0.00	0.00	0.00	0.00
= International Reserves, Bank of Mexico	0.72	0.07	-0.56	1.64	1.10	-0.61	1.44	4.23	-6.02	-0.02	0.76	1.83	-0.13	0.81	-1.67	-3.17	2.39	3.26

N.A. Not available.

Source: Author's calculations with data from SHCP, Banco de México, and INEGI. See Calderón–Madrid (1996a).

Changes in the Composition of Private Saving between Companies and Households

Table 5.5 breaks down private sector saving into its two main components: saving by households and undistributed corporate earnings. These flows are related to the corresponding notions of financial wealth for the two sectors, as it is represented in Table 5.4. Private investment expenditure of companies (net of foreign direct investment) was financed by a combination of four sources: changes in the net debtor position of the companies with the banking system; a decline in holdings of government bonds; a net increase in foreign indebtedness; and the retention of profits generated during the year. With data on investment expenditure taken from the national accounts, and with the figures corresponding to the first three concepts obtained from our matrices of financial assets and flows, one can derive retained earnings. A corresponding identity for households allows their level of saving to be calculated as net accumulation of financial assets during the year plus investment in housing construction.

Unfortunately, lack of information on the proportion of domestic saving generated by Mexican companies limits our ability to resolve disagreements about appropriate policies to raise private saving in Mexico. For example, some authors assume that the contribution of households to total saving has little relevance, and they suggest that economic policy should be directed primarily at stimulating saving by companies, which supposedly make the largest contribution to private saving in Mexico (see, for example, García Alba, 1996). Others attribute little importance to the potential for growth in saving generated by companies and suggest that policies directed at encouraging saving among households—such as pension reform—will in time resolve the problem of low saving.[9]

Results obtained in this study help to quantify the important role played by retained corporate earnings in generating private saving in the eight years

---

[9] For an analysis of the importance of changes in the pension system in Mexico see Sales, Solís, and Villagómez (1996). For these authors, for example, the reforms will increase private saving by more than 2 percentage points of GDP in five years, making it possible for changes in the pension system to generate directly almost 25 percent of the required additional investment, in accordance with the National Development Plan, to achieve growth in GDP of 5 percent annually.

Table 5.5 Real Private Saving, Net of Inflation Tax: 1987–94 (percentage of GDP)

Year	Individuals	Companies	Total
1987	3.5	4.6	8.2
1988	6.3	7.6	13.8
1989	4.4	7.3	11.7
1990	4.1	4.6	8.7
1991	1.3	4.8	6.1
1992	1.8	5.5	7.3
1993	2.4	7.1	9.5
1994	2.8	7.4	10.1

Note: Total saving refers to adjusted savings as in table 5.1B. Figures may not sum to totals because of rounding.
Source: Author's calculations using Banco de México and INEGI data.

prior to the 1994 crisis. Table 5.5 confirms that during this period a large part of private saving was generated by companies. The table shows that, with the exception of 1990, the drop in private saving was caused by changes in the behavior of households. Saving by households went from accounting for roughly half of private saving in 1988 to accounting for little more than one fifth in 1991. The drop of 5 percentage points in the total private saving–GDP ratio from 1988 to 1991 is explained to a great extent by reduced saving among households. The results also indicate that an increase in private saving of more than 2 percentage points of GDP in 1993 was mainly due to higher corporate saving.

Estimates of saving by companies for 1990 and 1991 show, unlike in the other years analyzed, a reduction of more than 2 percentage points of GDP from the preceding two years, which is of particular interest and requires further analysis. This raises the question whether this result is due to an increase in the proportion of profits distributed by companies to their shareholders or to an overall drop in corporate earnings. If the latter, what changes led to the fall in retained earnings?

The fact that the Mexican economy grew faster in 1990 and 1991 than in 1988 and 1989, together with the drop in interest rates and the increase in stock prices, suggests that the rate of real growth in corporate profits probably exceeded that of GDP growth. For this reason, compared with the two previous years, the share of corporate profits, before distribution, in GDP should not have fallen after 1989.[10]

Data from the national accounts support this conjecture: retained earnings attributable to the private sector were a larger share of GDP in 1990–91 than in 1988–89. In addition, as a result of the acceleration in privatizations initiated in 1991, the share of publicly owned enterprises in GDP fell by more than 2 percentage points from its 1990 level, which suggests greater participation by privately owned companies. During 1990 and 1991, real GDP posted its fastest growth in 10 years; investment by private companies grew 13 percent in each of these two years.[11] This information, together with the analytical predictions of economic models that explain profit retention by companies, leads one to expect a larger proportion of retained earnings during these years than depicted in the results presented here.[12] One possible answer is that the tax system was changed to encourage the paying out of earnings.

Corporate Saving and Changes in the Tax System

In 1989, the tax code was revised to facilitate the flow of profits from companies to shareholders. Beginning in that year, dividends could be distributed without creating an additional tax burden for shareholders as long as taxes had already been paid by the company. These changes made it possible

---

[10] The tax burden arising from payment of corporate income tax in these years was less than in 1989. If private profits did not fall in 1990 and 1991, one would expect that this would be reflected in tax payments. Why were more taxes not collected? It may be that the growth in investment indicated previously is part of the explanation, since as a result of tax changes aimed at encouraging investment, it was possible to deduct a higher percentage of new investment. In 1987 a substantive change was made in the corporate income tax: the tax rate was lowered from 42 percent to 35 percent, and an inflation adjustment was introduced, which eliminated serious distortions. In 1989 a tax on corporate assets was introduced at a rate of 2 percent by value, which constituted a minimum income tax payment. This tax arose in response to the large number of zero income tax declarations, and as a complement to the income tax, it has served as a disincentive to tax evasion. See Sadka and Tanzi (1992).

[11] This was the fastest rate of growth since 1982; the rate in 1989 was only 7.5 percent.

[12] One model to explain how retained earnings are determined, which has received a lot of attention, is that of Fazzari, Hubbard, and Peterson (1988). This model was recently used by Agosin et al. (1996) to explain the increase in private saving in Chile.

to avoid paying the 55 percent tax on distributed dividends. Prior to 1989, profits generated in a given year and distributed in the following year, when no profits were generated, had been subject to double taxation: the corporate rate was 42 percent and the household had a top individual rate of 55 percent. The tax on distributed profits thus could reach 73.9 percent. This was seen as creating a disincentive to the distribution of dividends. In 1989, in addition to eliminating this double taxation, corporate and household tax rates were lowered to 35 percent.

These changes in the tax structure were designed to allow shareholders to receive a larger share of profits, which they could then channel toward investments in other firms. If this goal had been achieved, the increase in distributed profits in 1990–91 would have made it possible to cover the financial needs of other companies through the purchase of corporate stocks and bonds. This in turn would have meant that, in the aggregate, reinvested corporate earnings would not have been lower than in other years. This would imply that there were financial flows not recorded by our calculations, and that Table 5.5 underestimates the reinvestment of earnings in the aggregate.[13] However, available data on financial intermediation through the stock market refute this possibility.

Although it may be difficult to identify the net financing that private companies in fact received through the stock market,[14] available statistical information does indicate that *net* financing derived from the stock market was no greater than 1.7 percent of GDP during 1991 (Mexican Stock Exchange, 1992, p. 25). Another 1.25 percent of GDP may be added to this figure owing to new placements by Mexican firms abroad.

When all of these data are compared with data on external financing of Mexican firms registered on the stock exchange[15] and, exclusively through

---

[13] In the breakdown of private saving presented here, it is not possible to capture the purchase and sale of stocks and direct investment that individuals have made in companies, if these transactions were not recorded using the formal financial intermediation system.

[14] This is due to the difficulty in isolating variations in stock prices and changes in net issues by companies that participate in the stock market (which, furthermore, are not constant in number) from changes in the value of the stock market.

[15] That is, when compared with the $6.3 billion (equivalent to 2.1 percent of GDP in that year) that, according to the capital account of the balance of payments, was invested by foreigners in the Mexican stock exchange, plus $1.1 billion that entered the country through the acquisition of bonds issued in foreign currency by the private sector.

the Mexican stock market, the net flow of funds from abroad into the stock market in Mexico in 1991 was greater than the net financing obtained by Mexican companies through the Mexican stock market to finance their investment. That is, in 1991, Mexicans who held stocks and bonds traded on the stock market became net sellers to foreign investors.[16] This dismisses the hypothesis that a greater distribution of corporate profits to shareholders led them to increase their financing of companies registered on the stock exchange.

These considerations make it impossible to rule out the possibility that the increase in the distribution of earnings by companies fueled spending on consumer goods and real estate. These expenditures were not necessarily made by the shareholders themselves: the distributions could have been deposited in the financial system and from there channeled to greater spending by the public in general, which would imply an overall drop in saving by households.[17]

Time-Series Analysis of the Behavior of Consumption, Saving, and Private Disposable Income

Table 5.6 shows that the 10 years prior to the 1994–95 crisis were characterized by important differences in the trends in income and expenditure in the private sector from one subperiod to another. To place the boom in private consumption spending in context, particularly that for the 1989–92 period,[18] one must look first at the change in the prospects for sustained growth. Beginning in 1989, a series of events seemed to point to a better economic future for Mexicans and a reduction in the uncertainty of future

---

[16] In 1990 the extraordinary amounts of revenue that flowed to the public sector through the sale of banks and state enterprises did not exceed half of 1 percentage point of GDP. In contrast, in 1991 this revenue rose to almost 3 percentage points of GDP. The calculations of private saving presented in Tables 5.1 and 5.5 are consistent with an (offsetting) operational surplus that excludes revenue from privatizations. The corresponding analysis including the latter would require the appropriate adjustments.

[17] In contrast to this hypothesis, Oks and Arrau (1992) suggest that the private sector has a very high marginal propensity to save income generated by interest. In that case the elevated level of saving in 1988–89 and its subsequent drop are explained to a great extent by the behavior exhibited by the domestic service of the public debt.

[18] For a macroeconomic analysis of the administration of President Carlos Salinas, see Calderón-Madrid (1997).

Table 5.6 Private Sector Income, Expenditure, and Saving: 1983–94 (percent)

	1983	1984–85	1986–87	1988	1989–92	1993–94
	Real Rates of Growth for the Period					
GDP	–4.2	6.1	–1.8	1.3	15	4.2
Private Disposable Income[a]	–0.38	3	–8.6	8.6	10	6.7
Private Saving	24.29	–10.4	–32.9	52.8	–48.7	39
Private Consumption:						
Total	–5.36	6.6	–2.7	1.8	23.5	3.9
Durable Goods	–22.1	19	–18.2	8.8	35	–3.4
Nondurable Goods	–3.3	7.1	–2.6	–0.3	22	3.6
Services	0.3	–0.2	4.5	2	19	4.8
	Shares (Average for the Period)					
Private Disposable Income (PDI) as Share of GDP[a]	78.7	74.9	73.0	76.7	73.6	75.1
Private Saving as Share of PDI[a]	20.9	17.0	14.3	18.7	10.6	11.3
Consumption of Durable Goods as Share of PDI[a]	7.5	8.5	8.0	7.8	9.0	8.7

a. Net of inflation tax.

income levels.[19] One of these events was the relatively successful renegotiation of the external debt, in keeping with the Brady Plan, and, after two recessionary adjustment programs agreed upon with the IMF, the advent of a period in which growth was encouraged. A second event was the control of inflation, which, after surpassing 100 percent in 1987, fell to 50 percent during 1988, the first year of the heterodox adjustment program. Inflation continued to fall steadily thereafter, to less than 15 percent by 1992. A third

---

[19] Carroll (1992 and 1994) and Hubbard, Skinner, and Zeldes (1994) set forth the relationship between private saving and the level of uncertainty with respect to expected income.

Figure 5.4
Open Unemployment Rate: 1985–95

event was the reduction in balance of payments pressures, reflected both in a drop in the real interest rate and in a reversal of expectations regarding the possibility of using the exchange rate as a nominal anchor. The latter can be deduced from the expected devaluation implicit in the interest rate differential between bonds denominated in pesos and the dollar-denominated bonds issued by the Mexican government. A fourth event was the return of Mexican companies to international capital markets, where they were able to obtain financing on very favorable terms,[20] and the accompanying massive entry of capital (see Krugman 1995). A fifth event was the resumption of real GDP growth, which amounted to 16 percent between 1987 and 1992, a period during which the population grew by only 10 percent. Figure 5.4 shows trends in the open unemployment rate,[21] which reflect these changes.

The positive growth rates of GDP per capita recorded beginning in 1988 are rather modest, but they should be seen in light of the economic

---

[20] According to some authors, this constituted such a huge inflow that it was capable of providing funds to cover beyond the next five years. See Mansell Carstens (1994).

[21] The figure shows the so-called alternative open unemployment rate. This indicator includes both the openly unemployed and the disguised unemployed (those who have stopped looking for work because they do not believe there is work for them) as well as those who say they are not working currently but already have a job lined up, which they will begin within one month at the most.

stagnation between 1983 and 1986. Furthermore, the turnaround in economic growth led to a widespread expectation of sustained growth in national income, especially after the announcement of the signing of the North American Free Trade Agreement (NAFTA) as well as Mexico's acceptance into the OECD.

To place the low level of saving of the early 1990s in context, consider also the changes in the value of private sector wealth and the associated effects of financial deregulation at the end of the 1980s. In 1988 a boom in the stock market underscored the optimism surrounding Mexico's economic prospects and produced one of the highest cumulative real rates of return in the world. The stock market boom had important effects on wealth; the impact was limited, however, by the small number of shareholders in the country. In contrast, a significant segment of the population—homeowners—did benefit from the boom in real estate prices beginning in 1988 (Figure 5.5).

The sustained increase in real housing values as a percentage of private disposable income between 1988 and 1994 contrasts with the evidence in Figure 5.6, which shows net financial wealth of households as a percentage of private disposable income. The drop in this measure was basically determined by the increase in credit granted by the commercial banking system. This faster extension of credit, in turn, was associated with the radical financial deregulation begun in 1988, and with the reduction in obliga-

Figure 5.5
Real Annual Appreciation of Real Estate: 1986–95

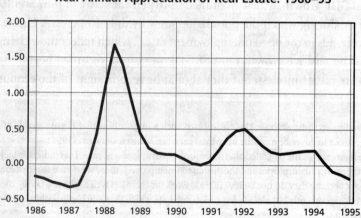

Figure 5.6
Net Private Financial Wealth: 1985–95
(thousands of constant pesos)

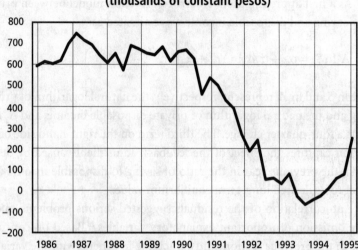

tory reserve ratios for banks, the elimination of interest rate caps, and other initiatives such as the reprivatization of state-owned banks. Changes in these variables play an important role in estimating a private saving function for Mexico.[22]

This study benefited from the availability of quarterly data on private saving in Mexico[23] and its main determinants for a sufficiently long period (from the fourth quarter of 1986 to the fourth quarter of 1995) to conduct an econometric time-series analysis. This analysis establishes and quantifies what caused the drop in private saving during the years prior to the 1994 crisis. A model was constructed that follows closely that used by Muellbauer (1994) to study the consumption boom in England in both analytical and empirical terms. Other authors have employed the same

---

[22] A brief description of the work done to estimate saving functions in Mexico is found in Villagómez (1993).

[23] These were constructed using operational surplus data from the public sector (net of the inflationary component of the debt), calculated for each of these periods. With these data, data on the current account and private investment, and an estimate of the inflation tax, it was possible to calculate saving in real terms.

method to analyze declines in saving in Australia and the Scandinavian countries. Some modifications have been made to adapt it to the Mexican case.

As a first approximation, an error-correction model between private sector saving and disposable income was estimated as:[24]

$$\Delta_4 \ln S_t = \alpha_0 + \alpha_1 \Delta_4 \ln Yd_t + \alpha_2 \left(\ln S_{t-4} - \ln Yd_{t-4} \right)$$

where $\ln S$ and $\ln Yd$ represent, respectively, the natural logarithm of private saving and the natural logarithm of private disposable income, and Δ_4 represents a four-quarter change. The third term on the right-hand side of the equation captures the effect of the feedback adjustment caused by deviations in the previous year in the ratio of saving to disposable income with respect to its desired long-term equilibrium value.

Autocorrelation of the residuals suggested serious problems caused by the omission of important explanatory variables.[25] Based on considerations in the previous section, and coinciding in general with the variables incorporated by the authors mentioned above, a revised model was estimated that included additional variables.[26]

To capture the prospects for economic growth and the uncertainty associated with income expectations, the open unemployment rate, *DES*, was introduced into the equation. The sign of the regression coefficient for this variable would be expected to be positive.

Under the hypothesis that, as a result of financial deregulation, property owners could use their real estate as collateral to obtain consumer credit, a second variable, the value of housing as a proportion of disposable income (*VIV/Yd*), was introduced. This variable was incorporated both directly and as multiplied by a binary variable, D_1, which takes the value 0 for dates prior to the first quarter of 1990 and 1 for subsequent dates.

---

[24] For a pioneering work in this type of estimation see Davidson et al. (1981).

[25] This suspicion was confirmed using the Cochrane-Orcutt method in estimating and obtaining a substantial improvement in the R^2 goodness-of-fit measure, from 0.60 to 0.90.

[26] After verifying that the time series corresponding to saving and private disposable income are integrated on the first order, the existence of a cointegral relationship was established. As is well known, a cointegral relationship implies a long-term relationship in terms of proportionality of the variables involved and the possibility of approximating an error-correction model. For a discussion of the long-term properties implied by an error-correction model, see Hendry et al. (1984).

To proxy for net financial wealth, a variable representing the proportion of private disposable income represented by total liquid assets (L) was added: these assets include money and government bonds held by households plus their net credit position with the commercial banking system. To capture explicitly the wealth effects associated with the boom in housing prices, a variable representing capital gains from the changes in real prices of housing, as a proportion of private disposable income (V/Yd), was included as well. Other variables that may have also affected private saving, including the interest rate and certain variables associated with the stock market boom, were included but were found not to have a significant impact.

The results of the estimation are as follows:

$$\ln S_t - \ln S_{t-4} = 0.535 + 4.203\left(\ln Yd_t - \ln Yd_{t-4}\right)$$
$$(4.014)\ (9.559)$$

$$-0.258\ln\left(S_{t-4} - \ln Yd_{t-4}\right) - 0.002\left(V\right)Yd_t$$
$$(-2.959)(3.841)$$

$$+0.086\,DES_t - 0.017\,VIV_{t-1}\left(Yd_t\right)$$
$$(4.402)(-0.149)$$

$$-2.319\,L_{t-1}\left(Yd_t\right) - 0.205\,D_t VIV_{t-1}\left(Yd_t\right)$$
$$(-4.861)(-2.219)$$

$$R^2 = 0.928 \quad (DW) = 1.85 \quad Q(9-0) = 7.175$$

Only one of the regressors in the final equation, housing value as a proportion of disposable income, failed to reach statistical significance. However, when this variable was multiplied by the binary variable that was set at zero prior to 1990, the resulting variable was significant at a confidence level of 5 percent. Its negative sign indicates that the ability of owners of real estate to increase their borrowing reduces saving.

Even if not all of the coefficients of the explanatory variables fall in the expected ranges, they do have the appropriate signs. In particular, the coefficient for the growth rate of disposable income rose with the inclusion of more variables. This may have happened because expectations of economic growth and the reduction in the level of uncertainty related to expected income levels were captured by inclusion of the open unemployment rate. In turn, capital gains associated with the increase in housing values did have a wealth effect on the drop in private saving.

Other regressions were estimated in an attempt to improve the goodness of fit and/or improve our understanding of the factors that determine the behavior of private saving. In a first exercise, the net wealth variable was disaggregated into gross assets and gross credit received. However, in this estimation, no significant statistical difference between the coefficients of these two components of net financial wealth was identified. This indicates that gross credit granted by the banking system to households has an explanatory capacity, given that it is part of net wealth and not a proxy for financial deregulation.

The real interest rate variable, when included in the equation, did not reach statistical significance. The same result was obtained when stock market indicators were included, either in the form of a variable representing total real market capitalization or in the form of a variable representing appreciation in stock prices as a proportion of disposable income.

Incorporating other regressors led to rejection of the hypothesis of a structural change in the relationship between the growth rates of saving and of disposable income. A variable constructed by multiplying the annual growth rate of disposable income by the binary variable D_1 did not turn out to be significant when added to the equation.

Cross-Sectional Analysis of Saving Behavior

The types of analysis used in the previous section do not allow an assessment of the importance of certain possible determinants of private saving, most of them suggested by microeconomic models of consumer behavior. Among these are the level of formal education of the head of household, his or her age, the number of minors under 12 years of age in the household, and other demographic variables. To include these determinants, a cross-sectional analysis was conducted based on data collected by the INEGI in its national surveys of household income and expenditures for 1989, 1992, and 1994.

Of particular interest for this study is whether the survey respondent owns the home in which he or she lives, and if so (if the house has not been paid for in full), whether the respondent carries a mortgage. It is also possible to discern from other responses to these surveys whether the respondent has a credit card and access to credit other than a mortgage. This information is required to complement the results on the importance of real estate after 1990, in the context of the abundance of credit available to households in 1992 and, to a lesser extent, in 1994.

In addition to assessing the importance that financial deregulation and greater availability of credit have in determining the fall in savings, consider if, as Bayoumi suggests (1993), financial deregulation has temporary effects in the initial periods, when restrictions to access to credit are relaxed, i.e., if the effects registered in 1992 are more important than those in 1994.

A hypothesis widely held by most studies dealing with the fall in saving is that this was associated with the price boom, since homeowners adjusted upward the estimated value of their wealth, acting as if the windfall increase was permanent. In spite of the plausibility of this hypothesis it is not possible to state, a priori, that aggregate private saving falls when the value of real estate increases. This is because those who do not own a house—generally the younger ones—will reduce their expenditure, relative to income, so as to count in the future on the resources needed to buy one. The hypothesis to be considered is whether the boom in real estate prices affected the saving decisions of homeowners differently from those not owning their home.

Data from these surveys were obtained with the aim of nationwide coverage, in which the households surveyed were representative of different socioeconomic strata. As the three surveys conducted were comparable to one another, the characteristics of economic agents who in 1992—and to a lesser extent in 1994—reduced their saving with respect to 1989 levels may be inferred.[27]

The analysis here is focused exclusively on households in the upper four deciles of the national income distribution. These households receive

---

[27] Household saving was calculated as the difference between income flows and expenditure on consumer goods. Although the data on current monetary income and current monetary expenditure necessary for calculating saving do not require modification to make the surveys comparable, data referring to household access to types of credit other than mortgages (credit card and other lending) require greater disaggregation for comparison. Excluded from the analysis were all current sources of income that were not compatible with national accounting, such as the sale of automobiles and second-hand durable consumer goods. An alternative way of calculating household saving is to use net changes in physical and financial assets held by households, but this method did not yield suitable results, since the survey does not register changes in the ownership of housing by households.

more than 74 percent of the country's total monetary income and, as indicated in Table 5.7, account for the bulk of saving identified as the aggregate of macroeconomic interest.[28] These households are more likely to have access to the formal credit market and be able to purchase housing with mortgage credit, two variables of particular importance for this analysis.

To extract the systematic regularities in this data set, regressions were estimated adding explanatory variables to the following function:

$$S/Y = \exp(\alpha_1 D_1 + \alpha_2 D_2 + \alpha_3 D_3)Y^{\beta}$$

For each household, S represents current monetary saving; Y represents current monetary income; exp indicates an exponential function; and D_1, D_2, and D_3, are dummy variables representing, respectively, home ownership (0 if not a homeowner and 1 if a homeowner), access to consumer credit (1 if the household has access and 0 if not), and level of formal education (0 for a head of household with no education, 1 for primary school, 2 for middle school, 3 for high school, and 4 for university or postgraduate level).

Other explanatory variables included are age, the number of income earners in the household, number of minors under 12, and size of the household.

The results obtained for the dummy coefficients in the regressions are presented in Table 5.8.

To consider the extent to which aggregate saving becomes more sensitive to such factors as wealth and the real interest rate, a set of regressions that explicitly separates homeowners from nonhomeowners was also estimated. This was achieved not by assigning a dummy value of 1 to homeowners, but rather by including as a variable the value that, as a percentage of income, the household surveyed declared in response to the question, What is the estimated amount to lease your house? For nonhomeowners this variable is set at zero.

---

[28] This stylized fact of the Mexican economy was highlighted previously by the consulting firm Grupo de Economistas y Asociados, which indicates in one of its reports that "increasing domestic savings is difficult, when one considers the fact that according to the 1992 Household Income-Expenditures Survey, only 40 percent of the population (the four deciles with the highest incomes) saved a part of their income."

Table 5.7 Income, Lease Value of Home, and Saving by Population Decile

Population Decile by Income	Current Monetary Income (Percentage of Total, Cumulative)	Lease Value of Home as a Percentage of Current Monetary Income	Saving as a Percentage of Current Monetary Income
1989			
First (lowest)	1.42	21.57	−55.55
Second	4.11	19.43	−33.58
Third	7.79	19.42	−12.74
Fourth	12.52	20.64	−5.58
Fifth	18.42	20.27	0.20
Sixth	25.73	21.11	2.58
Seventh	34.94	20.30	4.20
Eighth	46.31	21.65	8.26
Ninth	61.98	22.21	16.55
Tenth (highest)	100.00	22.63	30.47
1992			
First (lowest)	1.28	33.48	−39.84
Second	3.80	27.78	−20.11
Third	7.36	25.08	−11.47
Fourth	12.01	24.27	−2.59
Fifth	17.52	26.23	−5.44
Sixth	24.59	24.63	2.90
Seventh	33.28	25.62	8.94
Eighth	44.43	25.96	8.80
Ninth	60.25	26.63	15.13
Tenth (highest)	100.00	22.86	30.68
1994			
First (lowest)	1.28	35.52	−37.52
Second	3.83	26.30	−6.36
Third	7.32	27.61	−4.77
Fourth	11.80	27.42	1.32
Fifth	17.32	26.75	0.68
Sixth	24.14	26.70	7.91
Seventh	32.42	28.45	8.21
Eighth	43.59	26.87	17.19
Ninth	59.64	25.38	18.74
Tenth (highest)	100.00	23.16	31.08

Source: INEGI–SPP, *National Household Income and Expenditures Survey,* 1989 (ENIGH–89); and INEGI, *National Household Income and Expenditures Survey,* 1992 (ENIGH–92) and 1994 (ENIGH–94).

Table 5.8. Regression Coefficients for Dummy Variables Representing Homeownership (α_1), Access to Consumer Credit (α_2), and Level of Formal Education (α_3)

Year	α_1	α_2	α_3
1989	0.0	−0.24	−0.08
1992	−0.24	−0.16	−0.17
1994	−0.16	−0.18	−0.13

Source: Author's calculations.

Homeownership and Access to Credit as Determinants of the Drop in Saving

When housing value was included in the time-series econometric model presented in the previous section, this variable did not constitute a determining factor in the behavior of private saving for the years before 1990. Beginning in the first quarter of 1990, however, it did. This conclusion is also inferred from the cross-sectional regressions.

As the results in Table 5.8 show, the α_1 parameter corresponding to 1989 was indistinguishable from zero, whereas that for 1992 equaled −0.24: in contrast to what happened in 1989, owning the home in which the person lived affected significantly the decision to save in 1992 and, to a lesser extent, in 1994.

One explanation for this result is that the wealth effect associated with the real estate price boom registered prior to 1994 was not considered to be of a transitory nature.

Also compatible with these results is that, in the context of financial deregulation and greater availability of credit after 1990, it was property owners who, using their real estate as collateral, decided to increase their consumption, in view of windfall capital gains in real estate: adding the effects of the parameters α_1 and α_2 —having a property and access to credit— represents a more important effect in 1992 than in 1989.

It is noteworthy that the value of α_1 falls in 1994, relative to 1992, indicating that, as Bayoumi suggests (1993), financial deregulation has temporary effects in the initial periods, when restrictions on access to credit are relaxed.

The results suggest that in 1992, unlike in 1989, two people with identical access to credit, level of income, and level of formal education saved different amounts if one was a homeowner and the other was not. The nonhomeowner saved 27 percent more in 1992, but only 17 percent more in 1994.

The previous section referred to the boom in property prices that occurred before 1992 in Mexico. Such a boom took place in England in the 1980s, and just as in the disputes that arose in the analysis of its impact on consumption, the increase in housing values was not necessarily the most significant explanation of the reduction in saving. As King (1990, commenting on the work of Muellbauer) and Attanasio and Weber (1994) indicate, as a consequence of the boom in housing prices, "there will be households (probably the youngest) who will believe it necessary to reduce their consumption of goods other than housing services, with the aim of saving to acquire housing in the future" (Attanasio and Weber, 1994, p. 1270).

The results for Mexico indicate that these observations are relevant. Although variables such as the age of the household head were not significant when included as regressors, the data in Table 5.9 are nonetheless of interest.[29]

Educational Level and Expectations of Higher Future Income and Less Uncertainty

The drop in saving in 1992 corresponds not only to more widespread homeownership and access to credit but also to an increase in the value attached to having human capital, captured in our regressions by the educational level of the head of household. Thus, dissavers were those who, owing to their level of formal education, anticipated not only higher income but also a lower risk of losing their jobs. This suggests an alternative hypothesis for explaining the consumption boom. As Table 5.10 shows, based on the α_2 values in Table 5.8, expectations of higher future income and less uncertainty had an inverse effect on present savings. These results clearly indicate

---

[29] As Bosworth, Burtless, and Sabelhaus (1991) found, there were large discrepancies in the percentages of household saving at the individual level, which may be due both to real variability in the population and to difficulties in administering the survey and the reliability of the answers given. This problem was reduced by using only the average saving rates of specific socioeconomic groups.

Table 5.9. Saving Rate by Age of Household Head, Homeownership, and Access to Nonmortgage Credit

Ownership Status and Year	Age of Head of Household (years)				
	25–34	35–44	45–54	55–64	Over 65
Own Home, Have Access to Credit					
1989	–0.25	–0.04	–0.02	0.18	0.17
1992	0.03	–0.03	0.07	0.17	–0.01
1994	0.01	–0.03	0.07	0.13	0.11
Own Home, Lack Access to Credit					
1989	0.14	0.11	0.15	0.19	0.17
1992	0.10	0.10	0.16	0.22	0.23
1994	0.13	0.12	0.17	0.19	0.23
Do Not Own Home, Have Access to Credit					
1989	0.00	–0.19	0.07	0.07	0.20
1992	–0.10	–0.11	0.03	0.21	0.08
1994	0.09	0.09	0.14	0.21	0.24
Do Not Own Home, Lack Access to Credit					
1989	0.10	0.07	0.07	0.12	0.07
1992	0.12	0.13	0.16	0.26	0.29
1994	0.13	0.11	0.14	0.23	0.24

Source: Author's calculations based on data from ENIGH–89, ENIGH–92, and ENIGH–94.

Table 5.10. Saving among Persons without a Professional Education, as a Ratio to Saving among Persons with a Professional Education

Year	Level of Education			
	None	Primary	Secondary	University
1989	1.38	1.27	1.17	1.08
1992	2.00	1.67	1.41	1.19
1994	1.68	1.48	1.30	1.14

Source: Author's calculations.

Table 5.11. Saving Rate by Age of Household Head and Level of Education

| Education Level and Year | Age of Head of Household (years) | | | | |
	25–34	35–44	45–54	55–64	Over 65
Basic Education					
1989	0.14	0.09	0.13	0.19	0.17
1992	0.10	0.09	0.15	0.24	0.22
1994	0.10	0.10	0.15	0.19	0.23
Middle-School Education					
1989	–0.01	0.01	0.05	0.02	0.09
1992	0.00	–0.11	0.10	0.11	0.08
1994	0.08	0.02	0.08	0.25	0.15
Higher Education					
1989	0.05	0.03	0.11	0.11	0.11
1992	0.05	0.04	0.09	0.06	0.12
1994	0.11	0.08	0.15	0.13	0.23

Source: Author's calculations based on data from ENIGH-89, ENIGH-92, and ENIGH-94.

that in 1992, economic agents saved substantially less when they had more formal education.

In addition, young heads of household (those 25–44 years of age) were found to save at a lower rate than heads of household between 45 and 64. Heads of household with lower levels of education compensated for their lack of formal education with higher saving rates (Table 5.11).

These results, together with those in Table 5.9, indicate that the age structure of the population is an important determinant of saving. Households where the head is between 35 and 64 years of age save on average more than do those with heads between the ages of 25 and 34. However, there is no evidence in the sample analyzed for the Mexican case that savings accumulated during a person's working life are consumed at a faster pace during old age;[30] that is, there is no drop in the saving rate among people older than 65 compared with younger groups.

---

[30] The fact that older people save more may be explained by the inheritance motive: the well-being of younger generations is an argument in the utility function of the parents, so that saving in old age is not irrational behavior.

Results of the Regressions

The saving function to be estimated was specified as follows:

$$\ln S = \alpha_0 + \alpha_1 \ln TCMI + \alpha_2 DVIV + \alpha_3 CREDIT + \alpha_4 EFJ$$

$$+ \alpha_5 HS + \alpha_6 NE + \alpha_7 EFJ + \alpha_8 HS + \alpha_9 NE + \alpha_{10} DEi.$$

The variable $TCMI$ is total current monetary income (see Calderón-Madrid, 1999, for further descriptions of the variables). $DVIV$ is a dummy variable that acquires the value of 1 if the household surveyed is a homeowner and belongs to the category "house and land paid in full" and 0 otherwise. The access to credit variable ($CREDIT$) is also included as a dummy variable: it assumes the value of 1 if the household has access to any type of credit other than a mortgage, and 0 if it does not. EFJ represents level of education. The variable HS is the size of household, NE represents the number of income earners in the household, $M12$ is the number of minors under 12, and DEi represents age. (In the equation below, DEG represents household head aged 65 or older.) The results of this regression are as follows (numbers in parentheses are t statistics):[31]

1989
$$\ln S = -7.5520 + 1.4163 \ln TCMI - 0.2447 CREDIT - 0.0898 EFJ$$
$$(-17.46) \quad (48.79) \qquad\qquad (-4.42) \qquad\qquad\qquad (-6.98)$$

N = 3,814 cases
$R^2 = 0.40$
DW = 1.90

1992
$$\ln S = -8.4054 + 1.4814 \ln TCMI - 0.2439 DVIV - 0.1599 CREDIT$$
$$(-16.59) \quad (44.99) \qquad\qquad (-3.37) \qquad\qquad (-3.40)$$

$$- 0.1714 EFJ - 0.0236 HS - 0.0878 NE$$
$$(-10.34) \qquad\quad (-2.70) \qquad (-4.28)$$

N = 3,141 cases
$R^2 = 0.43$
DW = 1.79

---

[31] The test statistic for each coefficient was evaluated at a level of significance of 5 percent.

1994

$$\ln S = -4.7924 + 1.41421n\ TCMI - 0.1639\ DVIV - 0.1818\ CREDIT$$
$$(-18.40)\quad(47.12)\qquad\qquad(-2.44)\qquad\qquad(-4.13)$$

$$-\ 0.1332\ EFJ - 0.0396\ HS + 0.0688\ M12 + 0.1371\ DE6$$
$$(-8.95)\qquad(-4.05)\qquad(2.50)\qquad\qquad(2.51)$$

N = 3,921 cases
$R^2 = 0.42$
DW = 1.92

Comparing the coefficients of the dummy credit and homeowner variables makes it possible to analyze the effects of financial deregulation and the boom in housing values.[32] Although the influence of current monetary income was constant during these years, beginning in 1992 the real possibility of using houses as collateral made it more important to be a homeowner. The coefficient for housing value (*DVIV*) went from –0.01 in 1989 (insignificant in the regression, so it does not appear in the results) to –0.2439 in 1992 and –0.1639 in 1994.

Variables related to access to credit, taken alone, lose their significance between 1989 and 1992. However, they underscore the relevance of the combination of owning a home and having additional access to consumer credit in 1992.

Changes in the formal education of the head of household should also be noted. These gain importance when compared with education in 1989 and the appearance in 1992 and 1994 of other explanatory variables, such as size of the household, number of income earners, number of minors under 12, and age of the head of the household.[33]

---

[32] Between 1988 and 1992, an autonomous drop in saving occurred, which largely reversed itself in 1994.

[33] In 1994, the behavior of households whose heads were over 65 years old deviates significantly from that of the rest of the group. The coefficient is 0.13, which practically neutralizes the effect of the change in the value of the home. The signs of the coefficients for number of earners (negative) in 1992 and minors under 12 (positive) in 1994 are contrary to what is theoretically expected, but the coefficients are small and do not appear in the two regressions in a normal fashion (the estimated t-statistics cover only the requirements of statistical significance). These two variables have important covariations with income, which may explain in part their entry as explanatory variables and their sign.

As a variant of the estimations presented above, in the following regressions the value attributed to a home becomes 0 for households that do not own a home, and 1 for households that own their home outright, whether on their own land or on so-called unregularized land, and for those who are still paying for their house (once again, credit is a dummy variable).

1989

$$\ln S = -7.4458 + 1.4272 \ln TCMI - 0.1291\, DVIV - 0.2425\, CREDIT$$
$$\quad\ (-15.83)\ \ (45.03) \qquad\qquad (-2.26) \qquad\quad (-3.95)$$

$$\quad - 0.1031\, EFJ - 0.0467\, HS + 0.0569\, M12$$
$$\quad\ (-6.92) \qquad (-4.90) \qquad (2.11)$$

N = 3,163 cases
$R^2 = 0.41$
DW = 1.94

1992

$$\ln S = -8.1274 + 1.4462 \ln TCMI - 0.2559\, DVIV - 0.1578\, CREDIT$$
$$\quad\ (-16.40)\ \ (44.94) \qquad\qquad (-3.65) \qquad\quad (-3.66)$$

$$\quad -0.1360\, EFJ$$
$$\quad\ (-8.91)$$

N = 3,141 cases
$R^2 = 0.42$
DW = 1.81

1994

$$\ln S = -4.7475 + 1.393 \ln TCMI - 0.216692\, DVIV - 0.1677\, CREDIT$$
$$\quad\ (-19.02)\ \ (48.43) \qquad\qquad (-3.30) \qquad\qquad (-3.75)$$

$$\quad - 0.1142\, EFJ$$
$$\quad\ (-8.60)$$

N = 4,123 cases
$R^2 = 0.41$
DW = 1.91

The disaggregation according to homeownership changes the results significantly. Changes in the relative importance of the value assigned to the house are not of the same magnitude as in the previous set of regressions. The coefficient assigned to this variable in 1989 was –0.13 and was indeed significant. The fall in the coefficient to –0.21 in 1994 (after rebounding from –0.26 in 1992) echoes the implications of the other regressions.

Financial deregulation may imply permanent changes in the behavior of aggregate consumption. In particular, young consumers, whose access to credit was restricted under the financial regime prior to deregulation, begin to allocate their consumption over time under the new regime. As a result, aggregate saving becomes more sensitive to such factors as wealth and the real interest rate.

To analyze these considerations empirically, the following set of regressions explicitly separates homeowners from nonhomeowners.[34] This distinction was achieved not by assigning a dummy a value of 1 for homeowners, as in the previous section, but rather by including as a variable the value that, as a percentage of income, the household surveyed declared in response to the question, What is the estimated amount to lease your house? This variable is represented by PVEVIV. (For nonhomeowners this variable takes a value of zero.) In this analysis, access of households to different types of credit (whether through a credit card or through any other type of loan other than a mortgage) is included as a binary variable equal to that used in the previous section.

The comparative analysis was done at two different aggregate levels. A regression of the type specified above was run for all households interviewed in the three surveys, and subsequently for three subgroups. The first subgroup consisted of households whose home has been completely paid off and who own the land on which their home sits (that is, those that may use their home as collateral in the acquisition of bank credit). The second subgroup consists of households with a mortgage. The third subgroup consists of households that do not own a home.

The results of these regressions are presented below. The first set of results consists of those at the aggregate level, including all households:

---

[34] This includes homes paid for in full on land owned by the homeowner, homes paid for in full on communal land, and homes paid for in full on unowned land or with a mortgage.

1989

$$\ln S = -7.4149 + 1.425 \ln TCMI - 0.1280 \, PVEVIV$$
$$(-15.58) \quad (44.51) \qquad\qquad (-2.21)$$

$$- 0.2498 \, CREDIT - 0.1009 \, EFJ - 0.0535 \, M12 - 0.0452 \, HS$$
$$(-4.02) \qquad\qquad (-6.71) \qquad (-1.97) \qquad (-4.70)$$

N = 3,113 cases
$R^2 = 0.41$
DW = 1.94

1992

$$\ln S = -8.1243 + 1.4701 \ln TCMI - 0.3662 \, PVEVIV$$
$$(-15.44) \quad (42.95) \qquad\qquad (-5.18)$$

$$- 0.1686 \, CREDIT - 0.1694 \, EFJ - 0.0344 \, HS - 0.0856 \, NE$$
$$(-3.44) \qquad\qquad (-9.75) \qquad (-3.89) \qquad (-4.08)$$

N = 2,764 cases
$R^2 = 0.43$
DW = 1.81

1994

$$\ln S = -4.7145 + 1.4073 \ln TCMI - 0.2419 \, PVEVIV - 0.1790 \, CREDIT$$
$$(-18.05) \quad (46.77) \qquad\qquad (-3.59) \qquad\qquad (-3.953)$$

$$- 0.1305 \, EFJ - 0.0398 \, HS + 0.0663 \, M12 + 0.144608 \, DE6$$
$$(-8.76) \qquad (-4.07) \qquad (2.41) \qquad (2.65)$$

N = 3,651 cases
$R^2 = 0.42$
DW = 1.92

The structural changes in the saving function of households in the four highest income deciles in Mexico may be summarized as follows:

- The autonomous part of saving (captured by the constant term in the regression) varies a great deal. The constant term ranged from −7.4149 in 1989 to −8.1243 in 1992 and −4.7145 in 1994.
- The influence of the value assigned to housing leases also varies. That coefficient ranged from −0.1280 in 1989 to −0.3662 in 1992 and −0.2419 in 1994.

- The influence of households' access to any type of credit falls over the period. The coefficient assigned to this variable ranged from −0.2498 in 1989 to −0.1686 in 1992 and −0.1790 in 1993.
- The significance of the level of formal education of the household head for the level of household saving varies: the coefficient for this variable ranged from −0.1009 in 1989 to −0.1694 in 1992 and −0.1305 in 1994.
- The size of the household and, in 1992, the number of income earners were significant variables. In 1994 the number of minors under 12 and, of particular note, saving is greater in households where the head is older than 65 (variable $DE6$).
- The coefficient assigned to income is practically the same in the three regressions, which implies a high sensitivity of saving to significant changes in income.
- In the three surveys, there are significant positive correlations (greater than 0.30) among income, formal educational level of the head of household, and access to credit.

The next set of results is for regressions performed on the subgroup of households that own their own homes on regularized and titled land:

1989

$$\ln S = -7.0743 + 1.4013 \ln TCMI - 0.1470\, PVEVIV$$
$$\quad (-14.86) \quad (44.02) \qquad\qquad (-2.60)$$

$$\quad\quad - 0.2379\, CREDIT - 0.0861\, EFJ - 0.0340\, HS$$
$$\quad (-3.64) \qquad\qquad (-5.52) \qquad (-4.27)$$

N = 2,634 cases
$R^2 = 0.45$
DW = 1.96

1992

$$\ln S = -8.4332 + 1.4840 \ln TCMI - 0.2300\, PVEVIV$$
$$\quad (-13.43) \quad (36.44) \qquad\qquad (-2.84)$$

$$\quad\quad - 0.1584\, CREDIT - 0.1400\, EFJ - 0.0775\, HS + 0.1200\, M12$$
$$\quad (-2.61) \qquad\qquad (-6.56) \qquad (-5.95) \qquad (3.21)$$

N = 1,749 cases
$R^2 = 0.48$
DW = 1.88

1994

$$\ln S = -4.6176 + 1.4050 \ln TCMI - 0.2920 \, PVEVIV - 0.2101 \, CREDIT$$
$$(-14.31) \quad (38.63) \qquad\qquad (-3.69) \qquad\qquad (-3.78)$$

$$- 0.1171 \, EFJ - 0.0569 \, HS + 0.1071 \, M12 + 0.1476 \, DE6$$
$$(-6.33) \qquad (-4.77) \qquad (3.18) \qquad (2.41)$$

N = 2,265 cases
$R^2 = 0.45$
DW = 1.95

The value assigned to housing leases has particular relevance for this group, which is in effect the household category with a real possibility of gaining access to mortgage credit as yet another way of distributing consumption over time. The coefficients in this case are greater than those for the entire sample. In this case, two households with the same level of income and education, the same household size, and the same access to credit, but different in that one household owns its home whereas the other does not, will have considerably different levels of saving: the homeowner saves less. The year in which the survey was taken (1992) was relatively close to the time when the availability of credit in the economy increased. A reduction in the requirements to qualify for credit of any type may explain why the coefficient assigned to the value attributed to leases for this group in particular turns out to be lower than the corresponding coefficient for all households surveyed.

The third set of results is from regressions on the subgroup consisting of households with mortgages:

1989

$$\ln S = -9.2322 + 1.5151 \ln TCMI$$
$$(-2.56) \quad (6.35)$$

N = 22 cases
$R^2 = 0.66$
DW = 1.45

1992

$$\ln S = -11.4570 + 1.6563 \ln TCMI - 0.2473 \, EFJ$$
$$(-4.40) \quad (9.71) \qquad\qquad (-2.97)$$

N = 181 cases
$R^2 = 0.35$
DW = 1.91

1994

$$\ln S = -4.5607 + 1.3073 \ln TCMI$$
$$\quad\quad (-4.71) \quad\quad (12.49)$$

N = 216 cases
$R^2 = 0.42$
DW = 2.11

Only in 1992, the survey year closest to the increase in the availability of credit, does another variable besides income appear as an explanation of the saving of these households. In fact, this may be explained by the lower effective disposable incomes of these households. In all of the regressions, the high correlation between income (interpreted as disposable family income) and saving for this group means that, given that they have to pay a mortgage, their effective disposable income is lower than that of families who are not carrying a mortgage (either because they have paid off their home or because they do not own one). The residual saving is basically explained by variations in the household's total current monetary income. In 1992 the high correlation between income and the formal educational level of the head of the household is another reason why this variable is added to the saving function for that year. These households are also a very small part of the sample.

Conclusions

The dearth of information on the proportion of domestic saving generated by companies in Mexico has limited the resolution of disagreements related to the choice of policies to raise private saving in Mexico. The results obtained here make it possible to quantify the significance of corporate retained earnings during the eight years prior to the 1994 crisis in generating private saving. During this period, a large proportion of private saving came from companies, and except in 1990, the drop in private saving resulted from the behavior of households. Saving by households fell from half of all private saving in 1988 and 1989 to only one fifth two years later. The drop by more than 7 percentage points between 1988 and 1991 in the proportion of total private saving in GDP is explained to a great extent by reduced saving among households. This is the same explanation as for the drop from 1988 to 1992.

The estimate of corporate saving for 1990 and 1991 shows, contrary to what happened in the other years analyzed, a drop of more than 2 percentage points of GDP with respect to the values registered in 1988 and 1989. Changes in taxation, aimed at producing a flow of profits from companies to their shareholders, may have produced this result.

From a quarterly time-series model of the behavior of private saving from 1986 to 1995, it was determined that, although variables associated with a reduction in the degree of uncertainty of future income fostered a drop in saving in Mexico, this was explained in large part by variables related to financial deregulation and the boom in real estate. The analyses in this chapter both quantify these results and make it possible to specify the magnitude of the increase in average private sector saving in response to more rapid income growth.

Including housing values in the time-series estimations revealed that, prior to 1990, this variable was not a determining factor in the behavior of private saving, but it became one beginning with the first quarter of 1990. This result was also obtained in income-expenditure surveys for 1988, 1992, and 1994.

The results indicate that, unlike in 1989, in 1992 two people with the same access to credit, level of income, and level of formal education saved different amounts if one was a homeowner: the nonhomeowner saved 27 percent more. The corresponding calculation for 1993 indicates that this difference fell to 17 percent. The singular importance of access to bank credit as a determinant of the drop in saving was also measured and made clear. One explanation is that, when financial deregulation occurs and more credit is available to households, property owners, who can use their real estate as collateral, increased their consumption. However, the explanation of the drop in saving in 1992 is not just related to homeownership and access to credit. Human capital, captured in the estimations by the level of education of the head of household, explains that households who lowered their saving anticipated both higher and less uncertain income.

Finally, it was determined that age is a determinant of saving decisions; on average, households where the head was between 35 and 64 years old saved more than did other households.

Summary

Three types of complementary analysis were conducted to understand the determinants of the marked drop in private saving in Mexico since 1988.

The first approach quantified the significance of profits retained by companies during the eight years prior to the 1994 crisis for the generation of private saving. We found that in this period a large proportion of private saving came from companies. With the exception of 1990, the drop in private saving is driven by the behavior of individuals.

A second approach to the problem was based on econometric analysis of the determinants of quarterly data (from 1985 to 1995) using private saving. Significant among these variables were those related to capital gains produced by the boom in real estate prices and the rise in stock prices, as well as those associated with the financial deregulation that began in 1988.

Given that the same conceptual framework was used in the design of INEGI's Household Income and Expenditures Surveys in 1989, 1992, and 1994, we had the basis for a third approach. In particular, the value of housing was not a determining factor in the behavior of private saving in the first sample but thereafter became one. The singular relevance of access to bank credit as a determinant of the drop in saving was also brought out and quantified. The explanation for the drop in saving in 1992 is not just related to homeownership and access to credit; human capital, captured in our estimations by the level of education of the head of household, explains that individuals who lowered their saving levels had expectations not only of higher incomes but also of lower risk of losing their jobs owing to their level of formal education. Lastly, it was established that the age structure is a determinant of saving decisions; households where the head is between 35 and 64 save more than other households on average.

References

Agosin, M. et al. 1996. "Explicaciones del aumento del ahorro en Chile." Departamento de Economía, Universidad de Chile. Mimeograph.

Arriazu, R. 1987. "Un enfoque de flujo de fondos a la macroeconomía." Mimeograph.

Attanasio, O.P. and Weber, G. 1994. "The UK Consumption Boom of the Late 1980s: Aggregate Implications of Microeconomic Evidence." *Economic Journal*. 104: 1269–1302.

Banco de México. Various years. *Informe Annual*.

Bayoumi, T. 1993. "Financial Deregulation and Household Saving." *Economic Journal*. 103:1433–43.

Bosworth, B., Burtless, G. and Sabelhaus, J. 1991. "The Decline in Saving: Evidence from Household Surveys." *Brookings Papers on Economic Activity*. 1: 183–257.

Buira, A. 1994. "The Main Determinants of Savings in Mexico." Paper presented at the conference on The Role of Saving in Economic Growth, Federal Reserve Bank of Dallas, March.

Calderón-Madrid, A. 1996a. "Low Household Savings and Unsustainable Current Account Deficits: A Study of Private Savings Using Intersectorial Matrices of Financial Assets for the Mexican Economy." Documento de Trabajo VII-1996. Centro de Estudios Económicos, El Colegio de México.

———. 1996b. "Speculative Attacks and Exchange Rate Devaluations in Mexico: Why is the 1994 Episode Different?" Paper presented at the 1996 Annual Meeting of the Society for Economic Dynamic and Control (ITAM), June, and at the 10th Meeting of the Latin American Econometric Society, Rio de Janeiro, Brazil, August.

———. 1997. "Incomplete Adjustment, Private Savings and Current Account Deficits in Mexico since 1982." In K. Jansen, and R. Vos, editors *External Finance and Adjustment: Failure and Success in the Developing World*. London: Macmillan.

Carroll, C.D. 1992. "The Buffer Stock Theory of Saving: Some Macroeconomic Evidence." *Brookings Papers on Economic Activity*. 2: 61–156.

———. 1994. "How Does Future Income Affect Current Consumption?" *Quarterly Journal of Economics*. 109: 111–47.

Davidson, J., Hendry, D., Srba, F. and Yeo, S. 1981. "Econometric Modelling of the Aggregate Time-Series Relationship between Consumers' Expenditure and Income in the United Kingdom." *Economic Journal*. 88: 661–92.

Fazzari, S., Hubbard, R.G. and Peterson, B.C. 1988. "Financing Constraints and Corporate Investment." *Brookings Papers on Economic Activity*. 1: 141–95.

Garcia Alba, P. 1996. "La función del ahorro intemo en el crecimiento económico." *Revista Ejecutivos de Finanzas*. 35 (9): 21–34.

Hendry, D. et al. 1984. "Dynamic Specification." In Z. Griliches and M.D. Intriligator, editors. *Handbook of Econometrics*, Vol. 2. Amsterdam: Elsevier.

Hubbard, R.G., Skinner, J. and Zeldes, S.P. 1994. "The Importance of Precautionary Motives in Explaining Individual and Aggregate Saving." *Carnegie-Rochester Conference Series on Public Policy*. 40: 59–125.

Jappelli, T. and Pagano, M. 1994. "Saving, Growth, and Liquidity Constraints." *Quarterly Journal of Economics*. 109: 83–109.

Khadr, A. and Schmidt-Hebbel, K. 1989. "A Method for Macroeconomic Consistency in Current and Constant Prices." World Bank Policy Research Working Paper 306. Policy Research Department, Washington, DC.

King, M. 1990. "Discussion of Muellbauer and Murphy," *Economic Policy.* 11: 345–83.

Krugman. P. 1995. "Dutch Tulips and Emerging Markets." *Foreign Affairs.* July-August.

Mansell Carstens, C. 1994. "The Internationalization of the Mexican Financial System." Paper presented at the conference on the Global and Comparative Analysis of Financial Institutions, Rockefeller Foundation, Bellagio Conference and Study Center, May.

Mexican Stock Exchange. 1992. *Anuario Bursátil.* Mexico.

Muellbauer, N. 1994. "The Assessment: Consumer Expenditure." *Oxford Review of Economic Policy.* 10 (Summer): 1–41.

Oks, D. and Arrau, P. 1992. "Private Saving in Mexico, 1980-90." Policy Research Working Paper 861. Policy Research Department, World Bank, Washington, DC.

Sadka, E. and Tanzi, V. 1992. "A Tax on Gross Assets of Enterprises as a Form of Presumptive Taxation." Working Paper WP/92/16. International Monetary Fund, Washington, DC.

Sales, C., Solís, F. and Villagómez, A. 1996. "Pension System Reform: The Mexican Case." National Bureau of Economic Research, Cambridge, Mass.

Villagómez, A. 1993. "Los determinantes del ahorro en México: Una reseña de Ia investigación empirica." *Revista Economia Mexicana.* 2 (2): 305–27.

CHAPTER 6

Domestic Saving and Structural Adjustment in Peru: 1990–95

Efraín Gonzales de Olarte, Cecilio Lévano Castro,
and Pedro Llontop Ledesma[1]

The Peruvian economy experienced sustained stable growth from the 1950s through the mid-1970s. It then experienced a decline that lasted through the end of the 1980s and caused per capita GDP to shrink to the levels of the 1970s. One of the main reasons for this negative growth and crisis was the trend in investment and its effects on output. Growth began to recover in 1991, sustained by an increase in investment (Gonzales, 1996). The problem is that domestic saving was sufficient to finance investment only until the early 1970s. Since then, Peru has required more external saving for growth. The country has a chronic insufficiency in domestic saving to finance investment that results in an average saving rate of 18.9 percent, moderate by Latin American standards.

In 1990, Peru embarked on a structural adjustment program that is transforming the economic and institutional context of the past 25 years and will have an impact on saving and investment determinants; in other words, it is changing the accumulation system.[2] However, it does not seem to be changing the problem of insufficient domestic saving with regard to total investment—despite the recovery of the domestic saving rate since 1991—which is clearly an impediment to ensuring the viability of long-term growth.

---

[1] The authors are associated with the Instituto de Estudios Peruanos (IEP).
[2] The accumulation system is the process of generating saving and converting it into investment in order to increase the stock of capital, which allows for stable, self-financing economic growth.

To understand this problem demands an analysis of the determinants of domestic saving in Peru, in both the long and short term. Historical analysis should be able to provide clues about the permanent determinants of domestic saving, how they are affected by structural adjustment, and whether these changes favor an increase in domestic saving and its future stability.

In Peru, domestic saving is one of the main sources of financing for private investment, and external saving has played an important role in financing public investment, since public saving has proven insufficient. As a result, private saving has been a key piece of the accumulation process, which is why this analysis focuses on its determinants.

The saving rate has been moderate because long-term factors, such as disposable income, which drive saving, have been counteracted by factors that inhibit it, such as the degree of urbanization, unequal income distribution, and negative fluctuations in the terms of trade. Disaggregating private saving into household and business saving allows a better understanding of the effect income distribution, credit, and the terms of trade have on private saving after the application of structural reforms. Hyperinflation (1988–90) and structural adjustment (1990–96) have changed the composition of saving since 1990; business saving now constitutes two thirds of all private saving, and the saving rate is expected to vary, given the increased weight exercised by determinants of business saving. Up to now, recovery has only been observed for the average historical rate.

Economic Trends and Stylized Facts

Between 1950 and 1995, the Peruvian economy went through two distinct phases. Through the mid-1970s, growth was stable and averaged an annual 5.4 percent with an inflation rate of 9.5 percent per year (see Table 6.1). However, from 1976 to 1995 just the opposite occurred: the GDP growth rate was only 0.8 percent, meaning that per capita GDP actually declined, while inflation reached an unprecedented average rate of 704 percent per year. Over these 45 years, the per capita GDP growth rate was only 0.7 percent per year—a truly poor performance. What was gained in the first phase was lost in the second. On the other hand, the effective product was close to its potential through the early 1970s, dropping remarkably since the 1980s (see Figure 6.1a).

**Table 6.1 Economic Trends: 1950–95
(percent)**

	Annual Growth Rate		Annual Growth Rate of Saving	Saving/ GDP	Annual Growth Rate	Investment/ GDP	Average Annual Inflation Rate
	GDP	GDP Per Capita					
1950–95							
Average	3.4	0.7	5.8	18.8	6.0	21.1	309.8
Standard Deviation	5.5	5.4	17.3	0.03	19.6	0.03	1,230.3
Variability Rate	1.6	7.7	3.0	6.0	3.3		4.0
1950–75							
Average	5.4	2.4	7.8	18.7	8.8	21.5	9.5
Standard Deviation	2.7	2.5	16.7	0.03	18.4	0.04	5.4
Variability Rate	0.5	1.0	2.1		2.1		0.6
1976–95							
Average	0.8	–1.4	3.1	19.2	2.3	20.6	704.9
Standard Deviation	7.0	7.2	18.3	0.04	21.2	0.03	1,823.7
Variability Rate	8.8	–5.1	5.9		9.2		2.6

Source: INEI, *Statistical Annex 1992–93, 1994, 1995* (Lima, 1993, 1994, and 1995).

This dynamic is explained, in part, by the annual growth rates of domestic saving and investment, which were high (7.8 percent and 8.8 percent, respectively) in the growth phase of the long-term cycle and went down in the declining phase (3.1 percent and 2.3 percent), until domestic saving and per capita investment experienced negative rates. However, the high rates of saving and investment variability, which increased substantially from one phase to the other, signaled one of the greatest Peruvian economic growth problems: its strong instability since the 1970s (see Figure 6.1a). An additional aspect of this dynamic has been that during the expanding phase of saving and investment, it grew to similar rates, while in the declining phase, saving grew at a higher rate, which suggests the utilization of a portion of saving for purposes other than investment.

Throughout the entire period under study and in both phases, the domestic saving rate has been lower than the investment rate, and both have fluctuated slightly around their averages of 18.8 percent and 21.1 percent, respectively (see Table 6.1).

Figure 6.1a
Effective and Potential GDP, Disposable Income, Domestic Saving, and Investment: 1950–94
(millions of 1979 soles)

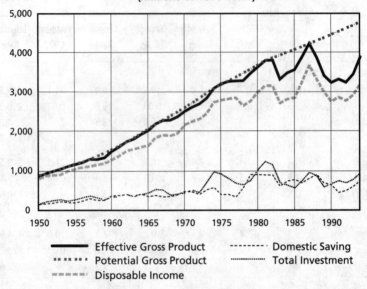

Figure 6.1b
Domestic Saving and Investment: 1950–94
(percentage of GDP)

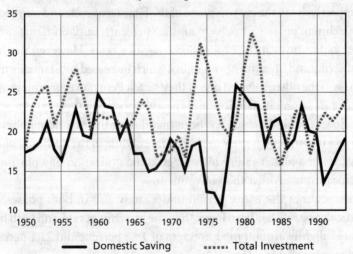

The Structural Adjustments

There were three structural adjustments between 1950 and 1995: two liberal and one statist. The adjustment cycle began with a liberalization under General Manual A. Odría (1948–56); twenty years later, the government of General Juan Velasco introduced a new state-centered reform; and 22 years after that, the government of Alberto Fujimori implemented a new set of liberal reforms, this time within an international neoliberal and global context.

In the midst of a profound economic and institutional crisis in 1990, the Structural Adjustment Plan (SAP) began with a drastic stabilization program known as "Fujishock," with two objectives: to combat inflation and reinsert Peru into the international financial system by paying foreign debt. The main goals of the plan were to eliminate the tax deficit, correct and stabilize public revenue, and unify and liberalize the exchange rate. In addition, shortly after a slight devaluation, a "monetary anchor" was selected under a system of floating exchange rates, complemented by severe monetary control.

Simultaneously, foreign trade was liberalized, first by eliminating quantitative restrictions, then by reducing average customs duties from 66 percent to 32 percent and establishing three levels of customs duties: 15 percent, 25 percent, and 50 percent. In early 1991, without waiting for the trade liberalization to have an impact on investment and spur industrial reconversion, the capital account was liberalized and public companies began to be privatized. Thus, the economic reforms were launched almost simultaneously with the stabilization plan.

This plan helped annual inflation decline from 7,650 percent in 1990 to 139 percent in 1991 and 11.9 percent in 1996, even as Peru became progressively reinserted into the international financial system. In addition, dollarization increased from 70 percent in 1990 to 79 percent in 1991 and then an average of 80 percent through 1994. Dollarization allowed international reserves to recover rapidly to above US$8,540 million in December 1996—an unprecedented level. However, it also contributed to an appreciation of the exchange rate, which was fed by an inflow of capital attracted by high interest rates, generated by the combination of financial liberalization and strict monetary policy. The seeds were thus planted for a persistent exchange rate overvaluation that inhibited export promotion while it increased imports and the consumption of durable goods, which had repercussions on investment and saving. Peru was returning to a primary commodity export model in sectors similar to those of the 1950s—mining, fishing, and petroleum. All of these are prone to external shocks and belong to foreign capital, making external saving an important variable for the accumulation system, both for the input of initial capital and for future outputs of business saving.

Although the inflation problem has been beat, recent economic trends in Peru still show no signs of having prepared the ground for stable growth since there is a growing external gap and a current account deficit that reached 5.7 percent of GDP in 1996. This reflects a saving-investment imbalance that signals the failure of structural adjustment to resolve the insufficiency of domestic saving and shows that investment is high thanks only to external saving.

Stylized Saving Facts and Growth: 1950–94

The saving rate (S/GDP) in the Peruvian economy has been approximately average for Latin America: 21.6 percent during the 1950–94 period, reaching a maximum of 31.1 percent in 1981 and a minimum of 15.2 percent in 1972.[3] The domestic saving rate (Sd/GDP) was an average of 18.9 percent and the external saving rate (Sx/GDP) 2.7 percent during the same period (see Table 6.2). The domestic saving rate had two stages: a declining trend from 1950 to 1977 that recovered between 1978 and 1979 with the orthodox adjustment of the military government, and another decline from 1980 through the early 1990s (see Figure 6.1b). Domestic saving has been procyclical, falling during periods of adjustment and recovering relatively quickly after the structural adjustments (see Figures 6.1a and 6.1b).

Domestic saving has not been enough to finance investment. The average domestic saving deficit in relation to total investment was 2 percent during the 1950–94 period. That is why external saving has been critical for sustaining the accumulation system and has experienced compensatory trends, particularly for public saving (see Figures 6.2 and 6.3). The importance of foreign saving lies in its ability to finance public investment, which has been unable to finance itself on the basis of public saving, as shown in Figure 6.5.

---

[3] Data unadjusted for inflation tax are used to describe the stylized facts.

Table 6.2. Saving and Investment: 1950–94
(percent)

	1950–94			1979–90			1991–94		
	Avg.	S.D.	C. V.	Avg.	S.D.	C.V.	Avg.	S.D.	C. V.
FBKF/GDP (I/Y)	21.1	3.5	0.17	20.3	3.6	0.2	20.5	3.2	0.2
Total Saving/GDP	21.6	3.8	0.18	23.9	3.9	0.2	20.3	2.5	0.1
Internal Saving/GDP	18.9	3.5	0.19	21.6	2.6	0.1	16.3	2.4	0.1
External Saving/GDP	2.7	3.1	1.15	2.3	3.4	1.5	4.0	0.1	0.0
Private Saving/GDP	18.8	3.4	0.19	22.7	2.0	0.1	16.3	2.4	0.1
Government Saving/GDP	0.06	2.3	38.3	–1.1	2.7	–2.5	0.84	0.65	0.8
Business Saving/GDP				6.3	2.4	0.4	10.9	1.3	0.1
Household Saving/GDP				16.4	2.7	0.2	5.3	1.4	0.3
Business Saving/Total Saving				26.7	11.1	0.4	54.3	4.0	0.1
Household Saving/Total Saving				70.1	15.0	0.2	25.9	5.0	0.2
Government Saving/Total Saving				–5.1	11.9	–2.3	4.4	2.3	0.5
External Saving/Total Saving				8.3	13.1	1.6	19.9	2.1	0.1

Note: Saving information is only available up to 1994.
Avg., Average; S.D., standard deviation; C.V., coefficient of variability.

The average rate of private saving (*Sp/GDP*) has been similar to that of domestic saving (18.9 percent) and has enabled financing of private investment (Gonzales, 1996). Private saving has not observed a precise trend in the 1950–94 period (see Figure 6.4) and has oscillated significantly. This oscillation has been associated with variations in disposable income, which confirms one stylized fact noted by Thorne (1986).

Since 1979, the saving structure has had two markedly distinct periods: 1979–90 and 1991–94. Between 1979 and 1990, households contributed 70.1 percent of total saving (16.4 percent of GDP) and companies only 26.7 percent; the government, for its part, had a dissaving of –5.1 percent, compensated by external saving of 8.3 percent. However, the structure of saving changed dramatically after 1991. Companies became the principal source of saving, contributing 54.3 percent of total saving; households reduced their share to 25.9 percent; the government increased its to 4.4 percent; and external saving also increased to 19.9 percent (4 percent of GDP), contrary to the previous experience (see Table 6.2 and Figure 6.4). This drastic change in the structure of saving had its root in the hyperinflation of 1988–

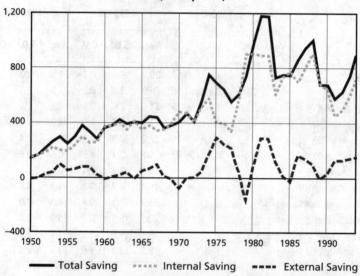

Figure 6.2
Total, Internal, and External Saving: 1950–94
(1979 prices)

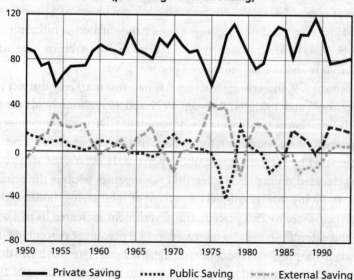

Figure 6.3
Structure of Saving: 1950–94
(percentage of total saving)

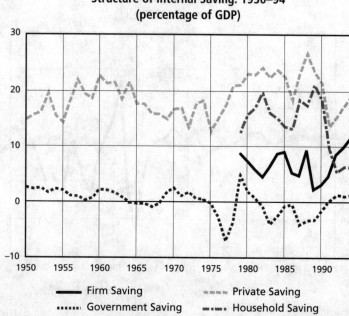

Figure 6.4
Structure of Internal Saving: 1950–94
(percentage of GDP)

Firm Saving   Private Saving
Government Saving   Household Saving

90 and the structural adjustment begun in 1990, which together had a significant impact on disposable income. In other words, these two phenomena seem to have changed the determinants of saving.

Household and business saving have followed very different trends since the end of the 1980s, since apparently there was a distributive conflict (profits/wages) with repercussions on the saving of households and businesses. Since the drastic change in the composition of saving from 1991, both evolved parallel to disposable income. Moreover, household saving is negatively affected by crises and economic adjustments (1983–85, 1989–91) and is slow to recover; on the other hand, business saving increased precisely during these periods. Finally, until the end of the 1980s, household saving "pushed" the domestic saving trend; in the 1990s, business saving has played this role.

In a primary-export and semi-industrial economy like Peru's, the behavior of the external sector has influenced domestic saving through the terms of trade, whose oscillations and tendency to decline have been a fac-

Figure 6.5
Public Saving and Investment: 1950–94
(millions of 1979 soles)

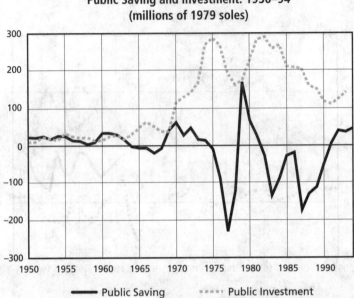

——— Public Saving   ••••• Public Investment

tor that has made domestic saving fluctuate, in both the short and long term (see Figure 6.6). Thus, the major recovery of domestic saving between 1978 and 1979 seems to be associated with the improved terms of trade, just as the fall in the saving rate between 1980 and 1990 coincides with the deterioration in the terms of trade.

On the other hand, demographic variables have also had repercussions on domestic saving, especially in households. In the first place, the rate of dependency, defined as the relationship between the economically inactive population over the active, has followed an inverted-U trend (see Figure 6.8). The rate increased until the mid-1960s and then began to decline steadily, reflecting a young population that does not save and an old population that dissaves. Second, the intense development process over the past 50 years has converted Peru from a rural country (in 1950, about 59 percent of the population was rural) to an urban one (in 1994, a full 70 percent of the population was urban; see Figure 6.9). This migration from the country to the city has affected saving due to the rural-urban differences in income, wages, access to credit, and educational attainment.

Figure 6.6

Internal Saving, Private Credit, Terms of Trade, and Profit-Wage Ratio: 1950–95

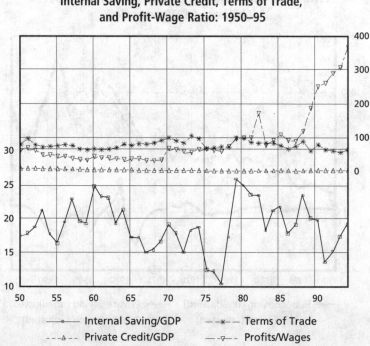

A final factor that impacts saving is restricted liquidity. Figure 6.6 shows us that the ratio of private sector credit to GDP follows the opposite trend from domestic saving. However, its changes are much less dramatic than those of saving.

Saving Data Corrected for the Inflation Tax

To see whether the inflationary process significantly affected the measurement of saving in domestic accounts, the data on private and government saving have been corrected for the inflation tax (see Figure 6.7). Corrected private saving diminished in moderate inflationary periods compared to uncorrected saving; the opposite occurred with government saving. During the hyperinflation of 1988–90, the inflation tax became practically null, which is why government saving was not favored, unlike the 1950–88 period, when inflation was a tax equivalent to 1.2 percent of GDP. However, hyperinflation negatively affected private saving and favored the recovery of public saving.

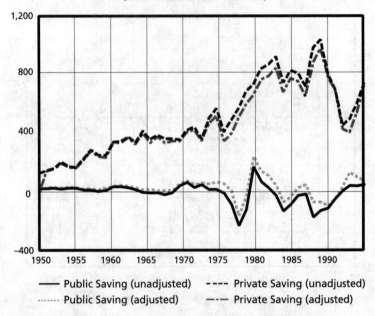

Figure 6.7
Private and Public Saving, Adjusted for Inflation: 1950–95
(millions of 1979 new soles)

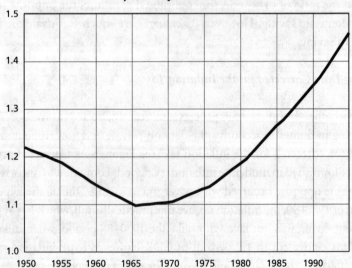

Figure 6.8
Dependency Ratio: 1950–94

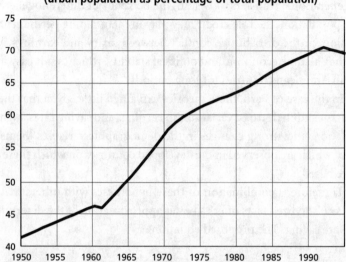

Figure 6.9
Change in Urbanization: 1950–94
(urban population as percentage of total population)

Determinants of Domestic Saving

Private Saving

Several recent studies, including those of Held and Uthoff (1995), Schmidt, Serven and Solimano (1996), and Deaton (1995), agree there are several determinants of domestic saving in developing countries, which derive from different theories. The usual ones are:

- The life-cycle hypothesis (Modigliani and Brumberg, 1954; Modigliani and Ando, 1963; Modigliani, 1979), which posits that the saving behavior of individuals depends on their age (children and adolescents do not save yet, and the elderly dissave). Consequently, saving depends on the age structure of the population and the behavior of maximizing intertemporal profits. Thus, the larger the working-age population, the greater the saving.

- The permanent income hypothesis (Friedman, 1957), which postulates that saving is a more or less constant proportion of future expected or permanent income and that temporary changes in income translate into saving before changes in consumption.

Several authors, including Casillas (1993) and Thorne (1986), point out the limitations of these hypotheses. They do not adequately explain intergenerational transfers of wealth, the behavior of different generations of the population, the role credit may play in maintaining permanent consumption, or the distributive conflict between salary and earnings. Moreover, they assume economic and political stability, which is not easy to find in Latin American countries for long periods.

In the case of Peru, these theories explained little, given that the stylized facts exhibited strong variations in earnings and saving rates, high rates of inflation, and strong changes in the demographic variables themselves, none of which are observed in the developed countries on which these theories are based.

Therefore, a combination of these hypotheses with others that arise from Peru's stylized facts offers a better approximation of the determinants of private saving. The proposed equation is:

$$
\begin{array}{ccccccccc} + & - & ? & + & - & - & + & ? & ? \end{array}
$$
$$
Sp = i\,(Ydisr,\ Crp,\ inf,\ Tadep,\ Purb,\ (P/W),\ TI,\ Sg\,,\ Sx)
$$

where Sp is private saving, $Ydisr$ is real disposable income, Crp is credit to the private sector, inf is annual inflation rate, $Tadep$ is dependency rate, $Purb$ is urban population over total population, (P/W) is earnings over wages, TI is terms of trade, Sg is public saving, and Sx is external saving.

The expected signs are based on the following theoretical hypothesis:

Over the long term, according to the permanent income hypothesis, growth in real income should increase private saving if the changes in income are perceived as temporary, or if earnings at the level of permanent consumption derived from increased permanent income occur more slowly than earnings in permanent income.

The a priori effect of the inflation rate on private saving is unclear. According to the risk aversion or precaution motive, high inflation rates are associated with high saving rates, which is why a drastic reduction in inflation may have negative effects on private saving. On the other hand, if inflation is perceived as a tax that reduces income and the changes that result from consumption are less than the reduction in income, then one can expect a negative association between the rate of inflation and private saving. The negative association between saving and inflation is also justified from the viewpoint of yield, since a lower inflation rate increases the yield savers obtain on their deposits in the financial system.

The dependency rate is connected to the life-cycle hypothesis, which is a positive sign since working-age people make up a larger portion of the population.

Greater credit to the private sector as a result of an easing of restrictions in financial markets together with trade liberalization may have negative effects on private saving in the short term since imported goods that were relatively more expensive are now being consumed (Jappelli and Pagano, 1994; Muellbauer and Murphy, 1990; Attanasio and Weber, 1994; Rossi, 1988). This hypothesis contrasts with the prevailing hypothesis in economic literature that financial liberalization impacts favorably on domestic saving.

According to post-Keynesian theory (Lewis, 1954; Kaldor, 1957; Passinetti, 1962) the distribution of income between profits and wages is associated with private saving. Assuming that capitalists have a higher rate of saving than workers, the redistribution of wages to profits increases saving. However, that relationship may be modified if the companies are owned by the state and have a lower propensity to save than workers. In that case, the redistribution of wages to profits reduces private saving.

In addition, government saving is included, but its sign will depend on whether the hypothesis of Ricardian equilibrium is met or not. The importance of external saving in the stylized facts suggests including this variable, whose effect on private domestic saving depends on a complementary or exclusionary relationship.

Interest rates have not been included because their effect on private saving is unclear. Also, authors like Edwards (1995) and Thorne (1986) have found that there is no significant relationship with respect to saving for Latin America and for the Peruvian case, respectively. One additional problem is the absence of an appropriate series of interest rates that covers the period of analysis.

Empirical Verification

Annual data from official sources are used and presented in Gonzales, Lévano, and Llontop (1998). The periods of analysis are 1950–90 (prior to the reforms) and 1950–94 (which includes the effects of structural reforms applied in 1991).

To avoid spurious correlations between the variables, the order of respective integration was analyzed first. The three versions of the augmented Dickey-Fuller (1981) test were used: with constant and trend, with constant, and with neither constant nor trend. Information criteria from Akaike (1973) were used to determine the optimum lag. The results are shown in Gonzales et al. (1998).

The test indicated that there was a unit root of up to 5 percent of significance in both periods for the following variables: real private saving, real disposable income, real credit to the private sector, growth rate of the dependency rate, growth rate of the urban population, and the profit relationship between compensation and terms of trade. They are stationary in the first differences. For the remaining variables—inflation, public saving and external saving—the hypothesis of unit root is rejected in favor of the hypothesis of stationariness up to 5 percent and 10 percent of significance. Thus, the following equation is presented for private saving:

$$LSP = f[LYDISR, LCRP, INF, DTADEP, DPURB, L(P/W), LTI]$$

where:

LSP is real private saving in 1979 new soles, expressed in logarithms.

LYDISR is real disposable income in 1979 new soles, expressed in logarithms.

LCRP is real credit from the banking sector to the private sector, in 1979 new soles. It is the proxy variable for the liquidity restriction and is expressed in logarithms.

INF is the annual rate of inflation.

DTADEP is the dependency rate fluctuation. The ratio of the increase in the economically active population to the increase in the economically inactive population was used as the proxy variable.

DPURB is the variation rate of the urban population with respect to total population.

L(P/W) is the ratio of real profits to real compensation. It is the proxy variable for income distribution and is expressed in logarithms.

LTI is the terms of trade, expressed in logarithms.

The Johansen and Juselius (1990) method reveals the long-term relationships between private saving and integration order (I/1) variables shown in Table 6.3.

Table 6.3 Long-Term Relationships: Dependent Variable, Real Private Saving

Variable	1950–90	1950–94
Real Disposable Income	0.981	1.027
Change in the Dependency Rate	0.427	0.297
Change in the Urban Population Rate	−1.834	−1.062
Profits-Salaries Ratio	−2.738	−0.727
Terms of Trade	2.633	0.551

Notes: All the variables are expressed in logarithms. The unit root test applied to the residual values of each cointegration relationship rejects the existence of unit roots.

Applying the Engle and Granger (1987) error-correction mechanism yields the short-term equations incorporating other explanatory integration order I(0) variables shown in Tables 6.4 and 6.5.

Statistically, there is a long-term relationship between private saving, disposable income, the dependency rate, terms of trade, the urbanization rate, and the proxy for income distribution (profits-salaries ratio). There is no long-term relationship between private saving, the inflation rate, credit to the private sector, government saving, and external saving. It is important to note that before and after 1990, from the long-term perspective, private saving is related in the same "sense" to the other variables; in other words, the relationship occurs after introducing the structural reforms. There is a positive association between private saving, the dependency rate, and the terms of trade, and a negative association with respect to the profits-salaries ratio and the rate of urbanization. There is also greater stability in the long-term elasticity of private saving with respect to disposable income (approximately 1) and the rate of dependency (0.3–0.4). Elasticity values (but not the sign) for private saving vary with respect to the rate of urbanization (from −1.8 to −1.1), the profits-salaries ratio (from −2.7 to −0.7), and terms of trade (2.6 to 0.6).

With respect to the determinants of short-term private saving, before and after the structural reforms, the lags of this variable are statistically significant, corroborating the notion that temporary shocks to private saving persist over time, as already shown by the unit root test. With the exception of the inflation rate, after structural reform, all the other variables assume greater importance for private saving. In the short term, the increments in

Table 6.4 Short-Term Relationships: Dependent Variable, Real Private Saving*

Variable	1950–90	1950–94
Constant	0.068	0.099
	(1.99)	(3.29)
Correction Vector of Errors (–1)	–0.06	–0.078
	(–2.19)	(–2.11)
Private Saving (–1)*	–0.488	–0.363
	(–2.69)	(–2.28)
Private Saving (–2)*	–0.514	–0.374
	(–3.08)	(–2.83)
Real Disposable Income (–1)*	0.022	0.159
	(0.04)	(0.33)
Private Credit (–1)*	0.149	0.177
	(0.71)	(0.97)
Terms of Trade (–1)*	0.102	0.089
	(0.48)	(0.44)
Profits–Salaries Ratio (–1)*	–0.0001	–0.064
	(–0.001)	(–0.59)
Change in the Urbanization Rate (–1)**	–9.29E-05	0.001
	(–0.002)	(0.02)
Change in the Dependency Rate (–1)**	–0.103	–0.127
	(–0.87)	(–1.14)
Inflation Rate (–1)**	–9.34E-05	–7.42E-05
	(–0.82)	(–3.00)

* In the first differences of the variable in logarithms.
** In the first differences of the variable without logarithms.
Notes: The short-term regressions are free of statistical problems, as shown in Table 6.5. The Cusum and Cusum 2 tests applied to the residuals of these regressions are presented in Gonzales et al. (1998) and are stable for the periods analyzed. Numbers in parentheses are *t*-statistics.

disposable income, private credit, and terms of trade have a positive effect on private saving; the reductions in the dependency rate also have a positive effect on private saving; and the increase in profits with respect to compensation has a negative effect on saving. None of these is statistically significant, however.

Table 6.5 Statistical Test Applied to the Short-Term Equations

---

1950–90

$R^2 = 0.49$ DW = 2.02   F = 2.61   LM(1) = 0.41, Pr = 0.53   LM(2) = 1.0, Pr = 0.38

LM(3) = 0.65, Pr = 0.59   White = 0.71, Pr = 0.77

ARCH-LM(1) = 1.24, Prob = 0.27

ARCH-LM(2) = 0.74, Prob = 0.49

ARCH-LM(3) = 0.75, Prob = 0.53

1950–94

$R^2 = 0.54$ DW = 2.09   F = 3.69   LM(1) = 1.0, Pr = 0.3   LM(2) = 1.7, Pr = 0.19

LM(3) = 1.20, Pr = 0.33   White = 0.58, Pr = 0.89

ARCH-LM(1) = 1.17, Prob = 0.29

ARCH-LM(2) = 0.95, Prob = 0.4

ARCH-LM(3) = 0.74, Prob = 0.53

The vector of error correction (VEC) is statistically significant, showing that almost 10 percent of the short-term saving variation is corrected in each period.

There is no evidence for accepting the precautionary saving hypothesis based on trends in inflation rates. The inflation rate is statistically significant considering the 1950–94 period. However, the low elasticity shows that it must be reduced drastically before it causes a significant increment in private saving, which may explain why private saving increased after inflation was reduced beginning in 1991 (Table 6.6).

On the other hand, there is no basis to confirm the permanent income hypothesis in the sense that private saving is associated with an increase in

Table 6.6 Matrix of Annual Correlation of Private Saving with Respect to the Other Variables: 1991–94

Variables Correlated with Private Saving	Correlation
Disposable Income	0.892
Profits-Salaries Ratio	0.983
Terms of Trade	−0.025
Inflation Rate	−0.869
Bank Credit to the Private Sector	0.955

disposable income over the long term. In the short term, although they are positively associated, it is not statistically significant. The Modigliani and Ando (1963) life-cycle hypothesis is also confirmed since the larger the working-age population, the higher private saving is in the long-term equation.

Income distribution that favors profits over salaries has, in the long term, had a negative incidence on private saving, although this effect seems to reverse itself after 1991, as shown in Table 6.6. Still, it has not been strong enough to reverse the long-term relationship.

This result is related to the change in the composition of private saving after 1991. During the 1980s, household saving represented 75 percent of private saving while business saving represented the remaining 25 percent. However, the figures reversed themselves in the 1990s, when business saving represented 75 percent of private saving. This may be related to the change in the propensity to save on the part of households and firms beginning in 1990. Several facts support this hypothesis. Households' propensity to save fell from 0.21 in 1991 to 0.16 in 1994, and the weight of profits in determining business saving increased, particularly among large companies. (See Gonzales et al., 1998.)

The rapid increase in the urbanization rate has signified a trend towards lower private saving. This result reflects a decline in the propensity to save on the part of urban households from 0.24 to 0.15 between 1991 and 1994, while the propensity to save of households in rural mountain areas increased from 0.06 to 0.15. The increase in credit is a variable that helps explain such behavior (see Gonzales et al. 1998). Credit directed to urban households eases liquidity restrictions and promotes consumption, while that directed to rural households is utilized in production, given that credit is scarce in rural areas.

At the macroeconomic level and in statistical terms, there is no evidence to support the financial restriction hypothesis that says that an increase in credit reduces private saving. The positive correlation between credit and private saving during the 1991–94 period (Table 6.7) may be the result of financial system liberalization and improved financial intermediation. This is a stylized fact that requires more detailed analysis.

Improvements in the terms of trade also bring improvements in private saving. Given the structure of Peruvian exports, an improvement in the terms of trade mainly benefits mineral export companies, which account for approximately 40 percent of business saving.

Table 6.7 Relationship between Private, Public, and External Saving: 1950–94

$$\text{SPRIVGDPt} = 0.21 - 0.43\text{SGOBGDPt} - 0.37\text{SEXTGDPt} + 0.64\text{AR(1)}$$
$$\qquad\quad (17.78)\quad (-1.93)\qquad\qquad (-2.39)\qquad\qquad (5.33)$$

$R^2 = 0.51 \qquad DW = 1.90 \qquad F = 13.68$

Note: SPRIVGDPt, SGOBGDP, and SEXTGDPt are the ratio to GDP of private, public, and external saving, respectively.

In combining these results with the stylized facts, the recovery of private saving between 1990 and 1994 should be due to the recovery in disposable income, the decline in the rate of urbanization, the increase in the terms of trade, a change in the profits-salaries ratio, and the drastic drop in the inflation rate.

The Relationship between Private, External, and Public Saving

Given that the annual series of private, public, and external saving show varying degrees of integration, it is impossible to formulate a long-term relationship among them. This limitation is corrected by using a series of annual ratios for private, public, and external saving compared to GDP, which are shown to be stationary during the 1950–94 period.

The method of ordinary least squares is used, since the data are stationary. The result is shown in Table 6.7.

The results show that there is a 94 percent probability of a negative statistical association between private saving and public saving, which is proof in favor of the Ricardian hypothesis. This hypothesis says that there would be a negative relationship between private saving and public saving as a result of the behavior of private sector agents, who would internalize the changes in public indebtedness, associating them with modifications in future taxes and thus in permanent income. According to this interpretation, an improvement in the fiscal position would imply a reduction in future taxes owed, an increase in disposable permanent income, and a drop in current private saving (Schmidt-Hebbel and Servén, 1997).

External saving has not behaved like private saving (Table 6.8). The most plausible explanation for this is that the flow of capital associated with imports (derived from the increase of credit or currency appreciation) increases consumption and reduces private saving.

Table 6.8 Relationship between Public and External Saving: 1950–94

SEXTGDPt = 0.01 + 0.66SEXTGDPt–1 – 0.26SEXTGDPt–2 – 0.44SGOBGDPt + 0.64SGOBGDPt–1
         (3.41) (4.75)   (–1.89)   (–2.19)   (3.22)

R^2 = 0.55   DW = 2.08   F = 11.54

External saving has been negatively associated with public saving in the long term because the absence of public saving is generally compensated by an increase in external saving to finance investment and public expenditures.

Conclusions

From 1950 to 1994, the accumulation system was characterized by a growth in production that depended largely on investments financed by private domestic saving and public investment financed by external saving. Economic reforms introduced in 1990 do not appear to have affected this pattern since external saving has become even more important in financing public investment. What has changed between 1988 and 1991 is the structure of private saving, which is now composed of two thirds business saving and one third household saving; this structure is exactly the opposite of what it was before.

However, domestic saving has been chronically insufficient for financing investment over this period. The main reasons for this deficit are that the long-term determinants of private saving, with negative sign (rate of urbanization and income distribution), have been weighing on the more important positive determinant: disposable income. In other words, the hypothesis that permanent income is a principal determinant is confirmed, but the demographic characteristics of Peru have given the life-cycle hypothesis much less impact and have not allowed an increase in the average long-term saving rate much beyond 19 percent of GDP.

Public saving and private saving have had a significant negative association over the long term, which suggests fulfillment of the Ricardian equilibrium in Peru. External saving has been negatively associated with private and public saving over the long term. That is, external capital flows compensate for the absence of domestic saving with respect to the desired investment but perversely increase the consumption of imported goods, exercising a negative effect on private saving. This constitutes a problem for future growth in that it does not create the conditions needed to increase public saving or resort to external saving without causing a reduction in private saving. This is a far-reaching subject that requires further research.

In the short term, the most significant determinant of private saving (1950–94 period) has been the inflation rate, and its drastic reduction in the early 1990s explains the growth in private saving during 1991–94.

The dramatic change in the composition of private saving since 1991—business saving increased its share from 25 percent to 75 percent—is associated with the recovery in the growth of private saving in the 1990s. Between 1991 and 1994, there was a return in the negative association between the profits-salaries ratio and the rate of private saving, which, faced with a growth in disposable income that favors growth in profits, lends more weight to business saving over household saving. However, it is still impossible to know if this change will last over time and thus imply a structural change in the long-term determinants of private saving.

This point implies an additional problem. Business saving comes not only from profits but also from the depreciation companies undertake. In 1992 and 1994, depreciation expenses represented approximately 90 percent of saving by large companies, which account for 99 percent of business saving. This means that the business saving for financing new capital generation grows from a very low level. Since this characteristic cannot be changed, the creation of new investment (that is, not simply replacement of capital) must be financed with external saving.

At the aggregate level, there is no evidence in favor of the hypothesis of financial restriction on private saving. However, an analysis of the decrease in household saving shows that the increase in credit has a significant impact. Relief from financial restrictions between 1991 and 1994 explains, in large part, why household saving has declined, especially in urban and high-income sectors with access to consumer credit. Rural sectors that do not have access to these sources save relatively more to finance their agricultural and livestock production.

The terms of trade are positively associated with private saving through their effect on companies and help explain the growth in private saving between 1993 and 1994. Mining companies account for 40 percent of business saving. Given the nature of their production and the Peruvian export structure, they are the principal beneficiaries of favorable terms of trade, which increase their earnings and business saving.

These results are significant for economic policy. On the one hand, while disposable income grows, saving will grow, and therefore a fiscal policy that reduces taxes may be critical in increasing private saving. On the other hand, credit and monetary policy may play an active role in regulating private saving, for example, by discouraging excessive consumption. There is, however, some uncertainty with regard to the effect of structural adjustment on capital flows, since to the extent that the primary export sector is being promoted and there is excess foreign currency, the external shocks become less foreseeable and will have negative effects on saving. Clearly, a review of trade and foreign exchange policies may stabilize domestic saving.

References

Akaike, H. 1973. "A Maximum Likelihood Estimation of Gaussian Autoregressive Moving Average Models." *Biometrika.* 60: 255–65.

Alarco, G. and del Hierro, P. 1989. *La inversión en el Perú: Determinantes, financiamento y requerimientos futuros.* Lima: Friedrich Ebert Foundation.

Alarco, G., Lora, E. and Orellana S. 1990. *Técnicas de medición económica.* Lima: Friedrich Ebert Foundation.

Attanasio, O. and Weber, G. 1994. "The UK Consumption Boom of the Late 1980s: Aggregate Implications of Microeconomic Evidence." *Economic Journal.* 104: 1269–1302.

Brocun, R.L., Durbin, J. and Evans, J.M. 1975. "Techniques for Testing the Constancy of Regression Relationship over Time." *Journal of the Royal Statistical Society.* Series B, N137: 149–92.

Bosworth, B., Dornbusch, R. and Labán, R., editors. 1994. *The Chilean Economy, Policy Lessons and Challenges.* Washington, DC.: The Brookings Institution.

Casillas, L.R. 1993. "Ahorro privado, apertura externa y liberalización financiera en la América Latina." *El Trimestre Económico* (México). 60 (4), 240: 807–83.

Carroll. C.D. and Weil, D.N. 1994. "Saving and Growth: A Reinterpretation." *Carnegie-Rochester Conference Series on Public Policy.* 40: 133–92.

Chirinko, R.S. and Schaller, H. 1995. "Why Does Liquidity Matter in Investment Equations?" *Journal of Money, Credit and Banking.* 27 (2): 527–48.

Corbo, V. and Rojas, P. 1992. "Crecimiento económico de América Latina." *Cuadernos de Economia.* 29 (87): 265–94.

Deaton, A. 1995. "Growth and Saving: What Do We Know, What Do We Need to Know, and What Might We Learn?" Research Program in Development Studies. Princeton University, Princeton, N.J. Mimegraph.

Dickey, D.A. and Fuller, W. 1981. "Likelihood Ratio Statistics for Auto-regressive Time Series a Unit Root." *Econometrica.* 49: 1057–72.

Edwards, S. 1995. "Why Are Saving Rates So Different across Countries? An International Comparative Analysis." NBER Working Paper 5097. National Bureau of Economic Research, Cambridge, Mass.

Engle R. F. and Granger C. W. J. 1987. "Cointegration and Error Correction: Representation, Estimation and Testing." *Econometrica.* 55.

Fazzari, S.M., Hubbard, R.G. and Peterson, B.C. 1988. "Financing Constraints and Corporate Investment." *Brookings Papers on Economic Activity.* 1: 141–95.

Feldstein, M. 1974. "Social Security, Induced Retirement and Aggregate Capital Formation." *Journal of Political Economy.* 82 (5).

———. 1995. "Social Security and Private Saving: New Time Series Evidence." NBER Working Paper 5054. National Bureau of Economic Research, Cambridge, Mass.

Feldstein, M. and Bachetta, P. 1991. "National Saving and International Investment." In B.D. Bernheim and J.B. Shoven, editors. *National Saving and Economic Performance.* Chicago: University of Chicago Press.

Feldstein, M. and Horioka, C. 1980. "Domestic Saving and International Capital Flows." *Economic Journal.* 90 (June): 314–29.

FitzGerald, E.V.K. 1979. *The Political Economy of Peru 1956–1978. Economic Development and the Restructuring of Capital.* Cambridge University Press.

Friedman, M. 1957. "A Theory of the Consumption Function." Princeton, N.J.: Princeton University Press.

Gersovitz, M. 1988. "Savings and Development." In H. Chenery and T.N. Srinivasan, editors. *Handbook of Development Economics*. Vol. 1. Amsterdam: North-Holland.

Gonzales de Olarte, E. 1993. "Economic Stabilization Adjustment under Fujimori." 35(2). *Journal of Interamerican Studies and World Affairs*.

————. 1994. "Peru's Difficult Road to Economic Development." In J. Tulchin and G. Bland, editors. *Peru in Crisis, Dictatorship or Democracy?* Woodrow Wilson Center Current Studies on Latin America. Boulder, Colo.: Lynne Rienner Publishers.

————. 1996. "Inversión privada, crecimiento y ajuste estructural en el Perú, 1950–1995." Documento de Trabajo. Consortio de Investigación Económica, Instituto de Estudios Peruanos, Lima.

Gonzales de Olarte, E. and Samamé, L. 1994. *El péndulo perunao: políticas económicas, gobernabilidad y sub-desarrollo, 1963–1990*. Serie Análisis Económico 14. 2d ed. Instituto de Estudios Peruanos, Lima.

Gonzales de Olarte, E., Lévano Castro, C. and Llontop Ledesma, P. 1998. "Determinantes del ahorro interno y ajuste estructural en el Peru." Working Paper R-327. Office of the Chief Economist, Inter-American Development Bank, Washington, DC.

Held, G. and Uthoff, A. 1995. "Indicators and Determinants of Saving for Latin America." Working Paper 25. ECLAC, Santiago.

Iguíniz, J. 1983. "Perspectivas y opciones frente a la crisis." *Revista Pensamiento Iberoamericano*. No. 4. Madrid: ICICEPAL.

IDB (Inter-American Development Bank). 1994. *Annual Report 1994*. Washington, DC.

Jappelli, T. and Pagano, M. 1994. "Saving, Growth and Liquidity Constraints." *Quarterly Journal of Economics.* 109: 83–109.

Jiménez, F. 1987. "El comportamiento de la inversión privada y el papel del Estado: Notas sobre la acumulación de capital en una economía no integrada." *Revista Socialismo y Participación.* No. 38: 13–28. CEDEP, Lima.

Johansen, S. and Juselius, K. 1990. "Maximum Likelihood Estimation and Inference on Cointegration, with Applications to the Demand for Money." *Oxford Bulletin of Economics and Statistics.* 52 (2): 169–210.

Kaldor, N. 1957. "A Model of Economic Growth." *Economic Journal.* 57.

Kaplan, S. and Zingales, L. 1995. "Do Financing Constraints Explain Why Investment Is Correlated with Cash Flow?" NBER Working Paper 5267. National Bureau of Economic Research, Cambridge, Mass.

Keynes, J. 1972. *The Collected Writings of John Maynard Keynes.* Macmillan.

Klein, L.R. 1960. "Entrepreneurial Saving." In I. Friend and R. Jones, editors. *Proceedings of the Conference on Consumption and Saving.* Vol. 2. Philadelphia: University of Pennsylvania.

Lewis, W.A. 1954. "Economic Development with Unlimited Supplies of Labor." *The Manchester School.* 22: 139–91.

Modigliani, F. 1979. "Utility Analysis and the Consumption Function: An Attempt at Integration." In A. Abel, editor. *The Collected Papers of Franco Modigliani.* Vol. 2. Cambridge, Mass.: MIT Press.

Modigliani, F. and Ando, A. 1963. "The Life Cycle Hypothesis of Saving: Aggregate Implication and Tests." *American Economic Review.*

Modigliani, F. and Brumberg, R. 1954. "Utility Analysis and the Consumption Function: An Interpretation of Cross-Section Data." In K. Kurihara, editor. *Post-Keynesian Economics.* New Brunswick, N. J.: Rutgers University Press.

Muellbauer, J. and Murphy, A. 1990. "Is the UK Balance of Payments Sustainable?" *Economic Policy*. 5 (October): 348–95.

Passinetti, L. 1962. "Rate of Profit and Income Distribution in Relation to the Rate of Economic Growth." *Review of Economic Studies*. 29: 267–79.

Pinzás, T. 1993. "Interpretaciones de la relación entre sector externo y la economía global." Documento de Trabajo. Consorcio de Investigación Económica, Instituto de Estudios Peruanos, Lima.

Romero, L. 1991. "El sistema financiero peruano después de la reforma." Documento de Trabajo. Consorcio de Investigación Económica, Instituto de Estudios Peruanos, Lima.

Rossi, N. 1988. "Government Spending, the Real Interest Rate, and the Behavior of Liquidity-Constrained Consumers in Developing Countries." *IMF Staff Papers*. 35: 104–40.

Schmidt-Hebbel, K., Servén, L. 1997. *Saving across the World: Puzzles and Policies*. World Bank Discussion Paper 354. Washington, DC.

Schmidt-Hebbel, K. and Servén, L. and Solimano, A. 1996. "Saving and Investment: Paradigms, Puzzles, and Policies." *The World Bank Research Observer*. 11 (1): 87–117.

Seminario, B. 1995. "Reformas estructurales y política de estabilización." Working Document 22. University of the Pacific Consortium.

Seminario B. and Buillón, C. 1992. "Notas sobre el crecimiento económico del Perú." Red. Macroeconómica Latinoamericana, V Reunión, Cochabamba (Ms).

Surinach, J., Artis, M., Lopez, E. and Sansó, A. 1995. *Análisis económico regional. Nociones básicas de la teoría de la cointegración*. Barcelona: Bosch and Gimpera Foundation.

Thorne, A. 1986. *The Determinants of Saving in a Developing Economy: The Case of Peru 1960–1984.* Ph.D. thesis. University of Oxford, Oxford, U.K.

Thorne, A., Iguiniz, J., Ferrari, C. and Polar, A. 1987. "Ahora interno y financiamiento del desarrollo." Research Studio, Friedrich Ebert Foundation, Lima.

Thorpe, R. and Bertram, G. 1978. *Peru, 1890–1977: Growth and Policy in an Open Economy.* New York: Columbia University Press.

Vega, M. 1989. "Inversiones y cambio técnico en el crecimiento de la economía peruana." *Economía.* 12 (24): 9–48. Catholic University of Peru, Economics Department, Lima.

White, H. 1980. "A Heteroskedasticity-Consistent Covariance Estimator and a Direct Test for Heteroskedasticity." *Econometrica.* 48: 817–38.

CHAPTER 7

Determinants of Domestic Saving in Uruguay

Nelson Noya, Fernando Lorenzo, and Carlos Grau-Pérez[1]

This chapter analyzes the determinants of domestic saving in Uruguay using time series of macroeconomic aggregates for two periods: 1955–94 (yearly aggregates) and 1975–94 (quarterly aggregates). It analyzes separately those factors that relate to private saving and those that relate to public saving. It focuses on the consequences of Uruguay's financial deregulation (begun in 1974–76 and not reversed) for private saving and on two exchange rate–based stabilization experiments. The first of these, in effect between October 1978 and November 1982, used prior announcements of changes in the exchange rate (following an exchange rate table, or *tablita*), and the second, in effect since March 1991, uses a floating rate within a band.

An econometric analysis of private consumption assesses the determinants of private saving. To assess public saving, fiscal policy is broken down into its discretionary and nondiscretionary components. The results suggest that the drop in the private saving rate observed since 1992 may be interpreted as transitory, generated by circumstances surrounding the stabilization plan, namely, an expansion in bank credit, in particular bank consumer credit, and growth in income.

[1] Nelson Noya is the former director of the Centro de Investigaciones Económicas (CINVE); Fernando Lorenzo and Carlos Grau-Pérez are senior researchers at CINVE.

Basic Data on Domestic Saving

Stylized Facts

Uruguay has a low rate of domestic saving even when compared with the rest of Latin America, where saving rates are typically lower than those elsewhere in the world. Over the last 40 years Uruguay's saving rate has averaged 13.5 percent of GDP, within a range between 9 and 17 percent. Between the 1982 external debt crisis and 1991 the saving rate remained practically unchanged at 15 to 16 percent of GDP. However, between 1992 and 1994 that rate dropped to 12.5 percent. Figures 7.1 and 7.2 show the trends in Uruguay's domestic and external saving rates. Domestic saving has evolved in almost symmetrical fashion with external saving. The same is true of both the private and the public components of domestic saving: increases in both have corresponded to decreases in external saving (Figure 7.2).

Figure 7.2 also shows that the drop in domestic saving in the 1990s is due entirely to a drop in private saving; public saving in the 1990s has risen to historically high levels. The drop in private saving began in 1990: this component of saving has fallen from more than 17 percent of GDP in 1989 to 9 percent in recent years.

Although the economy underwent important structural changes in the early 1970s, drastic changes in the behavior of domestic saving were not registered at first glance. Private saving, for example, is on average 12.1 percent of GDP, exactly what it was for the 20 years before and after 1975. Domestic saving was higher in the period following 1975, when the average public saving rate went from 0.7 percent to 1.9 percent of GDP.

The two periods in which exchange rate stabilization plans were in place coincided with reductions in the domestic saving rate (in 1978–82 and again in 1990–94), although the same is not true of private saving. Private saving showed no changes during the first of the two periods but fell considerably during the second. In Uruguay, the pattern of private consumption booms that characterizes this type of program is repeated, but in neither period does it translate into a drop in private saving. In both cases, capital inflows provide for an increase in external saving.

Other problems are inherent in the generic methodology of national accounting and are not specific to Uruguay—for example, the use of nominal rather than real interest rates. Tables 7.1 and 7.2 show possible measure-

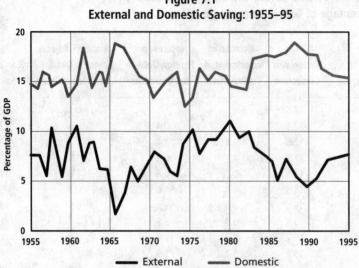

Figure 7.1
External and Domestic Saving: 1955–95

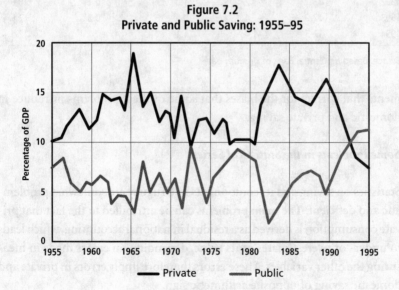

Figure 7.2
Private and Public Saving: 1955–95

**Table 7.1 Private Saving and Corrections: 1955–94
(percentage of GDP in current prices)**

Years	Saving w/o Correction	Valuation of Investment in Construction	Interest on Foreign Debt to Nonresidents	Inflation Adjustment in Dollars on External Debt	Corrected Saving
1955–64	12.5			–0.1	12.4
1965–74	12.3		0.4	0.3	13.0
1975–79	12.5	1.3	1.4	–0.1	14.9
1980	11.7	4.7	0.9	–1.6	15.7
1981	11.4	–0.2	0.8	–1.0	11.0
1982	11.3	2.1	1.6	0.3	15.3
1983	15.5	0.0	1.4	0.5	17.5
1984	15.9	–0.3	1.8	1.5	18.8
1985	15.7	–0.4	1.8	–0.3	16.7
1986	16.2	0.2	1.9	–2.4	16.0
1987	16.3	0.2	2.1	0.9	19.5
1988	17.2	0.1	2.7	1.4	21.4
1989	16.6	–0.2	2.8	1.4	20.6
1990	16.0	–0.4	2.5	1.3	19.4
1991	15.9	–0.9	1.9	0.1	17.0
1992	13.7	–1.2	1.0	0.1	13.6
1993	12.9	–1.4	0.9	0.2	12.6
1994	12.5	–1.4	1.1	0.1	12.4

Source: Based on Central Bank of Uruguay data.

ments that correct for the biases that some of these problems introduce in domestic and private saving.

Some Problems in the Statistical Series

Statistics on saving and its components in Uruguay are somewhat problematic and deficient. The main problems can be attributed to the fact that private consumption is derived as a residual in national accounting, which leads to under- or overestimates of its value, depending on errors made in measuring the other variables. These errors therefore imply errors in private and domestic saving of opposite arithmetic sign.

Adjustments to these estimates, however, lead to the conclusion that these errors do not radically change the most notable features of domestic

Table 7.2 Private Saving and Bank Losses: 1955–94 (percentage of GDP in current prices)

Years	Saving w/o Correction	Valuation of Investment in Construction	Interest on Public Debt to Nonresidents	Inflation Adjustment in Dollars on External Debt	Inflation Tax	Central Bank Parafiscal Deficit	Losses by Managed Banks	BHU Losses	Inflation Adjustment of Interest	Corrected Saving
1955–64	11.7			0.0	-1.6					10.1
1965–74	12.5			0.3	-2.7					10.2
1975–79	8.6	1.3	1.4	0.3	-2.0				-0.4	9.3
1980	7.5	4.7	0.9	0.6	-1.4				-0.1	12.28
1981	13.1	-0.2	0.8	0.6	-1.3				0.0	13.04
1982	16.8	2.1	1.6	0.7	-1.1	0.8			0.0	21.02
1983	19.5	0.0	1.4	0.2	-2.0	3.3			-0.1	22.43
1984	17.8	-0.3	1.8	0.5	-2.1	3.7			-1.0	21.32
1985	14.9	-0.4	1.8	-0.1	-2.3	3.0			-0.8	16.81
1986	14.0	0.2	1.9	-0.8	-2.4	3.7			-1.7	16.66
1987	13.9	0.2	2.1	0.3	-2.0	2.6			-1.5	17.18
1988	15.3	0.1	2.7	0.6	-2.5	2.7			-1.7	18.85
1989	17.2	-0.2	2.8	0.6	-2.7	3.0			-1.6	20.66
1990	14.0	-0.4	2.5	0.5	-1.9	3.3			-1.8	18.09
1991	11.0	-0.9	1.9	0.0	-1.4	2.1			-0.6	12.73
1992	7.1	-1.2	1.0	0.0	-1.2	1.4	0.1	0.4	-0.4	7.74
1993	8.8	-1.4	0.9	0.1	-1.3	0.8		0.1	-0.2	7.98
1994	9.1	-1.4	1.1	0.0	-1.1	0.6		0.0	-0.1	8.42

Note: BHU, Banco Hipotecario del Uruguay.

and private saving, or of external saving, in Uruguay. On the contrary, in the case of private and domestic saving, the adjustments accentuate the drop in the 1990s. In the econometric analyses conducted in the following sections, given that the only possible correction for all of the periods is related to the inflation tax, the series used take into account only this correction.

Determinants of Private Consumption

The procedure for identifying the determinants of private saving consisted of analyzing the determinants of private consumption. This agrees with most of the theoretical literature, which is based on consumption functions. The final conclusions, however, are expressed in terms of the determinants of private saving.

Similarly, the strategy does not attempt to identify the "true" model of private consumption but rather puts to the test some of the simple hypotheses frequently seen in the literature, with respect both to the determinants of consumption and to the effects introduced by stabilization or financial deregulation policies. In several cases this strategy was imposed by the availability and quality of the data.

First, a brief synthesis of the permanent income–life cycle hypothesis (PI-LC) is provided as the alternative to the liquidity constraint hypothesis. Second, the specification ultimately selected is used to compare the two hypotheses. Next, based on the same specification, the effects of the two exchange rate stabilization plans and the consequences of financial deregulation are analyzed. To the extent that this specification results in changes in consumption being viewed as the dependent variable, the comparisons provide information on the determinants of cyclical variations in consumption, since this is a first-order integrated variable. Reference is made to long-term determinants only in the last subsection, where the role played by the variables associated with fiscal policy is analyzed, putting the Ricardian equivalence hypothesis to the test.

Theoretical Framework

The PI-LC hypothesis in Hall's modern formulation (1978) is based on a representative consumer with rational expectations who maximizes expected utility over time.[2] The utility functions $U(C_t)$ for each period are assumed to be identical and separable. Given budgetary restrictions, the first-order condition, or Euler equation, is derived from the optimization program:

$$E_t U'(C_{t+1}) = \left[(1+\delta)/(1+r)\right]U'(C_t).$$

If the subjective discount rate δ is equal to the real interest rate r then the Euler equation says that the best predictor of marginal utility for the next period, $E_t U'(C_{t+1})$, is the marginal utility of the current period. If the utility functions for each period are assumed to be quadratic, the marginal utilities are linear, which may be expressed as follows:

$$C_{t+1} = C_t + \varepsilon_t$$

with ε being white noise. In other words, consumption follows a random walk, and there is no present variable that can predict future consumption.

This result presumes constant real interest rates, which is obviously an oversimplification, especially for countries like Uruguay where real interest rates have fluctuated by more than 20 percent over very short periods. Generalization of the above result to include changes in the real interest rate, conducted by Hansen and Singleton (1983) and Hall (1988), produces an equation like the following:

$$C_{t+1} = C_t + \theta r_t + \varepsilon_t$$

where the lower-case variables that represent quantities are expressed in logarithms (a convention followed from here on). Parameter θ is the intertemporal elasticity of substitution in consumption, which is constant only in the case where the utility functions of each period are isoelastic (CES).

However, beginning with Flavin's empirical work (1981), it has been found that the expected changes in current income have some predictive power over future consumption. For this reason, an additional determinant of variation in private consumption, according to Flavin's proposal, is constituted by variations in current income.

---

[2] See Deaton (1992), specifically chapter 3.

An alternative hypothesis is that some consumers face liquidity constraints. This hypothesis, according to Campbell and Mankiw (1989), may be formulated on the supposition that a proportion λ of representative consumers is constrained by lack of liquidity and consumes all of its income. In this way, the PI-LC hypothesis is grounded in a more general model that allows for the existence of liquidity constraints for a given group of consumers. If, for the rest, one adheres to the PI-LC hypothesis, then total consumption is derived from the aggregation of constrained and unconstrained consumers:

$$\Delta c_t = \mu + \lambda \Delta y_t + \theta r_t + \varepsilon_t.$$ [1]

In this way, the contrasting strategy consists of analyzing whether the parameter λ, corresponding to the variation in income for the current period, is significantly different from zero. If it is, the PI-LC null hypothesis is discarded, and one may conclude that liquidity constraints constitute a determinant of the trend in private consumption. In addition, this same parameter provides an estimate of the proportion of liquidity-constrained consumers.

The Campbell-Mankiw strategy is a way of contrasting liquidity constraints in their simplest forms with versions of the PI-LC hypothesis. However, this procedure has been criticized for interpreting the relationship between consumption variations and current income variations as not necessarily a product of liquidity constraints. That is, the simultaneous dependence of consumption on income can be sustained by factors other than liquidity constraints (for example, see Attanasio, 1994).

Permanent Income Hypothesis Comparison

The comparison was made with annual series for the 1955–94 period, and with quarterly series for the 1975–94 period. The annual series is based on official data from the Central Bank of Uruguay.[3] Although the central bank has prepared quarterly data equating supply and demand in constant prices

---

[3] For purposes of reconciling the different methodologies with those on which the most recent series and those prior to 1983 were based, the methodological criteria of the pre-1983 series had to be maintained, particularly to include interest earned by financial institutions in

since 1983, for purposes of this analysis series have been developed for the entire 1975–94 period based on the related series method of Chow and Lin (1971). The resulting series for the post-1983 period does not differ significantly from the official series.

According to the specification indicated by the theory, the variables that should be taken into account in the analysis are private consumption,[4] disposable income from the private sector,[5] and the expected real interest rate on deposits in domestic currency.[6] Estimates were also made using the real ex post interest rate, but the results are not appreciably different. Consumption and income were worked out in logarithms.

Specification tests indicate that private consumption, disposable income, and the expected real interest rate are first-order integrated variables. For this reason, including the level of the expected real interest rate in equations with differences of both disposable income and consumption leads to problems in the econometric specification. Therefore, two types of contrasting equations were tested, with and without the expected real interest rate,[7] and another equation was considered:

$$\Delta C_t = \mu + \lambda \Delta y_t + \varepsilon_t. \tag{2}$$

Equations [1] and [2] should be estimated using key variables, since consumption and income variations with one lag are not valid instruments (see Campbell and Mankiw, 1989). In the search for strong empirical re-

---

measuring GDP at market prices. For this reason, the figures used are not consistent with official figures from the years after 1983.

[4] Ideally, consumption of nondurable goods should also be considered, but a reliable estimate of this aggregate variable was unavailable.

[5] From the annual data, gross disposable income from the private sector (equivalent to national income minus direct taxes plus net transfers from the government to families) was corrected by the inflation tax, in all cases in constant 1983 prices. In the quarterly series, only GDP net of the inflation tax was considered as an approximation of disposable income from the private sector.

[6] Inflation expectations were estimated like the predictions for autoregressive models with seasonal price level components. The models were adjusted for each period using the available information from prior periods; that is, the sample of observations varied over time.

[7] Unit root comparisons were made for all of the annual and quarterly series under consideration. The results of these comparisons are not included but are available from the authors upon request.

**Table 7.3 Basic Comparison of the Permanent Income Hypothesis:
Key Variable, Estimation of Equation [1]
(annual data, 1955–94)**

Instruments	Actual Number of Observations	Results of OLS Regressions (a) Δy_t	$\hat{\lambda}$ (b)	Comparison of Constraints (c)
$\Delta y_{t-2}, \Delta c_{t-2}$	37	0.01	0.3638 (2.07)	−0.08
Δy_{t-2}	37	0.03	0.3664 (2.08)	−0.05
$\Delta y_{t-2}, \Delta y_{t-3},$ $\Delta c_{t-2}, \Delta c_{t-3}$	36	0.09	0.3386 (1.91)	−0.10
$\Delta y_{t-2}, \Delta y_{t-3}$	36	0.09	0.3730 (2.11)	−0.08
$\Delta y_{t-2}, \Delta y_{t-3}, \Delta y_{t-4},$ $\Delta c_{t-2}, \Delta c_{t-3}, \Delta c_{t-4}$	35	0.14	0.4936 (2.88)	−0.07
$\Delta y_{t-2}, \Delta y_{t-3}, \Delta y_{t-4}$	35	0.18	0.4781 (2.72)	−0.06

Note: Numbers in parentheses are t-statistics.
a. R^2 adjusted from the regression of the variable over the set of instruments.
b. Parameter estimated by key variables.
c. R^2 adjusted from the regression of equation [2] estimated by OLS over the instruments.

sults, different estimates were tested with different instruments. Variations of both variables between two and four lags were used as instruments. The results are shown in Tables 7.3 through 7.6.

In all cases the result is the same: the null hypothesis that the coefficient on variations in income is indistinguishable from zero is rejected. Therefore, the empirical results indicate that, during the period analyzed, the validity of the PI–LC hypothesis cannot be upheld and that liquidity constraints are important in explaining trends in consumption.[8] Estimates of the proportion of constrained consumers vary between 30 and 53 per-

---

[8] This result is compatible with the result obtained by Echenique (1995) using another methodology and different data. Echenique compared the generalized Euler equation for variable interest rates using the generalized time method and private consumption series prepared from tax receipts.

Table 7.4 Basic Comparison of the Permanent Income Hypothesis: Key Variable, Estimation of Equation [1] (annual data, 1955–94)

Instruments	Actual Number of Observations	Results of OLS Regressions (a) Δy_t	r_t	$\hat{\lambda}$ (b)	$\hat{\theta}$ (b)	Comparison of Constraints (c)
$\Delta y_{t-2}, \Delta c_{t-2}, r_{t-2}$	37	−0.03	0.28	0.3821 (2.13)	0.0966 (0.48)	−0.12
$\Delta y_{t-2}, r_{t-2}$	37	0.00	0.30	0.3829 (2.13)	0.0905 (0.45)	−0.08
$\Delta y_{t-2}, \Delta c_{t-2}$	37	0.01	0.20	0.3854 (2.15)	0.5121 (0.55)	−0.09
$\Delta y_{t-2}, \Delta y_{t-3}, \Delta c_{t-2}, \Delta c_{t-3}, r_{t-2}, r_{t-3}$	36	0.03	0.25	0.3785 (1.93)	0.0883 (0.48)	−0.17
$\Delta y_{t-2}, \Delta y_{t-3}, r_{t-2}, r_{t-3}$	36	0.04	0.27	0.4075 (2.15)	0.0974 (0.50)	−0.14
$\Delta y_{t-2}, \Delta y_{t-3}, \Delta c_{t-2}, \Delta c_{t-3}$	36	0.09	0.17	0.3016 (1.54)	−0.1965 (−0.44)	−0.09
$\Delta y_{t-2}, \Delta y_{t-3}, \Delta y_{t-4}, \Delta c_{t-2}, \Delta c_{t-3}, \Delta c_{t-4}, r_{t-2}, r_{t-3}, r_{t-4}$	35	0.05	0.20	0.5033 (2.92)	0.0303 (0.21)	−0.17
$\Delta y_{t-2}, \Delta y_{t-3}, \Delta y_{t-4}, r_{t-2}, r_{t-3}, r_{t-4}$	35	0.08	0.23	0.4928 (2.82)	0.0965 (0.60)	−0.20
$\Delta y_{t-2}, \Delta y_{t-3}, \Delta y_{t-4}, \Delta c_{t-2}, \Delta c_{t-3}, \Delta c_{t-2}$	35	0.14	0.12	0.4870 (2.84)	−0.116 (−0.42)	−0.07

Note: Numbers in parentheses are t-statistics.

a. R^2 adjusted from the regression of the variable over the instruments.

b. Parameter estimated by key variables.

c. R^2 adjusted from the regression of equation [1] residual values estimated by OLS over the instruments.

Table 7.5 Basic Comparison of the Permanent Income Hypothesis: Key Variable Estimation of Equation [2] (with Deterministic Seasonality) (quarterly data, 1975:I–1994:IV)

Instruments	Actual Number of Observations	Results of OLS Regressions (a) Δy_t	$\hat{\lambda}$ (b)	Comparison of Restrictions (c)
$\Delta y_{t-2}, \Delta y_{t-3}$	76	0.90	0.3598 (1.51)	0.02
$\Delta y_{t-2}, \Delta y_{t-3}, \Delta y_{t-4}$	75	0.91	0.4620 (1.95)	0.01
$\Delta y_{t-2}, \Delta y_{t-3},$ $\Delta y_{t-4}, \Delta y_{t-5}$	74	0.90	0.4739 (2.00)	0.00

Note: Numbers in parentheses are t-statistics.
a. R^2 adjusted from the regression of the variable over the instruments.
b. Parameter estimated by key variables.
c. R^2 adjusted from the regression of equation [1] residual values estimatd by OLS over the instruments.

Table 7.6 Basic Comparison of the Permanent Income Hypothesis: Key Variable Estimation of Equation [1] (with Deterministic Seasonality) (quarterly data, 1955–94)

Instruments	Actual Number of Observations	Results of OLS Regressions (a) Δy_t	r_t	$\hat{\lambda}$ (b)	$\hat{\theta}$ (b)	Comparison of Restrictions (c)
$\Delta y_{t-2}, \Delta y_{t-3}, \Delta y_{t-4},$ $\Delta c_{t-2}, \Delta c_{t-3}, \Delta c_{t-4},$ $r_{t-2}, r_{t-3}, r_{t-4}$	75	0.92	0.81	0.3987 (1.67)	0.0162 (0.23)	0.03
$\Delta y_{t-2}, \Delta y_{t-3}, \Delta y_{t-4},$ $r_{t-2}, r_{t-3}, r_{t-4}$	75	0.91	0.80	0.4831 (2.01)	−0.0184 (−0.25)	0.00

Note: Numbers in parentheses are t-statistics.
a. R^2 adjusted from the regression of the variable over the instruments.
b. Parameter estimated by key variables.
c. R^2 adjusted from the regression of equation [1] residual values estimatd by OLS over the instruments.

cent, although the majority of reliable estimates range from about 38 percent to about 49 percent.

Exchange Rate–Based Stabilization Plans and Liquidity Constraints

Many exchange rate–based stabilization plans have been accompanied by a drop in private saving (a consumption boom) and a substantial increase in external saving (a rise in the current account deficit). The Uruguayan experience is no exception.

The two episodes analyzed here share similarities as well as differences. In both cases there was a boom in consumption, although this began at least two quarters before the stabilization plan was launched. From that point, consumption grew at an increasing rate until it reached a maximum growth rate of about 4.5 percent approximately two years later. The 1970s witnessed a slowdown in this trend, although this does not differ from the 1990s. Whereas the plan put into place in 1991 remains in effect, that of the 1970s was abandoned at the end of 1982. One important difference here is that during the 1970s, as consumption grew, private saving did not drop simultaneously, whereas with the 1991 stabilization plan, when consumption increased, private saving fell.

The following arguments are usually used to explain the consumption boom associated with this type of stabilization plan:

- The stabilization program's lack of credibility leads private agents to shift their future consumption to the present, because the relative price of consumption is lower than it will be after the expected failure of the program (Calvo, 1986).
- The drop in inflation at the outset of the program generates a wealth effect owing to the increased value of government debt securities, which are presumed to be part of private wealth.
- Liquidity constraints exist and are reduced under the stabilization plan, owing to an increase in the availability of bank credit to the private sector. This can be the result of an increased demand for money as a result of the stabilization; a decrease in real public debt held by banks as a result of tight fiscal policies, which gives the banks greater lending capacity; or an increase in external bank holdings owing to capital inflows (Copelman, 1994).

In the case of Uruguay, Bruno's hypothesis does not apply because public debt fell in real terms during both stabilization plans. Conversely, Calvo's hypothesis presumes that the PI-LC hypothesis is valid.[9]

Having proved in the previous section that the PI-LC hypothesis is unacceptable and that liquidity constraints exist, the important effects of these constraints during stabilization plans will now be tested. This requires testing the hypothesis that the proportion of liquidity-constrained consumers decreases when these policies are in effect. Only the quarterly data will be considered here, using the following equation:[10]

$$\Delta c_t = \mu + \lambda_0 \Delta y_t + \lambda_1 D_{1t} \Delta y_t + \lambda_2 D_{2t} \Delta y_t + \varepsilon_t \qquad [3]$$

where the variables D_{1t} and D_{2t} are qualitative variables referring, respectively, to the first and second stabilization plans, and having a value of one during the period when the respective plan is in place, and zero when it is not. If, during the stabilization periods, the proportion of liquidity-constrained consumers is reduced, one would expect the estimated values for λ_1 and λ_2 to be negative.

The results presented in Table 7.7 indicate that, during stabilization, the liquidity constraints continue to be important; that is, variations in consumption continue to be sensitive to the behavior of current income. Yet although the signs of the estimates obtained by λ_1 and λ_2 are the expected ones, neither parameter is statistically significant. This lack of significance may be due to the fact that the constraints are eased gradually as credit expands, not in one fell swoop upon implementation of the stabilization plan. If this is so, the correct comparison hypothesis would establish that the λ parameter is, in reality, a function of credit expansion. Assuming that the parameter associated with the real interest rate also varies with credit

---

[9] Bergara and Licandro (1994) analyze the lack of credibility of the exchange rate band between 1991 and 1994, under time horizons ranging from one to six months, by adapting the Svensson test (1990), which consists of determining whether the expectations of devaluation calculated from the differential between local interest rates in domestic currency and in foreign currency imply exchange rates within or outside the band.

[10] Use of the extended version of this equation, which includes the effects of the expected real interest rate, does not affect the conclusions. The previous section pointed out that including the real interest rate presents certain difficulties, since it is a first-order integrated variable.

Table 7.7 Comparison of the Permanent Income Hypothesis during Stabilization Experiments: Key Variable, Estimation of Equation [3] (with Deterministic Seasonality)
(quarterly data, 1975:I–1994:IV)

Estimated Parameters	Set of Instruments		
	$\Delta y_{t-2},\ \Delta y_{t-3}$	$\Delta y_{t-2},\ \Delta y_{t-3},$ Δy_{t-4}	$\Delta y_{t-2},\ \Delta y_{t-3},$ $\sim\!\Delta y_{t-4},\ \Delta y_{t-5}$
$\hat{\mu}$	0.0035	0.0041	0.0033
	(0.55)	(0.66)	(0.65)
$\hat{\lambda}_0$	0.5889	0.7240	0.7075
	(1.97)	(2.51)	(2.48)
$\hat{\lambda}_1$	−0.1846	−0.2052	−0.1953
	(−0.95)	(−0.95)	(−1.05)
$\hat{\lambda}_2$	−0.0542	−0.0834	−0.0729
	(−0.27)	(−0.43)	(−0.37)
Adjusted R^2	0.86	0.89	0.90
Actual Number of Observations	76	75	74

Note: Numbers in parentheses are t-statistics.

a. Parameters estimated by key variables.

expansion, and that in both cases the relationship is linear, equation [3] becomes:

$$c_t = \mu + \lambda_0 \Delta y_t + \lambda \Delta y_t \Delta CRE_t + \theta_0 r_t + \theta_c r_t \Delta CRE_t + \varepsilon_t \qquad [4]$$

where ΔCRE_t is the variation between bank credit and income. To the extent that credit expands, one can expect that liquidity constraints will diminish, which implies that the expected sign of the coefficient associated with the variable $\Delta y_t \Delta CRE_t$ would be negative.

The results shown in Table 7.8 indicate that, in reality, credit expansion helps to reduce liquidity constraints. A second result is that, even when the effects of bank credit expansion on the liquidity constraints are accounted

Table 7. 8 Private Consumption and Credit to the Private Sector: Key Variable Estimation of Equation [4] (with Deterministic Seasonality) (quarterly data, 1975:I–1994:IV)

Estimate Parameters	Set of instruments [a] $\Delta y_{t-2}, \Delta y_{t-3}, \Delta y_{t-4}$ $\Delta c_{c\,t-2}, \Delta c_{t-3}, \Delta c_{t-4}$ $r_{t-2}, r_{t-3}, r_{t-4}$
$\hat{\mu}$	−0.0151
	(−0.99)
$\hat{\lambda}_0$	0.5440
	(2.36)
$\hat{\lambda}_c$	−14.8345
	(−2.11)
$\hat{\theta}_0$	0.0821
	(1.23)
$\hat{\theta}_c$	−6.5748
	(−2.32)
Adjusted R^2	0.91
Actual Number of Observations	74

Note: Numbers in parentheses are t-statistics.
a. Parameters estimated by key variables.

for, the effects of the current income variations on consumption variations are never fully eliminated. Credit expansion in relation to income is an important factor, but it is not the only thing that explains the existence of liquidity constraints.

The results in Table 7.8 are obtained by considering bank consumer credit, because this adjustment is slightly greater than that obtained with bank credit to the entire private sector. From the analytical standpoint of the stabilization episodes, the use of one or another type of credit modifies the evaluation of the episode, to the extent that the two episodes are different with regard to the growth of credit to the entire private sector in real terms, although they are similar with respect to consumer credit expansion. As shown in Figure 7.3, bank credit expansion to private sector resi-

Figure 7.3
Bank Credit, Total and Consumer
(1975=100)

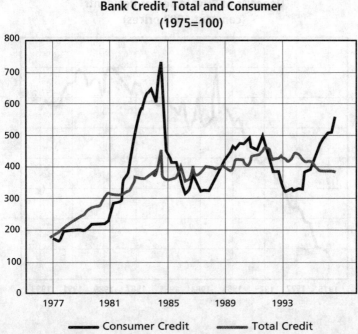

——— Consumer Credit ———— Total Credit

dents was important during the 1978–82 episode, whereas during the 1990 episode there was a real tightening of all credit to the private sector.[11]

There are also differences in the sources of credit expansion. In the 1978 episode the expansion came both from capital inflows (see Figure 7.6) and from recovery of intermediation levels (see Figure 7.4), which was mainly due to the increase in foreign currency deposits in the domestic banking system. However, whereas the recovery process for the degree of financial intermediation, as measured by deposits, began in 1975, capital inflows from nonresidents to the local system date back to the period of the stabilization experiment. In contrast, from 1978 to 1982, the improvement in fiscal revenues does not seem to have been a source of increased availability of bank credit (see Figure 7.5).

---

[11] The existence of problem portfolios, as a by-product of the 1982 financial crisis which persisted to the end of the 1980s, may be contributing to the distortion of credit measurement.

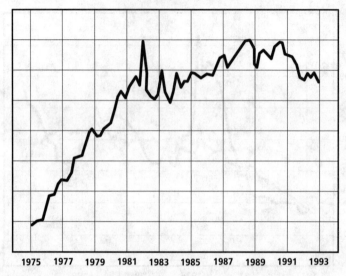

Figure 7.4
Deposits of Private Sector Residents
(constant 1983 prices)

Figure 7.5
Net Liabilities to the Public Sector
(constant 1983 prices)

Figure 7.6
Net Liabilities to Nonresidents except International Reserves
(constant 1989 prices)

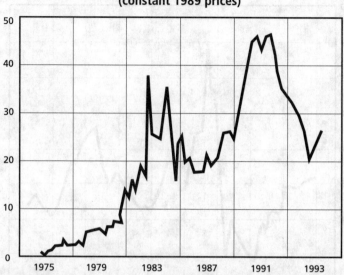

Figure 7.7 shows the growth in the degree of liquidity constraints, measured as the variable coefficient of income in equation [4], which is a function of the relationship between credit and income. From this we may observe that, in both episodes, liquidity constraints were eased. The coefficient fell by around 0.2 to 0.25 in both cases. To evaluate the importance of the different explanatory variables in both stabilization experiments, Figures 7.8 through 7.11 show their contribution to consumption growth (that is, the logarithmic difference) in the two stabilization episodes considered.

In both plans, contributions from the effects of income growth (direct or together with credit) have a time pattern similar to that of consumption growth, especially at the beginning of both episodes. The combination of the income growth effects and their interaction with credit contributes approximately 1.3 percent to the upturn. The direct effect of income is more important, but the positive effect of its interaction with credit is greater just a few years after the plan starts. This would indicate that, when consumption begins to shift downward, the easing of credit restrictions contributes toward sustaining consumption beyond what the income variations would

Figure 7.7
Degree of Liquidity Constraints: 1978–95

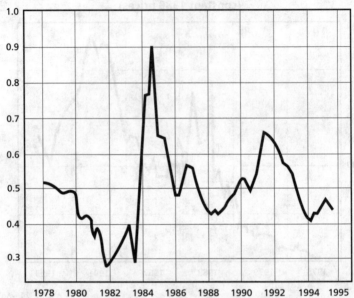

Figure 7.8
Contributions to Consumption Growth
(Income and Credit Income)

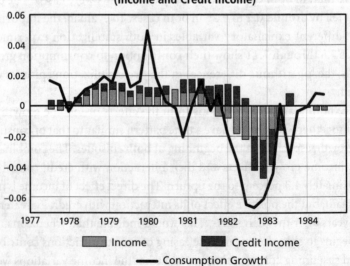

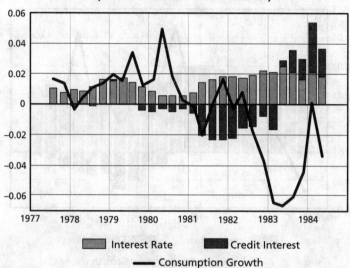

Figure 7.9
Contributions to Consumption Growth
(Interest Rate and Credit Interest)

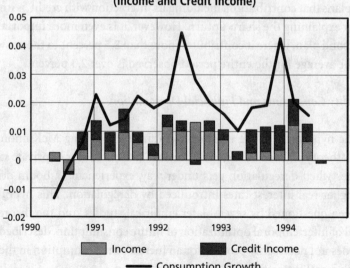

Figure 7.10
Contributions to Consumption Growth
(Income and Credit Income)

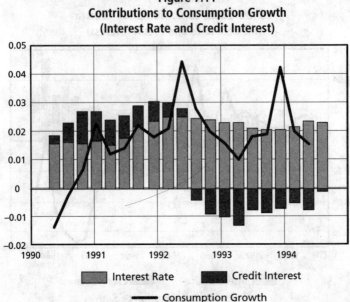

Figure 7.11
Contributions to Consumption Growth
(Interest Rate and Credit Interest)

allow. We have to consider that income falls in a more or less synchronized manner with consumption.

The role played by interest rate effects is different in each plan. In both plans that contribution, including its interaction with credit, is important in explaining the sharp upturn. However, it is even more important in the second plan, where it contributes more than 2.5 percent to the upswing, and the average for the entire period observed is over 2.3 percent.

Liquidity Constraints and Financial Deregulation

A basic hypothesis in the original literature surrounding McKinnon and Shaw's theory of financial deregulation is that the behavior of private saving changes when deregulation gets under way, experiencing a boom despite the higher real interest rates introduced by deregulation. This hypothesis has been questioned by several later empirical studies, and the theoretical model of intertemporal optimization of future consumption, described earlier, does not necessarily provide for an increase in consumption in the face of higher real interest rates.

However, that model deals only with solutions along the optimal consumption path—that is, with no credit squeeze. Given that previous comparisons indicate the existence of liquidity constraints, and that, at least in the post-1975 period, these constraints are manifested in terms of bank credit expansion to the private sector, it is natural to assume that the introduction of financial deregulation eases the liquidity constraint. This could explain the apparent insensitivity of private saving before and after financial deregulation. Financial deregulation and deepening, begun in Uruguay in late 1974 by allowing recourse to external capital flows, should have eased the credit restrictions and led to a smoother path of consumption than in the 1960s. In other words, consumption variations should have at least been sensitive to current income variations after financial deregulation

From an econometric viewpoint, a change in the intensity of the liquidity constraints implies that, in the regression of the comparison of the PI-LC hypothesis, the parameter that corresponds to income variation for the current period must be unstable. Moreover, its instability should be directly related to some measure of the degree of financial deepening. In this way, the problem may be introduced in a context similar to that used to analyze the stabilization experiments, that is, in terms of the stability of parameter λ beginning in 1976, when the process of liberalization and financial deregulation occurred in Uruguay.

Given that a profound financial crisis began in Uruguay in 1982, we have opted to distinguish two subperiods following 1976: 1976–81 (the period of deregulation, strictly speaking) and 1982–94 (the crisis and the period that followed it). In the postcrisis period, an increase in the sensitivity of variations in private consumption to variations in current income is expected in relation to the 1975–81 period, but not as much as existed prior to 1975. The empirical analysis is conducted on annual series.

Equation [1] is reformulated to determine whether parameter λ is significant in the two subperiods.[12] The comparative equation in this case then becomes:

$$\Delta c_t = \mu + \lambda_0 \Delta y_t + \lambda_4 D_{4t} \Delta y_t + \lambda_5 D_{5t} \Delta y_t + \theta r_t + \varepsilon_t \qquad [5]$$

[12] The results obtained are not affected by including the equation for the comparison of terms that explain the variation of the parameter that corresponds to the real interest rate.

Table 7.9 Private Consumption, Financial Liberalization, and Crisis, 1955–94: Estimation of Instrumental Variables of Equation [5]

	All Instruments [a]		
Estimated Parameter	$\Delta y_{t-2}, r_{t-2}$	$\Delta y_{t-2}, \Delta y_{t-3}$ r_{t-2}, r_{t-3}	$\Delta y_{t-2}, \Delta y_{t-3}, \Delta y_{t-4}$ $r_{t-2}, r_{t-3}, r_{t-4}$
$\hat{\mu}$	0.0053	0.0052	0.0041
	(0.49)	(0.49)	(0.41)
$\hat{\lambda}_0$	−0.095	−0.1184	0.0017
	(−0.38)	(−0.51)	(0.01)
$\hat{\lambda}_4$	0.5938	0.7683	0.5490
	(1.18)	(1.51)	(1.20)
$\hat{\lambda}_5$	0.6978	0.7341	0.9128
	(3.21)	(3.13)	(4.40)
$\hat{\theta}$	−0.0568	−0.0529	−0.0341
	(−0.85)	(−0.80)	(−0.56)
Adjusted R^2	0.80	0.79	0.83
Effective Number of Observations	36	35	34

Note: Numbers in parentheses are *t*-statistics.

a. Estimated parameter by instrumental variables.

where the variable D_{4t} is a qualitative variable that takes a value of zero up to 1975, of one between 1976 and 1981, and of zero again beginning in 1982, whereas the D_{5t} variable is set at zero up to 1981 and at one beginning in 1982 (Table 7.9).

The estimations offer a paradoxical result: during the period of stagnation and financial repression, the permanent income hypothesis offers a reasonable explanation for private consumption, to the extent that parameter λ_0 is not significant. Beginning with deregulation, we detect an initial phase in which the liquidity constraints are not significant, but starting in 1982 private consumption appears to be strongly conditioned by growth in current income.

One hypothesis that merits examination in future research is that of the existence of precautionary saving. The period before deregulation witnessed only slight variation in income and consumption, given the prolonged economic stagnation. In contrast, both income and consumption experienced significant fluctuations after 1975, to such an extent that the greater uncertainty regarding future income, approached through the income variations seen, may perhaps explain the closer relationship between consumption and income variations after financial deregulation.

Private Consumption and Ricardian Equivalence

As mentioned above, private saving and public saving in Uruguay have evolved in nearly symmetrical fashion (Figure 7.2). This pattern gives rise to the possibility that Ricardian equivalence is met. This classic hypothesis establishes a relationship of perfect substitution between public saving and private saving. The hypothesis, as formulated by Barro (1974), states that if the methods for financing a particular level of public expenditure are changed—for example, by reducing taxes and increasing public debt or by increasing the fiscal deficit (which amounts to the same thing)—private consumption does not change. Therefore, private saving increases to the extent that taxes decrease (a variation that is equal to higher disposable income).

The basis for this result is the notion that consumers internalize the public sector budgetary restriction over time. Although, from the time of that change, consumers have more disposable income because taxes are lower, they do not consume more, because their wealth has not changed: at some point in the future the government will have to impose higher taxes to amortize the debt issued today. Thus, public debt securities should not be considered part of the net wealth of the private sector.

To analyze the relevance of these hypotheses in the case of Uruguay, the approach proposed by Seater and Mariano (1985) is used. In an equation incorporating private consumption determinants, controlling for its most common determinants such as the interest rate or public sector consumption, if Ricardian equivalence holds, neither tax receipts nor public debt (nor, alternatively, changes in public debt) should be significant.

The econometric methodology adopted to compare this hypothesis was that of estimating a private consumption model with the cointegrated vector procedure proposed by Johansen (1988). The estimation includes one constant vector and, in the case of quarterly estimations, three deterministic seasonal variables. The six variables included ($n = 6$) are private consumption (C_t), income (GDP in the quarterly case, and gross disposable income from the private sector, in both cases net of the inflation tax Y_t), the real ex ante borrowing rate (r_t), government consumption (G_t), government revenues (T_t), and the variation in net public debt (ΔDP_t).[13] All variables are in constant 1983 prices.

Two interesting comparisons have been made on the basis of this estimation:

- A comparison that excludes the variables T_t and ΔDP_t from the cointegration vectors, which is equivalent to Ricardian equivalence
- The "equality with a different sign" comparison between the private consumption coefficient and the disposable income coefficient. In the normalized cointegration vector in private consumption, this restriction is (1–1). The validity of this restriction is essential in moving from an interpretation in terms of private consumption to the equivalent interpretation in terms of private saving.

The comparisons were made on the basis of the methodology proposed by Johansen and Juselius (1990). Table 7.10 shows the six estimated vectors for the variables that correspond to the quarterly series. The highest auto-value and the trace statistic coincide to identify a single cointegration relationship. A normalized cointegration vector in private consumption is shown in column 6 of Table 7.10. Notice that both the trace and highest eigenvalue statistics allow rejection (at the 1 percent level) of the null hypothesis that the rank of the long-term matrix is complete (six). The second eigenvalue is not significant, although the trace statistic rejects at the 5 percent level the null hypothesis that the rank of the cointegration matrix is four. As is typically the case in this type of analysis, the more conservative result is selected, where there is only one cointegration relationship among the six variables considered.

The comparison regarding the Ricardian equivalence—that is, excluding income from the public sector and the variation of net public sector debt from the cointegration vector—rejects that hypothesis: the chi-square statistic (2) associated with this restriction is equal to 10.58 and is significant at the 1 percent level. The "equality with a different sign" restriction between the consumption and income coefficients has a chi-square statistic

---

[13] In this case, unlike the specifications in previous sections, upper-case letters are used to designate that the variables are the actual numbers, not their logarithms. Logarithms cannot be used because the variations of net public debt are negative in many periods.

**Table 7.10 Cointegration Vectors and Long-Term Matrix Rank
(Model with Quarterly Data, 1975:1–1994:4)**

Variable	Normalized cointegration vectors $n - r$					
	6	5	4	3	2	1
C_t	1.000	1.000	1.000	1.000	1.000	1.000
Y_t	-1.068	-0.932	-1.346	4.067	-5.145	-1.273
r_t	0.467	-0.148	-0.128	-0.306	-0.624	0.087
G_t	-3.164	10.300	2.741	-2.700	27.762	4.043
T_t	0.952	-2.346	0.309	-9.724	-1.132	0.714
ΔDP_t	-0.226	-1.496	0.159	1.073	0.386	0.530
Estimated						
Eigenvalue	0.536	0.296	0.257	0.231	0.070	0.051
Maximum						
Eigenvalue Statistic	56.88*	25.94	21.95	19.44	5.40	3.91
Trace Statistics	133.51*	76.63*	50.69	28.74	9.30	3.91

* Indicates rejection of the null hypothesis that the long-term matrix rank is equal to $n - r$

Note: The transitory dynamic of the VAR model has been specified with five lags in the endogenous variables.

(1) of only 0.13, which indicates that the restriction is appropriate from a statistical viewpoint.

Determinants of Public Saving

This section analyzes the determinants of public saving or, more accurately, consolidated public sector revenue or the financial surplus—that is, public saving minus public investment expenditure. The analysis consists of breaking down the discretionary and nondiscretionary (or exogenous) components of aggregate public finance revenue. Whereas previous sections used information from the national accounts, this breakdown starts with budget performance data from the consolidated public sector, for the 1976–94 period. The public sector includes the central government, state enterprises, the social security system, and the Central Bank. Excluded from this aggregate, however, are departmental and municipal governments and the Banco Hipotecario del Uruguay (a state-run bank that specializes in promoting housing credit), because uniform records for the entire period could not be obtained.

Public revenues in Uruguay have behaved erratically over the past two decades. Although the public budget has been in deficit in most years, in some years revenue was positive, and deficit levels have varied significantly. Table 7.11 shows the sectoral pattern of fiscal performance according to the agents considered.[14]

The first section below establishes the definitions and criteria used to determine the nondiscretionary deficit and its components. The discretionary deficit is obtained as the difference between the total deficit and the nondiscretionary deficit. Later sections identify some of the components of discretionary fiscal revenue and extract key conclusions.

Nondiscretionary Revenue

Quantification of discretionary public revenue sheds light on the expansionary or contractionary (exogenous) nature of fiscal policy and differentiates it from revenue arising from external shocks. It therefore establishes a more direct and transparent relationship between political-electoral cycle revenue, or tests hypotheses regarding how those who formulate fiscal policy react to different kinds of macroeconomic disturbances.

An external shock to fiscal policy is any shock arising from the international economy or the domestic private sector, or from other nonfiscal areas of macroeconomic policy (including exchange rate or monetary policy). The nondiscretionary component is defined by combining the following: the activity cycle effect on central government and social security revenue, the Olivera-Tanzi effect on tax revenue, the flow of interest paid, the exchange rate growth effect on state enterprise earnings, and the effect of indexing expenditures on public disability, old-age, and survivor's insurance benefits beginning in 1989.

The fiscal revenue adjustment for the economic cycle requires specification of a revenue function with regard to the level of activity, as well as an estimate of potential GDP or the trend in GDP. Elasticities for taxes and

---

[14] The social security administration is only considered because of the deficit it generates, which is equal to central government financial assistance, recorded under expenditure.

Table 7.11 Composition of Fiscal Revenue and Expenditure in Uruguay (percentage of GDP)

	1976	1977	1978	1979	1980	1981	1982	1983	1984	1985	1986	1987	1988	1989	1990	1991	1992	1993	1994
Central Government																			
Revenue	14.0	14.8	14.1	14.6	16.2	17.4	15.2	16.0	13.5	14.7	15.9	15.2	16.1	14.7	16.8	17.5	18.3	18.3	18.8
Expenditure	16.6	16.0	15.4	14.4	16.1	17.5	23.9	20.0	18.8	17.6	17.1	17.2	18.0	17.9	16.8	17.1	18.0	19.3	20.9
Net Revenue	-2.6	-1.2	-1.3	0.2	0.1	-0.1	-8.7	-4.0	-5.3	-2.9	-1.2	-1.3	-1.9	-3.2	-0.1	0.4	0.3	-1.1	-2.1
Interest	1.2	1.0	0.9	0.6	0.4	0.3	0.6	1.2	1.8	2.0	1.8	1.5	1.6	1.8	1.8	1.6	1.4	1.4	1.3
Primary Surplus	-1.4	-0.2	-0.4	0.8	0.4	0.2	-8.1	-2.8	-3.5	-0.9	0.6	0.2	-0.3	-1.4	1.7	2.0	1.7	0.3	-0.8
State Enterprises																			
Revenue	12.8	12.1	11.2	10.6	13.1	12.9	13.3	14.6	17.4	15.4	13.6	12.3	12.7	11.9	13.8	13.2	12.6	12.0	12.1
Expenditure	12.7	11.8	10.8	10.4	12.1	12.7	13.4	13.9	16.1	16.1	13.0	12.4	12.5	12.1	13.2	12.5	11.7	11.7	12.4
Net Revenue	0.0	0.3	0.4	0.2	1.0	0.2	-0.1	0.7	1.2	-0.7	0.7	-0.2	0.1	-0.2	0.6	0.7	1.0	0.3	-0.3
Interest	0.0	0.0	0.0	0.1	0.1	0.2	0.1	0.7	1.8	1.7	1.3	0.9	0.9	0.9	1.0	0.5	0.5	0.4	0.4
Primary Surplus	0.1	0.3	0.4	0.2	1.1	0.4	0.0	1.4	3.0	1.0	2.0	0.8	1.0	0.8	1.6	1.2	1.5	0.6	0.0
Central Bank																			
Revenue	N.A.	N.A.	N.A.	N.A.	N.A.	N.A.	0.4	0.3	1.3	0.8	0.9	0.7	0.7	0.7	0.5	0.4	0.3	0.4	0.4
Expenditure	N.A.	N.A.	N.A.	N.A.	N.A.	N.A.	1.2	3.6	5.0	3.7	4.6	3.3	3.4	3.7	3.8	2.5	1.7	1.2	1.0
Net Revenue	N.A.	N.A.	N.A.	N.A.	N.A.	N.A.	-0.8	-3.3	-3.7	-3.0	-3.7	-2.6	-2.7	-3.0	-3.3	-2.1	-1.4	-0.8	-0.6
Interest	N.A.	N.A.	N.A.	N.A.	N.A.	N.A.	0.3	2.8	3.6	2.8	3.5	2.5	2.6	2.8	3.2	1.9	1.3	0.6	0.4
Primary Surplus	N.A.	N.A.	N.A.	N.A.	N.A.	N.A.	-0.5	-0.5	-0.1	-0.2	-0.2	-0.2	-0.2	-0.2	-0.2	-0.2	-0.2	-0.2	-0.3
Consolidated Public Sector																			
Revenue	26.8	26.9	25.3	25.2	29.3	30.2	29.0	30.9	32.2	30.9	30.4	28.8	29.5	27.3	31.1	31.1	31.2	30.6	31.3
Expenditure	29.3	27.7	26.2	24.8	28.2	30.1	38.6	37.6	40.0	37.5	34.7	32.9	34.0	33.7	33.9	32.1	31.4	32.2	34.3
Net Revenue	-2.6	-0.9	-0.9	0.4	1.1	0.1	-9.6	-6.7	-7.8	-6.6	-4.2	-4.1	-4.5	-6.4	-2.9	-1.0	-0.2	-1.6	-3.0
Interest	1.2	1.0	0.9	0.7	0.5	0.5	1.0	4.7	7.1	6.5	6.6	4.9	5.0	5.6	5.9	4.0	3.1	2.3	2.0
Primary Surplus	-1.4	0.1	0.0	1.1	1.6	0.6	-8.1	-1.4	-0.5	0.1	2.6	1.0	0.7	-0.6	3.3	3.2	3.1	1.0	-0.8

N.A., Not available.
Source: General Accounting Office, Central Bank of Uruguay, and the Office of Planning and Budgeting.

Table 7.12 Elasticities of Tax and Social Security Revenues at the Activity Level

	Tax Revenues [a]	Social Security Revenues [a]
Constant	−12.8	−1.87
GDP[a]	1.25	1.43
Student t	16.0	6.02
Number of Observations	19	19
DW	1.6	2.2
R^2	0.97	0.95

a. The estimations used the logarithm of the variables.

social security revenue at the activity level were calculated by the ordinary least squares method. The results can be found in Table 7.12.[15]

To estimate the trend in GDP, three alternatives were investigated: the breakdown between the Beveridge and Nelson (1981) trend and cycle, the breakdown suggested by Prescott (1986), and the Holt-Winters method of simple exponential smoothing. The magnitude of the differences between observed GDP and the GDP trend was highly sensitive to the choice of methodology. In the case of the Beveridge and Nelson breakdown, there is practically no significant difference between the observed GDP and the GDP trend. Estimations with the Holt-Winters method allow for control of the series smoothness level, and thus determine an intermediate level.

Starting from the elasticities and the GDP trend, the public sector revenue items affected by the level of activity are adjusted by the following:

$$T^a = T.\left(PBI^t / PBI\right)^\varepsilon$$

where T^a and PBI^t represent adjusted revenue and the GDP trend, respectively, and ε represents the elasticity at the activity level of revenue.

The second component of the nondiscretionary deficit is associated with the loss of real revenue through the Olivera-Tanzi effect. Given that

---

[15] For estimation purposes, binary-type variables were used to capture the tax structure modifications that affect the constant term of the regression rather than the elasticity. In the case of tax revenue, the variable is set equal to one in 1979, 1984, and 1989. In the case of social security revenue, the equation included one variable that takes the value of one between 1990 and 1994, and another that does the same in 1980 and 1984.

inflation was high during much of the period under analysis, this had a considerable impact on fiscal revenue. To evaluate it, the average payment term of the more important taxes was estimated, and the corresponding inflation rate was then applied.

In general, interest payments were considered nondiscretionary expenditure because they are the result of debts assumed to finance deficits incurred in the past. Therefore, current fiscal policy is unable to control these payments during the current period.

The fourth component of nondiscretionary revenues is the direct impact of changing the exchange rate. The exchange rate affects fiscal revenue basically through the payment of interest on public debt in foreign currency, but since all interest is considered to be nondiscretionary, this part of the impact is not taken into account. Another direct impact of the exchange rate is its influence on the value of public sector imports. However, public sector imports are principally those of the state enterprises. Therefore the exchange rate effect is measured by the influence it has on state enterprise earnings, because these have an input structure with an important imported goods component.[16] The effect was calculated as the product of the difference between the current real exchange rate and the long-term real exchange rate and the number of imported goods. The long-term real exchange rate was estimated using the same exponential smoothing methodology used in the GDP trend case.[17]

The fifth nondiscretionary component is retirement and annuity expenditure. In November 1989, as a result of a legislative initiative, a constitutional amendment was approved by plebiscite, establishing that retirement and annuity benefits would be adjusted in accordance with past growth in average nominal wages, whenever government wages are adjusted. In practice, this resulted in the indexation of social security benefits to growth in average wages in the previous four-month period. In this way, fiscal policy lost discretionary power with regard to an expenditure that represented more

---

[16] The 1983 product input matrix was utilized to determine the structure of state enterprise inputs.

[17] The real exchange rate was measured on the basis of the average real exchange rates of the nine main trading partners, taking wholesale price indices into account. Just as in the case of estimating the GDP trend, the Beveridge and Nelson methodology indicated no significant effects, even in periods of marked real currency appreciation or depreciation.

than 12 percent of GDP at that time. This nondiscretionary component was estimated as the product of real changes in a readjustment index of individual benefits times total expenditure.

Table 7.13 shows the composition of nondiscretionary revenues. Table 7.14, which includes a partial breakdown of the discretionary deficit, shows the discretionary portion of the same deficit as a residual. Figure 7.12 shows the results of this breakdown.

It was impossible to determine that, during the period studied, and especially beginning in 1982, the nondiscretionary portion of fiscal revenue dominated growth in total fiscal revenue. The principal factor behind this is the increase in interest payments following the debt crisis. Recent years have seen a marked drop in discretionary revenue due to the decrease in foreign

Table 7.13 Nondiscretionary Components of Fiscal Revenues (percentage of GDP)

Year	Cycle Effect	Olivera-Tanzi Effect	Revaluation Effect of Retirement and Annuity Benefits	Exchange Rate Effect	Interest Payments	Nondiscretionary Deficit
1976	-0.13	-0.31	0.00	0.08	-1.19	-1.55
1977	-0.16	-0.41	0.00	0.04	-1.03	-1.56
1978	0.05	-0.40	0.00	0.63	-0.87	-0.58
1979	0.56	-0.53	0.00	0.69	-0.69	0.02
1980	1.52	-0.42	0.00	0.67	-0.49	1.27
1981	1.89	-0.35	0.00	0.09	-0.54	1.09
1982	-0.14	-0.23	0.00	-1.19	-1.05	-2.61
1983	-1.19	-0.45	0.00	-0.65	-4.72	-7.00
1984	-0.82	-0.55	0.00	-0.42	-7.13	-8.91
1985	-0.85	-0.69	0.00	-0.24	-6.51	-8.29
1986	-0.20	-0.61	0.00	-0.06	-6.59	-7.46
1987	0.29	-0.45	0.00	-0.27	-4.87	-5.30
1988	0.00	-0.38	0.00	-0.15	-5.02	-5.55
1989	0.15	-0.43	0.00	-0.34	-5.61	-6.23
1990	-0.28	-0.58	-1.34	0.22	-5.93	-7.91
1991	-0.22	-0.46	-2.43	0.30	-4.02	-6.83
1992	0.33	-0.37	-1.45	0.27	-3.12	-4.33
1993	1.41	-0.34	-0.87	0.20	-2.30	-1.91
1994	1.41	-0.25	-0.81	0.54	-1.99	-1.10

Figure 7.12
Public Sector Revenues,
Discretionary and Nondiscretionary

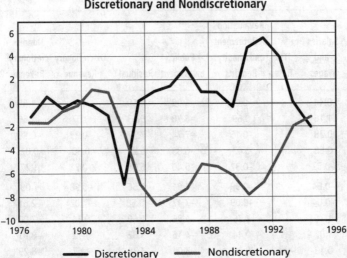

public debt securities following implementation of the Brady Plan. This factor has been accentuated in recent years by an important cyclical effect, which partially compensates for the interest payment effect, and the appearance of a new discretionary component resulting from the indexing of social security expenditure. The increase in the nondiscretionary deficit in the early 1990s is explained first by the indexation of retirement and annuity benefits. To the extent that the inflation rate stabilizes as the decade progresses, this nondiscretionary deficit component tends to disappear. The adjustment for the economic cycle effect on public sector revenue shows a similar trajectory during the two stabilization plans.

Discretionary Revenue and Its Components

This section identifies some of the components of discretionary fiscal revenue. This analysis takes into account the following variables subject to control by fiscal authorities: the change in the average index of real public wages, the real change in the social security benefits index in the period preceding the constitutional reform of 1989, the change in tax rates in real terms, and total public investment.

Table 7.14 Breakdown of Fiscal Revenues
(percentage of GDP)

Year	Salaries and Wages	Tax Rates	Revaluation of Retirement and Annuity Benefits	Public Investment	Residual	Discretionary Revenue	Nondis-cretionary Revenue	Total Revenue
1976	0.44		−0.06	−5.99	4.59	−1.02	−1.55	−2.57
1977	1.16		0.69	−6.70	5.53	0.67	−1.56	−0.89
1978	0.28		−0.15	−7.74	7.27	−0.33	−0.58	−0.91
1979	0.58		0.42	−6.88	6.25	0.38	0.02	0.40
1980	−0.52		−0.32	−5.40	6.03	−0.21	1.27	1.06
1981	−0.64		−0.99	−4.91	5.56	−0.98	1.09	0.11
1982	−0.04		−0.09	−7.47	0.58	−7.02	−2.61	−9.62
1983	1.76		1.76	−4.86	1.69	0.34	−7.00	−6.67
1984	1.02		0.44	−4.16	3.82	1.12	−8.91	−7.80
1985	0.13	−0.59	0.36	−3.01	4.78	1.67	−8.29	−6.63
1986	0.27	−0.24	−1.80	−3.32	8.33	3.24	−7.46	−4.22
1987	−0.04	−0.24	−1.23	−3.82	6.53	1.21	−5.30	−4.09
1988	−0.39	−0.28	−0.94	−3.78	6.43	1.05	−5.55	−4.50
1989	0.03	−0.36	−0.33	−3.94	4.46	−0.14	−6.23	−6.37
1990	0.63	−0.14	0.00	−2.63	7.19	5.05	−7.91	−2.86
1991	0.41	0.18	0.00	−3.89	9.09	5.80	−6.83	−1.04
1992	0.29	0.18	0.00	−3.27	6.96	4.16	−4.33	−0.17
1993	−0.75	0.39	0.00	−3.90	4.59	0.33	−1.91	−1.58
1994	0.15	0.63	0.00	−3.65	0.94	−1.92	−1.10	−3.02

The discretionary handling of public wages was quantified by adjusting the wage bill for consolidated public sector compensation to the impact of growth in public sector real wages. The same method used to analyze the nondiscretionary components in the post-1989 period was used to adjust pensions. Given that Uruguay's state enterprises operate as monopolies, their rates were considered to be the same as with the discretionary type.[18]

Obviously, one cannot make reliable inferences about the political-electoral cycle on the basis of the few available observations. However, two

[18] This hypothesis may overestimate the discretionary component, to the extent that earnings by state enterprises may be affected by the level of activity. A more precise measurement would consider the unit cost margin of state enterprises as discretionary.

results provide some indications. The first is that the two lowest levels of discretionary revenue (or the highest discretionary deficits) were recorded during the only two election years included in the observations: 1989 and 1994.[19] On the other hand, the second year of both administrations witnessed greater effort at fiscal policy (1986 and 1991). This is consistent with the fact that each new administration prepares its own budget during the first year of its term and begins to implement it during the second year.

The breakdown of the deficit's discretionary portion, also shown in Table 7.14, allows some conclusions regarding the room for maneuver and the tools used by fiscal authorities during different periods. Although the exceptionally negative fiscal revenues of 1982 were due in large part to external shocks, part of the large deficit of that year, equivalent to at least 2.5 percent of GDP, is due to an exceptional increase in public investment. Thus, adjustments in later years are basically explained by a reduction in public investment by some 2.6 percent of GDP, as well as by a drop in the wage bill and social security expenditure. The adjustment to the discretionary portion during the 1980s focused on the residual category and, to a lesser extent, on tax rates and public wages. It is the residual component that has changed dramatically during recent years, despite the fact that public wages and tax rates provide higher revenues.

Conclusions

The empirical evidence gathered here on the determinants of private saving in Uruguay does not support the validity of the life-cycle hypothesis but rather indicates the existence of a simultaneous dependence of private consumption on income. This may be interpreted as reflecting the existence of a large proportion of consumers with liquidity constraints. In this interpretation, the proportion of constrained consumers fluctuates, according to various estimates, between 38 and 49 percent of all consumers. Also, this proportion is not fixed but varies according to the real expansion of bank credit, particularly consumer credit.

Liquidity constraints are present even after the period of financial deregulation that began in the mid-1970s, and especially after the 1982 fi-

---

[19] The period from 1973 to 1985 was characterized by a de facto government.

nancial crisis. Moreover, the empirical evidence does not support the Ricardian equivalence hypothesis.

During the episodes of exchange rate–based stabilization plans, liquidity constraints were eased, thus stimulating an increase in consumption. However, that effect was insufficient to explain the expansion in consumption observed in both experiments. That is why limits on credit expansion are not recommended as an economic policy tool to contain the growth of consumption. To counteract the effects of the increase generated by the simultaneous expansion of current income, one would need not only limitations on credit expansion, but also strong credit tightening.

Liquidity constraints seem to play some role in the growth of consumption during stabilization plans, given the fact that income grows and there is a simultaneous dependence between consumption growth and income growth. However, the interest rate effect on consumption growth, arising from the intertemporal substitution effects caused by changes to the expected interest rates, although statistically less significant, helps explain consumption in a manner similar to income growth.

The fact that consumption growth begins before the plan takes effect suggests a direction for further research. This may be telling us that there are parallel factors unrelated to the plan, or factors that perhaps give rise to the decision to implement the plan, acting to unleash a consumption boom.

One of the unresolved puzzles in the case of Uruguay is that, although consumption grew in both stabilization plans, the same did not occur in terms of the decline in private saving, which characterized the 1990 episode but not the 1978–82 stabilization. This may be related to the difference in public saving behavior: in the first episode there were no significant changes in public saving except at the end of the period, whereas in the 1990s there was a significant increase. However, the positive effect of larger public debt on private consumption, determined in the Ricardian equivalence comparison, would not support this hypothesis.

The growth in public sector revenue (saving minus investment) is shown to be highly dependent on the nondiscretionary elements of fiscal policy, especially in the period following the external debt crisis. However, there are some indications that the discretionary components are related to the political-electoral cycle: discretionary deficits increase during election years and show a marked contraction in the first year in which the new authorities control the budget.

References

Attanasio, O. 1994. "The Intertemporal Allocation of Consumption: Theory and Evidence." NBER Working Paper 4811. National Bureau of Economic Research, Cambridge, Mass.

Barro, R. 1974. "Are Government Bonds Net Wealth?" *Journal of Political Economy* 81 (6): 1095–1117.

Bergara, M. and Licandro, J. A. 1994. "Credibility and Exchange Rate Policy: Recent Experiences in Argentina and Uruguay." *Revista de Economía.* 1 (1): 59–86, Second period. Central Bank of Uruguay, Montevideo.

Beveridge, S. and Nelson, C.R. 1981. "A New Approach to Decomposition of Economic Time Series into Permanent and Transitory Components with Particular Attention to Measurement of the Business Cycle." *Journal of Monetary Economics.* 7 (2): 151–74.

Calvo, G. A. 1986. "Temporary Stabilization: Predetermined Exchange Rates." *Journal of Political Economy.* 94: 1319–29.

Campbell, J. and Mankiw, N.G. 1989. "Consumption, Income and Interest Rates: Reinterpreting the Time Series Evidence." In O.J. Blanchard and S. Fischer, editors, *NBER Macroeconomics Annual 1989.* Cambridge, Mass.: MIT Press.

Chow, G. and Lin, A-L. 1971. "Best Linear Unbiased Interpolation, Distribution and Extrapolation of Time Series by Related Time Series." *Review of Economics and Statistics.* 53 (4): 372–75.

Copelman, M. 1994. "The Role of Credit in Post-Stabilization Consumption Booms." Department of Economics, Massachusetts Institute of Technology, Cambridge, Mass.

Deaton, A. 1992. *Understanding Consumption.* New York: Oxford University Press.

Echenique, F. 1995. "The Theory of Consumption: An Empirical Analysis for Uruguayan Data." Graduate thesis. School of Economic Sciences, Universidad de la República, Montevideo.

Flavin, M. 1981. "The Adjustment of Consumption to Changing Expectations about Future Income." *Journal of Political Economy.* 89: 974–1009.

Hall, R. 1978. "Stochastic Implications of Life Cycle–Permanent Income Hypothesis: Theory and Evidence." *Journal of Political Economy.* 86 (6): 971–87.

———. 1988. "Intertemporal Substitution in Consumption." *Journal of Political Economy.* 96: 339–57.

Hansen, L. 1982. "Large Sample Properties of the Generalized Method of Moments Estimators." *Econometrica.* 50: 1029–54.

Hansen, L. and Singleton, K. J. 1983. "Stochastic Consumption, Risk Aversion and the Temporal Behavior of Stock Market Returns." *Journal of Political Economy.* 91: 240–65.

Johansen, S. 1988. "Statistical Analysis of Cointegration Vectors." *Journal of Economic Dynamics and Control.* 12: 231–54.

Johansen, S. and Juselius, K. 1990. "Maximum Likelihood Estimation and Inference on Cointegration, with Applications to the Demand for Money." *Oxford Bulletin of Economics and Statistics.* 52 (2): 169–210.

Prescott, E. C. 1986. "Theory Ahead of Business Cycle Measurement." *Carnegie-Rochester Conference on Public Policy.* 25: 11–44.

Seater, J. and Mariano, R. 1985. "New Tests of the Life Cycle and Tax Discounting Hypotheses." *Journal of Monetary Economics.* 15 (2): 195–215.

Svensson, L. 1990. "The Simplest Test of Target Zones Credibility." NBER Working Paper 3394. National Bureau of Economic Research, Cambridge, Mass.

Talvi, E. 1994. "Uruguay: Stabilization Plans of October 1978 and December 1990." Paper presented to the International Economics Symposium on Stabilization Programs: Recent Experience in Latin America, Central Bank of Uruguay, Montevideo, August.

CHAPTER 8

Private Saving in Venezuela: Trends and Determinants

Luis Zambrano Sequín, Matías Riutort, Rafael Muñoz,
and Juan Carlos Guevara[1]

The most notable characteristic of the private saving rate in Venezuela has been the downward secular trend it has shown from the high levels of the 1970s. In addition to trending downward, saving has been very volatile.

This performance can be explained by the successive external and domestic shocks that have rocked Venezuela, as well as by the specific economic policies used to confront these shocks. The great swings in income generated by the impact of external events, especially following the 1983 external debt crisis, were compounded by economic policy shocks, specifically, the use of the exchange rate to adjust public finances.

The connection between terms of trade shocks and the behavior of saving has received an increasing amount of attention in the literature on private saving in developing countries. This literature has stressed the complexity of the interrelationships between the nature of shocks—temporary or permanent—and the not always evident channels by which these shocks affect income and relative prices.

The reaction of economic agents to the changes in relative prices and income generated by variations in the terms of trade will vary depending upon the institutional framework in which the changes are carried out.

[1] Luis Zambrano was head of the Economics Research Department in the Instituto de Investigaciones Económicas y Sociales (IIES) of the Universidad Católica Andrés Bello (UCAB) and is currently subdirector of the Oficina de Asesoría Económica (OAE) of the Venezuelan Congress; Juan Carlos Guevara also left IIES, UCAB for the OAE; Matías Ruitort and Rafael Muñoz are researchers at IIES, UCAB.

Within this institutional framework, the financial system is a major factor that can significantly strengthen or weaken the effects of external and economic policy shocks. This has received considerable attention within the context of an analysis of the effect of liquidity constraints on saving's sensitivity to changes in income and interest rates.

This frame of reference highlights the importance of an analysis of the changes in private saving in Venezuela over the past three decades, a period that has been characterized by successive and profound domestic and external shocks. The analysis focuses on three basic aspects: the effects of fiscal policy management on income and private saving, income volatility and changes in relative prices, and the presence of liquidity constraints that result from the imperfections and inefficiencies of the domestic financial system.

To analyze the consequences of income shocks and the presence of significant liquidity constraints, a basic model was developed to conduct a sensitivity analysis of the saving rate to the interest rate, controlling for (a) the existence of transitory shocks in the terms of trade, which are so important for Venezuela, and (b) domestic financial market imperfections. The basic variable used to control for both problems is the intertemporal elasticity of substitution.

Several factors explain the secular drop in both the level and rate of private sector saving. It is not enough just to relate the behavior of saving to the downward trend in domestic economic growth that has characterized the Venezuelan economy for the past two decades. The relationship between the private and public sectors must also be considered, as well as the transitory rather than permanent nature of the price and income shocks that have occurred during the time period analyzed here.

One basic aspect that has determined not only the transfer of resources from the public to the private sector but also the way in which the private sector reacts to government adjustment policies is the role that devaluation plays as a tax mechanism over economic agents. Given the fiscal importance of devaluation, it is not surprising that the inflation tax and public domestic borrowing in Venezuela have had relatively little importance in financing fiscal deficits. Capital flight and the consumption booms that traditionally precede fiscal adjustments in Venezuela are natural responses by economic agents faced with the collective expropriation of maxidevaluations. The use of devaluation as a tax mechanism has been a characteristic of economic policy in Venezuela since the onset of the external debt crisis in the early 1980s.

On the other hand, greater income volatility and more significant inter- and intratemporal changes in the structure of relative prices, most of which occurred following the first oil shock of the 1970s, clearly made saving less sensitive to interest rates just as the liquidity constraints in the domestic economy became greater. This confirms the ineffectiveness of monetary policy in influencing higher private saving in times of frequent and large shocks in the terms of trade, and important imperfections in the financial system, which constrain the liquidity of the private sector.

Private Domestic Saving: Trends and Volatility

In the past three decades, one of the most significant characteristics of the private saving rate in Venezuela has been its secular downward trend from an average 17 percent of GDP in the 1968–73 period prior to the oil shocks to less than 7 percent in the years following the 1989 adjustment program and the recent political-institutional shocks (see Table 8.1).[2]

This decline in the private domestic saving rate did not affect the overall domestic saving rate thanks to the offsetting growth in public sector saving. On the other hand, the reduction of the private saving rate was accompanied by an even more dramatic reduction in the private investment rate and by a downward trend in public investment, although less acute. The deterioration of the private investment rate, particularly since 1983, accounts for the obsolescence and low competitiveness of the manufacturing sector today.

The sustained level of the public saving rate (around 11 percent), with an upward trend after the 1989 adjustment plan, is basically associated with the tightening of expenditures precipitated by the external debt crisis and, more recently, with investments in the oil sector.

The downward trend of the private saving rate contrasts with the behavior of the private consumption rate. In fact, the rate of private consump-

---

[2] The 1968–94 period has been divided into four subperiods determined by the types of shocks that affected the Venezuelan economy: the oil boom of 1974–76 and 1979; the negative shock from the 1983 external debt crisis and the negative shock in oil prices in 1986; the implementation of the 1989 recessive adjustment program; and the institutional policy shocks of 1992 and 1993.

Table 8.1 Volatility Indicators Related to the Growth Rate of the Variables: 1968–94

Variable	Period	Variable in Relation to GDP	Growth Rate		
			Growth Rate	Standard Deviation	Coefficient of Variation
Gross Domestic Product	1968–94	—	0.028	0.045	1.586
	1968–73	—	0.049	0.018	0.366
	1974–82	—	0.033	0.035	1.066
	1983–88	—	0.015	0.043	2.794
	1989–94	—	0.017	0.063	3.798
Gross Domestic Saving	1968–94	0.233	0.047	0.217	4.587
	1968–73	0.226	0.079	0.120	1.516
	1974–82	0.254	0.013	0.261	20.024
	1983–88	0.209	0.048	0.222	4.653
	1989–94	0.236	0.072	0.196	2.711
Gross Domestic Private Saving	1968–94	0.119	0.016	0.230	14.822
	1968–73	0.172	0.077	0.097	1.249
	1974–82	0.136	−0.052	0.145	−2.781
	1983–88	0.095	0.093	0.134	1.435
	1989–94	0.067	−0.012	0.394	−32.099
Gross Domestic Public Saving	1968–94	0.114	0.173	0.586	3.388
	1968–73	0.054	0.144	0.423	2.930
	1974–82	0.118	0.209	0.756	3.609
	1983–88	0.114	0.042	0.468	11.242
	1989–94	0.170	0.273	0.483	1.765
Private Consumption	1968–94	0.526	0.043	0.052	1.200
	1968–73	0.395	0.065	0.027	0.400
	1974–82	0.528	0.084	0.053	0.600
	1983–88	0.596	0.013	0.042	4.012
	1989–94	0.587	0.023	0.062	3.184
Gross Private Investment	1968–94	0.131	−1.710	6.932	−4.053
	1968–73	0.205	0.040	0.123	3.072
	1974–82	0.169	−0.046	0.209	−4.597
	1983–88	0.082	−1.039	1.921	−1.848
	1989–94	0.042	−6.337	13.262	−2.093
Gross Public Investment	1968–94	0.107	0.077	0.288	3.733
	1968–73	0.070	0.138	0.374	2.720
	1974–82	0.148	0.147	0.189	1.289
	1983–88	0.088	−0.036	0.342	−9.384
	1989–94	0.100	0.035	0.215	6.075

— Not applicable.

Source: Banco Central de Venezuela, *Economic Reports: 1968–94.*

tion went from an average of 40 percent in the years preceding the 1974–76 oil boom to 53 percent during the 1974–82 subperiod, and then to around 59 percent in the past 11 years. The indicators that refer to the volatility illustrated in Table 8.1 show that the average standard deviation of the changes in the private saving rate in the various subperiods triples after the beginning of the 1989 adjustment and, overall, in the face of growing political and financial instability.

The evolution of the coefficient of variation shows that the volatility of the private saving rate markedly exceeds the already high coefficients for the other variables shown.[3] Compared with GDP, although this has become more volatile over time, its coefficient of variation is one ninth the corresponding rate of saving. Similar results arise if the comparison is made with nonoil GDP and consumption. On the other hand, the variation and volatility of the private saving rate are substantially higher than for combined savings, including that of public saving, which is also volatile. Finally, although the volatility of the saving rate increased significantly during the last subperiod (consistent with the greater political and economic instability of these years), the levels attained in the other subperiods are generally more pronounced than those shown by total and nonoil GDP.

Income Volatility and the Private Sector Domestic Saving Rate

The incidence of income volatility, as well as the distinction between its transitory and permanent effects on the saving behavior of private agents, has received increasing attention in the literature on the problems of economic growth and the determinants of consumption and individual saving.[4]

This theoretical and economic policy concern seeks to emphasize the precautionary nature of saving over other motivations. In other words, besides the level of economic activity, the instability associated with external and domestic shocks may affect the private sector saving rate. There-

---

[3] The coefficient of variation is calculated as the ratio between the standard deviation and the average of each variable. Given that the coefficient of variation is an index that does not depend upon the unit of measurement and is a way to standardize the standard deviation, it constitutes a more appropriate measurement for comparing the volatility between two different variables.

[4] Although there is a vast and growing bibliography on this subject, a good source of references on the issue may be found in Deaton (1990 and 1995).

fore, the variations in the total and private saving rates are not explained solely by changes in the level of economic activity, but also by whether these fluctuations are predictable or not. The income level and the mechanisms by which the different economic shocks are transmitted change the intra- and intertemporal valuations and thus alter consumption and saving decisions. Of course, the economy's productive structure, as well as the efficiency and size of the financial system (factors that are related to the possibilities for intra- and intertemporal consumption substitution), determine the reaction of saving to changes in the level and stability of economic activity.

In the case of Venezuela, the level and stability of income, combined with the composition of the productive structure and liquidity constraints, may explain the change in the private sector saving rate. The adverse and transitory nature of the shocks that occurred after 1983 may be determining factors in explaining why the private saving rate in Venezuela has declined so dramatically.

An analysis of Granger causality concludes that for the overall period under analysis, GDP seems to precede private sector saving.[5] As shown in Table 8.2, the F-statistic serves to reject the hypothesis of no causality between GDP and private saving during the 1968–94 period. This same conclusion is valid for the relationship between nonoil GDP and private saving. Yet, the causality from GDP to saving has weakened over time. For the 1983–94 subperiod, a relationship of simultaneity, rather than causality, exists between saving and GDP, which is consistent with a significantly more unstable period (see Table 8.2).

If the level of economic activity precedes saving, and not the other way around,[6] it then becomes important to analyze the relationship between the behavior of private saving and the volatility of economic activity. These are the results of a regression analysis between the variation in the rate of private saving (*VRPS*) and economic activity, measured as the rate of variation in the GDP growth rate (*VVRGDP*) for the 1970–94 period.

---

[5] The Granger causality test does not attempt to identify anything more than a temporal precedence. Therefore, the conclusion derived from the test may not take the place of a theoretical explanation of precedence.

[6] This may also be understood as the fact that economic growth precede savings, and not the other way around.

Table 8.2 Causality between GDP and Private Saving

Period	Alternative Hypothesis	F-Statistic	Probability
1968–94	GDP → PS	3.462	0.075
1968–94	NOGDP →PS	3.572	0.071
1968–84	PS → GDP	0.052	0.821
1968–84	PS → NOGDP	0.000	0.989

Notes: GDP, gross domestic product; NOGDP, nonoil gross domestic product; PS, private sector domestic saving.

$$VRPS = 0.010 + 0.016\,VVRGDP, \qquad [1]$$

$$R^2: 0.21, \qquad DW: 2.37 \qquad Student\ t: 2.532$$

These results suggest a positive relationship between the variation of the saving rate and instability in the level of economic activity. This relationship remains in place, without important variations, for different specifications of the period under consideration.

Interpretation of this final result must be done carefully. The regression indicates a correlation between the variations in the rate of aggregate saving and of total GDP. This is consistent with the results obtained when examining the Granger-causality test, suggesting once again that precautionary motives explain the conduct of aggregate saving. However, other elements (such as the economy's ability to substitute nontradable goods for tradable goods, and future consumption for present) must also be considered in order to understand this apparent relationship among the change in private saving, the transitory and permanent changes in the level of economic activity, and the volatility of real income.

National Disposable Income and Private Saving

It is possible to proceed in determining the behavior of private saving starting from a consideration of its residual nature in the context of national accounting.

Private saving may be expressed as what remains of GDP (Y) once we have considered private consumption (PC), the operating surplus of public companies (*SUPC*), direct and indirect taxes (*TA*), current transfers and payments from the public sector to the private sector for goods and services (*TRF*), net interest payments from the public sector to the private sector (*IDP*), and income (*ITRF**) and outlays (*ETRF**) for foreign transfers from the external sector. This may be stated as follows:

$$PS = GDP - PC - SUPC - TA + TRF + IDP + ITRF^* - ETRF^*. \quad [2]$$

Transforming this identity into real terms, utilizing the implicit private consumption deflator, and stating all the variables in relation to GDP yields the following equality:

$$\frac{ps}{y} = \frac{Py}{Pc} \cdot \frac{pc}{y} - \frac{supc}{y} - \frac{ta}{y} - \frac{tap}{y} + \frac{trf}{y} + \frac{idp}{y} + \frac{itrf^*}{y} - \frac{etrf^*}{y} \quad [3]$$

where *Py*, *Pc*, and *Y* are the implicit GDP deflator, the implicit private consumption deflator, and real GDP, respectively. The term *tap* is used to identify the oil taxes paid by the oil companies prior to their nationalization in 1976. All the other lower-case abbreviations have the same interpretation as their upper-case equivalents.

Table 8.3 shows the results of equation [3] for each year of the period under analysis. Table 8.4 shows the averages for each component in the different subperiods into which the sample has been divided.

Leaving aside the *Py/Pc* series, which reflects the changes in the price relationship between the implicit GDP deflator and the consumer price index, the tables clearly show some characteristics that explain the determinants of the change in the private saving rate in Venezuela.

To begin with, note the change in the consumption rate. This component increased rapidly and steadily throughout the 1974–82 subperiod until the 1983 external debt shock, from which point the rate of consumption has remained practically constant around 60 percent of GDP. Clearly, the oil boom of the 1970s influenced this change.

The decline in disposable income during the 1980s and 1990s affected the level of private consumption, although its relative level has not yet fallen. Of course, a constant consumption rate in the face of shrinking disposable income in part explains the drop in the rate of private saving.

Table 8.3 Derivation of the Private Saving Rate: 1968–94

Year	PS	Py/Pc	Pc	ta	trf	idp	itrf*	etrf*	supc	tap
1968	16.8	68.7	34.9	4.3	1.0	0.6	0.1	5.4	0.1	9.1
1969	15.4	66.3	35.6	4.4	1.0	0.6	0.4	4.9	0.1	8.0
1970	18.2	70.2	36.8	5.8	1.6	1.1	0.1	3.9	0.2	8.0
1971	15.3	64.2	32.3	6.3	0.9	1.9	0.0	4.0	0.3	8.9
1972	16.0	64.4	33.3	6.7	0.9	1.8	0.1	2.6	0.4	8.3
1973	17.9	69.6	33.4	6.5	1.1	2.0	0.6	3.8	0.9	10.8
1974	17.9	91.4	36.5	6.2	1.6	2.4	0.4	3.6	1.4	30.0
1975	14.6	81.2	38.7	7.8	2.0	2.6	0.7	2.1	1.5	21.8
1976	15.7	79.3	39.1	8.5	2.1	4.4	0.2	1.7	21.2	0.0
1977	15.5	80.0	41.2	9.1	2.1	4.7	0.3	1.8	19.6	0.0
1978	12.4	77.7	43.5	7.3	1.7	0.4	0.5	2.1	15.0	0.0
1979	10.6	83.6	44.4	7.9	1.9	−0.2	0.6	2.1	20.9	0.0
1980	12.2	88.4	47.1	8.4	3.0	0.4	0.8	1.9	23.1	0.0
1981	9.6	86.1	48.4	8.4	2.7	−0.3	1.3	2.0	21.4	0.0
1982	6.7	79.5	49.7	7.9	2.3	−0.1	0.7	2.0	16.0	0.0
1983	6.3	77.7	49.1	9.1	2.6	−1.3	0.8	1.1	14.2	0.0
1984	9.4	96.6	61.0	6.7	0.7	−0.9	3.4	1.7	20.9	0.0
1985	8.0	95.4	61.1	7.7	−0.3	−1.4	2.9	2.2	17.7	0.0
1986	9.7	86.2	59.0	7.7	1.7	−1.1	3.0	2.1	11.3	0.0
1987	13.9	89.4	59.3	8.6	4.6	−0.8	4.3	2.2	13.7	0.0
1988	13.3	86.1	58.8	8.0	4.9	−0.6	4.0	3.0	11.3	0.0
1989	10.2	92.0	60.5	5.5	5.4	−0.6	3.1	3.1	20.5	0.0
1990	7.2	94.1	58.5	5.8	3.0	0.8	3.4	2.8	27.0	0.0
1991	7.0	86.4	57.5	5.9	2.1	1.1	2.0	2.0	19.3	0.0
1992	6.0	85.0	59.2	6.4	2.0	0.1	1.8	2.5	14.8	0.0
1993	3.0	81.0	59.0	7.7	2.6	0.3	1.6	2.3	13.5	0.0
1994	6.1	82.7	59.3	8.0	4.8	2.3	1.7	2.4	15.9	0.0

Note: The variables are stated in relationship to GDP.
Source: Authors' calculations.

Significant changes have occurred in the relationship between the tax administration and the private sector. Tax pressures on the private sector have grown substantially since the positive oil shocks of the early 1970s, although they remain low by international standards. It is important to consider the changes in the tax structure as well as the tax mechanisms utilized. Table 8.5 shows the average values of the different types of taxes. Direct

Table 8.4 Derivation of the Private Saving Rate Average by Subperiods

Year	PS	Py/Pc	Pc	ta	trf	idp	itrf*	etrf*	supc	tap
1968–73	16.4	66.8	34.6	5.5	1.1	1.2	0.2	4.2	0.2	8.4
1974–82	12.8	83.0	43.2	8.0	2.2	1.6	0.6	2.1	15.6	25.9
1983–88	10.1	88.6	58.0	8.0	2.4	–1.0	3.1	2.0	14.9	0.0
1989–94	6.6	86.9	59.0	6.5	3.3	0.7	2.3	2.5	18.5	0.0

Note: The variables are stated in relationship to GDP.
Source: Authors' calculations.

taxes declined with the 1989 adjustment plan and have still not recuperated to previous levels despite efforts to improve income tax revenues.

In contrast, indirect taxes increased progressively over time. However, the causes for these variations must be identified. Devaluation, which in Venezuela acts as a tax on the use of foreign exchange, has become one of the main mechanisms for tax collection since the single, fixed exchange rate was abandoned in 1983. The importance of tax income generated by devaluation can be appreciated by comparing the rate of indirect taxation for the 1983–88 period (5 percent) with the years 1989–91 (3.6 percent) when the differential exchange system was abandoned. Later, beginning in 1992, the return to a fixed exchange rate, accompanied by successive and significant devaluations, granted new importance to this tax channel, although not as much as when the differential system was in effect. In addition to

**Table 8.5 Description of Tax Burdens
(percentage of GDP)**

Period	Direct Taxes	Direct Oil Taxes	Indirect Taxes	Other Tax Income
1968–73	2.8	13.1	3.4	2.3
1974–82	2.7	29.8	4.1	2.8
1983–88	2.8		5.0	1.3
1989–91	1.6		3.6	1.2
1992–94	2.0		5.7	1.1

Source: Authors' calculations.

Table 8.6 Federal Government Financing through Devaluation: 1982–93

Year	Fiscal Income from Devaluation (millions of bolivars)	Percentage of Federal Government Spending
1982	51	
1983	10,666	17.9
1984	16,828	28.0
1985	11,175	14.8
1986	17,296	21.9
1987	37,410	32.7
1988	3,701	2.6
1989	52,901	26.0
1990	17,817	4.7
1991	27,154	1.9
1992	41,685	5.8
1993	46,590	5.5

Sources: IMF, *International Financial Statistics*; Ministry of Energy and Mines, Oil and Other Statistical Data; Ministry of Finance, Annual Reports; Central Budget Office (OCEPRE), Explanation of Reasons for the Budget Bill; Central Bank of Venezuela, Economic Reports; authors' calculations.

devaluation, the implementation of a consumption tax in 1993 has led to a preponderance of indirect taxes over direct taxes.[7]

Table 8.6 shows the additional net income that the government obtained from devaluations from 1982 to 1993, a period in which manipulation of the exchange rate generated important tax resources exacted from the private sector. These inflows were very important, especially from 1983 to 1989, when they averaged 21 percent of all federal government expenditures.

The frequent use of exchange rate manipulation as a tax instrument has led economic agents to adopt precautionary measures in the face of expected devaluations. Capital flight, durable goods purchases, inventory

---

[7] In Venezuela, devaluation has not been the cause of tax deficits. It has been more a way of financing that the government has resorted to, given, in part, the inadequacy of the domestic tax structure and the tightness of the domestic financial market. For a detailed analysis of the financing mechanisms of the Venezuelan federal government, see Zambrano Sequín, Riutort, and Páez (1996).

accumulation, and real estate speculation have been among the mechanisms used to avoid such taxes. As shown in Table 8.4, net inflows to the private sector have been less significant due to interest on the internal national debt. Direct placement of internal national debt issues with the private sector has not been an important financing mechanism for the Venezuelan federal deficit.[8] Quasi-fiscal operations by the Central Bank through placement of securities in the money market, especially after the 1993 banking crisis, have gained in importance but have not further influenced nonfinancial private sector saving.

On the other hand, the relatively low government borrowing from the private sector has not generally led to a significant inflation tax. Table 8.7 shows the fiscal inflows due to the inflation tax for the period under analysis. Until 1986, there was virtually no inflation tax. Starting in 1987, although the relative weight of this taxation channel increases, its significance remains very low when compared to other chronic inflation countries in Latin America.

The change in income from transfers from the rest of the world reflects, among other things, returns on capital held abroad by private sector residents. Even if these transfers are underestimated, they follow the standard behavior of capital outflows experienced in the country, particularly after the 1983 external debt crisis and the adverse oil shock of 1986. The more recent relative reduction in the significance of this component, especially after 1992, is probably due more to capital control policies than to a reduction in the levels and returns on capital held abroad by residents. In any event, while a large portion of these revenues is accounted for in the current account, since they basically correspond to earnings on investments, a large portion of them will also be recorded as capital outflows when those earnings are capitalized in the markets where they are generated.

With respect to the changes in the relative weight of public companies' operating surpluses, the nationalization of the oil sector explains the

---

[8] Unlike other Latin American countries that also face the problem of external debt and continuous exchange rate shocks, the government of Venezuela has not had to resort, in any significant way, to domestic financing through the creation of money (Central Bank credits) or with private sector borrowing. This has been possible thanks to the high percentage of government revenues that comes from the external sector and relies on the exchange rate. Devaluation has been more advantageous to the government, since its net foreign inflows have always been positive.

Table 8.7 Inflation Tax Revenues in Relation to Fiscal Income and Nonoil GDP: 1968–94

Year	% Fiscal Income	% Nonoil GDP	% GDP
1968	1.1	0.2	0.1
1969	1.3	0.2	0.2
1970	1.3	0.2	0.2
1971	1.1	0.2	0.2
1972	1.4	0.2	0.2
1973	1.8	0.3	0.2
1974	2.1	0.7	0.4
1975	2.1	0.6	0.4
1976	2.6	0.6	0.4
1977	3.4	0.7	0.5
1978	3.4	0.5	0.4
1979	8.1	1.4	1.0
1980	6.8	1.4	1.0
1981	2.9	0.8	0.6
1982	2.4	0.5	0.4
1983	3.2	0.6	0.5
1984	5.7	1.8	1.4
1985	3.3	1.0	0.8
1986	5.7	1.4	1.2
1987	11.5	2.9	2.4
1988	12.2	2.6	2.2
1989	14.1	3.6	2.7
1990	7.7	2.5	1.8
1991	9.2	2.9	2.2
1992	11.9	3.0	2.4
1993	15.2	3.7	3.0
1994	16.9	5.0	3.7

Source: Authors' calculations.

changes between the first and second subperiods. This transfer of ownership from the private to the public sector should not have significantly affected private sector saving since the international companies did not in
fact save in the country; rather, they transferred their surpluses and profits
abroad. Once nationalized, saving on the part of oil companies clearly began, for the most part, to be accounted for as saving by residents.

Public and Private Saving

Is there a relationship between the behavior of public saving and its incidence on private sector saving? The literature refers to this subject as the problem of Ricardian equivalence. Basically, it says that the behavior of private saving could be influenced by changes in public saving if private agents perceive public saving as wealth.

This possibility, initially proposed by Barro (1974), establishes a relationship of perfect substitution between public and private saving. A change in the composition of financing public expenditures that implies a larger tax deficit (reduction of the marginal tax rate and/or increase in the issue of public debt) will have no effect on private consumption but will affect saving. Under this proposition, it is assumed that private agents do not include government bonds as a form of wealth. Although ownership of these bonds implies the promise of future interest payments by the government, it also implicitly entails higher future taxes so the government may pay the interest. Therefore, and according to the Ricardian equivalence approach, an increase in the marginal tax rate that implies an increase in public saving or a decrease in the deficit will generate a proportional decrease in the level of saving by private agents but will not affect their consumption as long as they internalize the future governmental budgetary restriction, which would allow for future tax reductions.

However, determining whether Ricardian equivalence holds or not must be done carefully. For example, a superficial analysis of the changes in public and private domestic saving during the 1983–88 subperiod may lead to an incorrect conclusion since outwardly, the two types of saving move in opposite directions. One aspect that should be controlled when discussing this hypothesis has to do with simultaneous changes in ordinary tax revenues. A drop in private saving provoked by increasing the indirect tax rate (for example, the devaluation tax) that occurs in tandem with an increase in public saving does not prove the existence of Ricardian equivalence. Therefore, confirmation of the Ricardian equivalence hypothesis requires controlling for the variations in ordinary tax revenues.

Figure 8.1 illustrates how the behavior of private domestic saving is not symmetrical (opposite) to public domestic saving in Venezuela. Perfect substitution does not exist between the two variables. However, a mere graphic visualization is not enough to contrast the Ricardian equivalence

Figure 8.1
Real Gross Domestic Saving
(millions of bolivars)

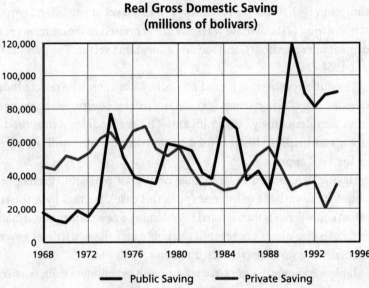

hypothesis. For that purpose, the results are presented as a regression between private gross domestic saving (SP) as a function of public saving (SG) for the 1968–94 period:

$$SP = 12.53 - 0.168SG \tag{4}$$

R^2: 0.56   DW: 1.91   Student t: −1.57

After accepting the cointegration hypothesis between these two variables, and having corrected the residual values for nuisance parameters, the results show that although a theoretically expected negative sign is obtained, the rate of public saving is less than one, and the coefficient is insignificant at conventional levels. However, to refute the hypothesis of Ricardian equivalence, tax collections and the level of public borrowing must be simultaneously controlled.

Starting from the approach proposed by Seater and Mariano (1985), a system of autoregressive vectors (VAR) is set up for six variables in which private consumption is assumed to be caused by the remaining system variables.

The variables used, all in real terms, deflated by the implicit GDP deflator are private consumption (pc), disposable national income (y), the real average deposit rate from the commercial banking sector (r), public consumption (gc), direct tax revenues (ta), and level of net federal government borrowing (D). All these variables are expressed in logarithms, except the deposit interest rate (r), and include a constants vector. The period analyzed is 1968–94.

The null hypothesis of Ricardian equivalence cannot be rejected when the rates for direct tax revenues (ta) and net federal government borrowing (D) are "simultaneously" insignificant. The methodology proposed by Johansen and Juselius (1990) is used to contrast the same null hypothesis under the VAR approach.

Having determined the existence of at least one cointegrating relationship for the variable of interest (pc in this case), the null hypothesis of Ricardian equivalence is then refuted by obtaining a new cointegration matrix that excludes the direct tax revenues variable and the net federal government borrowing variable (restricted matrix).

Table 8.8 shows the unrestricted normalized cointegration matrix in private consumption. At least one cointegrating vector exists, which is why the first column of Table 8.8 describes the long-term equilibrium relationship for private consumption:

$$pc = 2.8y - 1,667.7r + 1.831gc + 13.81ta - 58.6D. \qquad [5]$$

Finally, and after calculating the restricted cointegration matrix, the test of the probability rate was equal to 87.17. In contrast to the chi-squared statistic for (4) degrees of freedom, and equal to 14.86 at 1 percent significance, this allows us to reject the null hypothesis of the existence of Ricardian

Table 8.8 Unrestricted Cointegration Matrix: 1968–94

Pc	1	1	1	1	1	1
y	2.804	0.557	1.193	3.879	0.093	−1.988
r	−1,667.7	−5.866	0.052	0.004	0.0001	−0.002
gc	1.831	−0.475	1.249	3.403	−0.428	1.924
ta	13.811	−10.366	7.913	−1.243	−0.072	−0.131
D	−58.578	164.365	0.495	−0.087	−0.012	−0.002

equivalence for the case of Venezuela during the 1968–94 period. Not surprisingly, in an economy with relatively low tax pressure, insignificant domestic borrowing by the private sector, and a very low inflation tax, the hypothesis in question can be rejected.

External Shocks, Income Volatility and Private Sector Saving

Much of the income volatility in Venezuela is the product of consecutive external shocks, particularly those caused through the terms of trade. The effects of shocks in the terms of trade on the level of economic activity and income in a small, open economy have received growing attention in the literature on the determinants of saving.[9] Some relevant conclusions can be drawn from these studies. First, it is possible to demonstrate that only transitory shocks affect the saving rate. Permanent shocks are totally absorbed by consumption, while transitory ones are partially adjusted by the substitution between present and future consumption. Second, the effect of a transitory shock on saving depends, above all, on the possibilities for both intertemporal and intratemporal substitution. The degree of intertemporal substitution has been measured by the so-called elasticity of substitution between present and future consumption. Intratemporal substitution has been determined by the possibility of substituting nontradable goods for tradable ones, since shocks in the terms of trade affect the relative prices of these two types of goods—that is, the real exchange rate. In addition to the effects of inter- and intratemporal substitution, changes in income and wealth, the so-called effects on well-being, must also be considered. Since the substitution effects and effects on well-being occur in opposite directions, the net effect of shocks in the terms of trade depends, in each specific case, upon one prevailing over the other. If the income effects dominate the substitution effects, a negative and transitory shock in the terms of trade will decrease the saving rate. On the other hand, in economies where the substitution between tradable and nontradable and/or substitution between present and future consumption is high, a negative transitory shock in the terms of trade may increase the economy's private saving rate.

---

[9] For more information on this subject, see: Sachs (1981), Obstfeld (1982), Svensson and Razin (1983), Dornbusch (1983), and Ostry and Reinhart (1992).

Permanent and Transitory Shocks in the Terms of Trade

Given that transitory shocks are what finally affect the trajectory of private domestic saving, it is useful to separate the transitory component of the terms of trade from its permanent component. This sheds light on the severity and nature of the external shocks the Venezuelan economy has been subject to over the past 25 years. The transitory component by construction is stationary. Meanwhile, the permanent component is a unit root process.

The method suggested by Beveridge and Nelson (1981) and Stock and Watson (1988) was used to conduct the breakdown. The behavior of the transitory component of the terms of trade is illustrated in Figure 8.2.

The first oil shock of 1974 caused a 122 percent surge in the transitory component of the terms of trade. The external inflation shocks of 1976 and 1978 led to reductions of 37 percent and 34 percent, respectively, in the transitory component. The 1979–80 growth in oil prices brought about a 47 percent increase in the transitory component each year. For its part, the external debt shock in 1982 and 1983 led to declines of more than 30 percent each year, while the sharp drop in oil prices in 1986 brought about a 95 percent reduction in the transitory component of the terms of trade. Finally, the oil price recovery of 1990 boosted the transitory component of the terms of trade 153 percent.

Figure 8.2
Terms of Trade: Transitory Component

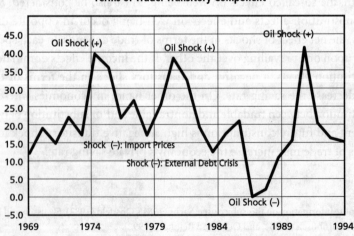

Such terms of trade volatility and the resulting pressures to which the Venezuelan domestic economy has been subjected have naturally affected the behavior of consumption and private sector saving.[10] These effects and their transmission channels should be developed within the context of an explanatory model that seeks to establish the determinants of saving in Venezuela.

Intra- and Intertemporal Substitution

Ostry and Reinhart (1992) developed an intertemporal and dynamic model that estimates the values of the key parameters that determine the net effect of transitory shocks in the terms of trade on private sector saving. The model is derived from a utility function for a representative agent characterized by additive and homothetic preferences, and a constant intra- and intertemporal elasticity of substitution.[11] Since the parameters are estimated directly from the utility function, the results are not affected by the economic cycle.[12]

The model to be estimated is the following:[13]

$$
u_t = \left\{ \frac{p_t\left(1+r_t^*\right)}{P_{t+1}} \left[\frac{am_t^{1-1/\varepsilon} + n_{t+1}^{1-1/\varepsilon}}{am_t^{1-1/\varepsilon} + n_t^{1-1/\varepsilon}} \right]^{\frac{\sigma-\varepsilon}{\sigma(\varepsilon-1)}} \left[\frac{m_{t+1}}{m_t} \right]^{-1/\varepsilon} \right\} - \frac{1}{\beta}
\tag{6}
$$

where u_t are the residual values of the estimation, σ and ε are the inter- and intratemporal elasticities of substitution, respectively; m and n refer to the real consumption of importable goods and nontradable goods, respectively;

---

[10]For a more detailed analysis of the macroeconomic effect of these shocks, see Hausmann (1991 and 1995).

[11]The hypothesis of an isoelastic utility function, the result of the proposition according to which the preferences are homothetic, also implies that the proportion of consumer expenditures does not depend on the level of wealth. For the rationale and validity of this hypothesis, see Friedman (1957).

[12]This means that the model estimated here is not vulnerable to the criticism of Lucas, as developed in Hall (1988). The parameters estimated here are stronger, and thus less unstable, than those that would be derived from conventional econometric equations.

[13]An explanation of the derivation of this model can be found in Zambrano, Sequín et al. (1996 and 1998).

β is the subjective discount factor; a is a parameter that represents the relative weight of the importable goods in the utility function for each period;[14] p is the relative price of importable goods; and r^* is the interest rate. The currency used is the price of exportable goods.

The estimation of the model is made under the assumption that the term u_t is not correlated with any of the remaining variables. Obviously, the model assumes nonlinear relationships among the variables, which is why it is estimated utilizing the generalized time method (GTM).[15]

The data series refer to the 1968–94 period. Real consumption of tradable and nontradable goods was estimated utilizing the definition and methodology followed by the Central Bank (BCV).[16] Those aggregates were used, together with the population figures published by the Central Office of Statistics and Information (OCEI), to calculate per capita consumption. The relative price of importable goods in terms of exportable goods was derived from the unit values of imports and exports published by the BCV. In relation to the interest rates in terms of exportable goods, bank interest rates for 90-day deposits were deflated by a price index for exported products, calculated on the basis of the unit export values.

The following instrument vectors were utilized:

$$INS_1 = \left[\text{Constant} , \ m_{t-1}/m_{t-2}, \ n_{t-1}/n_{t-2}, p_{t-2}\left(1+r^*_{t-2}\right)/p_{t-1}, \ m_{t-1}, m_{t-1} \right]$$

$$INS_2 = \left[\text{Constant} , \ m_{t-2}/m_{t-3}, \ n_{t-2}/n_{t-3}, p_{t-3}\left(1+r^*_{t-3}\right)/p_{t-2}, \ m_{t-2}, m_{t-2} \right]$$

$$INS_3 = \left[\text{Constant} , \ m_{t-1}/m_{t-2}, \ n_{t-1}/n_{t-2}, p_{t-2}\left(1+r^*_{t-2}\right)/p_{t-1}, \ m_{t-1}, m_{t-1}, p_{t-1} \right].$$

---

[14]Note that parameter a is restricted to being a positive value, but not less than one. For the case of a Cobb-Douglas–type utility function: $C = m^\alpha n^{1-\alpha}$, the parameter $a = \alpha/(1 - \alpha)$. If $0 < \alpha < 1$, this means that $a > 0$.

[15] Having previously estimated the parameters a and ε through an ordinary least squares (OLS) regression of the linearized version of the equation: $a(n_t/m_t)^{1/\varepsilon} = p_t/q_t$, where q is the relative price of the nontradable goods. This equation is nothing more than the nonstochastic condition that optimizes consumption in each period. That is, optimally, the marginal substitution ratio between m and n must equal the relative price of importable goods in terms of nontradable goods. The regression supplied consistent estimations of the parameters, given that the relative prices of the importable and nontradable goods constituted one cointegrated process. The estimated value of parameter ε (0.277) was used as one of the initial values for estimation by GTM.

[16] The BCV considers the following to be nontradable goods: all services, including electricity, gas, and water.

Table 8.9 Intra- and Intertemporal Elasticities of Substitution: 1968–94

Instrument	ε	σ	β	HJ	PV	DF
INS_1	0.165	0.534	0.928	2.326	0.676	4
	(2.792)	(0.898)				
INS_2	0.166	0.562	0.928	0.659	0.956	4
	(2.671)	(0.911)				
INS_3	0.177	0.642	0.928	3.604	0.607	5
	(3.273)	(1.119)				

Notes: The rates have been estimated using the generalized time method (GTM) incorporating a process of first-order moving averages, MA(1). The values in parentheses correspond to the student-t statistic. HJ is the J statistic from Hansen, and PV is its respective probability value according to the number of degrees of freedom (DF) associated with the test, which appears in the last column. The J statistic is distributed as an $\chi^2(4)$, and its critical value is 9.49 at a 95 percent level. For the case of 5 degrees of freedom, the J statistic is distributed as an $\chi^2(5)$, and its critical value is 11.1 at a 95 percent level.

Table 8.9 shows the parameter estimations using the different sets of instruments.

The values obtained for the parameters ε, σ, and β have the expected signs and fall within economically acceptable ranges.[17] The estimates shown indicate that the results are quite strong in relation to the instrument sets utilized, and none of the cases reject overidentification restrictions. According to the estimates, intratemporal elasticity of substitution for Venezuela fluctuates between 0.16 and 0.177. This is a relatively low elasticity compared with other countries. Ostry and Reinhart (1992), utilizing panel data for a set of African, Asian, and Latin American countries, found that the intratemporal elasticity of substitution fluctuates between 0.655 and 1.44. Gaviria (1993) estimated that this elasticity fluctuates around 0.6 for Colombia. For their part, Ogaki, Ostry and Reinhart (1995), in studying a set of 14 countries, found that intratemporal elasticities of substitution fluctuate between 0.38 and 2.16.

---

[17] Additional details related to the estimation procedure for these equations, as well as different versions and approaches to the model estimated here, may be found in Zambrano Sequín et al. (1996).

The intertemporal elasticity of substitution for Venezuela fluctuates between 0.53 and 0.64. This is highly coincidental with the study by Ogaki, Ostry and Reinhart (1995), who estimated that for Venezuela, the intertemporal elasticity of substitution fluctuates between a low of 0.449 and a high of 0.897, establishing a more likely central value of 0.648. In addition, that same study estimated the intertemporal elasticities of substitution for a set of countries utilizing panel data and determined that they ranged between 0.53 and 0.68. Finally, Ostry and Reinhart (1992) found that these intertemporal elasticities varied between 0.37 and 0.8.

For the purpose of examining how robust the estimates were in the face of different temporal specifications, the model for the 1974–94 sub-period was estimated, and the results are shown in Table 8.10. The results are not substantially different, although the levels of significance for the estimated parameters improve relatively. Therefore, the conclusions appear to remain valid for the period of strong terms of trade shocks. In Venezuela, since the substitution between tradable and nontradable goods is low and the substitution between present and future consumption is less than one, an adverse transitory shock in the terms of trade will reduce the economy's saving rate.

Table 8.10 Intra- and Intertemporal Elasticities of Substitution: 1974–94

Instrument	ε	σ	β	HJ	PV	DF
INS_1	0.156 (3.399)	0.382 (1.460)	0.928	2.984	0.560	4
INS_2	0.192 (3.392)	0.552 (1.049)	0.928	1.149	0.89	4
INS_3	0.198 (4.085)	0.476 (1.479)	0.928	5.017	0.41	5

Notes: The rates have been estimated using the generalized time method (GTM) incorporating a process of first-order moving averages, MA(1). The values in parentheses correspond to the student-t statistic. HJ is the J statistic from Hansen, and PV is its respective probability value according to the number of degrees of freedom (DF) associated with the test, which appears in the last column. The J statistic is distributed as an $\chi^2(4)$, and its critical value is 9.49 at a 95 percent level. For the case of 5 degrees of freedom, the J statistic is distributed as an $\chi^2(5)$, and its critical value is 11.1 at a 95 percent level.

This may explain the persistent drop in the saving rate in Venezuela following the long period of negative external shocks in 1983. The low substitution between tradable and nontradable goods, and between present and future consumption, verified in the period analyzed here, causes the income effects associated with changes in the terms of trade to predominate, and thus the effect of the shock tends to fall fully on the saving rate.

Terms of Trade and Private Saving: Simulating a Shock

Starting with the values of the estimated parameters, the effects of terms of trade shocks on private sector saving can be simulated with the aforementioned model. It attempts to determine the path over time of tradable and nontradable consumer goods, as well as the level of saving. The exercise was carried out assuming two periods, present and future, under the condition that the representative agent ends with a null net borrowing level.

Since the estimate requires values for the initial amounts, the per capita products of exportable, importable, and nontradable goods were calculated from BCV figures for 1994, and the price indices for tradable and nontradable goods are from the empirical estimate described above.[18] The amount for exportable goods was approximated by oil GDP. The GDP for importable goods was considered to be equal to that for tradable goods minus oil GDP. The nontradable GDP was taken directly from the published figures.

The real interest rate was assumed to be 0.15, and the initial level of borrowing was assumed to be equal to zero in order to facilitate the exercise.

With regard to the relative price of importable goods, the inverse of the terms of trade, and the relative price of nontradable goods, the inverse of the real exchange rate, initial values are equal to those calculated for 1994.

The basic model used for the simulations is:

$$\max_{m_0; n_0; m_1; n_1; s_0} \quad -1.13\left[\left(4.13m_0^{-5.25} + n_0^{-5.25}\right)^{0.17} + 0.93\left(4.13m_1^{-5.25} + n_1^{-5.25}\right)^{0.17}\right]$$

$$\text{s.a.} \qquad 1.76m_0 + 1.12n_0 + s_0 = 30{,}413$$

$$1.76m_1 + 1.12n_1 - (1+0.15)s_0 = 30{,}413. \qquad [7]$$

---

[18]Given the model used, the results are not determined by the specific values of the initial placements, which is why, in principle, their values may be arbitrary.

Two scenarios were constructed to simulate terms of trade shocks. Scenario 1 assumed a positive shock in the terms of trade generated by a 10 percent drop in the relative price of importable goods. Scenario 2, by contrast, assumes an adverse shock of the same absolute magnitude in the terms of trade caused by a drop in the relative price of exports. The effect a shock in the terms of trade has on the real exchange rate, the inverse of the relative price of nontradable goods, is theoretically ambiguous due to the substitution and income effects that operate simultaneously,[19] similar to what has been demonstrated in Khan and Montiel (1987) and Edwards (1989). For the Venezuelan case, Zambrano Sequín estimated the real exchange rate elasticity with respect to the changes in the terms of trade to be –0.09 for the 1974–88 and 1977–92 periods. This implies that a positive shock in the terms of trade would produce an appreciation of the real exchange rate or, what is equivalent, an increase in the relative price of nontradable goods. Thus, income effects would dominate over substitution effects, an expected result in a country where exportable goods are hardly consumed domestically or where they represent a relatively low share of total spending.

For the simulation exercise, it was assumed that, together with the positive transitory shock in the terms of trade, the relative prices of nontradable goods would increase, corresponding to a negative elasticity in the real exchange rate.

Table 8.11 shows the results of this simulation exercise. A positive and transitory shock in the terms of trade positively affects saving as long as the effects on the real exchange rate, the intertemporal change in prices, and the value of the resources of the representative economic agent have been simultaneously controlled.

This positive effect on saving is the result of the income effects dominating over the intra- and intertemporal substitution effects, discussed previously. The solutions are consistent with the Harberger-Laursen-Metzler (HLM) effect, that is, the increase in income associated with an improve-

---

[19]A drop in the terms of trade reduces real income, decreasing the demand for nontradable goods. The resulting imbalance implies a price reduction for those goods, causing the real exchange rate to depreciate. In addition to this direct effect, a substitution effect in the opposite direction also occurs. Depending on the intensity of both effects, the real exchange rate will appreciate or depreciate.

Table 8.11 Simulations Based on the Individual Optimization Model

	Terms of Trade	Real Exchange Rate	r	m	n	Level of Saving[a]
Base Scenario						
Period 0	0.568	0.893	0.15	10998	9422	504
Period 1	0.568	0.893	0.15	11396	9764	−580
Scenario 1						
Period 0	0.630	0.884	0.15	11464	9642	528
Period 1	0.568	0.893	0.15	11411	9776	−619
Scenario 2						
Period 0	0.517	0.900	0.15	10591	9227	496
Period 1	0.568	0.893	0.15	11393	9760	−570

a. Negative values are due to compliance with the condition of transversality.

ment in the terms of trade, by being transitory, raises the level of saving and the current account balance of the balance of payments.[20]

Obviously, the result is just the opposite when the relative prices of exportable products decline. The drop in income produced by the transitory loss in the purchasing power of exports in turn causes a depreciation in the real exchange rate, driven by the reduction in the demand and relative prices of nontradable goods. At the same time, it should make present consumption more expensive, which would increase saving for reasons of intertemporal substitution. As the model predicts, since the substitution effects that operate in the opposite direction from income are weak, savings diminish in the face of negative terms of trade shocks.

Private Saving Behavior and Liquidity Constraints

Another crucial element that helps explain the high sensitivity of private saving to variations in economic activity has to do with liquidity constraints in the economy.

---

[20]The models utilized here are obviously oversimplified, which prevents a rigorous analysis of the effects on the current account. For example, variations in the stock of capital would have to be considered, and through this channel savings and investment would be related to the changes in relative prices and the current account.

The existence of a perfect capital market allows the agents to smooth the trajectory of consumption over time despite fluctuations in income. Given that financial markets do not operate perfectly, some individuals may not have access to credit and, hence, cannot engage in intertemporal consumption smoothing. In this way, if liquidity constraints are prevalent in the economy, the capacity of the agents to defer their consumption is affected, regardless of how sensitive their temporal preferences may be to changes in the other determinants of consumption. Among other things, this implies that saving is less sensitive to variations in the interest rate, not because the elasticity of substitution is necessarily low, but because consumers do not have access to credit in the amounts they might wish. Thus, determining the presence and importance of liquidity constraints is key in determining not only the relationship between income volatility and private saving but also the ability of monetary policy to influence private saving.

Incorporating Liquidity Constraints into the Basic Consumption Model

In the literature on consumption and saving, the usual method for incorporating liquidity constraints is to modify the so-called standard model[21] by incorporating an additional restriction that establishes some limits on the borrowing capacity of the representative economic agent.[22] According to this approach, Venezuela does suffer from liquidity constraints (Zambrano Sequín et al., 1996). This is why it is important to estimate the intertemporal elasticity of substitution within the framework of a model that controls for credit restrictions.

Recent developments in this area have allowed for models in which the liquidity constraints, rather than exogenously imposed, are incorporated endogenously, thus improving the specification of the estimation

---

[21]Namely, the $\Delta c_t = -\rho\sigma + \sigma r_t + \sigma e_t$, where Δc is the consumption variation rate, $\rho > 0$ is the temporal discount rate, and σ is the intertemporal consumption elasticity of substitution. The detailed derivation of this linearized version of the Euler equation in the framework of an intertemporal stochastic decision model can be found in Blanchard and Fischer (1989, ch. 6).
[22]Examples regarding the use of this type of liquidity constraint may be found in Zeldes (1989) and Rossi (1988). In the case of Rossi (1988), the constraint depends upon the changes in income; therefore, this may vary over time.

models. Specifically, the modified version of the basic model developed by Wirjanto (1991 and 1995) is used.[23]

In the context of this model, instead of prohibiting individuals from freely borrowing against their future earned income, it is assumed that this is possible. However, the rate at which these individuals, subject to liquidity constraints, may do so is a growing function of the size of the credit. As a result, the consumption growth rate for these individuals will be related not only to the real interest rate but to their income growth rate, which explains why consumption is sensitive to changes in this last variable in the empirical analysis.

In this way, the Euler equation that describes the behavior of consumers subject to liquidity constraints is given by:

$$\Delta c_{2t} = \frac{\sigma_2 \rho_2}{1 - \xi_t \sigma_2} + \frac{\sigma_2}{1 - \xi_t \sigma_2} r_{2t} - \frac{\xi_t \sigma_2}{1 - \xi_t \sigma_2} \Delta y_{2t} + v_t; \quad E_{t-1}[v_t] = 0 \quad [8]$$

where subscript 2 indicates the variables and parameters corresponding to individuals with credit constraints, σ is the intertemporal consumption elasticity of substitution, ρ is the temporal preference rate, r_{2t} is the real lending rate, v_t is a term of random white noise, and $\xi_t < 0$ is the parameter that measures the severity of the liquidity constraints.

On the other hand, the Euler linearized equation for individuals not subject to liquidity constraints mirrors the standard model:

$$\Delta c_{1t} = -\rho_1 \sigma_1 + \sigma_1 r_{1t} + \sigma_1 e_t; \quad E_{t-1}[e_t] = 0 \quad [9]$$

where subscript 1 indicates the variables and parameters corresponding to this group of consumers and r_{1t} represents the real borrowing rate, since this is the relevant rate for consumer decisions in this case.

Assuming that $\rho_1 = \rho_2 = \rho$ and $\sigma_1 = \sigma_2 = \sigma$ and that consumption by the agents not affected by liquidity constraints has a weight of $(1 - \theta)$ in terms of total consumption, in aggregate terms, the rate of change in consumption is given by the following equation:

---

[23]A detailed description of the Wirjanto model (1995) is found in Zambrano Sequín et al. (1998).

$$\Delta c_t = \left(1-0\right)\left[-\rho\sigma + \sigma r_{1t} + \sigma e_t\right]$$

$$+ \; \theta\left[-\frac{\sigma\rho}{1-\xi_t\sigma} + \frac{\sigma}{1-\xi_t\sigma}r_{2t} - \frac{\xi_t\sigma}{1-\xi_t\sigma}\Delta y_{2t} + v_t\right] \qquad [10]$$

where θ is interpreted as the proportion of individuals subject to liquidity constraints in the economy.

Making $w_t = r_{2t} - r_{1t}$—that is, the differential between the lending and borrowing rate—equation [10] may be stated as:

$$\Delta c_t = \left(\frac{1}{1-\sigma\xi_t}\right)$$

$$\cdot \left[-\rho\sigma + \sigma r_{1t} + \theta\sigma w_t + \sigma\xi_t(1-\theta)\sigma\rho - \sigma\xi_t\theta\Delta y - \sigma\xi_t(1-\theta)\sigma r_{1t}\right]$$

a nonlinear equation for estimating the intertemporal consumption elasticity of substitution (σ) within the framework of an intertemporal selection model that (endogenously) incorporates liquidity constraints.[24]

Intertemporal Elasticity of Substitution in View of Liquidity Constraints

The following statistical series were used to estimate equation [11]:

Two alternative variables were employed for consumption: real per capita final consumption expense for households (CFH) to capture total private consumption, and per capita expenditures on nondurable goods and services (CNDS) to capture the consumption of nondurable goods and services. The assumption that the utility of the consumption of nondurable goods and services can be separated from other types of goods may be ques-

---

[24]To explicitly include ξ_t in the model and thus estimate equation [11], we follow Wirjanto (1995), incorporating a normalized quadratic function of w in the form

$$\xi_t = d_0 + d_1 w_t^n + d_2(w_t^n)^2$$

where $w_t^n = (r_{2t} - r_{1t})/r_{1t}$, as a proxy of the function (unknown) that governs the behavior of ξ.

tionable.[25] Therefore, when running tests with both variables, it is useful to verify this model's robustness with regard to this assumption. For income, real per capita disposable national income (IND) was deflated by the implicit deflator of the consumption variable. The average 90-day commercial bank nominal rate, deflated by the consumer price index, was used as the real borrowing interest rate. Finally, the real lending interest rate was calculated on the basis of general balance sheets and consolidated income statements from the commercial banking industry as income from interest in the average credit portfolio.[26]

After having rejected at significant levels the null hypothesis of unit roots in the variables to be used (income and consumption in their first difference and those related to interest rate levels), it was possible to estimate equation [11] for both real per capita final consumption by households (CFH) and real per capita consumption of nondurable goods and services (CNDS). The results of this estimate are shown in Table 8.12.[27]

The estimated values of σ are 0.84 and 0.9 for CFH and CNDS, respectively. In contrast to the results shown above, where liquidity constraints are not incorporated, both estimations are statistically significant at conventional levels. The HJ statistics, on the other hand, indicate that the model is not rejected by the data to significance levels of 5 percent.[28]

---

[25]See Wirjanto (1991) regarding this point.

[26]The problems of aggregation derived from the use of aggregate data may reduce the reliability of the statistical tests conducted on the estimates. It would be good to estimate equation [11] with individual information from households and for at least two consecutive periods. Unfortunately, as occurs in most countries, no such information is currently available for Venezuela, which is why aggregate data were used. Consequently, the results should be viewed in light of the limitations involved in the use of this type of data. Furthermore, the proxy variables employed for the estimation were unable to reflect what was theoretically desired, another reason for careful analysis of the estimations. This is particularly true for interest rates, which were controlled for most of the period under study.

[27] The temporal aggregation problems in annual consumption data, as Hall (1988) notes, introduce a process of first-order moving averages, MA(1), with one known parameter in the error term. Therefore, the covariance matrices for the explanatory variables are corrected by the said MA(1) configuration. This same fact forces the rejection of the set of key variables to be employed, beginning in the second period, in order to avoid inconsistent estimators that result in key variables being correlated with the residual values.

[28] Similar results have been obtained with specifications of the model where ξ_t is assumed to be constant. See Zambrano Sequín et al. (1996).

Table 8.12 Equation [11] Estimation: 1969–94

Δc_t	ρ	σ	θ	HJ	PV	DF
ΔCFH_t	−0.079	0.842	0.355	2.643	0.45	3
	(−4.497)	(3.963)	(3.969)			
$\Delta CNDS_t$	−0.063	0.904	0.534	0.351	0.95	3
	(−2.956)	(2.791)	(1.888)			

Notes: The rates have been estimated using the generalized time method (GTM) incorporating a process of first-order moving averages, MA(1). The values in parentheses correspond to the student-t statistic. HJ is the J statistic from Hansen, and PV is its respective probability value according to the number of degrees of freedom (DF) associated with the test, which appear in the last column. The set of key variables used is: Constant, Δc_{t-2}, Δc_{t-3}, Δc_{t-4}, $\Delta y_{2,t-2}$, $\Delta y_{2,t-3}$, $\Delta y_{2,t-4}$, $r_{1,t-2}$, w_{t-2}.

The estimated proportion of individuals subject to liquidity constraints (θ) is 36 percent for CFH and 53 percent for CNDS and in both cases is significant. Finally, a significant, but negative, value of the estimate of the temporal discount rate (ρ) was found. This result is contrary to the values established by consumption models for this parameter. However, other empirical research has indicated similar values in the estimations of ρ in developing countries, although not statistically significant (see Ogaki, Ostry, and Reinhart 1995).

These results suggest, first, the presence of important liquidity constraints in the period under analysis. The existence of these constraints, besides affecting the estimation of the intertemporal consumption elasticity of substitution, makes private saving less sensitive to interest rate variations, and therefore, the effect of income variation and volatility tends to predominate over the behavior of private saving.

The low response of private saving to changes in the interest rate and its high sensitivity to changes in income are due less to limited elasticity of substitution than to restrictions on access to credit that reduce the financing alternatives of economic agents and thus the possibility of compensating for the effects produced by income variation and instability.

In other words, if liquidity constraints are reduced, the model shows that the effects that changes in the interest rate have on the behavior of private saving will be substantially greater than those observed. Consequently, by improving the efficiency and coverage of the financial system and capital markets, and increasing the capacity of economic agents to ease the pace of their consumption, the effects that the high volatility of the level of economic activity have on the private saving rate can be reduced.

Conclusions

The sustained drop in the private saving rate over the past 20 years seems to be associated with the variable, unstable level of economic activity that has resulted from successive external shocks to the Venezuelan economy since the early 1970s. The temporal precedence, from GNP to saving, and the relationship between product volatility and variation of the rate of saving growth, are consistent with this conclusion.

Although these external shocks have also affected the public sector's ability to spend and save, there is no evidence of displacement effects on private spending through the conventional channels of domestic borrowing and/or the inflation tax. However, clearly the use of devaluation as a tax instrument has served as a basic mechanism for transferring resources to the government, particularly following the 1983 external debt crisis. The validity of the hypothesis that public saving displaces private saving, in the sense of Ricardian equivalence, could not be confirmed.

Moreover, the elasticities of substitution between tradable and nontradable goods, as well as intertemporal substitutability in private consumption, are not high enough to counteract the income effects associated with the transitory shocks in the terms of trade to which the economy has been successively subjected. The Harberger-Laursen-Metzler effect seems to be confirmed in the case of Venezuela, although the response of saving to transitory changes in the terms of trade is less than that predicted by a standard model in which changes in relative prices and liquidity constraints are not controlled. Importable and nontradable goods seem to be more complementary than substituted in Venezuela. However, the complementarity is not perfect. The modification of the terms of trade affects the real exchange rate and through this channel, the temporal consumption path, confirming the findings of Ostry and Reinhart (1992).

There is evidence that private saving is affected as much by relative price changes caused by transitory shocks in the terms of trade as it is by liquidity constraints. Saving tends to behave procyclically in the face of a transitory decline in the terms of trade. In principle, this suggests that such shocks should be "financed" to compensate for the effects on investment and international reserves. However, compensatory resource requirements may be overestimated by a model that does not control for the effects of substitution and liquidity constraints.

Thus, monetary policy seems to have little power to affect the level of saving if it uses interest rates as its main tool. The low elasticity of substitution in the consumption of tradable and nontradable goods and the inelasticity between present and future consumption cause private saving to be affected primarily by the fundamental adjustments to changes in the income level. However, a reduction of liquidity constraints would significantly increase the sensitivity of saving to the interest rate, and with it, the power of monetary policy to affect this aggregate.

References

Barro, R. 1974. "Are Government Bonds Net Wealth?" *Journal of Political Economy.* 81(6): 1095–1117.

Bayoumi, T. 1993. "Financial Deregulation and Household Saving." *Economic Journal.* 103: 1433–43.

Bester, H. 1985. "Screening vs. Rationing in Credit Markets with Imperfect Information." *American Economic Review.* 75: 850–55.

Beveridge, S. and Nelson, C. R. 1981. "A New Approach to Decomposition of Economic Time Series into Permanent and Transitory Components with Particular Attention to Measurement of the Business Cycle." *Journal of Monetary Economics.* 7 (2): 151–74.

Blanchard, O. J. and Fischer, S. 1989. *Lectures on Macroeconomics.* Cambridge, Mass.: MIT Press.

Browning, M. and Lusardi A. 1985. *Household Saving: Micro Theories and Micro Facts.* Center for Economic Research, Tilburg University, The Netherlands.

Campbell, J. 1987. "Does Saving Anticipate a Decline in Labor Income? An Alternative Test of the Permanent Income Hypothesis." *Econometrica.* 55 (November).

Campbell, J. and Lawrence, S. 1991. "Consumption Growth Parallels Income Growth: Some New Evidence." In B. D. Bernheim and J. B. Shoven, editors. *National Saving and Economic Performance.* Chicago: University Press for the National Bureau of Economic Research.

Deaton, A. 1990. "Saving in Developing Countries: Theory and Review." *Proceedings of the World Bank Annual Conference on Development Economics 1989.* Washington, DC.

———. 1995. "Growth and Saving: What Do We Know, What Do We Need to Know, and What Might We Learn?" Research Program in Development Studies. Princeton University, Princeton, N. J.

Dornbusch, R. 1983. "Real Interest Rates, Home Goods, and Optimal External Borrowing." *Journal of Political Economy.* 91 (February): 141–53.

Edwards, S. 1989. "Tariffs, Capital Controls, and Equilibrium Real Exchange Rates." *Canadian Journal of Economics.* 22: 79–92.

———. 1995. "Why Are Savings Rates So Different Across Countries? An International Comparative Analysis." NBER Working Paper 5097. National Bureau of Economic Research, Cambridge, Mass.

Flavin, M. 1981. "The Adjustment of Consumption to Changing Expectations about Future Income." *Journal of Political Economy.* 89: 974–1009.

Friedman, M. 1957. *A Consumption Function Theory.* Madrid: Alianza Universidad.

Gaviria, A. 1993. "Private Savings and Terms of Trade: The Colombian Case." *Ensayos sobre Política Económica.* No. 23 (June).

Ghosh, A. and Ostry, J. 1994. "Export Instability and External Balance in Developing Countries." *IMF Staff Papers.* 41 (2): 214–35.

Giovannini, A. 1985. "Saving and the Real Interest Rates in LDCs." *Journal of Development Economics.* 18 (August): 197–217.

Gupta, K. 1987. "Aggregate Savings, Financial Intermediation, and Interest Rate." *Review of Economics and Statistics.* 69 (May): 303-11.

Hall, R. 1978. "Stochastic Implications of the Life Cycle–Permanent Income Hypothesis: Theory and Evidence." *Journal of Political Economy.* 86 (6): 971–87.

————. 1988. "Intertemporal Substitution in Consumption." *Journal of Political Economy.* 96: 339–57.

Harberger, A. 1950. "Currency Depreciation, Income and the Balance of Trade." *Journal of Political Economy.* 58 (February): 47–60.

Hausmann, R. 1991. "Dealing with Negative Oil Shocks: The Venezuelan Experience in the Eighties." Instituto de Estudios Superiores de Administración, Caracas.

————. 1995. "Quitting Populism Cold Turkey: The 'Big Bang' Approach to Macroeconomic Balance." In L. W. Goodman, et al., editors. *Lessons of the Venezuelan Experience.* Baltimore: Johns Hopkins University Press.

Hayashi, F. and Sims, C. 1983. "Nearly Efficient Estimation of Times Series Models with Predetermined, but Not Exogenous Instruments." *Econometrica.* 51 (May): 783–98.

Horioka, C. 1995. "Is Japan's Household Saving Rate Really High?" *Review of Income and Wealth.* Series 41 (4): 373–97.

Jappelli, T. and Pagano, M. 1994. "Saving, Growth and Liquidity Constraints." *Quarterly Journal of Economics.* 109: 83–109.

Johansen, S. and Juselius, K. 1990. "Maximum Likelihood Estimation and Inference on Cointegration, with Applications to the Demand for Money." *Oxford Bulletin of Economics and Statistics.* 52 (2): 169–210.

Khan, M.S. and Montiel, P. 1987. "Real Exchange Rate Dynamics in a Developing Country." Working Paper WP/87/44. International Monetary Fund, Washington, DC.

King, M. 1986. "Capital Market 'Imperfections' and the Consumption Functions." *Scandinavian Journal of Economics.* 88 (1): 59–80.

Laursen, S. and Metzler, L. 1950. "Flexible Exchange Rates and the Theory of Employment." *Review of Economics and Statistics*. 32 (November): 281–99.

Lehmussaari, O-P. 1990. "Deregulation and Consumption: Saving Dynamics in the Nordic Countries." *IMF Staff Papers*. 37: 71–93.

Liu, L-Y. and Woo, W. T. 1994. "Saving Behavior under Imperfect Financial Markets and the Current Account Consequences." *Royal Economic Society*. May.

Milde, H. and Riley, G. 1988. "Signaling in Credit Markets." *Quarterly Journal of Economics*. 103.

Obstfeld, M. 1982. "Aggregate Spending and the Terms of Trade: Is There a Laursen-Metzler Effect?" *Quarterly Journal of Economics*. 97 (May): 251–70.

Ogaki, M., Ostry, J. and Reinhart, C. M. 1995. "Saving Behavior in Low- and Middle-Income Developing Countries: A Comparison." Working Paper WP/95/3. International Monetary Fund, Washington, DC.

Ostry, J. 1988. "The Balance of Trade, Terms of Trade, and Real Exchange Rate: An Intertemporal Optimizing Framework." *IMF Staff Papers*. 35 (4): 541–73.

Ostry, J. and Reinhart, C. M. 1992. "Private Saving and Terms of Trade Shocks: Evidence from Developing Countries." *IMF Staff Papers*. 39 (3): 495–517.

Rossi, N. 1988. "Government Spending, the Real Interest Rate, and the Behavior of Liquidity-Constrained Consumers in Developing Countries." *IMF Staff Papers*. 35: 104–40.

Sachs, J. 1981. "The Current Account and Macroeconomic Adjustment in the 1970s." *Brookings Papers on Economic Activity*. No. 1.

Seater, J. and Mariano, R. 1985. "New Tests of the Life Cycle and Tax Discounting Hypotheses." *Journal of Monetary Economics*. 15 (2): 195–215.

Stock, J. and Watson, M. 1988. "Variable Trends in Economic Times Series." *Journal of Economic Perspectives*. 2 (3): 147–74.

Svensson, L. and Razin, A. 1983. "The Terms of Trade and the Current Account: The Harberger-Laursen-Metzler Effect." *Journal of Political Economy*. 91 (February): 97–125.

Tybout, J. and de Melo, J. 1986. "The Effects of Financial Liberalization on Savings and Investment in Uruguay." *Economic Development and Cultural Change*.

Wirjanto, T. 1991. "Testing the Permanent Income Hypothesis: The Evidence from Canadian Data." *Canadian Journal of Economics*. 24 (3): 563–77.

———. 1995. "Aggregate Consumption Behavior and Liquidity Constraints: The Canadian Evidence." *Canadian Journal of Economics*. 28 (4b): 1135–52.

Zambrano Sequín, L., Riutort, M. and Páez, K. 1996. "Financing Fiscal Expenditures, Monetary Dynamics and Inflation in Venezuela." *Temas de Coyuntura*. No. 33.

Zambrano Sequín, L., Riutort M., Muñoz R. and J. Guevara. 1996. "Elasticity of Substitution, Terms of Trade and Liquidity Constraints in Venezuela." Instituto de Investigaciones Económicas y Sociales, Universidad Católica Andrés Bello.

———. 1998. "El ahorro privado en Venezuela: tendencias y determinantes." Working Paper Series R-322. Office of the Chief Economist, Inter-American Development Bank, Washington, DC.

Zeldes, S.P. 1989. "Consumption and Liquidity Constraints: An Empirical Investigation." *Journal of Political Economy*. 97 (2).

III. LESSONS FROM EUROPE

III. LESSONS FROM
EUROPE

CHAPTER 9

The Determinants of Saving: Lessons from Italy

Tulio Jappelli and Marco Pagano[1]

Understanding the determinants of the aggregate saving rate is a crucial pre-requisite in designing a number of policy interventions, from the design of the tax and social security system to the layout of financial market regula-tion. It is, therefore, not surprising that the analysis of saving behavior has become one of the central issues in empirical macroeconomics (see Brown-ing and Lusardi, 1996, and Deaton, 1992, for recent surveys). This analysis of the Italian experience is a contribution to this large and growing body of empirical research. In fact, the behavior of the Italian saving rate deserves special attention, for at least two reasons.

First, in this century Italy turned from an underdeveloped, mainly agricultural economy into one of the main industrial nations in the world, and during this transition it experienced wide fluctuations in its saving rate. These fluctuations provide an interesting environment to understand if sav-ing has been the driving force of capital accumulation or rather has pas-sively responded to exogenous changes in the economic growth rate—one of the key unsolved issues in the literature (Deaton, 1995).

Second, in most of the postwar period, Italy featured an abnormally high saving rate compared to most other industrialized countries. But in recent years this is no longer true. Under any definition of saving, in the last decade the Italian saving rate has fallen below the average of developed coun-tries. Why was the Italian saving ratio comparatively high, and why has the decline been so dramatic? There are various potential answers to both of these questions.

---

[1] The authors are economists at the Università di Salerno, Italy.

This chapter looks at the evidence from three different standpoints, drawing on new data sets as well as on results already available in the literature. The starting point is an analysis of the long-run record, by drawing upon more than a century of time-series data. Then, the Italian saving experience is put in international perspective and compared with the evidence for the principal developed countries. Finally, the theories consistent with the macroeconomic evidence are evaluated in light of the microeconomic data available for the 1980s and early 1990s.

The main results can be summarized as follows. The long-run historical record and the international data point to a very strong contemporaneous correlation between national saving and growth. The data also reveal that in the Italian historical experience growth tends to lead saving, rather than the opposite. This finding is consistent with the predictions of several models, including Modigliani's (1986) life-cycle model and endogenous growth models.

In addition, two stylized facts characterize the dynamics of the Italian saving rate in the postwar period. In the 1960s and 1970s, the Italian national saving rate was comparatively high even conditioning on growth and government saving. In the 1990s, instead, the Italian saving rate was back in line with the international average. The macroeconomic evidence is consistent with several potential explanations for these dynamics: the fluctuations in productivity growth, the pervasive borrowing constraints and imperfections of insurance markets (followed by some liberalization in the late 1980s), the transition to an unfunded and increasingly generous social security system in the late 1960s and 1970s, the spectacular drop in fertility, the increasing tax pressure associated with the buildup of public debt, and the changing tastes of Italian households.

Some explanations of the changes in aggregate saving behavior have testable implications at the microeconomic level. For example, the growth-saving nexus suggested by the life-cycle model arises from the fact that productivity differs across generations, the young being more productive than the old. In a growing economy, net saving is positive because the young are richer than their parents, and it therefore increases with the income differential between successive generations. One testable implication of the theory is that a change in productivity growth should not affect the individual propensities to save of different generations, but rather the relative income shares of the young and the old.

When this prediction is tested with data drawn from the 1984–93 Survey of Household Income and Wealth, it garners very little support: microeconomic data suggest that almost all the reduction of household saving in the last decade is due to a fall in the saving rate for all the age groups, not to a change in their relative income shares and in their relative size. One possible explanation for this finding is that the declining saving rates of the last decade are due not to a decline in growth, as suggested by the time-series evidence, but rather to other shocks, such as asset price changes or preference shifts. Alternatively, one must abandon the life-cycle framework and turn to models in which productivity growth is positively correlated with individual saving rates, and not only with the aggregate saving rate.

The Long-Run Historical Record

Economic theory suggests that productivity and population growth are the main candidates to explain variations in saving rates, both across countries and over time. This prediction is validated by much empirical work showing that a positive correlation between saving and growth is one of the most robust stylized facts in macroeconomics (Levine and Renelt, 1992; Carroll and Weil, 1994). Although most of the empirical studies on saving have used postwar data, this correlation is not peculiar to that period.

The correlation is apparent in Figure 9.1, which shows the time series of the national saving rate and the growth rate of real GDP in Italy in the 1862–1990 period.[2] This figure shows that Italy has not always been a high-saving country, contrary to what is commonly held. The swings of saving and growth are very remarkable, reflecting the length of the period of observation, two major wars, and the succession of different regimes and political institutions. The period that runs from 1862 until the turn of the century is essentially characterized by economic stagnation. The years be-

---

[2] In the figures and regressions of this section, the growth rate is computed as the rate of change of net national income, government saving is defined as the public sector budget surplus net of investment outlays, and private saving is defined as national saving minus government saving. Data sources are as follows. For the 1861–1951 interval, net national saving and net national income are drawn from *Statistiche storiche italiane*, Istituto Italiano di Statistica (ISTAT), 1985, Table 115, pp. 217-18; government saving is drawn from Modigliani and Jappelli (1987). For the 1952–90 interval, net national saving, net national income, and government saving are drawn from Pagliano and Rossi (1992), Tables 15 and 17.

Figure 9.1
Saving and Growth: 1862–1990
(percent)

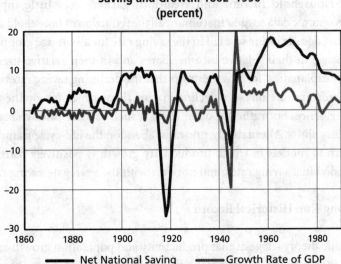

tween 1897 and 1907 represented, in all respects, the period in which the Italian economy grew the fastest; in fact, the national saving rate too rose to an average of 10.2 percent in the first decade of the century. After World War II, the net national saving rate increased tremendously during the "economic miracle" of the 1950s and 1960s, and then declined steeply in the 1970s and 1980s, reverting in 1990 to the level of the early 1950s.

The next figures offer greater detail about the secular behavior of the Italian saving rate. Figure 9.2 shows the time-series pattern of net national saving and of its breakdown into government saving and net private saving from 1862 to 1950, that is, from the unification of Italy to the inception of the "economic miracle." In the two world wars, net national saving dipped dramatically owing to the enormous dissaving by the government sector, reflecting the financing needs associated with the wars, while private saving held its level or even increased, largely due to the forced saving schemes imposed by the government.

The picture, however, changes considerably if private and government saving are adjusted for inflation, as is done in Figure 9.3. The inflation adjustment consists of deducting the reduction in the real value of government nominal debt due to inflation from private sector income and adding it to the revenues of the government. Since this adjustment captures infla-

Figure 9.2
Saving Components: 1862–1990

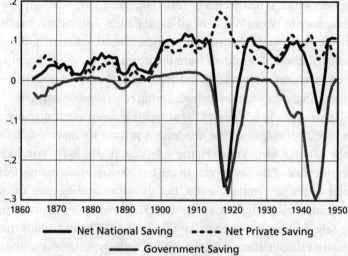

Figure 9.3
Inflation-Adjusted Saving Rates: 1862–1949

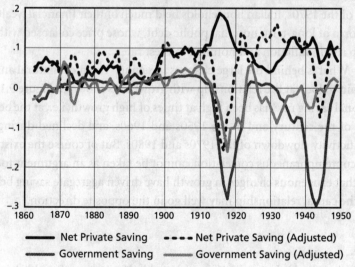

tion-induced transfers from the private to the public sector, it only applies to the saving rates of the private and public sectors, not to the national saving rate, which is unaffected by inflation. Due to the relatively low rates of inflation up to World War I, the adjusted figures do not differ much from the unadjusted ones. In the two war periods, instead, inflation induces massive redistribution of resources from the private to the government sector: adjusted government saving falls much less than the unadjusted figures, and correspondingly the adjusted private saving rate falls dramatically.

Figures 9.4 and 9.5 present the same breakdown of national saving for the 1950–90 period. Since the unadjusted private saving rate falls far less than the national saving rate (Figure 9.4), one may be led to conclude that the steep decline of the saving rate in the last 20 years arises mainly from the behavior of the government sector. But this is misleading once the saving rates are adjusted for inflation (Figure 9.5): the inflation-adjusted private saving rate declines much more steeply in the 1970s and 1980s than the unadjusted rate. Symmetrically, the decline in the government saving rate is far smaller after it is adjusted for inflation, especially in the 1970s. Again, this is because the high inflation rates of the 1970s and early 1980s effected a large transfer of wealth from the private to the public sector. The capital loss borne by the private sector was especially large because at the beginning of the 1970s, Italian households held much of their financial wealth in the form of long-term nominal public debt, whose price collapsed with the sharp rise in inflation and nominal interest rates.

What is behind the large changes in saving? The most natural answer is again to look at the relationship with growth. As shown in Figure 9.1, the national saving rate has been high at times of high growth, i.e., at the beginning of the century and in the 1950s and 1960s, and declined during the productivity slowdown of the 1970s and 1980s. But of course the existence of a contemporaneous correlation cannot be taken as an argument for the fact that exogenous changes in growth have driven aggregate saving behavior: the causal relationship may well go in the opposite direction.[3]

---

[3] A causal relationship from saving to growth is predicted by most growth models. In endogenous growth models, for instance, a preference shift that leads to a higher saving rate also increases the steady-state growth rate of the economy. In a neoclassical growth model, the same preference shift increases growth along the transition path to the new steady state.

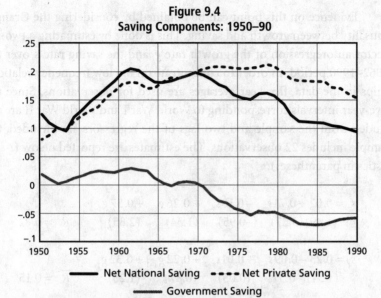

Figure 9.4
Saving Components: 1950–90

— Net National Saving   - - - Net Private Saving
▬▬ Government Saving

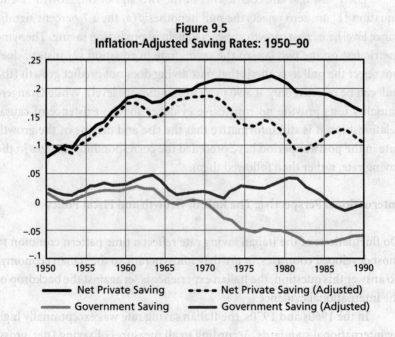

Figure 9.5
Inflation-Adjusted Saving Rates: 1950–90

— Net Private Saving   - - - Net Private Saving (Adjusted)
▬▬ Government Saving   ▬▬ Government Saving (Adjusted)

Evidence on this point can be obtained by considering the Granger causality between growth and saving. This is done by estimating a two-lag vector autoregression of the growth rate g_t and the saving rate s_t over the 1862–1990 period. In order to concentrate on the low frequency relationships in the data, five-year averages are used for observations. Since the five-year intervals corresponding to World War I and World War II are excluded from the sample and two lags of the regressors are included, the sample includes 22 observations. The estimates are reported below (t-statistics in parentheses):

$$s_t = 0.02 + 0.71 s_{t-1} - 0.18 s_{t-2} + 0.26 g_{t-1} + 0.57 g_{t-2} \qquad [1]$$
$$\quad (1.49)(3.27) \quad (-0.95) \quad (1.34) \quad (2.85) \qquad \overline{R}^2 = 0.82$$

$$s_t = 0.23 - 0.09 s_{t-1} + 0.01 s_{t-2} + 0.22 g_{t-1} + 0.32 g_{t-2} \qquad [2]$$
$$\quad (1.54)(-0.31) \quad (0.05) \quad (0.87) \quad (1.23) \qquad \overline{R}^2 = 0.15$$

The F test that the coefficients of the two lags of the growth rate in equation [1] are zero rejects the null hypothesis (at the 1.7 percent significance level), i.e., past growth appears to help in predicting saving. The symmetric test on the two lags of the saving rate in equation [2] instead does not reject the null hypothesis that past saving does not predict growth (the null can be rejected only at a 90 percent significance level). While Granger-causality tests provide no conclusive evidence for the existence of causal relationships, it is still informative that the rise and decline of the growth rate in the postwar period have preceded the corresponding changes in the saving rate, rather than followed them.

International Perspective: The Role of Growth and Fiscal Policy

Do fluctuations of the Italian saving rate reflect a time pattern common to most developed countries, or are they idiosyncratic to the Italian economy? To answer this question, the Italian experience is set against the backdrop of the international evidence.

In the 1960s and 1970s, the Italian saving rate was exceptionally high by international standards. According to all measures of saving (net, gross, national, private) in the G-10 only Japan exhibited a higher saving rate. As shown in Table 9.1, in those two decades Italy's gross national saving rate

Table 9.1 Gross National Saving (NS), Gross Private Saving (PS), and Government Saving (GS) in the G-10 (percentage of GDP)

	1960–69			1970–79		
	NS	PS	GS	NS	PS	GS
United States	20.1	20.3	–0.2	19.8	20.7	–0.9
Japan	34.4	29.0	5.4	35.3	30.9	4.4
Germany	27.3	22.7	4.6	24.4	21.1	3.3
France	26.3	21.2	5.1	25.9	22.2	3.7
Italy	28.3	29.1	–0.8	26.0	30.9	–4.9
United Kingdom	18.5	13.7	4.8	17.9	15.5	2.4
Canada	21.5	17.8	3.7	22.4	21.0	1.4
Belgium	22.6	21.4	1.2	23.2	23.5	–0.3
Netherlands	27.6	—	—	24.9	21.8	3.1
Sweden	24.0	14.5	9.5	21.1	14.7	6.4
Average	25.1	21.1	3.7	24.1	22.2	1.9

	1980–89			1990–94		
	NS	PS	GS	NS	PS	GS
United States	17.8	20.3	–2.5	15.4	18.5	–3.1
Japan	31.8	27.5	4.3	33.5	26.4	7.1
Germany	22.4	21.1	1.3	22.2	21.7	0.5
France	20.4	18.9	1.5	20.1	20.4	–0.3
Italy	21.8	28.2	–6.4	18.4	24.7	–6.3
United Kingdom	16.5	16.4	0.1	13.7	15.7	–2.0
Canada	20.1	22.9	–2.8	14.2	19.0	–4.8
Belgium	16.7	22.7	–6.0	21.4	25.8	–4.4
Netherlands	23.0	23.7	–0.7	24.4	25.5	–1.1
Sweden	17.3	17.7	–0.4	14.6	18.3	–3.7
Average	20.8	22.2	1.9	20.8	21.9	–1.1

Notes. All variables are divided by GDP. The averages are unweighted averages of all countries.
Source: Group of Ten (1995), Tables 2, 3, and 4.

exceeded the average rate of the G-10 by 3.2 and 1.9 percentage points, respectively. For private saving, the difference was even larger: 8 percentage points in the 1960s and 8.7 points in the 1970s. But in the 1980s the saving gap between Italy and the other developed economies started to narrow: it fell to 1 percentage point for national saving and 6 percentage points for private saving. And in the early 1990s the situation reversed, at least as far as the national saving rate is concerned: Italy's national saving is currently below the G-10 average, and its private saving rate is below that of Japan, Belgium, and the Netherlands.

So the Italian saving rate started from a higher level in the immediate postwar years but declined more rapidly than in other developed countries: in the last 35 years, gross national saving declined by 9.9 percentage points versus 4.3 in the G-10. Only half of this decline can be attributed to the reduction of government saving, which went from –0.8 percent to –6.3 percent of GDP. This represents a striking difference relative to the other G-10 countries. On average, this group experienced no change in its gross private saving rate between the 1960s and the early 1990s: the 4.3 fall in its national saving rate reflects precisely its fall in government saving.

Net national saving is the appropriate indicator of the resources available for capital accumulation, because it subtracts capital consumption (depreciation) from gross national saving. Table 9.2 reports net national saving and its breakdown into private and government saving. Both components of the national saving rate are inflation-adjusted. Due to the increased share of depreciation in GDP, the decline in net national saving is almost twice as large as the gross saving figures. But the comparison between Italy and the other countries is unchanged compared with Table 9.1. Italy still appears to be a high saver in the early postwar period and turns into a below-average saver in the early 1990s. And the decline of its national saving rate now appears to almost entirely reflect the fall in its private saving rate (11.1 out of 11.6 percentage points), in contrast with the G-10 average (where it explains 3.1 out of 7 percentage points).

Based on the evidence analyzed above, the growth performance of the Italian economy is a natural candidate to explain why Italy's saving rate performed differently. Figure 9.6 plots time averages of each country's net national saving against the corresponding averages of the real GDP growth rate. There are 4 observations for each G-10 country, corresponding to the 1960–69, 1970–79, 1980–89, and 1990–94 intervals (40 observations).

The scatter confirms that growth and saving are positively correlated. The correlation is also captured by the fitted values of the simple regression of saving on growth (the estimated coefficient of growth in this regression is 2.09, with a t-statistic of 5.81). The four observations for Italy (ita60, ita70, ita80, and ita90) are omitted from the regression. The purpose is to investi-

Table 9.2 Net National Saving (NS), Net Private Saving Adjusted for Inflation (PS), and Government Saving Adjusted for Inflation (GS) in the G-10

	1960–69			1970–79		
	NS	PS	GS	NS	PS	GS
United States	10.0	8.8	1.2	8.2	7.0	1.2
Japan	21.9	16.4	5.5	22.3	17.3	5.0
Germany	18.0	13.4	4.6	13.5	9.8	3.7
France	17.7	—	—	15.3	10.8	4.5
Italy	18.0	17.7	0.3	14.6	11.3	3.3
United Kingdom	10.0	1.8	8.2	7.4	-2.9	10.3
Canada	9.7	5.1	4.6	11.3	8.9	2.4
Belgium	12.8	—	—	13.8	9.6	4.2
Netherlands	18.1	—	—	15.6	10.4	5.2
Sweden	13.2	—	—	10.2	5.4	4.8
Average	14.9	10.5	4.1	13.2	8.8	4.4

	1980–89			1990–94		
	NS	PS	GS	NS	PS	GS
United States	4.5	5.4	-0.9	3.0	4.7	-1.7
Japan	18.2	13.2	5.0	18.1	10.6	7.5
Germany	9.8	7.7	2.1	9.2	7.5	1.7
France	7.9	5.7	2.2	7.0	6.7	0.3
Italy	9.8	7.4	2.4	6.4	6.6	-0.2
United Kingdom	4.8	1.2	3.6	3.0	3.4	-0.4
Canada	8.4	9.5	-1.1	2.0	5.4	-3.4
Belgium	7.2	8.2	-1.0	11.6	12.5	-0.9
Netherlands	12.2	11.9	0.3	12.9	12.2	0.7
Sweden	4.7	4.4	0.3	1.0	4.2	-3.2
Average	8.8	7.5	1.3	7.4	7.4	0.0

Notes. All variables are divided by GDP. The averages are unweighted averages of all countries.
Source: Group of Ten (1995), Tables 2 3, and 4.

gate if and when the Italian saving rate has been comparatively "high" or "low," conditioning on the relation between growth and saving prevailing in the rest of the sample and on the observed growth rate in Italy. The observations corresponding to the first two subperiods are above the fitted regression line. So the Italian saving rate was abnormally high, even after

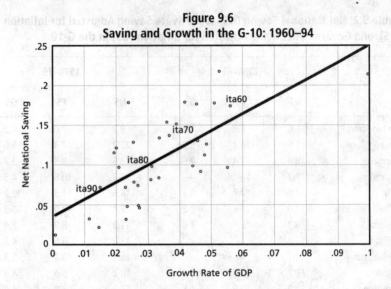

Figure 9.6
Saving and Growth in the G-10: 1960–94

taking into account that growth was comparatively high in those subperiods. The observations corresponding to the 1980s and 1990s, instead, are almost on the regression line, indicating that the lower level of the Italian saving rate in the last 20 years is in line with its lower growth rate. The growth slowdown thus emerges as a likely candidate explanation for the decline in the national saving rate.

However, the univariate correlation with growth captured by Figure 9.6 may be misleading, since other factors may have contributed both to the comparatively high initial level of Italian national saving and to its subsequent decline. Government deficits may be responsible for a reduction in national saving; furthermore, the initial level of per capita income can contribute to explain cross-country differences in private saving rates, if preferences are nonhomothetic. To control for these two factors, estimates have been made of a regression of the national saving rate on the growth rate of real GDP, inflation-adjusted government saving, and the logarithm of initial per capita real GDP, using the same panel of G-10 data (excluding the observations for Italy) used in Figure 9.6. Table 9.3 reports the regression results obtained with OLS and robust estimation methods, with and without the inclusion of time dummies among the regressors. In all the regressions, the coefficient of government saving is positive, large, and highly significant. The coefficient of 0.7 in Table 9.3 implies that the 4.1 percent-

Table 9.3 Regressions for National Saving

G-10 Countries (Excluding Italy)

Regression	Method	Constant	Growth	Government Saving	Log of Initial Per Capita GDP	Time Dummies	$\overline{R}^2$
1	OLS	−0.30 (−1.47)	1.83 (3.92)	0.70 (3.63)	0.04 (1.75)	No	0.61
2	OLS	−0.26 (−0.93)	1.88 (3.82)	0.68 (3.13)	0.03 (1.01)	Yes	0.59
3	Robust estimation	−0.32 (−1.41)	1.86 (3.61)	0.73 (3.42)	0.04 (1.67)	No	
4	Robust estimation	−0.28 (−0.92)	1.90 (3.47)	0.70 (2.88)	0.03 (0.98)	Yes	

Italy (percent)

	1960–69	1970–79	1980–89	1990–94
Predicted Values of Regression				
1	9.6	5.4	2.9	1.4
2	9.5	6.8	3.1	1.5
3	9.4	5.1	2.6	1.2
4	9.3	6.6	2.8	1.2
Actual Values	18.0	14.6	9.8	6.4

Notes. National saving and government saving are divided by GDP. Government saving is adjusted for inflation. Numbers in parentheses are *t*-statistics. For each decade, the beginning-of-period per capita GDP is expressed in real U.S. dollars.
Source: Group of Ten (1995), Tables 2, 3, and 4.

age point decline in G-10 government saving between the 1960s and the 1990s explains 2.8 of the 7.5 percentage point decline in net national saving (see Table 9.2). This represents a rejection of the Ricardian equivalence proposition, according to which an increase in government saving induces an equal reduction in private saving, leaving national saving unaffected.[4] The coeffi-

---

[4] This proposition applies to an increase in government saving achieved by increasing taxes, reducing debt, and holding public consumption constant. If instead the increase in govern-

cient of initial per capita GDP is positive, lending some support to the view that in rich countries households save more; however, this coefficient is not precisely estimated, in particular when time dummies are included in the estimation.

The differences between the actual values and those predicted by these regressions are reported in the bottom part of Table 9.3. Even though the regressions control for growth, government saving, and initial per capita income, they underpredict the Italian national saving rate in all periods (contrary to Figure 9.6, where sizable forecast errors occurred only in the earlier decades). The underprediction is larger in the 1960s and 1970s (8–9 percentage points) than in the 1980s and 1990s (about 5–6 percentage points). As a result, the regressions explain a good fraction of the decline of the Italian national saving rate—8.2 of 11.6 percentage points in the specification of row 1. Summing up, the international time-series evidence shows that growth and fiscal policy are important determinants of the decline in the Italian saving rate but do not explain its level and cannot account fully for its decline.

Other Reasons for the Decline in Saving

Since differences in growth and in fiscal policy cannot explain the evidence fully, what other factors may explain the high Italian saving rate of the 1960s and 1970s and its sharp decline in the 1980s and 1990s? The factors that in the Italian experience deserve the closest scrutiny are the level of development of its credit and insurance markets; the changes in the social security system; and the sharp demographic change in Italian society in the last two decades.

Credit and Insurance Markets

Italian households have traditionally met with highly imperfect markets for consumer credit, housing loans, and insurance, although in the late 1980s these markets have become more accessible owing to a partial liberalization.

---

ment saving is achieved by cutting public consumption, the fall of private saving will offset it completely only if the drop in government consumption is perceived to be permanent (otherwise, national saving will increase).

When the markets for consumer credit and housing loans are imperfect, young households are prevented from borrowing the desired amount to finance current consumption and must save to accumulate the funds needed to purchase consumer durables or homes. Similarly, insurance market imperfections induce households to accumulate wealth for precautionary reasons. In both cases, the saving rates of young households are higher than they would be otherwise. Jappelli and Pagano (1994) show that, for any given level of growth rate, the presence of borrowing constraints produces a higher aggregate saving rate and increases the sensitivity of the aggregate saving rate to changes in the growth rate. An identical change in growth—for instance, from zero to positive growth—generates a greater change in saving in an economy with liquidity constraints than in an economy with perfect capital markets.

This argument indicates that the interaction between saving, growth, and liquidity constraints can explain not only why Italy's saving rate was high in the 1960s and 1970s but also why the slowdown in economic growth reduced it more sharply in the 1980s and 1990s. The theory predicts that if indeed Italy featured less developed markets for household credit and insurance than other developed economies, the same reduction in growth performance would have caused a larger reduction of the aggregate saving rate in Italy than elsewhere. The partial liberalization of the consumer credit, housing loan, and insurance markets begun in the late 1980s may have added further impetus to this process.

The fact that in Italy the markets for household debt and insurance are "more imperfect" than in most other developed economies has been extensively documented by Jappelli and Pagano (1989 and 1994) and Guiso, Jappelli, and Terlizzese (1994). Some of the most striking findings of these studies are reported in Table 9.4 and summarized below.

Column 1 reports the share of consumer credit in total consumption expenditure in 1988; in Italy this figure was the lowest among the developed economies (4 percent). This did not reflect a comparatively low propensity to buy consumer durables by Italian households, as shown in column 2. Further evidence in this direction is provided by the simulations in Jappelli and Pagano (1989), which show that the earnings profiles and the age structure of the population do not have a pattern that should induce Italian households to borrow less than their OECD counterparts. The explanation for the small size of the consumer credit market is more likely due to the terms on which consumer credit is supplied by banks and finance companies. In 1989, the spread between the interest rate charged by consumer credit companies and the after-tax rate on one-year T-bills was 13.2 percentage points, compared with a spread of 6.5 points in the United States in 1986 and 3.5 points in the United Kingdom in 1987.

In the market for housing mortgage loans, the difference between the indebtedness of Italian households and that of their foreign counterparts is even more striking, as shown in column 3. In 1982, the ratio between outstanding mortgage loans and private consumption expenditure was a mere 6 percent in Italy, compared with figures ranging from 25 to 65 percent for the other countries in the table, and in particular with an average value of 44 percent for the G-10 countries. Microeconomic data show that in 1991 only 10.2 percent of the households interviewed had mortgage debt, with an average outstanding balance amounting to only 2.4 percent of the gross value of the house. But this comparatively low indebtedness does not reflect a comparatively low propensity to acquire homes by Italian households: as shown by column 4, in Italy the percentage of homeowners exceeds the G-7 average.

As for consumer credit, the low recourse to the credit market appears to be due mainly to the behavior of Italian financial intermediaries, rather than to that of households. Column 5 shows that the maximum loan-to-value ratio in the Italian mortgage market is much lower than in all the other countries. Moreover, mortgage loans are characterized by short maturities (10–15 years is the standard) and high interest spreads relative to government bonds of similar maturity (in the early 1980s this spread was 3 percent, compared with 1.8 in the U.S., 0.5 in the U.K., and 0.8 percent in Sweden and Japan).[5]

A variety of factors can account for these imperfections. Until the mid–1980s, regulation imposed a maximum loan-to-value ratio of 50 percent. Furthermore, legal costs inhibit the functioning of mortgage markets. The process of repossessing collateral is extremely cumbersome in Italy: on average, it takes 5.5 years for a bank to repossess the collateral, and in case of default the average net repossession by the bank is less than 60 percent of the value of the loan, after legal costs are accounted for.

[5] See Jappelli and Pagano (1989), Table 2, p. 1095.

The consequence of the scarcity and dearth of mortgage lending is that Italian households finance their home purchases mainly out of their accumulated savings. Thus, to buy their first home they have to wait much longer than households in the U.S., the U.K., and Japan, as shown by the figures in column 6 of Table 9.4.

The propensity to save of Italian households may also be affected by the working of insurance markets (health, casualty, and life). As shown in Table 9.5, the average Italian buys less private insurance than the average citizen of any other G-10 country (and, for that matter, of any OECD country except Greece). On the one hand, this may be explained by the availability of extensive public insurance arrangements (such as the National Health Service, which offers universal coverage and covers all health risks for any amount). But another factor accounting for the small size of the insurance

Table 9.4 Credit Markets and Home Acquisition: An International Comparison

	Consumer Credit (percentage of private consumption, 1988) (1)	Durables (percentage of private consumption, 1988) (2)	Mortgages (percentage of private consumption, 1982) (3)	Home-ownership (percent) (4)	Maximum Loan-to-Value Ratio for Mortgages (1981–87 average) (5)	Average Age of First-Time Home Buyers (6)
Canada	22	16	60	62	80	—
U.S.	23	11	61	65	89	28
Japan	18	7	25	60	60	40
France	8	9	44	47	80	—
Germany	15	—	65	37	80	36
Italy	4	11	6	59	56	41
U.K.	10	11	45	59	87	29
G-7 average	14	—	44	56	76	—
Finland	39	13	42	61	85	—
Norway	48	10	60	67	80	—
Sweden	39	12	61	57	95	—

Note: The figures in columns 1 to 4 are drawn from Guiso, Jappelli, and Terlizzese (1994), Table 1.3, p. 32; those in column 5 are from Jappelli and Pagano (1994), Table 1, p. 92; those in column 6 are drawn from Guiso, Jappelli, and Terlizzese (1994), p. 44, for Italy, U.S., and U.K., and from Hayashi, Ito, and Slemrod (1988). The figures in column 4 refer to 1981 except for Canada, Japan, France, and Germany, for which they refer to 1978.

Table 9.5 Ratio of Insurance Premiums to GDP: An International Comparison

	Total (1)	Life Insurance (2)	Other (3)
Canada	5.4	2.6	2.8
United States	9.1	3.7	5.4
Japan	8.7	6.4	2.3
Belgium	4.2	1.2	2.9
France	5.1	2.2	2.9
Germany	6.4	2.9	3.5
Italy	2.4	0.5	1.9
Netherlands	6.3	2.9	3.4
Sweden	4.5	2.5	2.0
United Kingdom	8.4	5.3	3.1
G-10 average	6.5	3.4	3.1
OECD average	5.5	2.7	2.9

Note. The data are drawn from Guiso, Jappelli, and Terlizzese (1994), Table 1.5, p. 37.

market is a regulatory regime that stifles competition by creating high entry barriers and severe restrictions on the admissible contracts. As a result, insurance policy premiums typically feature high markups over fair premiums: for instance, in 1991 the cost of insuring against fire and theft a property whose value is 90,000 ECU was 370 ECU, compared with an EC average of 207 ECU (Gerardi, 1994). Faced with an unattractive market for purchase of insurance, Italian households must buffer themselves against risk with a greater cushion of precautionary wealth.

These market imperfections help explain not only why the Italian private saving rate is high relative to that of other developed economies, but also why in the last two decades it was more sensitive to the decline in the growth rate.

An additional factor in explaining the decline in private saving in the last decade is that Italian credit and insurance markets have been gradually deregulated. The maximum loan-to-value ratio was increased to 75 percent in 1986, and to 100 percent in 1995. In addition, some of the banking and insurance regulations that traditionally restricted competition were lifted in the late 1980s, mainly under the pressure of EC Directives. Restrictions on bank branching have been removed, limits on maturities in the mortgage loan market have been abolished, life insurance policies are now indexed to inflation, and foreign intermediaries have been allowed to operate on equal grounds with domestic ones.

Social Security

Social security provisions are generally held to be key determinants of the national saving rate. In fact, replacing a funded social security system with a pay-as-you-go system reduces national saving unless people fully discount the implied burden of future social security contributions. In Italy, a growing body of empirical research has analyzed the effect of this transition on the household saving rate, and the likely outcome of recent reforms aimed at rebalancing the social security system.

Until 1952, the Italian social security system was fully funded. Starting in that year, the government set minimum pensions, gradually extended compulsory contributions to farmers and the self-employed, and supplemented the system with unfunded social security benefits. However, pension benefits were still strictly linked to contributions. Thus, between 1952 and 1968, the social security system, though unfunded, was still balanced.

The link between contributions and benefits was severed in 1969, with three major innovations. First, benefits were made proportional to the number of years of contributions and to the average earnings over the three years preceding retirement. Second, the system became entirely pay-as-you-go: anyone above 65 was entitled to a "social pension," irrespective of the contributions during his or her working life. Third, the maximum pension rose to 80 percent of the last salary, and benefits were indexed to the cost of living.

The 1970s witnessed a series of reforms relaxing the eligibility criteria. This led to a rapid growth in social security benefits, from 7.5 percent of GDP in 1970 to 10.2 percent in 1980 and 13.9 percent in 1990. In 1975 the indexation system was changed: minimum pensions were indexed to the earnings of employed workers, leading to automatic increases in the real value of benefits. As the increase in contributions did not keep pace, the result was a growing social security deficit (Rossi and Visco, 1994).

Up to 1992, the eligibility requirements for pension benefits were 35 years of contributions, or a minimum of 15 years of contributions, and 55 and 60 years of age for women and men, respectively. For all private sector employees, yearly benefits were determined as $0.02nS$, where n is the number of years of contributions (maximum 40), S is the average yearly salary over the last five years, adjusted for the increase in the cost of living, and 0.02 represents the yearly accrual rate.[6]

This highlights the particularly high benefits and broad eligibility criteria that the Italian social security system featured until 1992. In most other OECD countries, social security benefits compared to earnings are lower, either because they are unrelated to the earnings history or because only a fraction of the benefits is so related, as in the U.K. And where benefits are proportional to past salaries, eligibility requirements and pension award formulas are less generous than they were in Italy: the minimum retirement age is higher; pension benefits are computed not on the basis of the last 5 years' earnings but of the last 10 (France) or the entire career (Germany and Belgium); the accrual rate ranges from 1.33 percent in Belgium to 1.9 percent in Austria, as against 2 percent in Italy; the maximum pension as a fraction of salary is lower everywhere, except in Germany; benefits are indexed to prices, rather than salaries as in Italy; and the rules concerning double pensions and benefits paid to survivors are stricter than in Italy.

As a result of these differences, in 1985 the ratio of social security benefits to the yearly salary of men with 40 years of contributions was 80 percent in Italy, against 60 percent in Germany, 55 percent in Belgium, 50 percent in France, and 25 percent in the U.K. (CREL, 1990, p. 62). The increasing generosity of Italian eligibility rules and award formulas is witnessed by the fact that the ratio of the average retirement pension to the average salary rose from 26 percent in 1960 to 44 percent in 1987.

To what extent have these changes in the social security system contributed to the decline of the Italian private saving rate? Rossi and Visco (1994 and 1995) carefully construct an estimate of aggregate social security wealth in the postwar period, taking into account changes in legislation, population structure, labor force participation rates, and survival probabilities. In their time-series regression analysis, they relate the private saving rate to the growth rate, the real interest rate, the wealth-income ratio, the gross pension wealth–income ratio, and the ratio of pension benefits to income. Their results indicate that three main factors contribute to explain the fall in private saving between the 1960s and the 1980s: the growth slow-

[6] For public employees S is equal to the last yearly salary.

down, the increase in the wealth-income ratio, and the changes in pension wealth and benefits. Each of the first two factors explains 6.2 points out of an estimated 13.1 percentage points decline in saving. The increase in social security wealth accounts for a further reduction of 5.7 points, but this is offset by the effect of pension benefits, amounting to 4 percentage points. So the net effect of changes in the social security system is only 1.7 out of 13.1 percentage points reduction in saving.

Alternative estimates of the effect of social security wealth on private accumulation can be obtained by using cross-sectional data. This has been done by Jappelli (1995), who computes measures of social security wealth using various years of the Survey of Household Income and Wealth and finds that pension wealth is only an imperfect substitute for private net worth. An increase of social security wealth displaces only 20 percent of private wealth, a result that is broadly consistent with the time-series evidence.

One possible explanation for the relatively low displacement effect is that the very increase in benefits and the rapid aging of the Italian population may foster the perception that the current system cannot be sustained indefinitely. If so, perceived social security wealth is lower than the present discounted value of the net benefits implied by the rules of the current regime. In recent years this perception has been validated by a sequence of reforms aimed at rebalancing the accounts of the social security system.

The two major attempts in this direction have been the 1992 Amato reform and the 1995 Dini reform (from the names of the corresponding prime ministers). As a consequence of these reforms, the social security system has become less generous. Over the next decade, the minimum retirement age will be gradually raised from 60 to 65 for men and from 55 to 60 for women; the minimum period of contribution will gradually increase; and the period of the working life over which the pension benefits are computed will be gradually extended to the entire working life of employees. Finally, to encourage private retirement saving, private pension funds have been regulated and employers' contributions to pension funds will gradually replace severance pay.

To summarize, there is evidence that the increasing generosity of the social security system in the postwar period has mildly contributed to the decline in the private saving rate, although this effect is much smaller than that of the productivity slowdown. In the future, the effect of changes in social security legislation will go in the opposite direction, since the pension reforms aiming at reducing future benefits will promote household saving. According to Rossi and Visco (1995) and Attanasio and Brugiavini (1996), the first symptoms of this reversal are already apparent in the 1993 data.

Demographic Factors

A potentially important determinant of private household saving is the age distribution of the population. In Italy, this distribution has changed sharply in the past 20 years. The fertility rate has declined sharply, and the number of elderly in the population has increased dramatically since the early 1970s.[7] According to the life-cycle model, these changes in the age structure should have reduced saving. However, Cannari (1994) presents evidence that saving has not been reduced by the changing age structure. The main reason is that in Italy the elderly save at a rate that is considerably higher than predicted by the stylized version of the life-cycle model. As will be seen below, this result is confirmed by our microeconomic estimates.

Starting in the mid-1970s, the labor force participation rate of women has increased by 17 percentage points, from 33 to 50 percent. This change may reduce saving for two reasons. First, it may induce a substitution away from home-produced goods towards market-produced goods. Second, to the extent that it increases the share of households with more than one income recipient, it reduces households' earnings uncertainty and the need for precautionary saving. Evidence for this link is provided by Attanasio and Weber (1997), who find that households with working wives tend to save less than households in which the woman is not in the labor force, other things equal. However, the increase in households with multiple income recipients can hardly account for any significant decline in aggregate saving.

Do Micro Data Help Explain the Decline in Saving?

Microeconomic data offer an alternative to national income accounts data in studying trends in saving patterns. This independent evidence is particu-

[7] Currently the Italian fertility rate is the lowest in the world. What is surprising is the speed of the demographic transition. The rate of growth of the population went from 0.67 in 1971 to

larly important. Even if microdata are not fully consistent with the pattern of national accounts data, they provide a unique source of information for checking if plausible macroeconomic explanations for the saving decline are borne out at the individual level.

In Italy, the main source of microeconomic data is the Bank of Italy Survey of Household Income and Wealth (SHIW), which collects detailed information on demographics, household consumption, income, and balance sheets.[8] The SHIW was conducted on a yearly basis from 1965 to 1987 (with the exception of 1985). Up to 1984 the number of participant households in a typical year was around 4,000. In 1986 the sample size was doubled, and since 1987 the survey has been run every other year.

The data set used in this section includes six independent cross-sections (1984, 1986, 1987, 1989, 1991, and 1993), a total of 44,792 observations. Two macroeconomic episodes characterize the 1984–93 period. The recovery from the 1981–83 recession started in early 1984 and grew in intensity in 1987–88: the average growth rate of GDP during this expansionary period was 3 percent. The recovery was led by a consumption boom. In fact, in all years between 1985 and 1989 the growth of aggregate private consumption outpaced output and disposable household income. Then the economy went into a recession in the second half of 1989; at the end of the sample period the recession was at its worst.

The survey is representative of the Italian population (probability selection is enforced at every stage of sampling). The unit of observation is the family, which is defined to include all persons residing in the same dwelling who are related by blood, marriage, or adoption. Individuals selected as "partners or other common-law relationships" are also treated as families.[9] The use of sample weights is recommended, particularly for 1987, a year in which the survey oversampled wealthy households (Brandolini and Cannari, 1994). All statistics reported here use sample weights.[10]

---

about zero in the early 1990s. At the same time the fraction of the population older than 60 years increased by more than 6 percentage points between 1971 and 1992.

[8] This data set has been used extensively for analysis of the behavior of Italian households.

[9] The interviews are conducted during the first three months of the year; thus flow variables refer to the previous calendar year, and stock variables are end-of-period values.

[10] Disposable income and consumption are converted into 1991 lire using the CPI deflator.

The comparison between the national accounts and the SHIW is not easy because the SHIW measures of income and consumption underestimate the aggregate data. For instance, disposable income is underestimated by about 20 percent. Brandolini and Cannari (1994) find that in the 1989 SHIW the difference between the aggregate and survey measures of disposable income arises mainly from self-employment income (underestimated by half), pension benefits (by a third), and financial income.[11] Part of these differences is due to the fact that in the national accounts the household sector also includes unincorporated business.

In order to use microeconomic data to explain macroeconomic facts, one must check if the trends observed in the data are similar. Table 9.6 reports the two measures of the household saving rate for the period 1984–93.[12] No attempt is made to adjust the SHIW income for inflation[13] and limit the comparison to the traditional definition of saving. The broad trends in the two data sets are similar: the table shows that both measures of saving rates declined by over 6 percentage points between 1984 and 1993. However, the timing of the saving decline is rather different. The aggregate data indicate two marked drops in 1985 and in 1993. Instead, the survey data show a marked decline only in 1987; afterwards, the saving rate stays roughly constant up to 1993.

Decomposition of the SHIW Saving Rates

The microeconomic data can be used to check if the reduction in saving observed between 1984 and 1993 depends on changes in the relative size and income levels of the different age groups, or rather on changes in their behavior. It is also interesting to identify which population groups, if any, have been responsible for the decline in saving observed in the last decade. For instance, the liberalization of the market for household debt may have reduced the saving of the young more than that of the old. The increased

---

[11] The figures for rents and transfers are consistent, and wages and salaries are slightly overestimated with respect to the national accounts data.

[12] The household saving rate reported in Table 9.6 differs from the private saving rate in Table 9.2 because the latter includes business saving.

[13] This adjustment would require reliable data for the stock of financial assets, and unfortunately the available data on financial wealth are vitiated by severe measurement errors due to underreporting and nonreporting.

Table 9.6 National Account and Microeconomic Household Saving Rate

	National Accounts	Microeconomic Data (SHIW)
1984	20.2	31.5
1986	17.6	30.3
1987	17.6	25.6
1989	16.3	26.4
1991	16.5	24.0
1993	14.5	25.0
(93)–(84)	–6.7	–6.5

Note: The aggregate data of column 1 are authors' estimates based on the 1995 annual report of the Bank of Italy. The SHIW saving rates in column 2 are computed dividing total saving by total disposable income using sample weights and the entire data set for each survey.

labor force participation of women and the implied substitution from home-produced to market-produced goods can affect differentially the saving rate of households with multiple incomes. Migration and differences in population growth have changed the geographical composition of households between South and North. And changes in social security legislation have induced a redistribution of resources between generations and occupational groups with different propensities to save.

Following Bosworth, Burtless, and Sabelhaus, (1991) and Cannari (1994), the aggregate saving rate S_t in period t is expressed as:

$$S_t = \sum_{i=1}^{G} w_{it} y_{it} s_{it} \qquad [3]$$

where
w_{it} = fraction of household heads in the ith group;
y_{it} = ratio of average income in the ith group to the overall average;
s_{it} = saving rate of the ith group;
G = number of groups.

Table 9.7 reports the results of this saving accounting. The first column in each panel reports the SHIW saving rate in 1984–93, obtained by dividing the average saving of all survey respondents by their average in-

Table 9.7 Saving Rates by Specific Population Groups: 1984–93

	SHIW Saving Rate	Age and Population Shares Constant	Age and Income Shares Constant	Population and Income Shares Constant
1984	31.5	31.5	31.5	31.5
1986	30.3	31.5	31.4	30.3
1987	25.6	31.6	31.4	25.4
1989	26.4	31.7	31.3	26.2
1991	24.0	31.7	31.2	23.4
1993	25.0	32.2	30.8	24.9
(93)–(84)	–6.4	0.7	–0.7	–6.6

Note: Groups are defined as follows: household head less than 40 years old; 35–60; greater than 60.

	SHIW Saving Rate	Area and Population Shares Constant	Area and Income Shares Constant	Population and Income Shares Constant
1984	31.5	31.5	31.5	31.5
1986	30.3	31.4	31.3	30.2
1987	25.6	31.6	31.5	25.5
1989	26.4	31.1	30.6	26.3
1991	24.0	32.2	31.1	23.9
1993	25.0	31.6	31.5	24.8
(93)–(84)	–6.4	0.1	0.0	–6.6

Note: Groups are defined as follows: residents in the North, Center, and South.

	SHIW Saving Rate	Children and Population Shares Constant	Children and Income Shares Constant	Population and Income Shares Constant
1984	31.5	31.5	31.5	31.5
1986	30.3	31.5	31.6	30.3
1987	25.6	31.6	31.6	25.3
1989	26.4	31.7	31.5	25.9
1991	24.0	31.7	31.6	23.4
1993	25.0	32.0	31.6	24.4
(93)–(84)	–6.4	0.5	0.1	–7.1

Note: Groups are defined as follows: households with no children less than 18 years old; households with 1 or 2 children; households with more than 2 children.

Table 9.7 (continued)

	SHIW Saving Rate	Recipients and Population Shares Constant	Recipients and Income Shares Constant	Population and Income Shares Constant
1984	31.5	31.5	31.5	31.5
1986	30.3	32.3	30.1	31.1
1987	25.6	32.7	30.7	25.5
1989	26.4	33.4	30.4	25.9
1991	24.0	33.0	30.8	23.4
1993	25.0	31.3	32.4	23.9
(93)–(84)	–6.4	–0.2	0.9	–7.6

Note: Groups are defined as follows: households with 1 income recipient; 2 income recipients; more than 2 income recipients.

	SHIW Saving Rate	Cohort and Population Shares Constant	Cohort and Income Shares Constant	Population and Income Shares Constant
1984	31.5	31.5	31.5	31.5
1986	30.3	31.2	31.5	30.5
1987	25.6	31.4	31.4	25.8
1989	26.4	31.0	31.3	26.9
1991	24.0	30.8	31.4	25.0
1993	25.0	29.5	31.2	25.8
(93)–(84)	–6.4	–1.9	–0.2	–5.6

Note: Groups are defined as follows: household head born before 1925; born between 1925 and 1945; born after 1945.

	SHIW Saving Rate	Employment and Population Shares Constant	Employment and Income Shares Constant	Population and Income Shares Constant
1984	31.5	31.5	31.5	31.5
1986	30.3	31.8	31.0	30.3
1987	25.6	31.3	31.8	25.5
1989	26.4	31.9	30.7	26.4
1991	24.0	32.6	29.7	23.6
1993	25.0	34.0	28.5	25.5
(93)–(84)	–6.4	2.5	–3.0	–6.0

Note: Groups are defined as follows: employees, self-employed, not in the labor force.

come. The second column shows the saving rate that would have been observed if the population weights w_{it} and the group-specific saving rates s_{it}
did not vary, and therefore the effect of the redistribution of income between groups did not vary. The third column reports the saving rates that
would have been observed if the income shares y_{it} and the saving propensities s_{it} had been constant and thus captures the effect of changes in the relative size of the various population groups. The fourth column repeats the
exercise holding w_{it} and y_{it} constant, reflecting the effect of changes in the
saving behavior of various groups. The last row of each panel reports the
change in saving between 1984 and 1993 that can be attributed to each of
the three determinants of the aggregate saving rate (w_{it}, s_{it}, and y_{it}), holding
the other two constant.

The first panel of Table 9.7 is of particular interest. The G groups are
defined as households younger than 35, between 35 and 60, and older than
60. The table shows that the entire decline in saving should be attributed to
a fall in individual propensities to save (the s_{it} terms, which are kept constant in the last column), rather than to the changing composition of the
population (the w_{it} weights) or to changes in the distribution of income
between the young and the old (the y_{it} terms). The second column shows
that changes in y_{it} have increased the aggregate saving rate by 0.7 percentage
points; changes in w_{it} have reduced it by 0.7 points; and changes in s_{it} have
reduced it by 6.6 points.[14] Using the life-cycle hypothesis as the reference
model, this finding conflicts with the idea that the decline in productivity
growth is responsible for the decline in saving. According to that model, the
effect of changes in the growth rate should affect aggregate saving via changes
in the income distribution between the young and the old (the y_{it} terms) or
in their relative numbers (the w_{it} terms), contrary to what was found in the
data.

The dynamics of individual propensities to save are not visible in Table
9.7. Therefore, Figure 9.7 plots the saving rates of the different age groups
over the period 1984–93. It is important to stress that there is a control for
the presence of age effects in saving rates because Figure 9.7 tracks the saving rates of the same age group over the sample period. Such control is

---

[14] The sum of these three effects does not add up precisely to the total observed decline in the
saving rate reported in the first column (–6.4 percent) because of the presence of interaction
terms.

Figure 9.7
Mean Saving Rates by Age Group

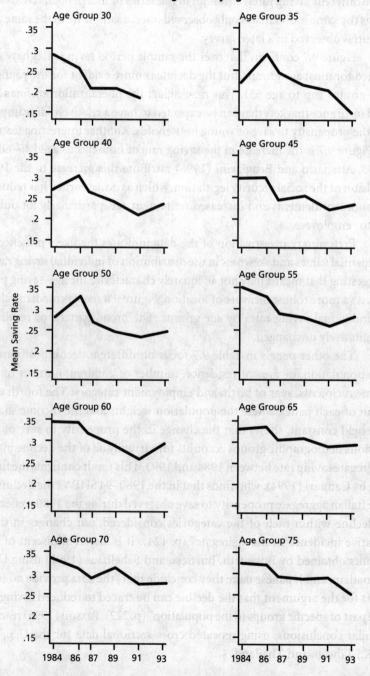

important because the life-cycle model predicts that the various age groups have different saving rates: although in the series of independent cross-sections the same individual is only observed once, a sample from the same age group is observed in a later survey.

Figure 9.7 confirms that over the sample period saving rates have declined for most age groups, but the decline is more evident for the younger age groups (up to age 55). This may reflect the liberalization of financial and insurance markets that can be expected to have a relatively large impact on the propensity to save of young households. Another interesting feature of Figure 9.7 is the increase in the saving rate of households aged 40–60 in 1993. Attanasio and Brugiavini (1996) attribute this increase to the 1992 revision of the social security legislation, which as noted earlier, has reduced pension entitlements and increased retirement age, particularly for public sector employees.

Preliminary investigation of the data indicates the likely presence of influential values and skewness in the distribution of individual saving rates, suggesting that means may not adequately characterize the age-saving profile. As a more robust measure of location, Figure 9.8 reports median values of individual saving rates by age groups. The broad pattern of results is qualitatively unchanged.

The other panels in Table 9.7 focus on different decompositions of the population, by area of residence, number of children, number of income recipients, year of birth, and employment category. The fourth column of each panel, where the population weights and the income shares are held constant, shows that the change in the propensity to save of the various demographic groups accounts for virtually all of the decline in the aggregate saving rate between 1984 and 1993. This result confirms the finding by Cannari (1994), who finds that in the 1980–94 SHIW "the decline in the Italian aggregate propensity to save observed during the 1980s reflected a decline within each of the categories considered, not changes in their relative incidence in the aggregate" (p. 124). It is also reminiscent of the results obtained by Bosworth, Burtless, and Sabelhaus (1991) using U.S., Canadian, and Japanese data: they conclude that "the data provide no support for the argument that the decline can be traced to reduced saving on the part of specific groups in the population" (p. 222). Paxson (1996) reaches similar conclusions, using repeated cross-sectional data for the U.S., the U.K., Taiwan, and Thailand.

Figure 9.8
Median Saving Rates by Age Group

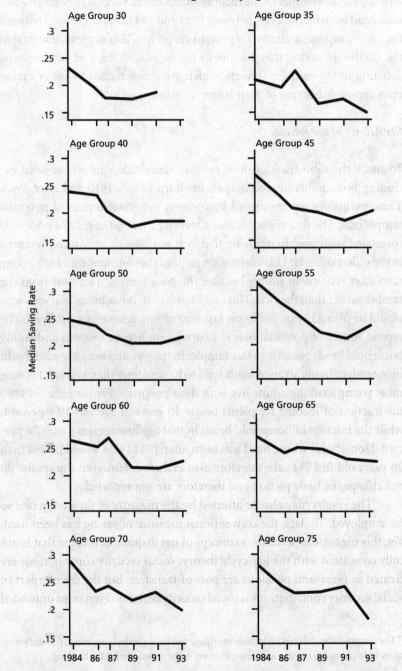

In the Italian case, the only significant exception to this general pattern is that the changes in the income shares of the various cohorts (household head born before 1925, between 1925 and 1945, and after 1945) reduced the aggregate saving rate by 1.9 percentage points. This suggests that part of the decline in saving may be due to the increased share of total income accruing to the younger cohorts, which are characterized by lower saving rates (possibly because of their lower thriftiness).

Sensitivity of the Results

To check the robustness of these results, the calculations are repeated excluding households headed by persons born before 1910 and after 1964. These exclusions are motivated by concern over two sources of potential sample bias. The first arises because survival probabilities may be positively correlated with wealth, implying that rich households are overrepresented in the oldest cohorts. This correlation implies that one may find high saving rates after retirement simply because the poor tend to disappear from the sample earlier than the rich. Thus 1,758 pre-1910 households (persons who would be over 83 years old in the last year of our sample) are dropped. The second source of potential bias is a correlation between wealth and young household heads peculiar to our sample. In Italy, young working adults with independent living arrangements tend to be wealthier than average, because most young working adults live with their parents.[15] For instance, in 1989 the fraction of income recipients below 30 years of age was 19.8 percent, while the fraction of household heads in that age bracket was a tiny 7.6 percent. Households whose head was born after 1964 (who would be less than 20 years old in 1984) are therefore also excluded. However, the results do not change the basic picture and therefore are not reported.

The results may also be affected by the measure of the saving rate so far employed. To date, the conventional measure of saving has been used. Yet, this measure is based on a concept of net disposable income that is not fully consistent with the life-cycle theory: social security contributions are treated as taxes, and pensions are part of transfers. But the counterpart of social security contributions is social security benefits (even in an unfunded

---

[15] The reasons for such behavior include mortgage market imperfections, which prevent young households from borrowing, and imperfections in the rental market for housing.

system). Since households expect to receive a pension upon paying contributions, one may argue that the latter should be treated as part of income. Correspondingly, during retirement, pension benefits are offset by the reduction in the annuity value of social security wealth; accordingly, pensions should not be included in the disposable income of retirees.

Thus, pensions are subtracted from disposable income and contributions are added to social security. In the survey, earnings are reported net of taxes and contributions. The contribution tax rate is a flat tax, increasing gradually from 24 percent in 1984 to 27 percent in 1993. Thus, earnings—the largest component of disposable income—are "inflated" by the contribution rate. The adjustment implies that disposable income is about 20 percent higher for workers and falls substantially after retirement. Table 9.7 is then repeated with this modified definition of saving. The results are broadly similar: saving falls for every population group, and the decline in aggregate saving is not explained by the changing shares of the groups. The only novelty is that now the changing composition of the population and income shares explain about 15 percent of the decline in the aggregate saving rate.

Assessing the Microeconomic Evidence

The microeconomic evidence suggests that the decline in the aggregate saving rate between 1984 and 1993 cannot be traced to changes in the behavior, resources, or size of a single population group. Rather, it is driven by an across-the-board reduction in the propensity to save of all groups. In particular, the fall in the propensity to save is shared by all age groups, and the decline in aggregate saving does not result from changes in their income shares or relative sizes, in contrast to the prediction of the standard life-cycle model about the relation between aggregate saving and growth.

There are significant exceptions to this pattern, however. One third of the reduction in the aggregate saving rate can be attributed to the redistribution of resources towards younger cohorts, characterized by lower thriftiness. Moreover, the propensity to save of young households has fallen relatively more than in other age groups, possibly as a reflection of financial liberalization. Finally, in 1993 the saving rate of the middle-aged has increased, a likely response to the announcement of a reduction in future social security benefits.

Conclusions: Can the Macro and the Micro Evidence Be Reconciled?

The time-series and cross-country evidence suggests a strong positive correlation between growth and aggregate saving. Based on that evidence, the productivity slowdown, together with the timid deregulation of the credit and insurance markets and the changes in the social security system, appear as the main candidates to account for the changes in the Italian private saving rate. But while several models predict a positive correlation between aggregate saving and growth, they have quite different predictions about the correlation between individual saving rates and growth. So the observed behavior of individual saving rates provides an opportunity to subject the competing explanations about the saving behavior of Italian households to a sharper test. This task is taken up with a series of repeated cross-sections drawn from the Survey of Household Income and Wealth.

The life-cycle model predicts a positive relation between growth and saving that arises only from the process of aggregation. An increase in the rate of income growth, caused by an increase in productivity or in the rate of growth of the labor force, raises the resources of the young (who are net savers) relative to those of the old (who dissave). This raises the weight of young households relative to that of the old in the aggregation of individual saving rates. In the basic version of the model, Modigliani (1986) further assumes that productivity growth is generation-specific and that earning profiles are flat over individual lives. Under these assumptions, individual saving rates do not respond to aggregate changes in productivity; the fall in aggregate saving results only from the reduction in the income share and in the number of young households relative to the retired. When income growth is also individual-specific and earnings profiles are upward sloping, a reduction in expected income growth will generally reduce young households' borrowing and increase individual saving rates.[16] With both types of growth (within and across generations) taking place, the aggregate correlation between saving and growth is a priori ambiguous, but at the individual level the correlation between saving and growth should still be zero or negative.

---

[16] Given the limited amount of borrowing of Italian households, the effect of expected income growth on individual saving rates should not be very important.

Other models share with the basic version of the life-cycle model the prediction of a positive correlation between aggregate saving and growth. For instance, in the standard infinite-horizon growth model, an increase in productivity growth shifts up the marginal productivity of capital; then if the elasticity of intertemporal substitution is sufficiently high, the individual saving rate will increase.[17] Since this is a representative agent model, this prediction also applies to the aggregate saving rate. The same prediction arises from models where households have a target wealth-income ratio, such as the buffer-stock model of saving emphasized by Deaton (1995) and models with habit formation. In these models, an increase in income triggers a gradual adjustment of consumption and thus leads to an increase in saving, at least in the short run. The infinite-horizon growth model and models with wealth-income ratio targets cannot be distinguished from the life-cycle model at the macroeconomic level. However, they carry opposite implications for the relationship between growth and saving at the individual level.

The microeconomic data show that the fall in the aggregate saving rate observed in the 1980s and 1990s is not only a result of the aggregation across households during the productivity slowdown, as the life-cycle hypothesis would predict. To the contrary, it mirrors an across-the-board decline in individual saving rates—a result that the life-cycle model cannot easily reconcile with a decline in productivity growth. Provided that the microeconomic data are not vitiated by systematic measurement errors, this may have one of two alternative interpretations. The first possibility is that the life-cycle model is not consistent with the data, and one should turn instead to models that predict a positive correlation between saving and growth *both* at the micro level and at the macro level. The second interpretation is that the decline in the Italian aggregate saving rate has little to do with the growth slowdown of the last decades. The reason for the decline in saving should then be sought in other phenomena that affected all house-

---

[17] The standard permanent income model with infinite horizon, perfect markets, and exogenous factor prices predicts that an increase in income growth raises permanent income and reduces current saving. Thus, it produces a negative correlation between growth and saving and cannot account for the macroeconomic evidence above. In the infinite-horizon growth model, where factor prices are endogenous, this wealth effect is outweighed by the substitution effect, if the elasticity of substitution is high.

holds simultaneously, such as changes in asset prices or preferences. Clearly, much further research is needed to sort out this issue, and in the process it is quite possible that still other ways to reconcile the macro and the micro evidence may emerge.

References

Attanasio, O.P. and Brugiavini, A. 1996. "L'effetto della riforma Amato sul risparmio delle famiglie italiane." Note di Lavoro 96.05. Università di Venezia.

Attanasio, O. P. and Weber, G. 1997. "I consumi delle famiglie italiane: quali cambiamenti destinati a durare?" In F. Galimberti, F. Giavazzi, A. Penati, and G. Tabellini, editors. *Le Nuove Frontiere della Politica Economica.* Milano: Il Sole 24 Ore.

Brandolini, A. and Cannari, L. 1994. "Methodological Appendix: The Bank of Italy's Survey of Household Income and Wealth." In A. Ando, L. Guiso, and I. Visco, editors. *Saving and the Accumulation of Wealth: Essays on Italian Household and Government Saving Behaviour.* Cambridge, U.K.: Cambridge University Press.

Browning, M. and Lusardi, A. 1996. "Household Saving: Micro Theories and Micro Facts." *Journal of Economic Literature.* 34: 1797–1895.

Bosworth, B., Burtless, G. and Sabelhaus, J. 1991. "The Decline in Saving: Evidence from Household Surveys." *Brookings Papers on Economic Activity.* 1: 183–257.

Cannari, L. 1994. "Do Demographic Changes Explain the Decline in the Saving Rate of Italian Households?" In A. Ando, L. Guiso, and I. Visco, editors. *Saving and the Accumulation of Wealth: Essays on Italian Household and Government Saving Behaviour.* Cambridge, U.K.: Cambridge University Press.

Carroll, C.D. and Weil, D.N. 1994. "Saving and Growth: A Reinterpretation." *Carnegie-Rochester Conference Series on Public Policy.* 40: 133–92.

CREL 1990. "La previdenza integrativa in Italia: analisi, tendenze e prospettive." Rome. Mimeograph.

Deaton, A. 1992. *Understanding Consumption.* Oxford, U.K.: Oxford University Press.

———. 1995. "Growth and Saving: What Do We Know, What Do We Need to Know, and What Might We Learn?"Research Program in Development Studies. Princeton University, Princeton, N.J.

Gerardi, D. 1994. "Insurance Market Imperfections and the International Differences in Saving Rates." Discussion Paper 94-3. Università Bocconi, Istituto di Economia Politica.

Group of Ten. 1995. "Saving, Investment and Real Interest Rates." October. Mimeograph.

Guiso, L., Jappelli, T. and Terlizzese, D. 1994. "Why Is Italy's Saving Rate So High?" In A. Ando, L. Guiso, and I. Visco, editors. *Saving and the Accumulation of Wealth. Essays on Italian Household and Government Saving Behaviour.* Cambridge, U.K.: Cambridge University Press.

Hayashi, F., Ito, T. and Slemrod, J. 1988. "Housing Finance Imperfections, Taxation and Private Saving: A Comparative Simulation Analysis of the United States and Japan." *Journal of the Japanese and International Economies.* 2: 215–38.

Jappelli, T. 1995. "Does Social Security Wealth Reduce Private Accumulation? Evidence from Italian Survey Data." *Ricerche Economiche.* 49: 1–32.

Jappelli, T. and Pagano, M. 1989. "Consumption and Capital Market Imperfections: An International Comparison." *American Economic Review.* 79 (December): 1088–1105.

———.1994. "Saving, Growth and Liquidity Constraints." *Quarterly Journal of Economics.* 109: 83–109.

Levine, R. and Renelt, D. 1992. "A Sensitivity Analysis of Cross-Country Growth Regressions." *American Economic Review.* 82: 942–63.

Modigliani, F. 1986. "Life Cycle, Individual Thrift, and the Wealth of Nations." *American Economic Review.* 76: 297–313.

Modigliani, F. and Jappelli, T. 1987. "Fiscal Policy and Saving in Italy since 1860." In M. Boskin, J. Flemming, and S. Gorini, editors. *Private Saving and Public Debt.* Oxford, U.K.: Basil Blackwell.

Pagliano, P. and Rossi, N. 1992. "Income and Saving in Italy: A Reconstruction." Temi di Discussione 169. Banca d'Italia, Rome.

Paxson, C. 1996. "Saving and Growth: Evidence from Micro Data." *European Economic Review.* 40: 255–88.

Rossi, N. and Visco, I. 1994. "Private Saving and Government Deficits." In A. Ando, L. Guiso, and I. Visco, editors. *Saving and the Accumulation of Wealth: Essays on Italian Household and Government Saving Behaviour.* Cambridge, U.K.: Cambridge University Press.

———1995. "National Saving and Social Security in Italy." *Ricerche Economiche.* 49: 329–56.

Modigliani, R. 1986. "Life Cycle, Individual Thrift, and the Wealth of Nations." American Economic Review 76: 297–313.

Muellbauer, J. and Lattimore, J. 1992. "The Wealth Effect and Savings in Italy." In Saving and Bequests, edited by M. Flemming and Le Ingrà Italians. Forthcoming and Behaviour, Ontario, UK: Basil Blackwell.

Pagano, P. and Rossi, N. 1997. "Income and Saving in the Italian economy." Econ. Tavol di Discussion, no. 67. Banca d'Italia, Rome.

Paxson, C. 1996. "Saving and Growth: Evidence from Micro Data." European Economic Review 40: 255–88.

Poterba, J. and Venti, S. 1994. "Private Saving and Government Policy. In A Study Guide and L. Weiss, editors, Saving and the Accumulation of Wealth: Essays on Italian Household Savings Behaviour and Consumer Behavior." Cambridge, UK: Cambridge University Press.

———. 1994. "National Saving and Social Security in Italy." Paper forthcoming, no. 29, etc.

CHAPTER 10

Trade Liberalization and Private Saving: The Spanish Experience, 1960–95

Michele Boldrin and Juan Manuel Martin Prieto[1]

Understanding the long-run determinants of the aggregate saving rate is of paramount importance for the design of sound economic policies to foster stable economic development. There are a number of reasons why the evolution of Spanish private and national savings from 1960 to 1995 is particularly interesting.

During this period, Spain transformed itself from an economically backward country into an advanced economy in which the composition of output and the labor force is essentially identical to that of Italy, France, and other major European countries. In this rapid process of economic transformation, four episodes of structural change played a central role: three trade liberalization reforms and a successful transition from a dictatorial political system to a parliamentary democracy.

During these 35 years, both the private and the national saving rates oscillated widely from very high levels in the 1960s to historical lows in the early and mid-1980s to a strong recovery in recent years. For the purposes of policy making, it would be interesting to know which of the structural changes had an impact on savings and which did not. More precisely, can some form of relatively stable "saving function" be recovered from the data, and how has this saving function performed during the trade reform subperiods?

---

[1] The authors are associated with the Universidad Carlos III in Madrid.

A stable and economically meaningful "saving function" can be derived from first principles and consistently estimated using Spain's annual macroeconomic data. The theoretical underpinnings of the model are those of traditional intertemporal optimization by a representative agent, facing a complete set of borrowing/lending opportunities and an exogenous income process. The representative agent is endowed with a "habit formation" utility function. This helps explain a crucial feature of the data; i.e., the strong and positive impact that innovations in the growth rate of income have upon saving (either national or private).

Each of the three trade liberalization processes is treated as a sequence of shocks that changes the growth rate of income, and the democratization experience is treated as another sequence of shocks that changes the saving behavior of the public sector and, as a consequence, its fiscal pressure on the private sector. When these two exogenous variables—innovation in income and growth rate of total fiscal pressure—are accounted for, the three trade reforms have no other systematic effects upon saving. The only other aggregate economic variable that retains significant explanatory power for the growth rate of private saving is the distribution of income between labor and capital as measured by the growth rate of the gross profit margin.

By definition, national saving is the sum of private and public saving. Public saving is considered exogenous, while private saving is interpreted as the equilibrium outcome of a process in which an aggregate representative agent reacts to variations in per capita income growth, its distribution, the long-run rate of return on investment, and public sector taxing and spending decisions, among other things. In this sense, only private saving is implicitly modeled here, while all other variables are taken as exogenous. This is, therefore, only a partial equilibrium exercise, and the restrictive assumptions upon which it is founded should be discussed and clarified at the outset.

Certainly, public saving is not exogenous to the overall evolution of an economic system. Its two fundamental components, tax revenues and public expenditures, are affected in both the short and the long run by movements in national income. In the short run, for given fiscal and expenditure systems, changes in national income and in its distribution among individuals will automatically affect tax revenues and outflows. In the long run, the overall system of taxation and public expenditure must be seen as the outcome of the political and economic game played by the country's citizens, whose interests, in turn, depend upon the growth rate and distribution of national income.

In principle, a political-economic model is needed that takes as exogenous the stochastic processes representing Spain's technological advances and institutional evolution and deriving the growth rate of per capita income and the dynamic paths of taxes and public expenditure as equilibrium outcomes. No model of this kind exists that can be brought to the data; hence, the assumption of an exogenous process for the government's propensity to save out of national income. This implies the ancillary hypothesis, according to which private agents take per capita private disposable income as the relevant exogenous variable: taxes and transfers will not be treated as an equilibrium outcome in this environment.

Again, there is no good reason to be satisfied with such an assumption. Private disposable income depends not only upon taxes and transfers but also upon private agents' decisions to work, save, and invest. Hence, a good intertemporal model of saving would have to include a general equilibrium determination of rates of return and capital accumulation, which is not covered in this chapter.

The list of exogenous variables should not be limited to those mentioned so far. Apart from the obvious one—the real rate of return on investment—historical analysis and economic theory suggest that a number of other factors should also be considered. Central among them are the structural changes undergone by Spain's economy during the 35 years encompassed by this investigation: three trade liberalization reforms and a rapid successful transition (1975–78) from a dictatorial political system to a parliamentary democracy.

The liberalization efforts span three subperiods (1960–69, 1970–85, and 1986–95) characterized by very different fiscal policies, exchange rate regimes, patterns of international trade, and labor cost dynamics, as well as wide oscillations in the real rate of return on financial assets, demographic changes, and immigration flows. The social security system expanded continuously throughout all three periods, but particularly after 1976. All of these variables may, in principle, have a strong impact on private saving behavior. One important step is to isolate the pure liberalization process from other factors that may reasonably be seen as independent.

The working hypothesis is that Spain's trade liberalization experiences should be formalized as exogenous increases in the expected growth rate of permanent income. Such an increase in the exogenous growth rate is induced either by a more efficient allocation of factors or by the adoption of new, more efficient technologies. While the beginning of each reform period was marked by either the signing of an international treaty or the approval of some major legislative reform, none of them occurred rapidly. In each case, the implementation took many years, and the opening process was always relatively slow and at times monotonous. Furthermore, none of the reforms (with perhaps the exception of the third one) involved using the exchange rate as a crucial policy instrument.

Periodizing the stochastic process of private saving propensity according to the dates of trade reform is rejected by the data. One cannot reject the hypothesis that a structural break occurred in 1960, but the shortness of the time series available before that year greatly reduces the information that can be extracted from this statistical finding. Altogether, these considerations suggest modeling Spain's trade reforms as positive innovations to the exogenous stochastic process of per capita income. This leads to an attempt to quantify their impact on saving from within the framework of permanent income and intertemporal consumption smoothing.

Received theory of consumption-saving behavior (see, e.g., Deaton 1992), based on the permanent income hypothesis and intertemporally separable Von Neumann-Morgenstern preferences for consumption, suggests that confronted by permanent innovation in the income sequence, the representative consumer should react by temporarily running down his accumulated assets in order to move to the new permanent consumption position. The actual magnitude of such a movement will depend on the preference parameters and on the simultaneous changes in the expected rate of return on saving. In an open economy context or, better, in a "more open" economy context like Spain's, this will typically imply running down the current account surplus and generating a growth rate of imports that, for a few years, will exceed the growth rate of exports. In any case, a temporary reduction in national saving and an increase in consumer goods imports would not constitute, from such a partial equilibrium point of view, much of a puzzle.

In a general equilibrium model, with endogenous investment and labor supply decisions, a positive shock to the production possibility set that sufficiently increases the expected rate of return would bring about an increase in the level of investment. In a closed economy, this implies an increase in saving, while in an open economy this would induce an external capital inflow. In any case, the channel through which a positive innovation in per capita income induces an increase in domestic saving propensity should be the rate of interest.

If private saving in Spain had behaved according to either one of these simple models, the task would be easily accomplished. But this is not the case. The overall correlation between national and private saving propensities, on the one hand, and income growth rates, on the other, turn out to be positive. This is even more so when the appropriate pairs of income and saving variables are compared. As a matter of fact, only for the third liberalization period after 1986 do the data show a *small and temporary* drop in private saving. It will be argued later that this fact is more coherently explained by other temporary factors than by the permanent increase in income that Spain's entrance into the European Union may have caused. The evidence, in any case, rules out the simple partial equilibrium and constant interest rate approach.

The general equilibrium and rate of interest route, while theoretically more appealing, is not convincingly supported by the data, at least as long as one maintains the view that (for a given level of the expected rate of return) saving propensities are negatively correlated with positive innovations in per capita income. Measures of real interest rates display either very weak or no correlation with output and saving growth rates. Furthermore, a proper handling of this approach would require the construction of a fully specified dynamic general equilibrium model with endogenous production and labor supply, a task that clearly goes beyond the scope of the present research.

Still, there is need for a minimal consistent model of intertemporal consumption saving behavior capable of accommodating at least an overall positive impact of income growth upon saving propensities. The suggestion is a simple representative agent model in which saving propensities are more often than not an increasing function of income growth rates. This has been argued recently by a number of authors (e.g., Boldrin, Christiano, and Fisher, 1994; Carroll and Weil, 1994; Carroll, Overland, and Weil, 1995) on the basis of various specifications of the habit formation preferences model originally analyzed by Ryder and Heal (1973) and then again by Abel (1990) and Constantinides (1990) in the context of asset pricing. Indeed, Boldrin, Christiano, and Fisher (1994) argue that the strongly procyclical behavior of stock market prices and activity can and should be interpreted as an important piece of evidence supporting the proposed specification of preferences. Here, a simplified, partial equilibrium version of this model is the starting point of the empirical analyses and does reasonably well in explaining the Spanish annual data.

Once this basic relation has been established, one can move on to investigate the impact that other economic factors may have had upon private saving. Between 1975 and 1978, Spain moved rather rapidly and peacefully from dictatorship to democracy. In the data set, this shows up in a very simple form: around those same years, the amount of outstanding public debt, which as a percentage of GDP had been steadily declining since the early 1960s, starts to grow at a remarkably quick pace. Indeed, no matter which year one chooses within that interval, the hypothesis that a structural break in the stochastic process determines public saving propensity cannot be rejected. This sharp change in the government's propensity to save represents the direct economic impact of the exogenous change in the political regime.

This framework of analysis is based upon the figment of a representative agent. Indeed, on the back of this simple model, the existence of a number of fictitious representative agents, corresponding to the public, private, household, and business saving ratios, is assumed. This is a drastic simplification: arguing that public saving affects private saving but that this occurs at less than a one-to-one ratio is equivalent to recognizing that the splitting of the national pie between the public and the private agents has an impact upon the aggregate saving rate. A full examination of this issue (i.e., of the so-called Ricardian equivalence hypothesis) would, nevertheless, require the availability of reliable microeconomic data that are not available for Spain. Hence, the analysis suffices with a simpleminded estimation of the aggregate impact that variations in fiscal pressure or public sector income have upon private saving once the effects of income and interest rates are accounted for.

In Spain, the transition from dictatorship to democracy and the opening to international trade flows also meant a substantial redistribution of power among the major social groups. This redistribution of power has generated or been accompanied by changes in the distribution of income large enough to potentially affect the average private propensity to save. From an intuitive point of view, this may occur in two forms: either income flows from one income distribution decile to the others affect the average propensity to consume, or, due to some violation of the assumptions underlying the Modigliani-Miller equivalence results, shifts in the functional distribution of income bring about nonnegligible changes in the average propensity to save of the private sector. A simple measure of the variation of gross profit margins in Spain's private sector income is used to capture the empirical importance of this channel.

Spain's Saving in the Past 40 Years

Data Analysis and Description

The following set of saving ratios is used:

s: Spain's per capita, annual, national gross saving rate over the period 1954–95, defined as the ratio of gross national saving (S) to gross national disposable income ($GNDI$). S is obtained by deflating nominal saving with the implicit investment deflator while $GNDI$ is deflated with the implicit GDP deflator, s_t reported in Figure 10.1.[2]

From a purely statistical viewpoint, the most appropriate time-series representation for s_t is as an AR(1) process, with OLS estimates (standard deviations in parentheses)

$$s_t = 0.034 + 0.85\, s_{t-1} \qquad\qquad [1]$$
$$(0.017)\ (0.074)$$

and $R^2 = 0.78$. From equation [1] Dickey-Fuller tests can be computed, and neither of them rejects the null hypothesis of s_t behaving like a random walk. Furthermore, there is no apparent structure in the residuals of [1], which look like normally distributed white noise.

No special economic significance is attached to this purely statistical finding or to its implication that a simple cointegration relation between S and $GNDI$ does not exist. The economic framework does not require, a priori, the existence of any stable linear relationship between income and saving. The finding that Spain's saving rate behaves like a random walk is only evidence of its high persistence and volatility during the sample period, the

---

[2] Reliable data from 1954 are available only for national saving. Disaggregated values are available for only the 1964-95 period.

Figure 10.1
National Saving Ratio: 1954–95

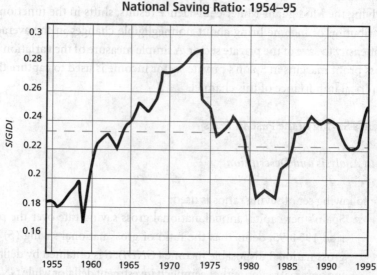

explanation for which must be found in the movements of other relevant economic variables.

   sp: Spain's annual gross private saving rate over the period 1964–95, defined as the ratio of gross private saving (*SP*) to gross private disposable income (*GPrDI*). The latter is deflated by the implicit GDP deflator, while the former is deflated by the implicit investment deflator. The values for *sp* are reported in Figure 10.2.

If anything, the evidence of random walk–like behavior is even stronger for sp_t. The OLS regression of sp_t gives (standard deviations in parentheses):

$$sp_t = 0.04 + 0.83sp_{t-1} \tag{2}$$
$$(0.03)\ \ (0.13)$$

and $R^2 = 0.58$. Considerations completely analogous to those already made for s_t also apply here.

   sg: Spain's annual gross public saving rate over the period 1964–95, defined as the ratio of gross public saving (*SG*) to gross national disposable income (*GNDI*). Also, the implicit investment deflator is used for the numerator and the implicit GDP deflator for the denominator. Values for *sg* are reported in Figure 10.3.

Figure 10.2
Private Saving Ratio: 1964–95

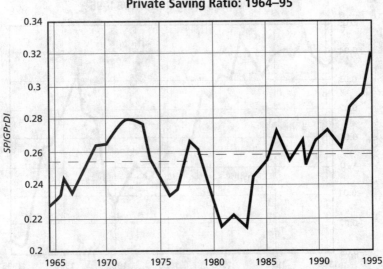

The choice of the implicit investment deflator to compute the real value of saving and consequently the saving ratios is, admittedly, unusual. The common practice is to divide nominal saving by nominal *GNDI* or *GPrDl*, thereby implicitly assuming that the GDP deflator is also the appropriate price of saving.

The choice of deflator makes a nonnegligible difference for some of the analytical conclusions. As Figure 10.4 displays, the implicit GDP and investment deflators behave rather differently over the sample period. More to the point, their ratio displays a very clear downward trend, which seems to become more pronounced right after the liberalization episodes of 1960 and 1986.

Normal economic testing confirms this intuition. The overall regression shows the relative price of capital decreasing at a rate of –0.832 percent per year over the 1954–95 interval. During various subperiods, though, one finds significantly different trends:

	1954–59	1960–69	1970–85	1986–95
Trend (percent)	–0.78	–1.87	0.15	–1.87

This finding suggests that during the postwar period, Spain, like most advanced countries, has witnessed a remarkable decrease in the relative price

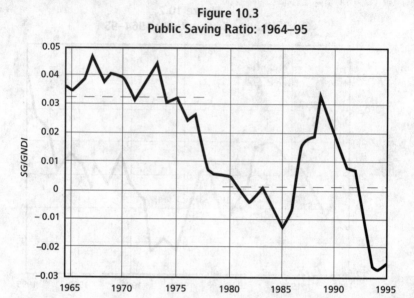

Figure 10.3
Public Saving Ratio: 1964–95

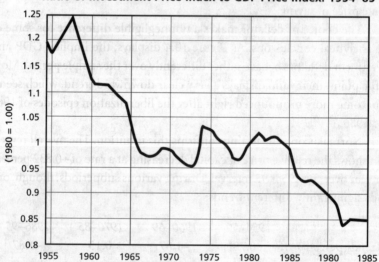

Figure 10.4
Ratio of Investment Price Index to GDP Price Index: 1954–85

of investment goods.[3] Second, it lends credit to the working hypothesis of treating the trade liberalization process as equivalent to a sequence of permanent positive technological shocks. Such positive shocks materialize as, among other things, drops in the cost of new productive capital. Under this interpretation our statistical results confirm the widespread view that 1960 and 1986 were the major liberalization episodes, relegating 1970 and the entire decade of the 1970s to a very secondary role.

These considerations have led to the conclusion that the appropriate price index for calculating the real value of saving is the investment deflator. This choice of deflator is the only one coherent with received economic theory. All theoretical models are based on the assumption that economic agents save in order to acquire assets that will generate a future stream of income. That is, the purpose of saving is not the postponent of current consumption but the generation of future consumption.

If this assumption is maintained, explaining saving amounts to explaining the quantity of those income-producing assets agents decide to buy at each point in time. All else being equal, if the cost (in current consumption units) of those assets decreases, forward-looking agents will react by increasing or decreasing the total quantity of purchased assets, depending upon the relative income and substitution elasticities of their demand for future consumption. A proper evaluation of the net outcome is possible only if one can measure productive assets in their own units. This requires dividing nominal saving amounts by the price of new capital goods.

While doing this does not reduce the wide oscillations in saving rates over the sample period, it substantially eliminates the impression of a long-run decrease in saving propensities, both national and private. Given the paramount importance of this fact, and in order to facilitate comparison, saving propensities calculated by dividing nominal saving by nominal income measures are also reported (see Figure 10.5) and explicitly discussed when relevant.

Private saving, *sp*, can be broken down further into two other measures:

---

[3] A number of papers, e.g., Greenwood, Hercowitz, and Krusell (1995) and Greenwood and Yorukoglu (1996) have stressed the implications of this phenomenon for understanding U.S. data.

sh: the household gross saving rate out of *GPrDl,* and

sb: the business gross saving rate out of *GPrDl.*

Their behavior is reported in Figure 10.6.

Visual inspection of Figures 10.1–10.3 tells the following story. National saving oscillated widely from a very low level at the beginning of the 1960s to its maximum in the early 1970s, to then collapse until 1982–83, when it started to recover, reaching relatively high levels during the last cyclical expansion. This remarkable swing was the product of a large decrease in public saving (from a maximum of about 4 percent to a minimum near – 3 percent) which began in the early 1970s. The private saving rate has suffered equally large variations in three full cycles over 30 years, ranging from a minimum of about 22 percent in 1981 to a recent maximum of 32 percent.

Visual inspection alone will not tell us, though, if any particular correlation pattern is present. For this purpose, a set of elementary statistics for *s, sp, sg, sh,* and *sb* is reported in Table 10.1. Three features of the data are apparent: public saving is negatively correlated with both private and business saving, the last two have a strong positive correlation with each other, and household saving moves in the opposite direction from business saving.

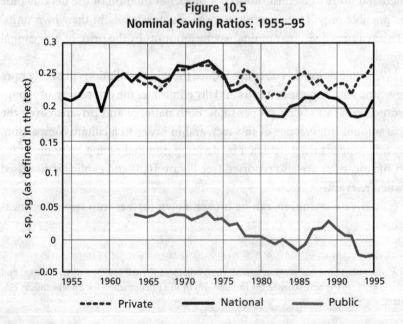

Figure 10.5
Nominal Saving Ratios: 1955–95

Figure 10.6
Household and Business Saving Ratios: 1964–95

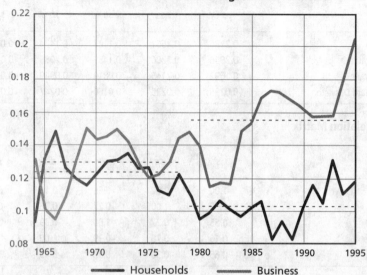

Besides looking at pairwise correlations, it is interesting to check whether either the trade liberalization reforms or the transformation to a democratic political system produced any structural break in the behavior of Spain's saving rates.

For the 1960 reform one must reject the hypothesis of a constant mean of the national saving rate, while for 1970 and 1986 the hypothesis of constancy cannot be rejected.

In spite of the statistical test's results, the idea that the year 1960 witnessed a fundamental change in the national propensity to save is dismissed. This decision is based not so much on the availability of very few observations for the years prior to 1960, as upon the more substantive fact that the last three observations before 1960 come from years of very low or even negative growth in national income. The data from Spain suggest the presence of a strong business cycle effect upon saving rates, even at the annual frequency. Drawing conclusions about structural breaks by comparing a mean from a sample where half of the points are recession years with another one in which recession years are not even a fifth of the total would be rather questionable.

Table 10.1 Basic Saving Ratio Statistics: 1964–95

	s	sp	sh	sb	sg
Mean	0.2285	0.2561	0.1127	0.1434	0.0159
Maximum	0.2846	0.3206	0.1489	0.2085	0.0452
Minimum	0.1692	0.2145	0.0819	0.0949	–0.0283
Standard Desviaton	0.0295	0.0235	0.0160	0.0247	0.0219

Correlation Matrix

	s	sp	sh	sb	sg
s	1.00	0.52	0.55	0.15	0.65
sp	0.52	1.00	0.27	0.78	–0.30
sh	0.55	0.27	1.00	–0.39	0.32
–sb	0.15	0.78	–0.39	1.00	–0.49
sg	0.65	–0.30	0.32	–0.49	1.00

Test of Mean Break

	s	sp	sh	sb	sg
1964–78	0.2546	0.2532	0.1236	0.1295	0.0334
1979–95	0.2213	0.2586	0.1030	0.1556	0.0004
t–statistic	–1.16	0.65	–4.73	3.47	–6.52

The other historical event that seems to have a strong influence upon Spain's saving behavior is the transition from a dictatorial to a democratic and parliamentary system. Statistical testing suggests that a change in the public's propensity to save occurred in the second half of the 1970s. The democratization process began around 1976 and came to its first institutional conclusion in 1978 with the approval of a new constitution. In accordance with a common convention, 1978 was chosen to date the test. The horizontal lines in Figures 10.1–10.3 and 10.6 indicate the sample mean values over the pre- and postdemocratization subperiods.

Table 10.2 reports sample statistics for the same set of saving propensities when the GDP deflator is applied to nominal savings. Some differences are worth noting. The volatility of all saving ratios is somewhat

Table 10.2 Saving Ratio Statistics: 1964–95 (GDP Deflator)

	s	sp	sh	sb	sg
Mean	0.2273	0.2210	0.0934	0.1176	0.0157
Maximum	0.2727	0.2355	0.1285	0.1502	0.0438
Minimum	0.1869	0.1823	0.0614	0.0820	−0.0240
Standard Desviation	0.0251	0.0152	0.0160	0.0150	0.0208

Correlation Matrix

	s	sp	sh	sb	sg
s	1.00	0.65	0.66	−0.51	0.83
sp	0.65	1.00	0.53	0.44	−0.13
sh	0.67	0.53	1.00	−0.52	0.48
sb	−0.05	0.44	−0.52	1.00	−0.38
sg	0.83	0.13	0.49	−0.39	1.00

Test of Mean Break

	s	sp	sh	sb	sg
1964–78	0.2515	0.2185	0.1067	0.1118	0.0330
1979–95	0.2049	0.2044	0.0817	0.1227	0.0005
t–statistic	−7.00	−2.92	−7.14	2.17	−7.10

reduced, while the already strong positive correlation between national and public saving is magnified. On the other hand, the negative relation between public and private saving now disappears, leaving only a negative correlation between public and business saving. What is more important, though, is that the use of the GDP deflator would suggest that, with the sole exception of the business sector, a drop in all saving propensities occurred after the mid-1970s. This appears to be a misleading conclusion, caused only by the adoption of an incorrect price measure. Figure 10.7 adjusts the gross public and private saving ratios for the impact of inflation on the real value of the outstanding public debt, whose time pattern is described in Figure 10.8. Besides the obvious increase in the average value of *sg* and the parallel reduction of *sp*, adjusting for inflation reinforces the conclusion

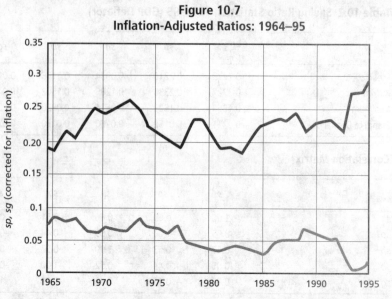

Figure 10.7
Inflation-Adjusted Ratios: 1964–95

Private

Public

Figure 10.8
Public Debt: 1964–95

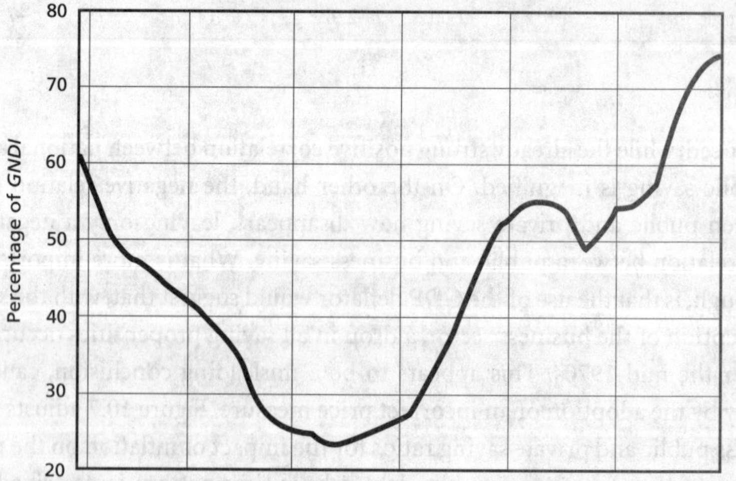

that a drop in public saving occurred around 1978, while leaving all other stylized facts unaltered.

Here is a summary of the stylized facts examined thus far.

Except for the 1960 liberalization, there is no statistical evidence of increasing or decreasing long-run trends or of abrupt changes of behavior in the national and private propensities to save, while a clear discontinuity exists in the average public saving ratio before and after democratization took place. In particular, there is no prima facie evidence that the 1986 entrance into the European Union and the associated liberalization of financial markets have been the causes of any sizable drop in national or private saving propensities.

Some of these results are sensitive to the choice of the price deflator. When the implicit GDP deflator is used, one cannot reject the hypothesis of a structural break in 1978 also for the means of s and sp. When the impact of inflation upon the real value of public debt is taken into account, the large drop in public saving after 1978 is somewhat reduced but not eliminated.[4] More importantly, correcting for the inflation tax does not change the dynamic behavior of sp_t.

The patterns of pairwise correlation are also worthy of some attention. Over the entire 1964–95 interval, government saving is negatively correlated with private saving, but in a relatively weak form. When a correlation matrix is computed for the two separate subperiods, 1964–78 and 1979–95, the following is observed: sg and sp are practically uncorrelated ($\rho = 0.02$) during the first period and become strongly negatively correlated during the second ($\rho = -0.55$).

If one computes the same correlations with inflation-adjusted data, the pattern is more uniform across subperiods: sp and sg have correlation coefficients equal to -0.45 in 1964–78 and -0.55 in 1979–95. This behavior is even stronger for (non-inflation-adjusted) household savings, which are again uncorrelated with sg until 1978 and display instead a -0.77 correlation coefficient between 1979 and 1995. These patterns are invariant to the choice of saving deflator and are in fact reinforced by the use of the implicit GDP deflator. To the extent that unconditional pairwise correlations can be

---

[4] Most Spanish observers interpret the short-lived positive jump in government saving around 1986–88 as a one-time accident, due mostly to the introduction of the value-added tax (VAT) and to the temporary positive effect this had on the level of tax revenues.

taken to convey any information about Ricardian relationships between public and private saving, they suggest that there is no reason to analyze the two subperiods separately.

The average saving ratios over the entire sample period are roughly within the EU and OECD range of values, even if they are below the level of very high performers such as Italy (but only until the mid-1980s) and Japan (over the whole sample period).

Looking at the ratio of private saving to gross private disposable income (sp) and its components sh and sb, there is a strong positive correlation between sp and sb (0.78) and a nonnegligible negative correlation between sh and sb (−0.39) which seem to be generated mostly by their behavior in the 1978–95 subperiods. A variety of specific tax provisions introduced in the last 15 years is commonly believed to be the main reason for the large amount of tax arbitrage carried out by the private sector through movements of income between the household and business sectors. Unsystematic evidence about the saving behavior of small and medium-size businesses supports this view.

Table 10.3 shows a pronounced positive correlation between the growth rate of national income and gross national saving, which is explained mostly by the strong correlation between sg and $GNDI$, since the correlation between sp and $GNDI$, while still positive, is substantially smaller. When $GPrDI$ is used, however, then sp also displays a high positive correlation with income growth rates. While statistics for sample subperiods are not reported, it is worth stressing that the described pattern is homogeneous across them.

Table 10.3 Saving Propensities and Income Growth Rates
Corr. with $\hat{y}$ (64–95)

	s	sp	sg	Sp
$\hat{y} - 2$	0.29	0.05	0.23	0.17
$\hat{y} - i$	0.52	0.15	0.42	0.18
$\hat{y}\,0$	0.69	0.17	0.63	0.42
$\hat{y} + I$	0.77	0.14	0.77	0.29
$\hat{y} + 2$	0.69	0.09	0.73	0.24

Note: For the first three columns, the measure of income is GNDI. For the fourth it is GPrDI.

The unconditional pairwise correlations are uniformly higher when each saving propensity is paired with the growth rate of "its own" income, i.e., *GNDI* for *s* and *sg* and *GPrDI* for *sp*. This reinforces our prior finding according to which, to a first approximation, each representative agent's saving propensity is determined by the information available about the stochastic process of his own income.

The behavior of aggregate demand and of its main components (Figure 10.9) does not exhibit any particular "jump" after each liberalization episode. A limited exception is the period 1986–90, which will be discussed in detail below. In addition, and contrary to what one would have anticipated, each trade reform except the last one brought about a short-run *surplus* in the current account, which was later eliminated by the increase in internal demand and imports (Figure 10.10). The post-1986 external deficit was generated by an unusually rapid growth of the imports/*GNDI* ratio and by the flat behavior of the export/*GNDI* ratio until 1990. This suggests the importance of finding out what was special in 1986.

Figure 10.11 plots national saving and investment as percentages of national income, their pairwise correlation being equal to 0.84. Visual in-

Figure 10.9
Components of Aggregate Demand: 1954–95

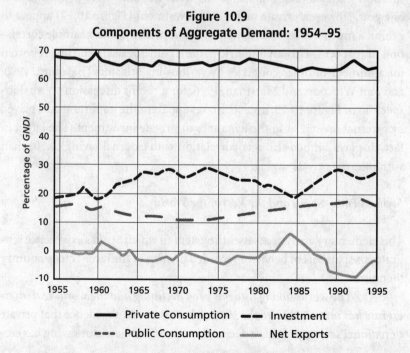

Figure 10.10
Imports and Exports: 1954–95

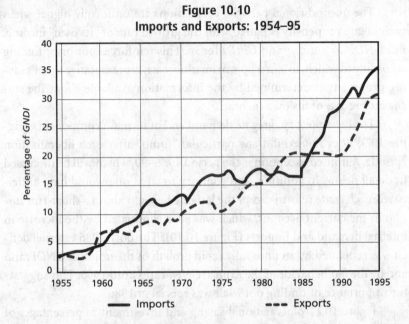

spection suggests that national saving leads national investment by about one year. However, private saving and investment (Figure 10.12) appear to exhibit a much weaker intertemporal relation, if any, with a sample correlation of just 0.18. This asymmetric pattern coincides with the one reported for a number of other countries by various investigators (Bayoumi, 1990, and Van Wincoop and Marrinan, 1996, for a recent discussion). Visual inspection of Figure 10.13, instead, makes apparent the important role played by external saving, *se*, in the dynamics of private investment. The latter, in fact, displays a much stronger correlation with external saving (0.50) than with internal private saving.

Stylized Facts: Spain and the Rest of the World

This elementary analysis assesses the extent to which Spain's experience replicates the patterns of behavior recorded in most of the recent cross-country literature.

(a) *The world saving rate has been declining and the world real interest rate has increased since the 1970s.* There is no clear evidence that private or national saving rates have declined in Spain. Public sector saving has cer-

Figure 10.11
National Saving and Investment: 1954–95

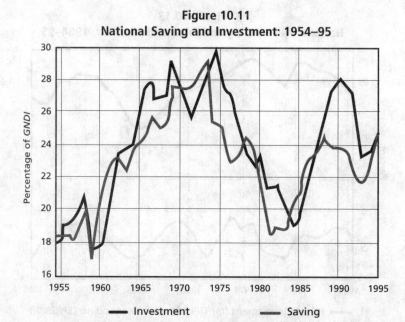

Figure 10.12
Private Saving and Investment: 1964–95

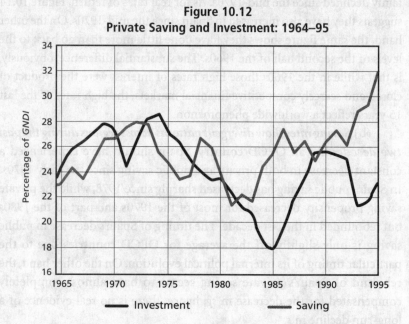

Figure 10.13
National Net Lending and Private Investment: 1964–95

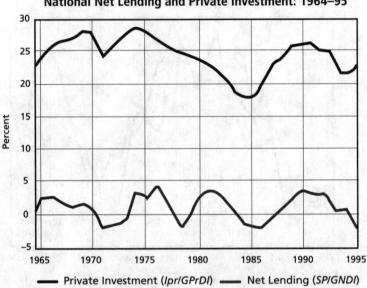

Private Investment (*Ipr/GPrDI*) — Net Lending (*SP/GNDI*)

tainly declined since the mid-1970s. As for real rates of return, Figure 10.14 suggests they have also increased in Spain since the mid-1970s. On the other hand, the same figure shows they have done little more than go back to the levels of the second half of the 1960s. The substantial difference, obviously, is that while in the 1960s those high rates of interest were the product of closed and scarcely competitive financial markets, the high rates of the last 15 years reflect a worldwide phenomenon.

(b) *Saving rates show divergent patterns across regions during the past two decades.* As an OECD country, Spain should have experienced a constant decrease in both private and public saving since the early 1970s. In Spain, public saving has decreased sharply since 1978, while the private saving propensity decreased for most of the 1970s and part of the 1980s but rebounded in the last decade. The timing of Spain's decrease in public saving is only slightly off the average for OECD countries due to the particular timing of its internal political evolution. On the other hand, the rebound of Spain's private saving seems to have almost completely compensated for the decrease in *sg*; hence, there is no real evidence of a long-run decline in *s*.

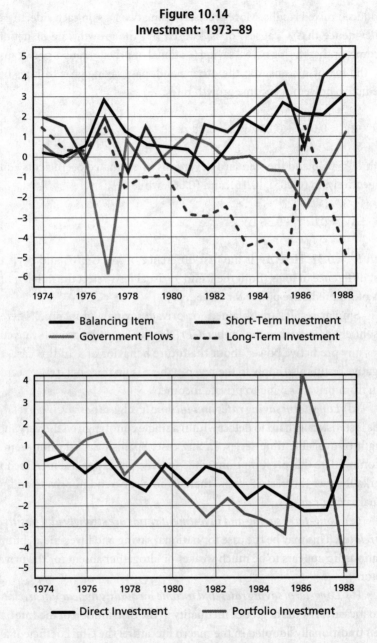

Figure 10.14
Investment: 1973–89

(c) *Long-term saving and growth rates are positively correlated.*
Pairwise correlations suggest this is the case in Spain as well. The test for
Granger causality between various measures of income growth and saving

produced mixed results. More precisely, using two lags on each side, there is no evidence that s "causes" or is "caused by" the growth rate of national income, or that the log of real saving (national or private) causes or is "caused by" the log of income. On the other hand, past saving growth rates have predictive power for income growth rates:

$$\Delta y_t = 0.017 + 0.23 \, \Delta y_{t-1} + 0.18 \, \Delta s_{t-1} \qquad [3]$$

with $R^2 = 0.46$ and the standard deviations of estimated coefficients equal, respectively, to (0.005), (0.16), and (0.06), while

$$\Delta y_t = 0.014 + 0.56 \, \Delta y_{t-1} \qquad [4]$$

with $R^2 = 0.32$. Here Δy_t is the first difference of $\log(GNDI)$ and Δs_t is the first difference of $\log s_t$. Both the F and χ_2 usual tests reject the null hypothesis of no predictive power for s in eq. [4].

Similar results are obtained for private saving and income. There is absolutely no evidence that either *GPrDl* or its log or its growth rate contains any predictive power about the future behavior of s. In this case, the negative results also apply to the reverse: there is no trace of Granger causation from private saving to private income.

(d) *Long-term saving rates and income levels are positively correlated.* This is statistically hard to detect within a single country given the very short length of available time series. In any case, Spanish data do not seem to accommodate this presumption: while income per capita has increased remarkably over the past 35 years, there is no clear trend in private and national saving rates.

(e) *Long-term saving and investment ratios are strongly and positively correlated.* This may be the case for national saving and investment, but the relationship appears to be much weaker or altogether absent for the private sector.

(f) *Long-term saving rates and income inequality appear uncorrelated.* Two measures of the degree of inequality in the distribution of income have been traditionally adopted in the macro literature: the Gini coefficient and the percentage of national income controlled by the middle class, where the latter is defined as consisting of households in the three central quintiles of the income distribution. No reliable time series for any of these indices could be reconstructed. The little evidence available, covering only the last 15 years, suggests a relatively sharp and monotone decrease in all measures of Spain's income inequality (see Ruiz Castillo, 1994, and references therein). Neither the national nor the private saving rates decreased over this time interval. Thus, the time-series evidence for Spain supports the stylized fact above.

On the other hand, the dispersion in the distribution of income among individuals is not the only channel through which the allocation of national product among different groups may affect saving. In the presence of credit frictions or market imperfections, other sources of heterogeneity among economic agents may become important, in particular, the functional distribution of income between capital and labor. Relatively reliable time series of the division of value added between firms and workers are available covering the years 1964–95. The effect of this income distribution variable on private saving propensities is examined below.

(g) *Trade and financial liberalization reforms are followed by sudden jumps in consumption and consequent sharp declines in private saving.* This did not occur in Spain after either the 1960 reform or the smaller 1970 reform. It is important to stress this because the 1960 plan allowed for the inflow of foreign capital and credit but maintained serious restrictions on the outflow of capital.

A small decline in the private saving ratio (and a sharper drop in household saving) did take place, nevertheless, between 1987 and 1990. On the other hand, the national saving ratio increased sharply in the few years after 1986, driven by a temporary but very strong increase in public saving.

(h) *Do higher interest rates cause higher saving propensities?* This additional question is added to the collection of stylized facts and will be answered subsequently.

Trade Reforms: A Chronicle

Trade Liberalization: 1960–86

Until the end of 1959, Spain was a very closed economy that prohibited free foreign trade of any kind of goods and services by private companies or individuals. All imports of raw materials and other basic inputs not available in the country were directly controlled by the central government and subject to item-by-item authorization. The same was true for the small exporting activity Spain was then able to generate.

As a consequence of this institutional environment and of the strongly autarkic policies, the degree of openness of the economy (imports + exports as a percentage of GDP) had been decreasing steadily over the decade, from 19.68 percent in 1951 to 13.62 percent in 1959 (Gámir, 1990, Table 1). Meanwhile, overall competitiveness was collapsing, with the ratio between exports and imports decreasing from 120.1 percent in 1951 to 62.6 percent in 1959.

The movement of labor and capital across national borders was practically impossible, and a complicated system of multiple exchange rates was in place. Again, a small inflow of foreign capital took place, but only under the direct control and authorization of the central government bureaucracy.

In spite of this, the economy had been growing at a healthy rate, averaging 6.12 percent per year over the period 1949–60. Due to a variety of internal and external circumstances, however, the situation deteriorated rapidly around 1958–59, with the growth rate of national income dropping to –2.7 percent in 1959.

On July 21, 1959, the Plan de Estabilización y Liberalización was adopted. This was the first and most ambitious effort to reform Spain's economic system in a free-trade direction. It allowed the convertibility of the peseta against most other important currencies, it permitted foreign investments to take place in Spain, and it also authorized some limited outflow of capital from Spain to foreign markets. More crucially, on the trade side a system of tariffs was introduced to replace the previous quotas and licenses. This transformed a completely centralized organization of international trade into one partially regulated by market transactions and based on the principle that the import of goods was free once the prescribed tariff had been paid.[5] This allowed the previously miniscule area of *comercio libre* (free trade) to begin growing at a very high rate.

As for capital, the inflow of foreign capital into Spain was highly liberalized, while most restrictions on the outflow of Spanish capital were maintained. Foreign commercial credit, direct investments (up to just under 50 percent of the firm's value), and real estate and portfolio investments were liberalized.

---

[5] A number of administrative authorizations were, nevertheless, maintained for both imports and exports.

During the three decades following the Plan de Estabilización y Liberalización, a slow and not always steady process of trade integration and liberalization took place, accompanied by a number of more or less small "competitive" exchange rate devaluations in 1967, 1971, 1973, 1976, 1977, 1980, and 1982. Spain was admitted as a member of the General Agreement on Tariffs and Trade (GATT) in 1963, which implied a further reduction in trade barriers between 1963 and 1965 and then again in 1967 as a consequence of the Kennedy Round.

In June 1970, a preferential trade agreement with the European Economic Community (EEC) was underwritten that brought the average tariff on Spanish imports to around 60 percent and reduced the average protection on Spanish goods exported to EEC member countries to 14 percent. At the same time, the Bank of Spain began to modernize the national banking system, introducing reserve requirements together with the first tools for the creation of a money market and scrapping a number of administrative controls and quotas on the allocation of bank credit. The process of liberalization and tariff reduction also progressed through a series of small steps, not all of which, however, went in the same direction.

A quantitative assessment of this long process is almost impossible to find, given the complex and often incoherent nature of the various systems adopted. From our vantage point two facts are relevant: (a) trade liberalization did not occur all at once and (b) by 1986, when Spain entered the EU and began the process of tariff harmonization with the other member countries, the extent to which it was still closed to foreign trade was already minimal.

Trying to quantify this argument, Table 10.4 reports some indicative measures of trade protection and openness drawn from various sources (see in particular Gámir, 1990, and De la Dehesa, Ruiz, and Torres, 1990).

Trade and Financial Markets Liberalization: 1986

On January 1, 1986, after the transition to a democratic political system was completed, Spain entered the European Union by signing the Tratado de Adhesión. This implied a total liberalization of trade with the members of the EU and the adoption of all the trade agreements established among the EU and other countries. It required the elimination, in the space of three to four years, of the residual quantity restrictions on imports and exports, as

Table 10.4 Measures of Trade Protection: 1960–86

Year	Average Tarriff[a] (percent)	ICGI/VAT[b] (percent)	Total	Imports (Lib.)[c]	(X + M)/Y
1960	16.50	0.00	16.50	40.0	19.6
1961	12.71	6.00	18.71	45.0	21.5
1962	11.90	6.24	18.13	55.0	23.7
1963	11.84	6.23	17.73	59.5	23.7
1964	11.61	7.31	18.91	63.5	25.6
1965	8.82	9.14	17.94	67.3	23.1
1966	9.97	9.39	19.28	71.2	25.2
1967	9.62	9.22	18.43	76.8	24.3
1968	7.97	8.05	15.19	75.9	24.5
1969	7.80	8.39	16.19	77.4	26.0
1970	7.29	8.15	15.44	76.2	27.9
1971	7.60	8.17	15.77	75.7	28.3
1972	7.86	8.43	16.29	74.2	31.1
1973	7.51	8.52	16.02	80.4	32.4
1974	5.21	6.67	11.88	85.2	32.1
1975	5.32	6.18	11.49	79.6	31.4
1976	5.15	6.03	11.17	78.6	33.4
1977	6.23	6.78	13.02	78.3	32.8
1978	5.15	6.86	12.02	80.0	33.8
1979	4.59	6.41	11.02	79.4	36.8
1980	3.82	6.08	9.90	91.0	37.0
1981	3.56	4.97	8.53	88.0	37.4
1982	3.77	5.45	9.22	87.0	39.2
1983	3.85	5.40	9.25	86.0	40.0
1984	3.65	5.36	9.01	88.3	42.4
1985	3.88	5.56	9.44	93.1	43.1
1986	4.95	10.51	15.46	100.0	43.3

a. Trade-weighted *pure* tariff protection.
b. Impuestos de Compensación de Gravámenes Interiores (ICGI) or, after 1986, the VAT.
c. Percentage of total imports under liberalized status.

well as the abolition of tariffs and the progressive replacement of the
Impuestos de Compensación de Gravémenes Interiores (ICGI) with the uniform European VAT rates. While the liberalization process was not instanta-

neous, about 70 percent of total trade in goods and services with EU countries was liberalized immediately, and free mobility of capital was practically complete by 1989. This rapid financial opening came to a brief halt between 1987 and 1990, when a number of exchange rate control measures were introduced, but continued rather smoothly after that.

The degree of trade liberalization that took place after Spain joined the EU, however, was far less than that put in place since 1960. What makes 1986 different from other years is not the lifting of some trading gate but instead the decision to peg the exchange rate of the peseta to the other European currencies participating in the European Monetary System (EMS) and the relatively rapid liberalization of private financial flows. Nothing like this had been done after 1960, except for a small simplification of exchange rate controls in March 1981.

Many observers have stressed the very strong reaction of private consumption in Spain to the 1986 reform. Beginning that year the (then positive) difference between private saving and investment starts dropping as export growth is unable to keep pace with import growth (see Figure 10.10, above).

The breakdown of imports between investment and consumption goods, available only from 1975, confirms but also qualifies the widespread impression of an EU "consumption binge." Figure 10.15 reports the series as percentages of *GNDI* when the appropriate deflators are used, while Figure 10.16 reports the same data as ratios of undeflated nominal variables.

While both sets of data confirm the increase in consumer goods imports, a very different story is told about the real behavior of investment goods. Additional information about the extent to which the sharp rise in imports was due only to consumption is provided in Figure 10.17, which reports separately the proportion of imported capital goods and consumer durables.

The sharp rise in consumer durable imports after 1986 is clear, as is their decline (in percentage of total imports) after 1989–90. The rise in imports of capital goods, no less strong in 1986, is more permanent and remains so even after the consumption binge is over.

Various hypotheses have been advanced to explain this relatively short-lived but intense jump in private consumption following the 1986 liberalization. In light of the analysis carried out so far, the following two factors provide a reasonable description of what happened.

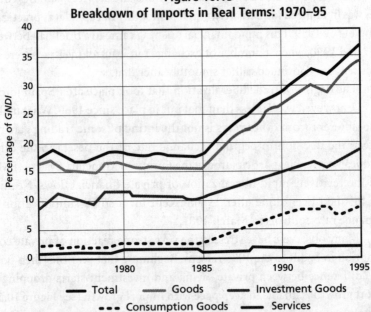

Figure 10.15
Breakdown of Imports in Real Terms: 1970–95

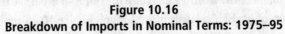

Figure 10.16
Breakdown of Imports in Nominal Terms: 1975–95

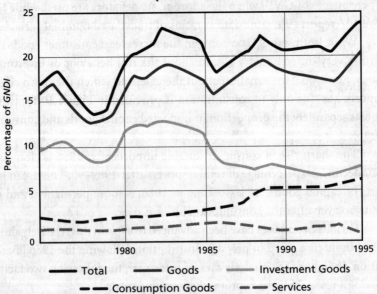

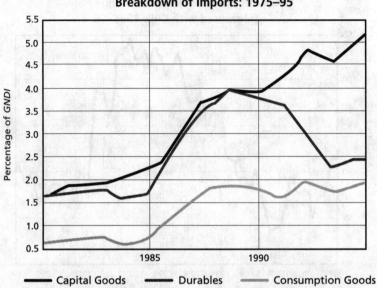

Figure 10.17
Breakdown of Imports: 1975–95

(1) First is the *overvalued peseta* and the related very high real interest rates adopted to attract foreign capital and to prepare for entrance into the EMS in 1989. The evidence supporting this hypothesis is mixed. While there is no doubt that Spain's real rates were kept high (relative to the EMS partners) during the four years between 1985 and 1989, the behavior of the exchange rate is less clear. Figure 10.18 shows the real effective peseta exchange rate with respect to the other EMS currencies over the 1980–95 interval when deflated by the consumer price index. The rise in the peseta's purchasing power is clear, but the timing is not. The sudden increase in consumer durable imports begins when the peseta exchange rate is still low (1986–88), and it is long over by the time the exchange rate reaches its maximum (1992).

The 1992 collapse of the peseta exchange rate reinforces the view that, perceiving the 1988–91 exchange rate as unsustainable, Spanish consumers rushed to purchase (temporarily) cheap foreign goods. There is nothing in the data or in the evolution of Spain's economic policies after 1992 to indicate whether the temporary nature of the real exchange rate evaluation should be attributed to

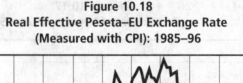

Figure 10.18
Real Effective Peseta–EU Exchange Rate
(Measured with CPI): 1985–96

lack of credibility or to the voluntary choice of an overvalued exchange rate as a disciplining device to curb internal inflationary
pressures. Regardless, the trade reforms have stayed, while inflation and the overvalued peseta are gone.

(2) Second is the easing of credit conditions; the consumption binge
is therefore explained as pure and simple *pent-up demand* which,
due to financial repression and the unavailability of credit, could
not be satisfied before the liberalization. There is little structural
evidence suggesting a drastic change in the conditions of Spain's
credit markets after 1986, especially in the area of consumer credit.
Once again, the progressive entrance of foreign banks had started
much earlier and continued thereafter in a relatively smooth fashion. The same is true for the increase in foreign capital inflows. It is
important to recall (see above) that inflows of foreign capital had
already begun to be liberalized in 1960 and it was the outflow of
capital that was still severely restricted until 1986.

Macro data can only confirm that a surge in consumer credit
took place but, this being an equilibrium outcome, they cannot
help much in discriminating the underlying mechanism. The year

1986 is a turnaround point in the dynamics of the ratio of total internal private credit to *GNDI*, as shown in Figure 10.19, and this increase in credit is particularly strong in the purchase of durable goods, as shown in Figure 10.20. Figure 10.19 also shows that, after all, internal credit to the private sector just returned to where it had already been in the mid-1970s, before the 1986 trade reforms occurred.

Furthermore, a comparison of Figures 10.17 and 10.20 highlights the parallelism in the temporary nature of the boom in durable imports and in the internal credit to durables. In summary, if any drop in private saving occurred because of financial liberalization and a run to the imports of durables financed by easy credit, it was certainly very short-lived.

Is There Anything Puzzling about Spain?

This simple examination of recent Spanish history and saving data suggests the following hypotheses.

Both the national and the private propensities to save out of current income have been very volatile in the past 35 years, but there is no prima facie evidence of any drastic change in their long-run behavior. Both saving

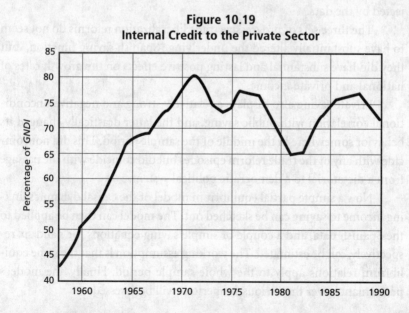

Figure 10.19
Internal Credit to the Private Sector

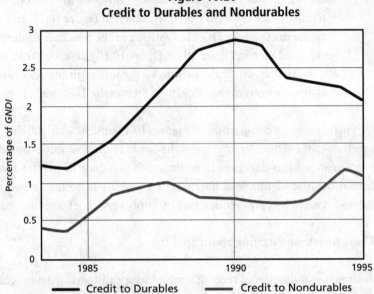

Figure 10.20
Credit to Durables and Nondurables

propensities exhibit a strong and positive unconditional correlation with movements in income, either national or private, but the hypothesis that past-income movements Granger-cause saving (or vice versa) is easily rejected by the data.

The three sets of progressive trade liberalization reforms do not seem to have substantially altered the underlying "Spanish saving function," but they did have substantial and lasting positive effects on the growth rates of national and private income.

Private saving also displays a relatively strong and negative unconditional correlation with public saving, and the latter drastically changed its behavior somewhere in the middle of the sample period. This did not coincide with any of the trade reform episodes but did coincide with the passage from a dictatorial to a democratic political system.

Now a simple partial equilibrium model of the causal dynamics linking income to saving can be sketched out. The model can then be applied to the Spanish data, and a couple of simple saving equations for s and sp, respectively, can be estimated. The working assumption is that the same equilibrium relations apply to the whole sample period. Finally, the model's performance over the various subperiods will be assessed.

The details of the model, as well as the derivation of the relevant equilibrium relationships, can be found in Boldrin, Christiano, and Fisher (1994). Let the stochastic process of per capita private disposable income be

$$y_t y_{t-1} \cdot \exp \theta_t \qquad [5]$$

where the growth rate θ_t obeys

$$\theta_{t-1} = (1-\rho)\,\bar{\theta} + \rho\theta_t + \varepsilon_t \qquad [6]$$

and ε_t is i.i.d. normally distributed with mean zero and constant standard deviation σ.

The representative agent intertemporal preferences for consumption are given by

$$U = \sum_{t=0}^{\infty} \delta^t \frac{(c_t - x_t)^{1-\varphi} - 1}{1 - \varphi} \qquad [7]$$

where x_t represents the habit stock, which evolves as follows

$$x_t = hx_{t-1} + bc_{t-1}$$

and the budget constraint is

$$a_{t-1} + c_t \leq (1 + r_t)a_t + y_t$$

where a_t is total financial assets, r_t is the real interest rate, and a_0 is taken as given. Denote with W_t the present value of individual total lifetime wealth as of period t. For illustrative purposes consider the case in which the random innovation in y_t is turned off (i.e., $\varepsilon_t = 0$ for all t) and the rate of return r_t on saving is fixed and equal to $(\gamma^{\varphi}/\delta)$ with $\gamma > 1$. One can show (see Boldrin, Christiano, and Fisher, 1994) that the equilibrium consumption policy is

$$c_t = \gamma^t \left[\psi^t x_0 + B_t Q \right] \qquad [8]$$

where ψ, B_t, and Q are simple functions of the underlying model parameters, of the time index t, of initial wealth W_0, and of x_0, the initial stock of habits. Algebraic manipulations allow one to compute the following derivative of current consumption with respect to unexpected innovations in total lifetime wealth:

$$\frac{dc_t}{dW_t} = \gamma\left(\frac{1}{\delta\gamma^{1-\phi}} - 1\right)\frac{\left(\frac{\gamma^\phi}{\delta} - (h+b)\right)}{\frac{\gamma^\phi}{\delta} - h}$$

[9]

While eq. [9] may look a bit complicated at first, careful inspection will show that whenever $b \neq 0$ and $\gamma \neq 1$, the standard predictions of time-separable permanent income theory do not apply to our model.

The latter says that current consumption should grow one-to-one with permanent income (i.e., with $dW_t \cdot r$ where r is the risk-free rate of interest). But in eq. [9] (dc_t/dW_t) is now a decreasing function of b and also a decreasing function of h whenever $b > 0$. With habit persistence, the optimal response to an increase in wealth is to use financial markets to slow down consumption growth so that the stock of habits has a chance to increase and therefore equalize marginal utilities over time. The flip side of this is that saving propensity may increase in the aftermath of a positive shock to permanent income. It is this prediction that constitutes the core of our simple econometric exercise.

More generally, the model implies that, given the specification eqs. [5]–[6] for the stochastic process of income growth, a general relation exists between variations in saving, $\Delta\log(S_t)$, and innovations in permanent income, ε_p in which the latter should have a positive impact on the former.[6]

A linear version of this relationship is our starting point of investigation, and it is estimated jointly with eqs. [5]–[6] by using annual data for Spain. This will be done first to relate national saving S to $GNDI$, and then for private saving Sp and $GPrDI$, respectively, over the 1954–95 and 1964–95 intervals. Estimation of [5]–[6] over the interval 1954–95, when y_t is per capita $GNDI$, gives

---

[6] Intuition suggests that one should be able to write a full general equilibrium model of endogenous growth in which past saving will have a negative impact on current saving. Even though this will not be attempted here, preliminary estimates say that this prediction for Spain is not rejected by the data.

$$\theta_t = 0.014 + 0.56\theta_{t-1} \qquad\qquad [10]$$
$$\quad (0.056) \ (0.13)$$

with $R^2 = 0.30$ and the first-order autocorrelation in the estimated e equal to 0.08.

Now, the estimated innovations in per capita GPrDI growth rates are used to run the following regression:

$$\Delta \log (S_t) = \alpha + \beta_1 \varepsilon_t \qquad\qquad [11]$$

which gives (standard deviations in parentheses) $\hat{\alpha} = 0.04 \ (-0.01)$, $\hat{\beta}_1 = 5.50$ (0.92), with $R^2 = 0.48$ and the first-order autocorrelation in the estimated residuals equal to -0.21 with a very normal-looking histogram.

Estimation of [5]–[6] over the interval 1964–95 when y_t is per capita GPrDI gives

$$\theta_t = 0.02 + 0.32\theta_{t-1} \qquad\qquad [12]$$
$$\quad (0.01) \ (0.18)$$

with $R^2 = 0.09$ and the first-order autocorrelation in the estimated residuals equal to -0.09. While eq. [12] gives a rather poor fit for the growth rate of GPrDI, it still is its optimal univariate representation according to the AIC criterion. There is nothing in the behavior of the residuals of eq. [12] suggesting they should not be taken as normal white noise.

Now use the estimated innovations in per capita GPrDI growth rates from eq. [12] to run the following regression:

$$\Delta \log(Sp_t) = \alpha + \beta_1 \varepsilon_t . \qquad\qquad [13]$$

OLS estimation gives (standard deviations in parentheses) $\hat{\alpha} = 0.04 \ (0.011)$, $\hat{\beta}_1 = 3.03 \ (0.44)$, with $R^2 = 0.63$ and the first-order autocorrelation in the residuals equal to 0.06.

Before moving on to characterize the impact that other factors may have had on private saving, pause and consider the quality of the fit that equations [11] and [13] provide for the post-1986 observations. Parameter estimates of both the income and the saving processes during the subperiods 1954(64)–85 are very similar to those obtained for the whole sample. Standard tests for a change in parameter values are largely consistent with the null hypothesis of constant values.

Furthermore, and somewhat surprisingly, if one concentrates on private income and saving behavior, it turns out that eq. [13] fits the last ten years *better* than it fits the previous period. Not only is there no trace of bias in the sign of the estimated residuals, but their variance is substantially lower (almost half the size) during 1986–95 than during 1954(64)–1985.

The conclusions: this simple model of national and private saving behavior performs remarkably well over the intervals 1954(64)–1995, and the entrance into the EU in 1986 did not cause any structural break in the equilibrium relation linking saving to innovations in per capita income growth.

Characterizing the Impact of Other Factors

Beginning with the estimates obtained in equations [11] and [13], it is now useful to focus attention on the determinants of private saving, Sp, other than the innovations in the private income process.

Real Interest Rates

It is well known that, from a theoretical point of view, the impact that changes in real rates should have on saving is ambiguous because of the contrasting income and substitution effects. The stylized model of consumption-saving behavior sketched above is no exception to this rule. An increase in the expected return on saving may generate a positive increase in wealth without necessarily increasing current income. This should increase current consumption and therefore decrease current saving ratios. But the usual substitution effect will act the opposite way, generating an ambiguous net variation in saving propensities.

Not surprisingly, any reasonable specification of eq. [13], including a measure of interest rates, fails to produce a statistically significant coefficient. Only one such specification, which is, in a statistical sense, quite representative of many others, is reported here.

$$\Delta\log(Sp_t) = 0.04 + 2.99\varepsilon_t - 0.19\,\Delta r_t \qquad [14]$$
$$(0.01)\;(0.47)\quad(0.53)$$

where $R^2 = 0.63$ and the autocorrelation in the residual is 0.07.

The measure of interest rate used in eq. [14] is a long-run rate. Alternative measures give completely similar results. Once income growth is introduced, real rates do not appear to have any explanatory power for private saving. Analogous results are obtained for national saving when measures of the real interest rate are added to eq. [11]. What is more important is that in conformity with most previous literature, real interest rates do not exhibit any explanatory power for saving rates even in univariate regressions. The value of the t-statistics is never above 1.2, and the R^2 coefficient is always practically zero.

Public Debt

It has already been shown that public saving ratios are strongly and negatively correlated with private saving. In light of the Ricardian equivalence debate, it is natural to ask whether variations in the public sector propensity to save have any effect on that portion of the variation in private saving that is not captured by the innovation in private income growth.

Coherently with the theoretical framework sketched above, the ratio of per capita government expenditure to national income can be taken as a given and any variation in the ratio of government saving to GNDI can be modeled as due to a change in individual tax rates. This is equivalent to variations in fiscal pressure or, which is roughly the same, in income of the government sector. This empirical analysis has considered two different but practically very correlated measures: one is fiscal pressure, FP, measured by the ratio between public income, GPbDI, and GNDI, and the other is the growth rate of public income. In both cases, the symbols denote log first differences.

$$\Delta\log(Sp_t) = 0.04 + 2.17\varepsilon_t - 3.10\Delta FP \qquad [15]$$
$$(0.01)\ (0.48)\quad (1.01)$$

with $R^2 = 0.72$ and first-order autocorrelation in the residuals equal to 0.04.

$$\Delta\log(Sp_t) = 0.05 + 2.66\varepsilon_t - 0.40\ \Delta\log(GPbDI) \qquad [16]$$
$$(0.01)\ (0.42)\quad (0.14)$$

with $R^2 = 0.71$ and first-order autocorrelation in the residuals equal to 0.05.

The relevance of the public saving variable is quite strong, and the sign is as expected. What is more interesting is that its introduction does not practically change the point estimate of the income growth coefficient. The specification eq. [15] will be used in the next exercise, but completely identical results would be obtained using eq. [16].

Changes in Income Distribution

What is the effect on the aggregate saving rate of a change in the distribution of income? The scarcity of evidence about the evolution of income dispersion among individuals prevents using such a variable in a time-series regression. And inspection of the data suggests that it is not likely to have a relevant impact on private saving rates.

On the other hand, there are a number of reasons to expect oscillations in the division of output between labor and capital to have some residual importance for private saving after an equation such as [15] or [16] has been estimated. To check this, compute the annual time series of the share of gross profit margin over total value added. Call it B_t. The following estimates are obtained:

$$\Delta \log(Sp_t) = -0.05 + 1.52\varepsilon_t - 3.60\Delta FP + 1.03\pi_t \qquad [17]$$
$$ (0.23)\ (0.53)\quad (0.97)\qquad (0.46)$$

with $R^2 = 0.77$ and first-order autocorrelation in the residuals equal to -0.11.

Equation [17] is a clear improvement over eq. [15] and, therefore, the way in which value added is shared between labor and capital seems to be relevant for the long-run evolution of private saving propensities.

Behavior after 1986

The stability of a new set of regression equations between the two subperiods 1964–85 and 1986–95 was also tested. In *every one* of the four regressions presented here, there is a substantial decrease in the variance of estimated residuals after 1986, quite similar to the one discussed earlier.

As an example, equation [15] yields

$$\text{var}\left[u_t(1964-1985)\right]=0.0038 \tag{18}$$

$$\text{var}\left[u_t(1987-1995)\right]=0.0007$$

which is quite remarkable. Figure 10.21, plotting the sample residuals, speaks for itself.

The interpretation is simple: *if* the 1986 reform did change the access of Spain's private sector to credit markets, it was by making it easier and less costly. Therefore, this should have made the condition of the actual "Spanish representative agent" closer to the one of the idealized individual in the simple model, who is assumed to have costless access to a full set of borrowing/lending markets. Since the post-1986 time series are generated by an environment closer to the one hypothesized in the model, a better fit should not come as a surprise.

Policy Implications and Conclusions

The following points have been argued here:

- In order to properly assess the evolution of national and private saving in Spain during the past 35 years, one must take into proper

Figure 10.21
Residuals of Equation [15]

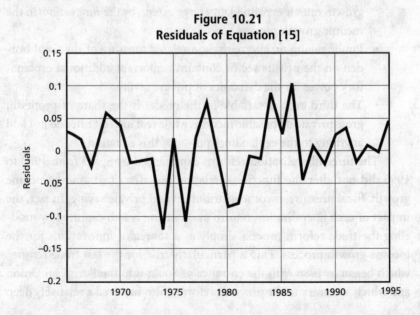

account the dramatic change in the relative price of new capital goods. The choice of a correct relative price to deflate nominal quantities allows one to compute real saving in a way that is consistent with economic theory and common sense and dispels the widespread belief that there was a dramatic drop in private saving propensities in the last 20 years. This is an important finding whose impact goes beyond the evaluation of the Spanish experience. The relative price of capital has been decreasing in most industrialized countries, and the speed of this process has actually accelerated during the last 20 years.

- A relatively stable saving function for Spain can be estimated using annual macroeconomic data over the period 1954(64)–95. The functional form of this saving function is the same for both national and private gross saving.

- The behavior of saving described by the estimated equation is consistent with intertemporal optimization on the part of a "representative agent" and can in fact be derived from a simple, explicit model of consumer behavior.

- The crucial explanatory variable to capture the dynamics of Spain's national and private saving is the growth rate of per capita national or private income. To be more precise, the variability in saving growth rates is explained, to a large extent, by the *innovations* in the income growth process.

- Public saving or, alternatively, a related measure of the fiscal burden on the private sector contains important additional explanatory power for the dynamics of private saving.

- The third crucial variable in the model is the share of profits in gross private disposable income, while real interest rates do not add anything to the explanatory power of this equation.

The three liberalization reforms experienced by Spain from 1960 to 1995 did not alter the functional relation just described among income growth, fiscal pressure, income distribution and private saving. In fact, the impact of each liberalization reform upon saving is well captured by modeling the trade reform process simply as a source of innovations for the income growth process. This is particularly true for the last trade reform, which began in 1986 with the entrance of Spain into the European Union and which, contrary to the previous reforms, also involved a relatively deep liberalization of Spain's financial markets. Contrary to widespread belief, there is no evidence of a permanent drop in private saving propensity after 1986. A short-lived drop in private saving was more than compensated by a surge in public saving, and when this decreased dramatically, private saving rebounded, basically in line with the estimated saving function.

In fact, the estimated saving function fits the post-1986 data better and more convincingly than for any other subperiod. In this sense, the temporary boom in consumption of durables that took place between 1986 and 1990 should not be interpreted as a pathological effect of trade and financial liberalization. Instead, it is the rational response of private agents to positive innovations in the income process and temporarily favorable exchange rates taking place in that period. In particular, the response of private saving to innovations in income observed after 1986 is in line with the quantitative predictions of the model even when the latter is estimated only from annual data prior to 1986.

From the perspective of economic policy, this suggests two main conclusions:

(a) Saving growth is determined by income growth. Hence, the policies that most favor national and private saving are those that most favor a long-run increase in the growth rate of national and private income.

(b) Trade and financial liberalization does not appear to modify the long-run structural relationship among income growth, public saving, and private saving. The impact of liberalization on private saving can be ascribed to its impact on the former variables. In particular, there is no evidence that trade and financial reforms should generate a permanent (or even temporary) reduction in the national and private propensity to save. Therefore, there is no reason to support a policy of controlled or limited financial liberalization on the grounds that this would help avoid unjustified and damaging consumption booms.

References

Abel, A. 1990. "Asset Prices under Habit Formation and Catching Up with the Joneses." *American Economic Review.* 80: 38–42.

Argimon, I. and Roldan, J. 1994. "Saving, Investment and International Capital Mobility in EC Countries." *European Economic Review.* 38: 59–67.

Bayoumi, T. 1990. "Saving-Investment Correlation." *IMF Staff Papers.* 37: 121–38.

————.1993. "Financial Deregulation and Household Saving." *Economic Journal.* 103: 1433–43.

Bayoumi, T., Masson, P.R. and Samiel, H. 1996. "International Evidence on the Determinants of Private Savings." Centre for Economic Policy Research. Discussion Paper Series 1368.

Boadway, R. and Wildasin, D. 1994. "Taxation and Savings: A Survey." *Fiscal Studies.* 15: 19–63.

Boldrin, M., Christiano, L. and Fisher, J. 1994. "Asset Pricing Lessons for Modeling Business Cycles." Third revision. NBER Working Paper 5262. National Bureau of Economic Research, Cambridge, Mass.

Bosworth, B. 1993. *Savings and Investment in the Open Economy.* Washington DC: Brookings Institution.

Calvo, G. 1988. "Costly Trade Liberalization: Durable Goods and Capital Mobility." *IMF Staff Papers.* 35: 461–73.

Carroll, C.D. and Weil, D.N. 1994. "Saving and Growth: A Reinterpretation." *Carnegie-Rochester Series on Public Policy.* 40: 133–92.

Carroll, C.D., Overland, J. and Weil, D.N. 1995. "Saving and Growth with Habit Formation." Brown University, Providence, R.I.: Mimeograph.

Constantinides, G. 1990. "Habit Formation: A Resolution to the Equity Premium Puzzle." *Journal of Political Economy.* 98: 519–43.

Corrales, A. and Taguas, D. 1991. *Series macroeconómicas para el periódo 1954–1988: un intento de homogenezación.* Monograph 75. Instituto de Estudios Fiscales.

Deaton, A. 1992. *Understanding Consumption.* Oxford, U.K.: Oxford University Press.

———.1995. "Growth and Savings: What Do We Know, What Do We Need to Know, and What Might We Learn?" Research Program in Development Studies. Princeton University, Princeton, N.J.

De la Dehesa, G., Ruiz, J.J. and Torres, A. 1990. "The Timing and Sequencing of a Trade Liberalization Policy: The Case of Spain." In M. Michaely et al., editors. *Liberalizing Foreign Trade.* Oxford, U.K.: Basil Blackwell.

Doshi, K. 1994. "Determinants of Saving Rate: An International Comparison." *Contemporary Economic Policy.* 12: 37–45.

Edwards, S. 1995. "Why Are Saving Rates So Different across Countries? An International Comparative Analysis." N.B.E.R. Working Paper 5097. National Bureau of Economic Research, Cambridge, Mass.

Feldstein, M. and Horioka, C. 1980. "Domestic Saving and International Capital Flows." *Economic Journal.* 90 (June): 314–29.

Ferson, W. and Constantinides, G. 1991. "Habit Persistence and Durability in Aggregate Consumption." *Journal of Financial Economics.* 29: 199–240.

Gámir, L. 1990. *Política Arancelaria.* ICE. December 1989–January 1990. 19–50.

Gavin, M., Hausmann, R. and Leiderman, L. 1995. "The Macroeconomics of Capital Flows to Latin America: Experience and Policy Issues." Inter-American Development Bank, Washington, DC. Mimeograph.

Greenwood, J., Hercowitz, Z. and Krusell, P. 1995. "Long-Run Implications of Investment-Specific Technological Change." Research Report 9510. Department of Economics, University of Western Ontario.

Greenwood, J. and Yorukoglu, M. 1996. "1974." Department of Economics, University of Rochester. Mimeograph.

Molinas, C. 1990. *MOISEES: un modelo de investigación y simulación de la economía española.* Barcelona. Antoni Bosch.

Ruiz Castillo, J. 1994. *La distribución de la renta en España en la E.P.F.* Documento de Trabajo 94-12. Departamento de Economía, Universidad Carlos III de Madrid.

Ryder, H. and Heal, G. 1973. "Optimal Growth with Intertemporally Dependent Preferences." *Review of Economic Studies.* 40: 1–31.

Taylor, A. 1994. "Domestic Saving and International Capital Flows Reconsidered." NBER Working Paper 4697. National Bureau of Economic Research, Cambridge, Mass.

Van Wincoop, E. and Marrinan, J. 1996. "Public and Private Saving and Investment." Discussion Paper 172. Department of Economics and Business, Universitat Pompeu Fabra.

CHAPTER 11

Swinging since the 60s: Fluctuations in U.K. Saving and Lessons for Latin America

David Begg and Stephany Griffith-Jones[1]

In the last three decades, gross national saving in the United Kingdom has fluctuated widely. Swings in components of national savings have of course been even more marked, since there are sound economic reasons to expect changes in one component (e.g., private saving) to be at least partially offset by changes in another (e.g., public saving). Moreover, since the start of the 1980s, national saving behavior has been characterized not merely by fluctuations but by trend decline, the recent upturn notwithstanding. These changes in U.K. saving and its components, as well as their theoretical and empirical explanations, have implications for policy design and provide lessons for Latin America.

Two variables—the ratio of saving to GDP and the financial surpluses or deficits of different sectors of the economy—are important for understanding U.K. saving. For each sector, the financial surplus is essentially its saving minus its investment (with a few minor adjustments, such as capital transfers). There are two key points about U.K. saving as a percentage of GDP. First, it has displayed large swings in the short run. Second, its trend decline in the longer run is largely attributable to the trend decline in public sector saving, which is itself a reflection of steadily lower levels of public sector investment.

---

[1]The authors are associated with Birkbeck College, London University, and the Institute of Development Studies, Sussex University, respectively.

The most amply discussed issue in the U.K. literature is aggregate consumption and saving by the household or personal sector. How well does modern intertemporal consumption theory explain changes in household saving behavior, and how much can be traced to the "usual suspects": financial liberalization and credit conditions, perceived changes in underlying productivity growth, demographic changes, the effect of inflation, and problems of (mis)measurement? Clearly, financial liberalization in the U.K. is important in understanding the collapse of household saving in the 1980s and its recovery in the 1990s. Still, the empirical evidence is consistent with what theory suggests: the effects of liberalization, although they may initially be dramatic, are unlikely to have permanent effects on the saving rate. Of equal significance, even the short-run swings in U.K. household saving cannot be entirely attributed to financial liberalization; other influences, most notably changes in confidence about future income growth and changes in demography, have also played important roles. As much of Latin America opens up its financial sectors, the U.K. experience can provide an interesting reference point.

Reviewing the relationship between private and public saving is also telling. The purpose is not merely to get some idea of the extent to which Ricardian equivalence does or does not hold, but to focus attention on the appropriate fiscal stance during periods in which substantial flow imbalances exist in the *private* sector. If, unfortunately, such private imbalances develop, it may be appropriate for the public sector to aim temporarily for a surplus. Dogmatic insistence on budget balance may then lead to quite inappropriate outcomes. However, particularly in Latin America, it may be inappropriate for the government to aim for large budget surpluses that are achieved by cutting essential government expenditure. If financial liberalization induces a temporary bout of private dissaving to an extent threatening macroeconomic balance, preference should be given to tax increases rather than public expenditure reduction. The need for any such fiscal cushioning will of course wear off again as any temporary surge in consumption is gradually unwound. More broadly, it is important to enact policies that do *not* lead to large private sector imbalances.

How does domestic saving affect the current account? Here again the U.K. offers interesting evidence for Latin America. In the late 1980s, the slump in U.K. private saving was reflected to a large degree in a current account deficit. While sterling floated, markets did not appear unduly wor-

Figure 11.1
Ratio of Total U.K. Saving to GDP: 1963–94

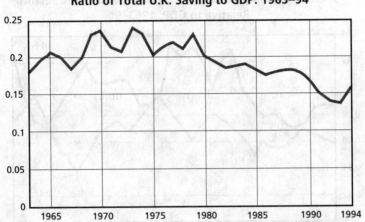

ried. Once the U.K. joined the exchange rate mechanism, a soft landing became much more difficult, and in practice the U.K. faced a dramatic exchange rate crisis in 1992 of a kind faced later by countries from Latin America to East Asia.

Saving and Sectoral Balances in the U.K., 1963–95

Figure 11.1 shows the ratio of total U.K. saving to GDP during 1963–95. Starting from around 18 percent in the early 1960s, it fluctuated markedly but in a rising trend, peaking at nearly 24 percent in 1973 and declining steadily after 1979 to fall below 14 percent by 1993 before recovering quite sharply in 1994. Saving fell slightly again in 1995 but was still above 1993 levels.

Figure 11.2 shows the three sectoral components of national saving—household, corporate, and public sector (the latter comprising central and local government and public sector corporations)—each also expressed relative to GDP.[2] Figure 11.2 makes clear that all three components fluctuate

---

[2]Although it is more usual to examine household saving relative to personal disposable income, the correlation of this with the ratio of household saving to GDP is very high for the U.K. during this period, implying that fluctuations are driven primarily by changes in household saving rather than in the relationship between disposable income and GDP.

Figure 11.2
Sectoral Saving (Household, Corporate, and Public Sector)
Relative to GDP: 1963–94

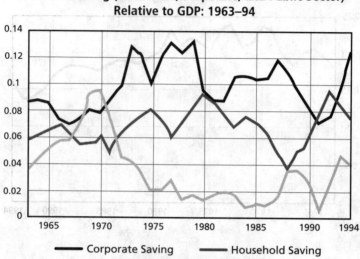

substantially but that there is no long-run trend in either household or corporate saving. In contrast, there seems to be a distinct downward trend in public sector saving over the 30-year period; in a very simple sense, this is what underlies the downward trend in national saving.

Since both the personal and the corporate components of private saving exhibit little trend, whereas public sector saving exhibits a clear systematically declining trend over a long period, formal cointegration analysis is unlikely to provide strong support for Ricardian equivalence.[3] This said,

---

[3] Although Ricardian equivalence identifies an extreme set of assumptions under which, for a given path of government spending on goods and services, changes in public saving should be offset by changes in private saving, government spending as a share of GDP fell under the Conservative government in power from 1979 to 1998. The U.K. government has since 1979 explicitly tried to reduce the share of public expenditure in GDP. As capital expenditure is the most flexible part of the budget, this has meant that falls in government spending have mainly been achieved by compressing public investment (OECD, 1990). As a consequence, increases in, and timely renewal of, infrastructure capital did not keep pace with growing demand (OECD, 1990). The decline in public investment helps explain the logic of declining public saving. It is necessary to control for this before reaching a final judgment on how to interpret correlations of different components of national saving. See Box 11.1.

Figure 11.2 shows that household saving does display a negative correlation with both corporate and public sector saving, and hence provides weaker support for the idea that households see through both the corporate and government veils. However, it is noteworthy that until 1973, household saving and corporate saving moved together and thus were positively correlated, whereas after 1973 they start displaying a clear negative correlation. It could be hypothesized that financial liberalization—which started in the early 1970s—changed the link between household and corporate saving, by lifting the credit constraint. However, by far the clearest trend since around 1970 is the systematic and sharp decline of public saving (see Figure 11.2).

One reason to make these points is to emphasize the likely interdependence of different components of national saving and hence the limits to what one can learn by focusing attention on one component alone. The latter, nevertheless, is what various literatures tend to do. The consumption function literature on aggregate household consumption and saving views the evolution of taxes and transfers as exogenous to the path of disposable income. The literature on fiscal policy, fiscal stance, and the appropriateness of government budget balance neglects the likely effect of swings in private saving on the size of the budget deficit. And the literature on the macroeconomic effects of companies has always focused much more on understanding corporate investment than on the study of corporate saving. Here, an effort is made to trace the linkages, though much remains to be done.

Sometimes saving should also be examined simultaneously with investment. National income accounts imply that sectoral surpluses, the excess of saving over investment, are linked through an identity: the private sector surplus must be reflected either in a public sector deficit or in a current account surplus on the balance of payments. Figure 11.3 shows how these three magnitudes (each normalized by GDP) evolved during 1963–94.

Through 1980, private sector surpluses fluctuated but remained generally positive and rising. These were accompanied after 1970 by fairly large public sector deficits, which are largely to blame for the current account deficits in the mid-1970s. Since 1980, the trends have changed. There was a sharp deterioration in the private sector balance, which bottomed out at around 5 percent of GDP in 1988. This was accompanied by an improving public sector balance, which peaked at 1.3 percent of GDP, also in 1988. It

Box 11.1 Econometric Estimates of Sectoral Linkages

Statistical inference about causality between highly simultaneous variables is fraught with difficulties. Post hoc propter hoc is a fallacy liable to make Granger-causality tests a misleading basis for inference about structural relationships: e.g., in the pure random-walk consumption model, lagged consumption predicts but does not cause future consumption.

Economics hints at two possible relationships between household saving and public sector saving: Ricardian equivalence implies causality from public sector to household saving, but exogenous tax rates as automatic stabilizers lead to causality from household saving to public sector dissaving. In what follows, investment is assumed to be more exogenous than saving: despite the Feldstein-Horioka puzzle, in open economies this seems a reasonable simplification to begin with.

Equation [B.1] regresses the saving-GDP ratio on sectoral investment rates (for households *IHO*, public sector *IPU*, corporate sector *ICO*), each normalized also by GDP, using annual data for 1963–95, standard errors in parentheses. Whereas equation [B.1] confirms a close relationship between investment and saving for households and the public sector—coefficients close to unity`—it suggests a different pattern for companies, which are generally less prominent in the results below.

$$S/Y = 0.06 + 0.95 IHO/Y + 0.94 IPU/Y + 0.33\ ICO/Y \qquad [\text{B.1}]$$
$$\quad (0.02)\ (0.40) \qquad\quad (0.11) \qquad\quad (0.14)$$

Next, the determinants of household saving are estimated directly within a framework in which Ricardian equivalence is possible. Corporate investment quickly drops out from estimation, and proceeding from general to specific yields as OLS regression for household saving, *HOS,* in terms of household investment, *HOI,* and the public sector surplus, *PUSU,* itself the difference between public saving and public investment (the data are consistent with equal and opposite coefficients on these):

$$HOS/Y = 0.08 - 0.59\ HOI/Y - 0.28\ PUSU/Y \qquad [\text{B.2}]$$
$$\quad (0.01)\ (0.24) \qquad\quad (0.07)$$

Equation [B.3] reestimates by instrumental variables, treating PUSU/Y as endogenous and using ratios of public and corporate investment to GDP as additional instruments:

$$HOS/Y = 0.06 - 0.24\ HOI/Y - 0.46\ PUSU/Y \qquad [\text{B.3}]$$
$$\quad (0.02)\ (0.38) \qquad\quad 0.17)$$

Thus, proceeding from general to specific estimation, it is hard to derive much econometric support for the proposition that an increase in public saving causes an equivalent reduction in household saving.

Box 11.1   (continued)

Next consider whether changes in household saving really drive changes in public sector saving. Again, general-to-specific methodology quickly reveals that corporate variables are much less relevant. Proceeding as before, OLS yields:

$$PUS/Y = -0.1 - 0.99\ HOSU/Y + 1.04\ PUI/Y \qquad\qquad [B.4]$$
$$(0.01)(0.17) \qquad\qquad (0.13)$$

The data easily accept that household saving and investment enter with equal and opposite signs—only the household surplus matters—together with public investment/GDP. Reestimating using household and corporate investment/GDP ratios as instruments for household surplus yields:

$$PUS/Y = -0.1 - 1.00\ HOSU/Y + 1.04\ PUI/Y \qquad\qquad [B.5]$$
$$(0.01)(0.19) \qquad\qquad (0.13)$$

Unlike [B.3], [B.5] finds not only evidence of a long-term relationship between public sector saving and investment (with unit coefficient) but also clear evidence of an almost exact offset between public and private saving. [B.5] should not be taken as definitive proof that it is changes in household saving that cause changes in public saving—differences between [B.5] and [B.3] are not statistically identified, and differences in estimated coefficients may be attributed to the extent to which the assumed orthogonality of instruments is in fact valid in each equation.

---

is, therefore, the very large private sector deficit that more than explains the large current account deficit in the 1987–89 period. Parallels could be drawn with the evolution in Mexico, where large current account deficits in the early 1990s were explained by private sector imbalance.

Returning to the U.K. context, it used to be argued in Cambridge, U.K., in what became known as the Cambridge theory of the balance of payments, that the private sector was usually close to sectoral balance—credit constraints prevented substantial deficits, and there was little appetite for sustained saving—when there was a close short-term connection between government deficits and external current account deficits. Figure 11.3 provides some evidence for this proposition up to 1980. But thereafter the correlation between public sector and external positions is clearly negative, and neither swings as much as the household sector, which, having gone on a credit binge of overspending in the late 1980s, had to save massively in the 1990s to meet its debt interest burden.

Figure 11.3
Sectoral (Household, Corporate, and Public Sector)
Surpluses Relative to GDP: 1963–94

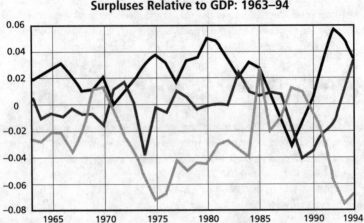

This initial examination of the data concludes with a brief comparison of the U.K. with other G-7 economies, data for which are given in Table 11.1. A first fact that emerges from Table 11.1 is that U.K. national saving is the lowest of the G-7 countries for the years analyzed.

Second, the final column of Table 11.1 shows that falls in national saving have been the norm, not the exception, in G-7 economies, with the

Table 11.1 National Saving in the G-7 : 1977–93
(percentage of GDP)

	1977	1981	1985	1989	1993	Change 1977–93
Japan	32.0	31.5	31.7	34.3	32.5	0.5
United States	19.7	20.8	17.6	16.6	14.9	– 4.8
Canada	20.9	22.6	19.6	19.4	13.3	– 7.2
Germany	21.7	20.3	22.0	25.7	19.9	– 1.8
France	24.4	21.1	18.9	21.8	18.7	– 5.7
Italy	26.0	22.5	21.6	20.0	18.0	– 8.0
United Kingdom	18.5	16.1	17.6	15.4	12.7	– 5.8

Source: OECD, *Economic Outlook*, various years.

clear exception of Japan. Since the previous discussion of the U.K. suggests that different components of national saving may behave very differently, Table 11.2 shows the behavior of household saving during the 1980s and 1990s for the G-7 economies.

Table 11.2 shows wide discrepancies in national rates of household saving, which is high in Italy and Japan but has for a long time been low particularly in the United States but also in the United Kingdom. Personal saving has been falling throughout the G-7 during the last two decades, though it has been remarkably steady in countries like Germany.

Having introduced the key facts about U.K. saving, both over time and in relation to other G-7 countries, a guided tour of institutional, policy, and other developments in the U.K. during the period helps identify factors potentially relevant to an analysis of saving in the U.K.

Institutional and Policy Features in the U.K.

Some key institutional and policy features of the U.K. may help explain U.K. savings and provide an overall context for further analysis. One of these key issues, and one of the key policy themes in the past few decades, has been the evolution of the current account deficit. From the mid-1970s, the current account improved sharply up to the early 1980s and deteriorated thereafter. In the 1988–90 period, the average annual deficit exceeded 3 percent of GDP, which is large by postwar standards in the U.K.

**Table 11.2 Household Saving in the G-7: 1982–93
(percentage of disposable income)**

	1982	1988	1993	Change 1982–93
Japan	16.7	14.3	14.7	– 2.0
United States	8.9	4.5	4.6	– 4.3
Canada	18.2	10.4	9.2	– 9.0
Germany	12.7	12.8	12.3	– 0.5
France	17.3	11.0	13.8	– 3.5
Italy	20.4	16.7	15.7	– 4.7
United Kingdom	11.3	5.7	11.7	0.4

Source: OECD, Economic Outlook, various years.

It is interesting that the initial response of those responsible for policy was to downplay the significance of such a large current account deficit, largely because the origin of the deficit was in the private sector, and therefore reject the need for any policy action. This position became known in the U.K. as the Burns Doctrine (Terence Burns was the chief economic adviser to the U.K. Treasury), whereas internationally it became known as the Lawson Doctrine. However, this analysis had respectable roots in economic thinking. Thus, Corden (1977) had argued: "the private sector can take care of itself . . . if private firms choose to increase their spending and finance this by borrowing abroad, and so generate a current account deficit, this does not call for any public concern or intervention." In broader terms, this was the position assumed by then U.K. Chancellor of the Exchequer Nigel Lawson in his speech to the IMF in October 1988. Lawson explained that "we are prisoners of the past, when U.K. current account deficits were almost invariably associated with large budget deficits, poor economic performance, low reserves and exiguous net overseas assets. The present position could not be more different."

Figure 11.4
The Current Account and Oil: 1971–89
(percentage of nominal GDP)

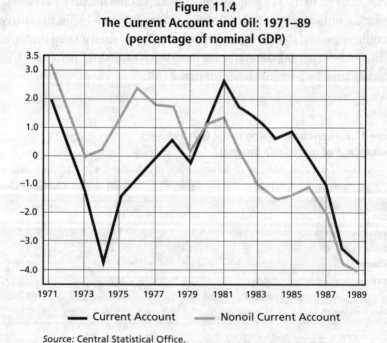

Source: Central Statistical Office.

The evolution of the current account during the 1970s and the 1980s (see Figure 11.4) was strongly influenced by developments in the oil sector. Until 1975, the United Kingdom imported the bulk of its liquid fuel needs. The rapid development of North Sea oil fields boosted oil output sharply in the late 1970s, and by 1979 the U.K. was self-sufficient in oil. By 1987, it had become the fifth largest liquid energy exporter in the world. Large oil exports in the first half of the 1980s were accompanied by particularly high prices of oil; but the oil price collapsed in 1986. In the late 1980s, oil exports were less than 0.5 percent of GDP compared to 3 percent at their peak in the first half of the decade.

The evolution of the oil account after the mid-1970s concealed a deterioration in the nonoil current account. Measured against GDP, the nonoil external position fell from a surplus of 2.5 percent in 1976 to a deficit of 4.5 percent in 1989. Until the mid-1980s, this deterioration was mainly explained by a downturn in the nonoil trade balance (particularly due to a sharp widening in the trade gap of industrial outputs, especially semimanufactured and intermediate goods). Particularly in the late 1970s and early 1980s, the increase in oil prices, combined with very tight monetary policy, led to a sharp appreciation of sterling, which was a major factor in explaining the briefness and small scale of current account surpluses in spite of high oil revenues.

An important theme in the analysis of U.K. savings is the impact of financial liberalization and its effect on credit. Financial deregulation has been an important phenomenon in many countries, particularly in the 1980s. In the U.K., regulation of financial institutions' assets and liability management were progressively relaxed during the 1980s, leading to greater competition between institutions for personal customers.

In the U.K., the process started when the move to targeting monetary aggregates made interest rates increasingly volatile. Furthermore, in 1979 the U.K. abolished exchange controls, which opened up its domestic credit markets to international capital movements. This was followed by the abandonment, in 1980, of the "corset"—the supplementary special deposit scheme that had restricted bank lending till then. The abolition of the "corset," together with difficulties with developing countries' debt, encouraged banks to enter the housing loan market. These markets therefore became much more competitive, as the cartel between building societies concerning interest rates was broken up. Furthermore, restrictions on building societies were relaxed; a new type of mortgage lender, often financed by overseas banks, entered the market. One of the most important changes was that modifications of building societies' regulations in 1986 and 1988 allowed them to expand their lending activity without an accompanying property transaction—for example, by mortgaging an already-owned property. This increased the attractiveness of credit-financed consumption since the interest rate fell from that of "high interest" personal loans to that of "low interest" mortgage loans.

There had also been important changes in the non-mortgage-related personal credit market in the 1980s. Hire-purchase controls were abolished in 1982, and financial institutions then aggressively marketed new personal credit facilities. Both housing loans and personal credit increased sharply relative to private consumption during the 1980s (see Figure 11.5).

From 1980 to 1989, household debt-to-income ratios in the U.K. more than doubled to one of the highest ratios in the world, and there was a

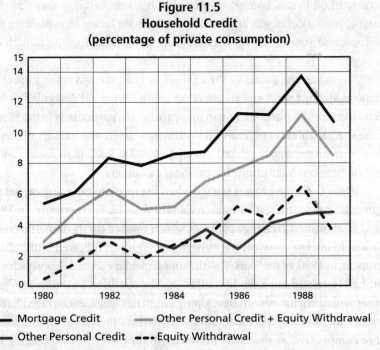

Figure 11.5
Household Credit
(percentage of private consumption)

━━ Mortgage Credit   ━━ Other Personal Credit + Equity Withdrawal
━━ Other Personal Credit   ●●● Equity Withdrawal

Source: Central Statistical Office, Financial Statistics and National Accounts; HM Treasury.

boom in housing prices in which real prices in the U.K. doubled over the same period (Muellbauer, 1994). These developments were not solely the result of financial deregulation, since there was sustained growth and falling unemployment from 1986 to 1990; however, there was obviously a connection.

Interestingly, similar financial liberalizations occurred in Scandinavia, with Denmark followed by Norway, then Sweden, and finally Finland. In all four countries, debt-to-income ratios grew strongly, real housing prices boomed, and household saving ratios fell sharply.

Household Saving in Theory and Practice

As a percentage of personal disposable income, the personal saving rate grew steadily if not smoothly, from 2 percent in 1950 to 9 percent in 1961, a level around which it then fluctuated for a decade before rising again in 1972 to peak at 13.4 percent in 1980. It then fell sharply to a mere 5.7 percent in 1988 but climbed back to 12.8 percent in 1992 before starting to edge down again.[4] Thus, how one sees the pattern of evolving personal saving depends very much on the chronological vantage point from which one looks. Those, like much of the literature, wearing recent spectacles tend to emphasize the secular decline since 1980; those (e.g. Chrystal, 1992) taking a much longer perspective begin by noting how exceptional the high saving levels were around 1980.[5] Chrystal even goes back to the early 1920s, when the personal savings rate was negative; the whole interwar average was only between 3 percent and 4 percent.

Within the broad framework of modern intertemporal consumption theory, U.K. evidence allows for the reinterpretation of some familiar and general issues in saving behavior—excess sensitivity and excess smoothness, the role of income expectations, the effects of financial liberalization, the importance of uncertainty, problems of inflation accounting, other measurement issues, (dis)aggregation problems and demographics, and forecasting failures.

---

[4] All data are from *Economic Trends*, U.K. Central Statistical Office.
[5] This period had two obvious features: high inflation (whose effect on measured income and saving is discussed shortly) and valuable North Sea oil revenues that, being temporary, should have induced some degree of intertemporal smoothing through saving.

Intertemporal Smoothing, Permanent Income, and Household Saving

Figure 11.2 and Table 11.2 reveal that the most dramatic episode in the behavior of household saving in the U.K. in the last 30 years was its sharp collapse and subsequent recovery during the 1980s. For quarterly data, household saving reached a mere 2.4 percent of disposable income in the fourth quarter of 1988 and then recovered to 13.3 percent by the second quarter of 1992. Lower saving in the 1980s had as its counterpart a substantial increase in household debt. The most obvious issues therefore are whether economic theory can explain such wild swings and whether econometric models of consumption and saving predicted this ex ante or, more modestly, can rationalize it ex post.

Deaton (1992) and Muellbauer (1994) give excellent summaries of the current state not merely of the intertemporal theory of household consumption and saving but also of econometric attempts to fit the data and discover remaining problems. Relative to the simplest rational-expectations permanent income hypothesis, encapsulated in Hall (1978), in practice aggregate consumer expenditure exhibits *excess sensitivity* to changes in the currently predictable component of future income. Simultaneously however, given the strong persistence in the process of income and output dynamics, current innovations in income, which should be extrapolated to have a large effect on permanent income, in fact lead to surprisingly little effect on current consumption, which therefore exhibits *excess smoothness* with respect to such income innovations. Caballero (1994) also notes that such "puzzles" about expenditure on nondurables apply even more strongly to expenditure on consumer durables. This implies that the predictable changes in income have relatively large effects on consumption, while surprise or unexpected changes in income have relatively small effects on consumption. These empirical trends seem to show that, even after financial liberalization, credit market imperfections remain that reduce the ability of households to smooth consumption when faced with unexpected changes in income.

Although these propositions were often formulated in respect to U.S. data and experience, they apply equally to aggregate consumption and saving behavior of U.K. households. "Solutions" to the puzzles have explored several avenues, notably the role of liquidity constraints, habits and evolving tastes or needs, uncertainty and precautionary motives, demography and disaggregation, and measurement difficulties. The large swings in U.K. household saving offer an ideal opportunity to test some of these propositions, and thereby to inform policy design.

As in the United States, U.K. personal saving during the last 30 years has displayed only small sensitivity to real interest rates. In theory, of course, although substitution effects apply universally, the signs of income and wealth effects depend on whether initially one is a saver and lender or dissaver and borrower. Aggregation, therefore, produces considerable netting out. Liquidity constraints also diminish the role of intertemporal substitution, both in theory and in practice. Interestingly, even without such constraints, an elasticity of substitution of around 0.5, which is quite plausible, would generate the small real interest rate effects typically found in empirical work prior to 1990 (see, e.g., Deaton, 1992).[6] This said, the traditional importance attached to inflation can be interpreted in part as an effect via real asset returns, and relaxation of credit constraints is unlikely to increase the role of real interest rates in saving decisions.

The 1980s Consumer Boom: Easier Credit versus Supply-Side Optimism

Many of these general issues can be crystallized in the debate about the causes of the U.K. 1980s saving collapse and its subsequent reversal. The literature was sparked by the interchange between Muellbauer and Murphy (1990) and King (1990) and Pagano (1990). Muellbauer and Murphy's central thesis was that financial liberalization had, for the first time, allowed homeowners to use housing wealth as collateral for loans for more general consumption spending, thereby relaxing previous credit constraints. King (1990) and Pagano (1990), instead, took the view that increasing confidence in a "Thatcher miracle" and the consequent belief in a sustainably higher rate of productivity growth had led to a sharp upward revision in estimates of permanent income. (For a summary of the debate on the impact of U.K. saving see Table 11.3.) Although this interchange took place before the reversal of saving behavior of the early 1990s was fully apparent, the competing explanations for reversal follow from the above: either (a) the end of a one-time adjustment plus the consequences of falling prices of housing and

---

[6] Elasticity of substitution is here defined as the measure of responsiveness of the ratio of consumption to relative prices (in this case to interest rates).

Table 11.3 Impact on U.K. Savings

Authors	Financial Deregulation	Expectation of Future Income	Inflation	Other
Muellbauer and Murphy (1990, 1993) Muellbauer (1994)	Yes, main factor; relaxing credit constraints facilities due to increasing "spendability" of financial assets.	Yes.		Yes, via effect on real interest rates.
King (1990) Pagano (1990)	More skeptical.	Yes, main factor; increased confidence in Thatcher reforms initially increased estimates of permanent income.		
Acemoglu and Scott (1994)	Not important.	Yes, main factor, linked to reduction in uncertainty about future income, more than increased mean of income.		
Deaton (1992)	Yes, initially, by diminishing need for precautionary saving.	Yes.		
Hendry (1994)	Yes, indirectly.		Yes, via departures from long-term value of desired ratio of liquidity-adjusted assets to inflation-adjusted income.	
Bayoumi (1993)	Yes.			

other assets as the U.K. experienced the chill wind of high real interest rates in the 1990s;[7] or (b) increasing awareness that many of the Thatcher improvements in productivity were more likely to be once-only increases in levels (caused by greater discipline, for example) than sustainable increases in rates of growth, for which more investment in human and physical capital was likely to have been necessary (see, e.g., Crafts, 1991).

Muellbauer and Murphy (1993) and Muellbauer (1994) extend their earlier econometric analysis of consumer spending and saving by refining operational measures of the "spendability" of assets to capture their changing liquidity as financial regulation and practice in credit markets alters over time. Indeed, financial liberalization, by making asset-backed credit more available, made previously more illiquid assets more spendable. With the appropriate measure, they claim a well-fitting consumption function in which financial deregulation and increasingly spendable financial assets play a major role in the collapse of saving in the U.K. in the 1980s. During the 1970s, when nominal interest rates failed to keep pace with inflation, substantially negative real interest rates, combined with large tax incentives (deductibility of *nominal* interest payments), created a large demand for credit that was held in check by rationing. Progressive deregulation of lending, especially for home purchases, led to lending spurts not merely in the U.K. but also in Denmark, Sweden, Norway, and Finland.

However, this effect is more subtle than it first appears. Several authors (Campbell and Mankiw, 1989; Jappelli and Pagano, 1989) have tried for several countries to estimate the percentage of credit-constrained households. Essentially, such tests rest on the idea that credit-constrained households have a close correspondence between current consumption and current income, whereas unconstrained households smooth consumption to an extent that vastly reduces its correlation with current income. These authors find that the percentage of credit-constrained households in the U.K. *increased during the 1980s.* The response of Muellbauer and Murphy is that deregulation, by allowing the use of housing asset collateral, made previously illiquid assets more liquid. The spendability of assets increased. More-

---

[7] This implies that alleviation of credit constraints might significantly raise the responsiveness of saving to real interest rates, a point emphasized in Pagano (1990). Note that the real interest rate effect operates not because intertemporal substitutability of consumption is directly enhanced but because real interest rates have a wealth effect via asset prices.

over, when borrowing for house purchase, consumer durables purchases, or intertemporal smoothing becomes a good idea, for whatever reason, it is not implausible that households not initially credit constrained now borrow up to a point at which they become credit constrained. Financial liberalization never meant the overnight appearance of perfect capital markets, nor should it have been expected to in a world of asymmetric information, adverse selection, and moral hazard.

The competing view, represented in King (1990) and Pagano (1990), is that an optimistic revision in the income generation process, thought at the time to be permanent but subsequently shown to have been temporary, may better explain the 1980s swings in U.K. household saving.[8] King, in particular, raises several doubts about the Muellbauer-Murphy thesis. First, financial liberalization had been proceeding throughout the 1980s, not merely during the period of sharply rising house prices. Second, prices of houses and other assets are endogenous. Hence, rising housing prices themselves are more a symptom than a cause.

This last point is not disputed. Muellbauer and Murphy see financial liberalization as the largest exogenous cause of the initial housing price boom. The subsequent literature (e.g., Miles, 1993) has also clarified other aspects of the argument. In particular, while privatization of state housing at subsidized prices unambiguously raises private sector wealth whenever Ricardian equivalence is incomplete, pure rises in real housing prices have two effects requiring careful disentangling and disaggregation. They increase the user

---

[8] One particular episode is agreed by everyone to have been (temporarily) significant. In the budget of spring 1988, Chancellor of the Exchequer Lawson announced that in the third quarter of 1988 one particular form of tax relief would be discontinued, namely the ability of unmarried cohabiting couples to claim two allowances for mortgage tax relief (married couples had always been entitled to only one such relief). Predictably, this announcement led to a spate of home buying by unmarried couples before the deadline expired, helping to explain the precise date of the peak in the housing market. Chancellor Lawson had engaged in similar tactics before and might therefore have been expected to foresee the outcome. Earlier in the 1980s, in switching from a regime of highly taxed corporate profits accompanied by high tax relief on new physical investment to a regime of lower corporate tax accompanied by abolition of investment allowances, he preannounced the phasing of the regime change over two years in such a way that, with no uncertainty, firms could invest today with full tax allowances, knowing that tomorrow capital taxation would be low. There was of course a dramatic spike in U.K. investment in 1984, accompanied by much lower levels in the two subsequent years, confirming the intertemporal substitution that had occurred in response to such a large, certain, and temporary fiscal incentive.

cost of housing, whose substitution effect reduces the demand for housing, and they have a wealth effect whose sign depends on one's existing housing assets relative to one's average demand for housing over the remainder of the life cycle.

Further Econometric Evidence

Acemoglu and Scott (1994) reexamine aggregate U.K. consumption spending in relation to excess sensitivity with respect to expected income, usually taken as implicit evidence of significant credit constraints. Interestingly, they find that when one includes *both* a lagged indicator of consumer confidence *and* the usual income measures based on information already available, the latter become insignificant, whereas the lagged confidence measure remains highly significant. Excess sensitivity applies not to income but to confidence. The authors conclude that this is compatible with a significant role for precautionary saving, the motive for which is easily linked with uncertainty and a desire for intertemporal smoothing. This and other evidence leads the authors to reject the importance of changes in credit market imperfection and to favor explanations based on perceived changes in income dynamics as the driving force for consumption and saving, albeit the latter now applies to uncertainty about future income, not just to views about its mean. The golden years of Mrs. Thatcher are thus to be interpreted as dispelling clouds of doubt, allowing the sunshine of optimism and greater certainty to shine on households. As uncertainty reemerged, precautionary saving took off again.

There is one reason to be skeptical of the conclusion that changes in credit constraints played no significant role in the 1980s: there is no easy theoretical partition between precautionary saving and capital market imperfections. As Deaton (1992) and Muellbauer (1994) make clear, by inhibiting future borrowing to meet future crises, credit constraints should raise significantly the return on precautionary saving that, by providing a buffer of accumulated assets, reduces the danger of future adversity. Conversely, initial relaxation of credit restrictions should diminish the need for precautionary saving, but, once new credit limits have been exhausted, the incentive at the margin for precautionary saving may be restored. None of this denies an additional role for changes in beliefs about income dynamics, or the degree of future income uncertainty.

One way in which to pursue this issue further is to turn to micro data and disaggregation. First, other econometric studies of aggregate macro time-series data for U.K. consumption and saving by households are discussed. Church, Smith, and Wallis (CSW) (1994) usefully survey the performance of such equations in the large number of U.K. macroeconometric models. Such models have perhaps been taken more seriously in the U.K. than in some other countries, to the extent that public grants help fund not merely modeling groups but also a unit to evaluate the models of the groups thus funded.

CSW provide a summary on the relevant equations of the main models and make four main points. First, different models come down on different sides of the fence about whether to model consumer durables and nondurables separately or whether to model them jointly as total consumption spending. They conclude that the empirical performance of the latter is clearly superior, presumably because substitution between the two components of consumer spending is hard to model reliably.

Second, operational empirical consumption functions adopt the cointegration framework of Engle and Granger (1987) presaged in Davidson, Hendry, Srba, and Yeo (DHSY) (1978) and Hendry and von Ungern-Sternberg (HUS) (1981), who first introduced error-correction models. Thus, modern equations can be viewed as first estimating the cointegrating vector (long-run relationship) and then estimating an error-correction mechanism to represent dynamic adjustment towards long-run equilibrium. CSW's second conclusion is that the routine updating of macroeconometric models to fit new data as they became available led to improvements in the dynamic adjustment equations but to no fundamental alteration of the cointegrating vector representing the long-run relationship. To the extent that within the overlapping cohorts of the real world, fundamental regime changes should be expected to alter not merely dynamics but the underlying long-run relationships, this conclusion is unwelcome evidence for those who believe that the sources of swings in household saving have been established definitively.

Third, CSW conclude that inclusion of unadjusted housing wealth in these models provides no magic solution to their previous difficulties in accounting for the substantial swings in household saving during the 1980s. The success obtained by Muellbauer and Murphy (1993) therefore reflects key but subjective judgments about the "spendability" of different assets. It will probably take many more years of data before there can be confidence in the reliability of such adjustments.

Fourth, CSW observe that the standard empirical models missed forecasting the large turnarounds in saving, both in the 1980s, when it fell more quickly than forecast, and then in the 1989–92 period, when it increased more quickly than forecast. They attribute this to "overfitting" equations that have picked up too much of the spurious noise during the period of estimation despite the battery of statistical tests to which they have been subjected.

All investigators have had to contend with dramatic revisions in U.K. macro data. For example, official statistics for household saving as a percentage of disposable income in 1974 originally estimated it at 15.3 percent. But by the early 1990s, the estimated figure for 1974 had been reduced to 10.6 percent, largely because the systematic amounts by which income-based GDP data exceeded expenditure-based measures of GDP had eventually led statisticians to search for ways in which expenditure might have been underrecorded (Hendry, 1994). Table 11.4 gives further details. Note that some of the largest revisions for 1974–75 data take place nearly 20 years later!

Table 11.4 Successive Revisions of Central Statistical Office Estimates for 1974–75

Calendar Date	Date at Which Estimated					
	1978	1980	1983	1986	1989	1992
1974						
Consumer Expenditure						
(£10 bn)	52.0	52.1	52.6	53.1	53.2	53.7
Personal Saving						
Rate (%)	14.1	14.2	12.2	11.1	11.9	10.0
1975						
Consumer Expenditure						
(£10 bn)	63.6	63.7	64.7	65.2	65.5	66.1
Personal Saving Rate (%)	15.3	14.7	12.6	12.8	12.0	10.6

Source: Hendry (1994).

Hendry (1994) also considers how these substantial data revisions affect the HUS model he had earlier estimated with von Ungern-Sternberg in 1981. The 1981 variant had emphasized the role of inflation through two distinct channels: (a) the need to replace actual income with adjusted income to reflect the effect of inflation (because of losses on assets, especially liquid assets, whose real return was effectively negative), and (b) through deviations in the ratio of liquid assets to income from the long-run value of that ratio, prompting a need to temporarily alter saving rates to rebuild liquid assets to more normal levels. With completely revised data and systematic changes in estimates of the saving rate, the original model now of course fits poorly. As a result, inflation plays a far smaller role in influencing saving than had been previously thought. However, Hendry shows that incorporating a Muellbauer-style variable to capture financial regulation effects on effective assets and liquidity is sufficient to allow successful reestimation in which many of the original channels survive. Specifically, Hendry concludes that short-run departures from the desired long-run value of the ratio of liquidity-adjusted assets to inflation-adjusted income continue to be critical in understanding the dynamics of saving behavior.[9]

The impact of inflation on interest rates was different before and after financial deregulation. Thus, after deregulation, declines in inflation have coincided with positive and high real interest rates.

This section has examined the macroeconometric literature on household consumption and saving. So far, four possible effects have been identified: changes in expected (long-run) income caused by changed perceptions of income dynamics; changes in perceived uncertainty and the need for precautionary saving; changes in inflation (effectively an effect via real interest rates on relevant assets including money); and changes in liquidity or spendability of assets caused by financial deregulation.[10] Muellbauer (1994)

---

[9] If inflation affects consumption by reducing real interest rates on liquid assets, sometimes to substantially negative levels, this is hard to reconcile with the view that real interest rates have little effect on consumption and saving. Where inflation simply raises the real tax burden because measured income fails to incorporate appropriate inflation accounting, no such effect is implied.

[10] Carroll (1992), reviewing U.S. data, attributes the decline in saving of U.S. households primarily to easier access to credit and to reduced uncertainty.

concludes his review of U.K. saving by using his latest estimate of a consumption function to decompose the 10 percentage point increase in the ratio of consumption to income in 1980–88 as follows:

Percentage points	Cause
+2.0	Forecast income growth
+2.5	Lower unemployment (more security)
+0.5	Lower income volatility (more security)
+0.5	Higher current income growth (for credit constrained)
+5.0	Rise in spendability-weighted net asset–income ratio
−1.0	Higher real interest rates
−1.0	Rise of inequality

According to Muellbauer, the biggest single contributor to the rise in the consumption-to-income ratio was the rise in the spendability-weighted net-asset-to-income ratio, which explains 5 percentage points (that is, half) of the rise. His analysis, because it is rigorous, clearly shows the importance of financial liberalization. However, as discussed above, other economists (such as King and Pagano) have argued for the significance of other factors such as income expectations. Given the existence of the debate, and the fact that Muellbauer is a strong advocate of financial liberalization, as well as the high quality of Muellbauer's estimates, this estimate for the impact of financial liberalization represents the upper bound of its influence.

Looking at the strong debate of the U.K. economists from another angle, one could perhaps argue that to some extent they are involved in discussing a false dilemma. King and Pagano attribute the increase in the consumption-to-income ratio to the perception of a "Thatcher miracle" (the perceived positive effect of a successful reformer), while Muellbauer attributes it largely to financial liberalization. Since financial liberalization was such an important part of the Thatcher reform package, the distinction is not as sharp as the debate would indicate, even though—in the abstract—one could conceive of financial liberalization without other structural reforms. Furthermore, the fact that both processes are integrated makes it difficult to disentangle empirically in a completely conclusive way which was the most important cause of the rise in the consumption-to-income ratio.

Additional insights into the analysis of the impact of financial de-regulation on household saving, with empirical tests for the U.K., based on its eleven standard regions, are provided by Bayoumi (1993). Bayoumi distinguishes two effects of financial deregulation: (a) an exogenous short-run fall in saving, some of which will be recouped over time, and (b) an increase in the sensitivity of saving to other variables, such as wealth, current income, real interest rates, and demographic factors.

Bayoumi's model for U.K. saving divides the fall in saving into three parts. The first is associated with changes in wealth and other factors, using coefficients in the saving function prevailing before liberalization. Another part is associated with changes in wealth and the shifts in the coefficients of the saving function associated with deregulation. Finally, part of the decline is attributed to the autonomous change in saving resulting from deregulation.

Bayoumi's results indicate that the main cause of the fall in saving was the increase in wealth sparked by the higher real value of houses and shares, which he estimates to have lowered the saving rate by over 5 percentage points over the 1980s. Some of this rise in asset values may have reflected the impact of deregulation on these markets; thus, deregulation may have had some indirect influence on this process. The direct effects of deregulation came through two channels. The first relates to the increased sensitivity of saving to wealth and other factors, estimated to have lowered the saving rate by 1.6 percent. Second, deregulation is, however, also estimated to have resulted in an autonomous 2.3 percentage point decline in the U.K. personal saving ratio. Interestingly, this result shows a slightly smaller direct impact of financial deregulation on saving in the 1980s than that of Muellbauer, (see above) but gives fairly similar results to those of Jappelli and Pagano (1994), whose alternative econometric approach finds that financial deregulation explains one third of the fall in saving over the 1980s.

Evidence from Micro Data

The U.K. Family Expenditure Survey contains detailed information on a large number of individual families and offers a further opportunity to examine the issues set out above. Although such data may be subject to their own measurement errors, they offer an important cross check, given the substantial revisions to macro data that have occurred. Attanasio and Weber (1994) use a time series of data on cohorts (by age) to explore both the consequences of disaggregation and the behavior of a synthetic but representative aggregate, in particular regarding the debate on the previous sections. They attempt to model both credit constraints and the perceived dynamics of the income generation process.

Disaggregating by age, Attanasio and Weber conclude that liberalization of credit and housing finance *can* explain much of the mid-1980s consumer boom for older households, whose lifetimes had been long enough to accumulate substantial equity in their homes, for whom housing price increases were beneficial, and who could use this collateral in liberalized credit markets as collateral for general consumption loans. Equally significant, Attanasio and Weber find that such factors *cannot* account empirically for the consumption boom of younger households, who quantitatively made up more of the total U.K. consumption boom prior to 1988. Rather, it appears that increased optimism about future incomes was the principal cause.

For the synthetic aggregate sample, the authors then simulate the consequences of an unexpected but permanent increase in productivity growth and expected labor income. In the short run, saving falls sharply as particular cohorts adjust to their altered circumstances. In the long run, however, the saving rate may actually increase.

Conclusions

What explains the behavior of household saving in the U.K.? Consumption functions have always been a popular area for empirical research in macroeconomics, attracting many of the leading empirical macroeconomists and econometricians; the U.K. is no exception. The preceding discussion describes the state of play. Much has been learned, and the interaction of theory and evidence continues to be fruitful.

The personal saving rate has not been stable, exhibiting both medium-term swings and abrupt short-term changes. The roles of income, liquid assets, uncertainty, and real returns are all established, although there remains a healthy dispute about their exact relative importance. Aggregate behavior conceals significant differences in disaggregated behavior. Disaggregating between durables and nondurables, although theoretically attractive, has to date had no empirical payoff with U.K. macro data. Disaggregation by cohort reveals much sharper differences.[11] In particular, it suggests that optimism and liquidity effects may each have their place, but in relation to different cohorts or age groups.

What lessons should a policy maker learn from all this? First, swings in household consumption and saving can be large. Given the share of consumption in output, and of household saving in national saving, considerable effort should be devoted to trying to understand what drives these variables.

Second, economic theory goes a long way toward providing a framework within which to interpret what is going on. As elsewhere in economics, simple one-liners (e.g., consumption is a random walk) should be understood for the insight they contain but then rejected in favor of something more complex. In the theory of saving and consumption, intertemporal analysis is not enough: one must also think about credit constraints, effective liquidity, nonlinearities, uncertainty, and hence the role of precaution and confidence. Against this ambitious list, empirical research has made substantial operational progress even if there is always much yet to do.

Third, the tide right now is always flowing one way. The late twentieth century is a time of increasing financial liberalization, not just in the United States and the U.K., but increasingly throughout the OECD, middle-income countries, transition economies, and beyond, though the pace of liberalization varies across countries. Reductions in capital market imperfections increase the relevance of intertemporal considerations and stock variables but eventually reduce the relevance of contemporaneous flow variables. In policy making this has several implications. Credibility, or the lack of it, by affecting a stream of expectations about the future, can potentially have a bigger effect today than was the case when the future was quarantined to a larger extent by capital market imperfections. A fortiori, when policies have large effects on relevant stocks (e.g., liquid assets or debts), the short-term implications for flow variables—consumption, saving, and output—may be large.

Fourth, despite country-specific shocks in policies, resources, and institutions, the U.K. has shared two characteristics of other economies. With

---

[11] Banks and Blundell (1994) show that many disaggregated effects are cohort specific rather than simply age specific: i.e., for a 50-year-old in 1996 it may be more important that he was born in 1946 than that in 1996 he was 50. If so, year of birth effects follow a cohort throughout its lifetime.

other G-7 economies, it has shared a longer-run trend for the saving rate to drift downwards; with the Scandinavian economies it shared the asset price inflation, consumer debt, boom-bust cycle of the last ten years. Simulations such as those by Attanasio and Weber (1994) suggest that there is no reason for credit liberalization to necessarily lead permanently to a fall in the saving rate: rather, it may represent a temporary adjustment (admittedly over very many years) to dramatic changes in the credit regime. The precise adjustment path is unlikely to be independent of the path of real interest rates, exposure to which is increased when households make more use of credit markets.

Fifth, this discussion of U.K. household saving is consistent with another belief about saving that is often expressed: demography and public pension provision both matter (and indeed interact). Not only does saving behavior change over the life cycle; the age structure of the population can have a large effect on the path of adjustment to other exogenous changes, whether in credit, interest rates, taxes, or output growth. Moreover, to the extent that the usefulness of the life-cycle approach has been established, this suggests that pension rights should affect household saving, a point often made to explain cross-country differences in private saving rates. In this context, one should be interested not merely in whether countries have or do not have generous state provision of pensions but also in whether or not unfunded state pension plans will credibly be honored once the baby boomers become the aged and there are few young workers to pay the taxes to support them. This raises the prospect, at least among the countries previously thought to have generous state pension provision, that increasing worries about future pension rights may gradually prompt a renewal of personal saving.

This indicates one channel through which private and public savings interact. Swings in household behavior are likely to have many implications for other sectors of the economy.

Government Saving, Public Finance, and Fiscal Policy

Figures 11.1 and 11.2 show not merely that U.K. saving has fluctuated during the last three decades but that it has done so around a declining trend and that the source of this trend must be traced not to personal or corporate saving but to a fall in public sector saving. Figure 11.3 shows, unsurprisingly, that there is no such trend in the overall surplus or deficit of the public sector. Intertemporal smoothing of tax rates might provide a motive for public sector surpluses today to cover, at least in part, for demographic changes that will surely have adverse effects—low tax payments and high pension demands—on public finances especially after the year 2010 (see e.g., OECD, 1995). However, governments with short-term reelection constraints find it politically difficult to sustain surpluses, and sustained deficits, properly measured, may lead eventually to threats of insolvency.

Figures 11.2 and 11.3 imply that lower national saving was attributable to lower public sector saving, and, since there was no trend in the overall public sector balance, the fall in public sector saving must have been roughly offset by a fall in public sector investment. Indeed, given the Conservative government's promise since 1979 to shrink the size of the public sector, it is more plausible to attribute causality in the reverse direction. As the government managed to reduce public sector investment, the perceived need for public sector saving was reduced, providing scope for cuts in tax rates.

An interesting question is, therefore, whether the cut in public sector investment was achieved by cutting government investment or by cutting fixed capital formation by public sector companies, either by constraining their activities or as a result of reclassification by privatization. Figure 11.6 shows that both components fell substantially in relation to GDP, but since 1979 it has really been cuts in investment by public corporations, not cuts in government investment, that have been the counterpart to reductions in public sector saving.

Figure 11.6 shows not merely that public sector saving and investment have been falling but also that public saving is much more volatile than public investment, generating the fluctuations in public sector deficits shown in Figure 11.3. Figure 11.7 shows how fluctuations in public sector surpluses compare with the separate components of private sector surpluses, those for households and for companies. The very strong negative correlation between surpluses of households and the public sector is evident.

Correlation does not, of course, determine causality. Causality may often flow from public to private, as, for example, when a tax increase leads to a reduction in the government deficit but an increase in the household deficit, in the direction if not the extent implied by Ricardian equivalence. But economics also teaches about automatic stabilizers and the effect of

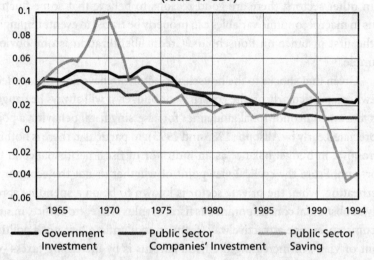

Figure 11.6
Public Sector Saving and Investment by Government and
by Public Sector Companies: 1963–94
(ratio of GDP)

Government
Investment   Public Sector   Public Sector
                    Companies' Investment Saving

Figure 11.7
Sectoral Surpluses
(Private Sector, Public Sector, and Current Account): 1963–94
(ratio of GDP)

Private Sector Surplus   Public Sector Surplus
                Current Account

the business cycles on budget deficits, examples in which a private spending boom, caused by dissaving, generates budget surpluses in the public sector. While the behavior of any sector should not be viewed in isolation from other sectors, there are good reasons to believe that some fluctuations in macroeconomic variables can properly be traced to events impinging in the first instance on households. Credit liberalization is one obvious example.

Given that shocks to the household sector can have first-order effects elsewhere, particularly on the government budget, it will always be dangerous to frame unconditional guidelines for assessing fiscal behavior, a point appreciated early by Allsopp (1985 and 1993). In particular, there is nothing sacrosanct in budget balance as an indicator of fiscal performance in the short run. From the cyclical viewpoint of whether or not the economy is overheating, when the private sector is known to be on a spending spree, only a substantial contemporaneous fiscal surplus is likely to suffice. In such circumstances, one attractive way (from an economic, albeit not a political point of view) of increasing the fiscal surplus is by increasing taxes—via either indirect taxes on consumption or direct taxes on households. These will both improve the fiscal balance and reduce the private sector imbalance, by dampening the consumption spree. In the U.K. context, the government resisted this option, due to its strong programmatic commitment not to increase (and indeed to decrease) taxes. The alternative implies, via national accounts identities, that the private deficit is allowed instead to spill over into a current account deficit, but the substitutability of traded and nontraded goods is (by definition!) too low to allow an additional supply of traded goods fully to discipline prices of nontraded goods. Nor may it be wise to promote substantial real adjustment between the two sectors. In the specific context of the U.K., one reason the so-called Lawson Boom of 1987–88 was allowed to escalate was that a government already achieving a budget surplus for almost the only time in postwar U.K. history[12] found it hard to believe that fiscal policy could be part of the problem,[13] given the massive private sector imbalances.

---

[12] The only years of budget surplus from 1953 to 1994 were 1969–70 (fiscal retrenchment following devaluation) and 1988–89.

[13] Monetary policy also mattered: the then policy of shadowing the deutsche mark from outside the European Monetary System (EMS) delayed the use of interest rate increases to cool

Figure 11.7 shows that after 1988 private saving increased dramatically, and public saving correspondingly collapsed. Causation is almost certainly in both directions. Faced with a consumer debt mountain and high real interest rates, households had to save hard merely to meet debt service obligations. A government aware of the preceding arguments and evidence might have taken a relaxed view of the burgeoning budget deficit, believing that once households overcame their debt problem and reduced their saving rate, public saving would correspondingly rise. For a government wishing to keep its European options open and looking over its shoulder at the criteria for fiscal prudence agreed at Maastricht in 1991, this was never an option. Hence, the comovements of household and public saving, and in particular the final reversal after 1992, were caused not just by gradual reductions in the burden of household debt and the consequent need to save, which was achieved most notably by cuts in interest rates after 1992. It was also caused by explicit government action (higher tax rates after the elections) to arrest the growing budget deficit.

Despite its drawbacks, IS-LM analysis conveys some important messages. One is that the mix of fiscal and monetary policy matters. Assessments of fiscal policy should not be independent of the monetary regime or the particular conduct of monetary policy. In a sense, the argument takes that proposition one step further: given the demonstrable empirical connection between household and public saving, it cannot be wise to frame fiscal policy without reference to pressures on households. Credit liberalization is potentially (and certainly, in the U.K., in reality) a massive shock to household behavior. And it is not simply because it is a change of regime, important as that is. During the subsequent regime of easier credit, one should expect larger fluctuations in saving rates precisely because households are no longer so constrained by current income. This is a lesson that fiscal policy ignores at its peril.

Saving and the Balance of Payments

The U.K. current account improved sharply through the early 1980s and deteriorated thereafter (see Figure 11.4, above). This evolution reflected the

down the economy. When interest rate rises were eventually judged to be the only solution, interest rates were increased very substantially.

dramatic increase in the oil trade balance since the mid-1970s, and the effect of sterling's appreciation on the nonoil current account.

Current account developments are by definition linked to changes in the balance between national saving and investment. As can be seen in Figure 11.8, the deterioration of the U.K. current account during the second half of the 1980s mainly reflected increased investment. However, in comparing the late 1980s with the second half of the 1970s, the decline in the national saving ratio explains the deterioration in the current account, since the investment ratio had recovered during the 1980s from its very sharp decline in 1980–81. Thus, at the peak of the current account deficit in 1989, the investment ratio was not higher than the average over the 1974–79 cycle, while the national saving ratio was significantly lower. The deteriorating balance between national investment and savings was mainly explained by the growing private sector deficit (see again Figure 11.3, above). From 1980 to 1987, this was mainly due to a sharp deterioration in the personal sector

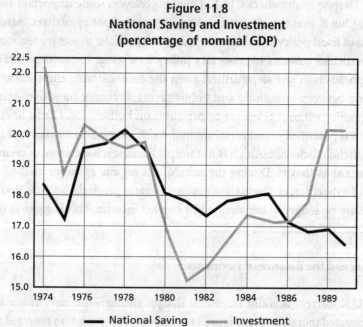

Figure 11.8
National Saving and Investment
(percentage of nominal GDP)

Note: National saving is derived from the expenditure-based measure of gross national product plus net transfers from abroad minus private and public consumption. Investment includes stockbuilding.
Source: Central Statistical Office.

financial balance (partly offset by some improvement in the business sector imbalance). However, during 1987–89, the deficit in the personal sector financial balance was added to a deteriorating—and negative—business sector deficit.

It is interesting to examine how the fairly large U.K. current account deficit in the late 1980s was financed. Particularly until 1989, financing the current account deficit did not pose any problem. In spite of a sharp widening of the current account deficit in 1987 and 1988, the authorities were faced with strong upward pressure on the exchange rate during most of this period. In 1989, however, the exchange rate came under repeated downward pressure, which forced the authorities to tighten monetary conditions significantly, and led to a major increase in interest rates. It is interesting that since late 1988, the current account deficit had suddenly become an important news item, even though it had been ignored during the period when the deficit was growing. Thus, changes in expectations during 1989 seemed to put more pressure on the exchange rate than was warranted by changes in fundamentals (OECD, 1995).

The dominant feature of U.K. capital developments in the late 1980s was the growth in short-term inflows required to finance widening current account deficits plus net outflows of long-term capital (see Figure 11.9). To the extent that capital classified as short term is more volatile than capital classified as long term, the capital inflows during the 1980s made the exchange rate more vulnerable to shifts in portfolio preferences of international investors, as was shown during the 1992 crisis.

Recorded long-run capital net outflows grew rapidly, as a proportion of GDP, in the first half of the 1980s, explained by both direct investment and portfolio flows. By 1986, recorded net long-term capital outflows totalled as much as 5.5 percent of GDP, while short-term capital inflows amounted to 3 percent of GDP. After a period of repatriation of portfolio investment following the stock-market crash in 1987, which led to net long-term capital inflows in that year, investment by U.K. residents in foreign bonds and shares restarted in 1988 and by 1989 had again reached 5.5 percent of GDP. Short-term capital inflows reached more than 5 percent of GDP in 1989.

The fact that, on a net basis, direct investment did not contribute to financing current account deficits is primarily due to the high propensity of British companies to invest abroad, (4.0 percent of GDP during 1986–89)

Figure 11.9
Balance of Payments
(percentage of nominal GDP)

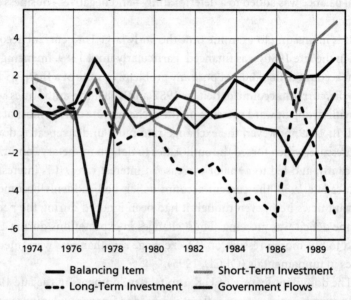

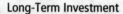

Long-Term Investment

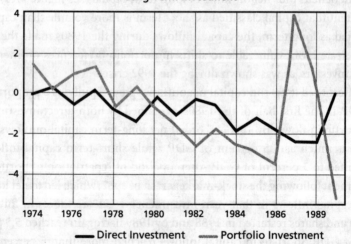

Source: Central Statistical Office.

rather than to a lack of inflows (1.8 percent of GDP during the same period, which is above the average for major OECD countries).

The abolition of foreign exchange controls in April 1979 appears to have been the main element behind the sharp outflow in the early 1980s (Artis and Taylor, 1989). In the pre-1979 regime, institutional investors such as pension funds and insurance companies were constrained in diversifying into foreign assets. After 1979, when all controls were lifted, the share of foreign assets in their total portfolio increased sharply; further portfolio outflows were caused by the rapid rise of these institutions' total assets. Another stimulus to outward portfolio investment came in 1988 when the government started retiring debt: lack of suitable domestic investment assets encouraged institutions to buy foreign assets.

The increase in short-term capital inflows in the first half of the 1980s was associated with a growing differential between U.K. and foreign short-term interest rates, which continued into the latter part of the decade.

Extracting the Lessons

What are the lessons from the U.K. experience? What is their relevance for Latin America? Above all, what are the policy implications?

First, the U.K. experience does offer important lessons for Latin America. Indeed, it could be argued that many parallels exist between the U.K. evolution during the 1980s and, for example, Mexico's economic evolution in the early 1990s, which Mexican economic authorities could have examined with benefit during the "euphoric" period. In both cases, liberalization of the domestic financial sector, as well as optimism partly generated by the perception of a very successful reform process, led to sharp increases in consumption, which were financed largely by an increase in credit from the newly liberalized financial system. In both cases, the resulting decline of national savings was a factor behind rising current account deficits, which were initially financed with ease, as international markets did not seem to "notice" the negative evolution of the current account deficit. Furthermore, in both cases, the growing current account deficit was financed mainly by short-term, potentially volatile, capital flows; this was facilitated by the previous liberalization of the capital account and made possible by short-term interest rates that were higher domestically than internationally. In both cases, but particularly loudly in the U.K., the economic authorities argued that current account deficits did not matter or were not so serious because they were caused not by budget deficits, but by imbalances in the private sector's accounts.

Naturally, there are also important differences in the macroeconomic evolution of the U.K. in the 1980s and Mexico in the 1990s. There are far larger differences in the structural features of both economies, as well as in the denouement to the period of declining national saving and growing current account deficits.

Returning to the U.K. experience and its lessons, the evidence and the literature show that the liberalization of the financial sector contributed to the consumption boom in the 1980s and the resulting decline in the national saving rate. The U.K. experience, combined with that of the Scandinavian countries that underwent similar processes of financial liberalization, seems to show that financial sector liberalization—even if radical and speedy—is likely to contribute to an increase in households' consumption. This consumption is also likely to be boosted by the optimism generated by the perceived success of the overall market reform program, of which financial liberalization is a part. However, in the U.K. case, household saving has recovered fairly significantly (see Figure 11.2). Though other factors are at play, this would seem to confirm what the literature affirms, that the post-financial-liberalization decline of households' saving is a temporary problem. In the U.K., the ratio of saving to GDP is still well below its 1970s peak, but this is mainly due to the sharp and systematic trend towards declining public sector saving (see again Figure 11.2).

However, very rapid and radical liberalization of the financial sector is a somewhat problematic policy in the context of a reform program. If one of its main goals is to encourage domestic saving, at least in the short term, it is likely to lead to a fairly important decline of household saving.

The fact that liberalization of the financial sector can be done far more slowly and gradually is illustrated by the fact that certain continental European countries (particularly Germany) have done just that. It is interesting that Germany has seen its saving rate fall far less than the U.K.. However, much further study would be required before concluding that this slower financial liberalization was a key factor in explaining lower declines of German saving.

Avoiding liberalization of the financial sector completely does not seem, however, a realistic option, both because of international trends and pressures and because liberalization of the domestic financial sector does bring important benefits, particularly of a microeconomic nature. The better option seems, as pointed out above, to liberalize the domestic sector far more gradually. This would lead to a more gradual decline in domestic saving, which would make particularly the management of the temporary decline of saving less problematic. In doing so, policy makers need to be aware that the financial liberalization will likely lead to higher interest rates. As other mechanisms disappear, the interest rate becomes the only way to ration credit and is likely to increase as a result.

Higher domestic interest rates, particularly in the context of a liberalized capital account, are likely to attract short-term capital inflows from abroad. This may lead to an appreciation of the exchange rate and a growing current account deficit. If this deterioration is excessive, the threat of a costly balance of payments crisis may emerge (see Ffrench-Davis and Griffith-Jones, 1995).

The U.K. experience seems to show that a further tightening of fiscal policy in the late 1980s (even though the fiscal position was already in surplus) may have led to better economic performance, and to higher saving, than the policy of very high interest rates pursued. In the context of middle- or low-income countries, with both important social and developmental needs being met by public spending, it seems difficult to argue for public spending cuts to achieve large public sector surpluses unless these relate to nonessential public spending, where cuts are to be welcomed. Economically (though probably not politically), a more attractive option may be to compensate for any household sector dissaving by increasing taxes. Increased taxes would not only increase public saving but would also do it in a way that discouraged household consumption.

However, the U.K. experience also shows that, once financial liberalization has been completed, increases in saving in one sector are often largely compensated by induced effects in the other direction in other sectors. Therefore, the task for policy makers of raising total saving becomes harder.

References

Acemoglu, D. and Scott, A. 1994. "Consumer Confidence and Rational Expectations: Are Agents' Beliefs Consistent with the Theory?" *Economic Journal.* 104 (January): 1–19.

Allsopp, C. 1985. "The Assessment: Monetary and Fiscal Policy in the 1980s." *Oxford Review of Economic Policy.*

———1993. "The Assessment: Strategic Policy Dilemmas for the 1990s." *Oxford Review of Economic Policy.* 9 (Autumn): 1–25.

Artis, M.J. and Taylor, M.P. 1989. "Abolishing Exchange Control: The U.K. Experience." Centre for Economic Policy Research Discussion Paper 294.

Attanasio. O.P. and Weber, G. 1994. "The U.K. Consumption Boom of the Late 1980s: Aggregate Implications of Microeconomic Evidence." *Economic Journal.* 104: 1269–1302.

Banks, J. and Blundell, R. 1994. "Household Saving Behavior in the United Kingdom." In J. Poterba, editor. *International Comparisons of Household Saving.* Chicago, Ill.: University of Chicago Press.

Barro, R. 1974. "Are Government Bonds Net Wealth?" *Journal of Political Economy.* 81(6): 1095–1117.

Bayoumi, T. 1993. "Financial Deregulation and Household Saving." *Economic Journal.* 103: 1433–43.

Caballero, R. 1994. "Notes on the Theory and Evidence on Aggregate Purchases of Durable Goods." *Oxford Review of Economic Policy.* 10 (Summer): 107–17.

Campbell, J. 1987. "Does Saving Anticipate Declining Labor Income? An Alternative Test of the Permanent Income Hypothesis." *Econometrica.* 55 (November): 1249–73.

Campbell, J. and Deaton, A. 1989. "Why Is Consumption So Smooth?" *Review of Economic Studies.*

Campbell, J. and Mankiw, N.G. 1989. "Consumption, Income, and Interest Rates: Reinterpreting the Time Series Evidence." In O.J. Blanchard and S. Fischer, editors. *NBER Macroeconomics Annual 1989.* Cambridge, Mass.: MIT Press.

Carroll, C. D. 1992. "The Buffer Stock Theory of Saving: Some Macroeconomic Evidence." *Brookings Papers on Economic Activity.* 2: 61–156.

Carroll, C.D. and Summers, L. 1991. "Consumption Growth Parallels Income Growth: Some New Evidence." In B. Bernheim and J. Shoven, editors. *National Saving and Economic Performance.* Chicago, Ill.: University of Chicago Press.

Chrystal, K.A. 1992. "The Fall and Rise of Saving." *Quarterly Review, National Westminster Bank Review.* February: 24–40.

Church, K., Smith, P. and Wallis, K. 1994. "Econometric Evaluation of Consumers' Expenditure Equations." *Oxford Review of Economic Policy.* 10 (Summer): 71–85.

Corden, W.M. 1977. *Inflation, Exchange Rates, and the World Economy: Lectures on International Monetary Economics.* 1st ed. Oxford, U.K.: Clarendon Press.

Crafts, N. 1991. "Productivity Performance in the U.K. in Historical and International Perspective." Discussion Papers in Economics and Econometrics 9103. Department of Economics, University of Southampton.

Davidson, J., Hendry, D., Srba, F. and Yeo, S. 1978. "Econometric Modelling of the Aggregate Time-Series Relationship between Consumers' Expenditure and Income in the United Kingdom." *Economic Journal.* 88: 661–92.

Deaton, A. 1991. "Saving and Liquidity Constraints." *Econometrica*. 153 (November): 1–42.

_____ . 1992. *Understanding Consumption*. Oxford, U.K.: Oxford University Press.

Engle, R. and Granger, C. 1987. "Cointegration and Error Correction: Representation, Estimation and Testing." *Econometrica*. 55.

Ffrench-Davis, R. and Griffith-Jones, S. 1995. *Coping with Capital Surges*. Boulder, Colo.: Lynne Rienner.

Flavin, M. 1981. "The Adjustment of Consumption to Changing Expectations about Future Income." *Journal of Political Economy*. 89: 974–1009.

Flemming, J. 1983. "The Consumption Function When Capital Markets Are Imperfect." *Economic Journal*.

Forsyth, P. and Kay, J. 1980. "The Economic Implications of North Sea Oil Revenues." *Fiscal Studies*.

Hall, R. 1978. "Stochastic Implications of the Life Cycle–Permanent Income Hypothesis: Theory and Evidence." *Journal of Political Economy*. 86(6): 971–87.

Hendry, D. 1994. "HUS Revisited." *Oxford Review of Economic Policy*. 10 (Summer): 86–106.

Hendry, D. and von Ungern-Sternberg, T. 1981. "Liquidity and Inflation Effects on Consumers' Expenditure." In A. Deaton, editor. *Essays in the Theory and Measurement of Consumers' Behaviour*. Cambridge, U.K.: Cambridge University Press.

Jappelli, T. and Pagano, M. 1989. "Consumption and Capital Market Imperfections: An International Comparison." *American Economic Review*. 79: 1088–1105.

King, M. 1990. "Discussion of Muellbauer and Murphy." *Economic Policy.* 11: 345–83.

_____ . 1994. "Saving, Growth, and Liquidity Constraints." *Quarterly Journal of Economics.* 109: 83–109.

Mankiw, G. and Shapiro, M. 1985. "Trends, Random Walks, and Tests of the Permanent Income Hypothesis." *Journal of Monetary Economics.* 16 (September): 165–74.

Miles, D. 1993. "House Prices, Personal Sector Wealth and Consumption: Some Conceptual and Empirical Issues." *Manchester School.*

_____ . 1993. "Housing Markets, Consumption and Financial Liberalisation in the Major Economies." *European Economic Review.* 36: 1093–1127.

Muellbauer, J. 1994. "The Assessment: Consumer Expenditure." *Oxford Review of Economic Policy.* 10 (Summer): 1–41.

Muellbauer, J. and Murphy, A. 1990. "Is the UK Balance of Payments Sustainable?" *Economic Policy.* 5 (October): 348–95.

_____ . 1993. "Income Expectations, Wealth and Demography in the Aggregate U.K. Consumption Function." Nuffield College, Oxford. Mimeograph.

Obstfeld, M. 1995. "International Currency Experience: New Lessons and Lessons Relearned." *Brookings Papers on Economic Activity.* 1: 119–211.

OECD (Organization for Economic Cooperation and Development). Various issues. *Economic Surveys:* Paris.

Pagano, M. 1990. "Discussion of Muellbauer and Murphy." *Economic Policy.*